D0850547

THE ORPHANS OF
BYZANTIUM

THE ORPHANS OF BYZANTIUM

Child Welfare in the Christian Empire

TIMOTHY S. MILLER

The Catholic University of America Press
Washington, D.C.

Copyright © 2003
The Catholic University of America Press
All rights reserved
The paper used in this publication meets the minimum re-
quirements of the American National Standards for Infor-
mation Science—Permanence of Paper for Printed Library
Materials, ANSI Z39.48—1984.
∞

Library of Congress Cataloging-in-Publication Data
Miller, Timothy S.
    The orphans of Byzantium : child welfare in the
Christian empire / Timothy S. Miller.
        p.   cm.
    Includes bibliographical references and index.
    ISBN 0-8132-1313-4
    1. Orphanages—Byzantine Empire. 2. Child welfare—
Byzantine Empire. 3. Alexius I Comnenus, Emperor of
the East, 1048–1118. 4. Guardian and ward—Byzantine
Empire. I. Title.
HV963 .M55 2003
362.73'2—dc21
2002001419

For my wife, Vicki, and our two sons, Justin and Matthew. Many times they have rescued *The Orphans of Byzantium.*

Interest in the ancient civilization of Greece and Rome and in the Christian world of the Middle Ages has declined in recent years. Most of my students find the names Demosthenes and John Chrysostom more difficult to remember than Lao Tzu and Montezuma. In such an atmosphere, I was especially delighted to discover that a group of physicians and independent scholars had organized the Hellenic Society Paideia of Virginia, a branch of a national organization founded in 1974, to encourage the study of Greek civilization from its beginnings in the Bronze Age to the present. This organization helped to support my research for this book and has also assisted many other scholars and students in reaching their academic goals. It is especially appropriate that the Hellenic Society Paideia put down strong roots in Virginia where more than two hundred years ago serious study of classical civilization gave birth to the ideals of a new nation.

4 July 2002
Salisbury, Maryland

CONTENTS

Orphans of Byzantium
tears too long forgot
how ironic is this innocence gazing to distant shore
immovable prow upon the reef hears now the slightest whisper
transverse thy broken ship on Heaven's mercy gleam
angels that we slaughered tis to thee we now implore
forgive
O breathe upon our unfurled swaddle
safely to thy harbor yet
how pink the inlet is
as if born just recently
and warm
a Mother and her child

vicki beth miller
10/26/02

Thus says the Lord:
'You shall not wrong any widow or orphan.
If ever you wrong them and they cry out to me
I will surely hear their cry.'
Exodus 22: 22, 23

PREFACE

When I began research for *The Orphans of Byzantium* in 1990, I planned it as a sequel to my first book, *The Birth of the Hospital in the Byzantine Empire* (published in 1985). Just as the East Roman Empire of Byzantium supported charitable medical hospitals to offer health care to people from all classes in society, so too did it maintain a series of orphanages to nurture boys and girls who had lost their parents. But as I examined more closely the primary sources describing orphan care, I discovered that the East Roman method of aiding homeless children had evolved along different lines than had its system of providing free access to physicians. The Byzantine method of assisting orphans relied primarily on the laws of guardianship, which required that members of the extended family assume responsibility for protecting the children of their deceased relatives.

My initial purpose in preparing this study was thus to describe how Byzantine society cared for orphaned and abandoned children and to examine how this child welfare program differed from the East Roman hospital system. As I pursued the project, however, I realized that many of the problems that Byzantine emperors, church leaders, and directors of orphanages faced did not differ from those confronting today's social workers, psychologists, and educators. The more I read studies of modern orphanages and child welfare issues, the more I saw that societies have been addressing the same problems in assisting homeless children for centuries.

Every grade school student has heard the saying that history repeats itself, and all of us have learned the necessity of experience in solving problems. Nevertheless, many modern experts in the field of child welfare know almost nothing about the history of how earlier societies have tried to assist abandoned and orphaned children. Is it unreasonable to believe that earlier generations might have found solutions to problems that we are facing today, solutions that have somehow slipped from our collective memory?

In researching my topic, I became increasingly aware of how little interest government agencies, politicians, and even child advocacy groups in the United States, and to some extent also in Europe, have shown in examining the successes and failures of ancient and medieval societies in their efforts to assist the poor and needy in general and to provide care for orphans and abandoned children in particular. Can this lack of historical perspective help to explain the unsatisfactory results of the current foster-care system for children, and perhaps the failure of other social welfare systems of the capitalist West?

As a result of these considerations, perhaps a more fundamental goal of this book is to awaken a greater awareness of the long and complex history of social welfare, a history which in fact began with the conversion of the Roman Empire to Christianity during the fourth century. Thus, a thorough understanding of how child welfare programs developed through the centuries requires that one begin with a detailed study of Byzantine efforts to assist orphans and abandoned children.

Rather than list the people who have contributed to this book, I would like to present a short description of how the project unfolded and who came to rescue me at crucial moments. After eight years of study, I had found in the surviving sources references to only six provincial orphanages in the Byzantine Empire. This was, nevertheless, a considerable achievement because a number of scholars, after combing medieval sources, had maintained that Byzantium knew only one orphanage, the Orphanotropheion (The Orphanage), located in Constantinople. Despite this limited success, I failed to find information on how many children lived in any of these institutions. The only information on the size of orphanages came from a twelfth-century monastery for women; the founder of this institution required that the nuns always maintain two orphan girls in the community.

From the evidence I had assembled it seemed likely that Byzantine orphanages could shelter only a few children at a time. Such a conclusion would have confirmed the views regarding East Roman hospitals that scholars such as Ewald Kisslinger and Michael Dols had expressed—namely, that most Byzantine philanthropic institutions had been small and could afford to provide only limited care to a few patients and poverty-stricken guests.

At this point Professor George Dennis, S. J., who directed my dissertation at The Catholic University of America, sent me one of his entertaining notes together with a photocopy of a letter by Theodore of Stoudios (early ninth century). Father Dennis had been reading the letters of Theodore in preparation for a study of Michael Psellos's letters when he noticed that Letter 211 of the Theodore collection described a privately funded orphanage just outside the Bithynian town of Prousa. Moreover, Theodore's letter specifically stated that this institution took care of forty boys and forty girls. Dennis's discovery altered the whole picture of Byzantine orphanages. If a private orphanage outside Prousa served eighty children, how many did the great Orphanotropheion of Constantinople care for?

In listing the men who served as *orphanotrophoi* (directors) of the Orphanotropheion of Constantinople, I noticed that in a few cases these officials had been monks or clerics. Dr. John Nesbitt, a research associate specializing in sigilography at the Byzantine Center, Dumbarton Oaks, Washington, D.C., suggested that this particular office could have been part of both an ecclesiastical and a secular *cursus honorum*. He decided to examine carefully lead seals of *orphanotrophoi* to determine how many directors came from clerical or monastic backgrounds. The results of his research will appear shortly in two articles: "St. Zotikos and the Early History of the Office of Orphanotrophos," to appear in a memorial volume for Nicholas Oikonomides, published by the Center for Byzantine Studies, Athens, Greece; and "The Orphanotrophos: Some Observations on the History of the Office in Light of the Seals," to appear in *Studies in Sigillography,* vol. 8. These articles will augment the information presented in Chapter Seven concerning the orphanage directors of Constantinople.

Throughout the years I spent in preparing this book, I had been thinking about a suitable illustration for the cover, an icon or manu-

xii PREFACE

script illustration that would capture the theme of Christian care for children. As late as May 2002, I still had found nothing that I could use. I discussed my dilemma with Dr. John Cotsonis, director of the Archbishop Jakovos Library, Hellenic College / Holy Cross Greek Orthodox School of Theology, and he immediately suggested a manuscript illustration depicting Christ blessing a little child, from Codex 587 in the Monastery of Dionysiou on Mount Athos. With the kind permission of Archimandrite Petros, kathegoumenos of the Dionysiou Monastery, this beautiful miniature appears on the cover of this volume.

Besides these colleagues, I want to thank Mr. Mark Zapatka for frequent assistance at the Dumbarton Oaks Library, and Mr. Joseph Mills for preparing the cover illustration. I would have been unable even to have begun this project without the hospitality of Dr. David Johnson, S.J., and Rev. Raymond Studzinski, O.S.B., who often offered me a room at Curley Hall when I needed to spend several days either at Dumbarton Oaks or at the Mullen Library of The Catholic University of America. At my home institution, Salisbury University, I would like to thank Susan Wheatley, Audrey Schadt, and Diane Abresch at Blackwell Library for their help with the bibliography. Finally, I should mention the excellent work of Philip Holthaus, Susan Needham, and Beth Benevides, all of The Catholic University of America Press, for their help and advice in preparing this manuscript for publication.

I extend special thanks to Dr. Aristides Sismanis of Richmond, Virginia, for his support of this project. His encouragement helped me through some difficult periods in completing this book. He also invited me to address the Hellenic Society Paideia of Virginia. The financial support from the members of this organization have made this book possible.

ABBREVIATIONS

AB   *Analecta Bollandiana.* Brussels, 1882– .

ACO   *Acta conciliorum oecumenicorum.* 4 volumes in 27 parts. Edited by Eduard Schwartz. Berlin and Leipzig: De Gruyter, 1922–1974.

ActaSS   *Acta Sanctorum.* Antwerp, 1643–. 3rd ed. 71 volumes. Paris, 1863–1940.

Bas   *Basilicorum Libri LX.* 17 volumes (including scholia). Edited by H. J. Scheltema and N. van der Wal. Groningen: Wolters, 1953–.

BGU   *Berliner griechische Urkunden. Ägyptische Urkunden aus den königlichen Museen zu Berlin.* 4 volumes. Berlin, 1895–1912.

BZ   *Byzantinische Zeitschrift.* Munich, 1892– .

CodTheo   *Codex Theodosianus.* 2 volumes in 3 parts. Edited by Theodor Mommsen and Paul M. Meyer. Berlin: Weidmann, 1905. Translated into English by Clyde Pharr. New York, 1952.

CSHB   Corpus Scriptorum Historiae Byzantinae. 50 volumes. Bonn: W. Weber, 1828–1897.

Dig   *See Corpus juris civilis,* vol. 1.

DOP   *Dumbarton Oaks Papers.* Washington, D.C., 1941–.

GCS   Die griechischen christlichen Schriftsteller der ersten Jahrhunderte. Leipzig and Berlin: Akademie-Verlag, 1897–.

Inst   See *Corpus juris civilis,* vol. 1.

JCod   See *Corpus juris civilis,* vol. 2.

JGR   *Jus Graecoromanum.* 8 volumes. Edited by Karl E. Zachariä von Lingenthal and prepared by Ioannes and Panagiotes Zepos . Athens: Phexi and Son, 1931; reprint, Aalen, 1962.

JNov See *Corpus juris civilis*, vol. 3.

MM   Miklosich, Franz, and Müller, Joseph, editors. *Acta et diplo-mata graeca medii aevi.* 6 volumes. Vienna: C. Gerold, 1860–1890: reprint, Aalen, 1968.

OCP   *Orientalia Christiana Periodica.* Rome, 1935–.

ODB   *Oxford Dictionary of Byzantium.* 3 volumes. Edited by Alexander Kazhdan, Alice-Mary Talbot, Anthony Cutler, et al. New York and Oxford: Oxford University Press, 1991.

PG   Patrologiae cursus completus. Series graeca. 161 volumes. Edited by Jacques-Paul Migne. Paris, 1857–1866.

PLips *Griechische Urkunden der Papyrussammlung zu Leipzig.* Vol.1. Edited by Ludwig Mitteis, with contributions by Ulrich Wilcken. Leipzig: Teubner, 1906.

PLond *Greek Papyri in the British Museum.* Vol. 5. Edited by H. I. Bell. London: British Museum, 1917.

POxy *The Oxyrhynchus Papyri.* London: Egypt Exploration Fund, 1898–1919 and Egypt Exploration Society, 1920–.

RE   *Paulys Realencyclopädie der classischen Altertumswissenschaft.* 24 volumes. Revised and edited by Georg Wissowa and Wilhelm Kroll. Stuttgart: J. B. Metzler, 1893–.

REB   *Revue des Études Byzantines.* Bucharest, 1947–1948; Paris, 1949–.

RP   Rhalles, Georgios, and Potles. Michael, editors. Σύνταγμα-τα τῶν Θείων ἱερῶν Κανόνων. 6 volumes. Athens: G. Chartophylax, 1852–1859.

SC   Sources Chrétiennes. Paris: Cerf, 1941–.

THE ORPHANS OF
BYZANTIUM

I   INTRODUCTION

From among the children who had been deprived of their parents and were pierced by the evil of *orphania* [orphanhood], the <emperor Alexios Komnenos> assigned some to relatives and others whom he knew to be pious to the superiors of the holy monasteries. The emperor commanded that <the monks> raise these <orphans> not as slaves, but as free persons, considering them worthy of a liberal education and instructing them in the Holy Scriptures. Some <orphans> he entrusted to the Orphanotropheion which he had constructed, handing them over to those in charge to be taught general education.[1]

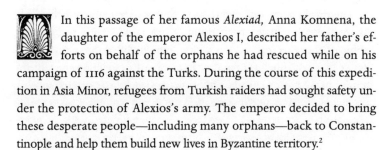 In this passage of her famous *Alexiad*, Anna Komnena, the daughter of the emperor Alexios I, described her father's efforts on behalf of the orphans he had rescued while on his campaign of 1116 against the Turks. During the course of this expedition in Asia Minor, refugees from Turkish raiders had sought safety under the protection of Alexios's army. The emperor decided to bring these desperate people—including many orphans—back to Constantinople and help them build new lives in Byzantine territory.[2]

To assist the children, Alexios had to find adults who were willing to shelter, nourish, and educate them. In Anna's compact prose, she listed three groups of orphans, each of which the emperor aided in a different way. The first group he assigned to relatives, the second group he entrusted to monasteries, and the third group he committed to the Orphanotropheion, a large state-run orphanage that Alexios himself had recently reorganized and refinanced.

1. Anna Komnena, *Alexiad*, 15.7.3 (3: 214).   2. Treadgold, p. 628.

Anna's description contains a great deal of information in just a few sentences. Indeed, her prose is so compact yet detailed that its precise meaning has escaped her modern interpreters.[3] To understand Anna's description the reader must have some knowledge of the Byzantine child welfare program. In a sense, the monograph that follows is an extended commentary on Anna's two-sentence passage regarding her father's actions on behalf of these refugee children.

For her learned contemporary readers, Anna provided just enough information to identify exactly what type of assistance each of the three categories of orphans received. The emperor Alexios was able to help the first group of children by enforcing the extant laws of guardianship, which required adult relatives to take in younger members of the extended family who had lost both their parents. The Byzantine state, or the East Roman Empire, had inherited most of these guardianship regulations from pre-Christian Roman society.

The emperor assisted the orphans in the second group by placing them in monastic schools. These children had no relatives in Constantinople, but they had received baptism and knew enough about the Christian faith that they could enter the capital's monasteries as students and potential members of these ascetic communities.

The third group assigned to the Orphanotropheion, on the other hand, had enjoyed no instruction in Christian doctrine and custom. Some of these were Turkish children who had fled the many clashes between Turkish tribesmen and Byzantine forces along the shifting border in western Anatolia. Others were Greek boys or girls who, in the chaos of early-twelfth-century Asia Minor, had never been taught

---

3. Cf. the translation by Sewter, p. 492: "All children who had lost their parents and were afflicted by the grievous ills of orphanhood were committed to the care of relatives and to others who, he knew, were respectable people, as well as to abbots of the holy monasteries, . . ." Sewter takes the accusative ὁπόσους to be an indirect object parallel with τοῖς τε συγγενέσι. In fact, it must be the direct object of the participle διανείμας ("assigning others to the monasteries"). In his French translation, Leib, the editor of the Greek text, understands ὁπόσους as modifying τοῖς συγγενέσι: "Tous les enfants qui avaient perdu leurs parents et qui, orphelins, étaient meurtris par cette cruelle épreuve, furent répartis par ses soins entre leurs proches, quand il les savait d'une honorabilité notoire, et les higoumènes des saints monastères, . . ." (Anna Komnena, *Alexiad*, 15.7.3 [3: 214]). Leib's translation thus has an accusative relative pronoun modifying a dative plural noun. The recent German translation of this passage by Dieter Reinsch (1996) agrees with the interpretation presented here.

the basic elements of their Christian faith. Anna's subsequent description of students at the Orphanotropheion leaves no doubt that by Alexios's reign this philanthropic institution received many barbarian students to instruct them in Christian doctrine and initiate them into the world of Hellenic civilization.[4]

Clearly, by the reign of Alexios, East Roman society had evolved a complex system of caring for children who had lost both parents. From ancient Roman society, the Byzantine Empire had inherited the laws of guardianship. From the Christian Church, it had received and expanded a system of charitable group homes and schools, many of which were administered by bishops or monasteries. Finally, from the unique historical forces shaping its capital city of Constantinople, it developed the Orphanotropheion, an institution that had begun as a simple episcopal orphanage for abandoned children from the streets of the city and had then evolved into a large and complex government agency supervising a wide range of welfare services including the care of barbarian children and other young victims of warfare. Anna's account thus presents a picture of child welfare based on several different approaches to providing food, shelter, and nurture, a system inspired by ancient legal traditions, Christian charity, and the classical concept of the *polis*.

As we noted above, modern scholars have failed to capture the correct sense of Anna's description because they did not have enough information available to recognize the distinctions that she was making. In fact, no modern historian has examined even superficially the program that the East Roman Empire evolved over many centuries to aid homeless children. In the past fifty years, scholars have begun to recognize how extensive was the general welfare program in the Byzantine Empire, a system supported by the imperial government, the Orthodox Church, the monastic movement, and private persons. Several monographs have described the network of almshouses *(xenodocheia* or *diakoniai),* old-age homes *(gerokomeia),* medical hospitals *(nosokomeia* or *xenones),* and orphanages *(orphanotropheia)* that East Roman society maintained to aid all kinds of needy people.[5] The aim of this present book is to focus on the institutions and programs that Byzantine socie-

---

4. Anna Komnena, *Alexiad,* 15.7.9 (3: 218).
5. Constantelos, *Byzantine Philanthropy,* and Volk, *Klostertypika.*

ty developed to assist orphans. It is my intention to provide enough information on guardianship laws, philanthropic institutions, and adoption practices so that readers will have some concept of how Byzantine society evolved the complex system that Anna briefly outlined in the *Alexiad*.

In 1985, I published a book on Byzantine hospitals, usually called *xenones* in medieval Greek. These philanthropic institutions had begun as simple almshouses in the fourth century, but rapidly evolved into centers of medical care. By the reign of the emperor Justinian (527–565), the best physicians of the empire dedicated a substantial portion of their professional efforts to curing indigent patients in these *xenones*. During the centuries that followed, these hospitals expanded their services and by the eleventh and twelfth centuries had become the major centers of health care in Constantinople and perhaps in other large Byzantine towns such as Thessalonike and Nicaea. By 1100, the Byzantine medical profession had reorganized its practice around these philanthropic institutions to provide in-house hospital care as well as outpatient services for the sick who remained in their own homes. Not only the poor, but people of the middle class, and under special circumstances even aristocrats and members of the imperial family, sought medical treatment in Byzantine hospitals.

After presenting evidence found in both published and unpublished sources, I reached several conclusions concerning Byzantine *xenones*, conclusions that challenged traditional notions of how medieval physicians practiced their profession. In place of a system based on private practitioners who charged fees to cure patients in their shops or to visit the sick in their own homes, the Byzantine health care service offered free medical care to all, but provided this treatment through the wards and outpatient clinics of the *xenones*.[6]

When I turned my attention to investigating the Byzantine child care system, I expected to find the same sort of institutional centralization around *orphanotropheia*, located in the empire's larger cities. Indeed, the emperor Justinian, the great legal reformer of the sixth century, placed *orphanotropheia* in the same legal category of pious

6. Miller, *Birth*, esp. "Introduction to the 1997 Edition," pp. xi–xxxii.

foundations as he did the hospitals. These orphanages, however, never came to dominate the child welfare system to the same extent that *xenones* eventually controlled the provision of medical care. Despite the attempt of the iconoclastic emperors (717–867) to place more children without parents in church-run group homes, Byzantine society preferred to leave orphans with relatives.[7] As a result, most state activity on behalf of orphans focused on reforming guardianship laws rather than on building large institutions to house and educate homeless children.

This study will trace these changes in the laws of guardianship and try to evaluate the success or failure of well-intentioned but sometimes ill-conceived reforms. It also will examine how the Byzantine system utilized orphanages and integrated their services into a complete system of care for orphans. Finally, this study will evaluate the success of each element of the child care system. Did family guardians actually provide good foster homes for orphans? Were children who stayed with an uncle or an aunt better off than those whose guardians were adult brothers or sisters? Did women make better guardians than men? Did the alumni of orphanages do better in later life than the children who found a home with a family member or perhaps with a stranger willing to adopt them?

Because of the primary role guardianship played in finding adults to care for orphans, this book deals not only with the evolution of a child welfare system in the East Roman Empire, but also with important areas of the Byzantine legal system—that is, family law and the law of wills. So crucial was knowledge of Byzantine law in assisting orphans that many directors of the Orphanotropheion in Constantinople (the *orphanotrophoi*) were selected from candidates with wide experience in the law courts of the empire. Historians are just beginning to use Byzantine legal manuals and casebooks to extract valuable information concerning the details of East Roman legal history as well as concerning aspects of social history, family organization, and economic development. Thus, this study will prove useful not only for the information it provides on the care of orphans, but also for the light it sheds on the

---

7. *Ecloga*, 7.1 (p. 198).

Byzantine legal system. How much did Byzantine legislation alter the rules and the spirit of ancient Roman laws? Did the laws issued by the emperors actually affect the daily lives of Byzantine subjects? Finally, what sort of information can historians expect to find in the legislative texts and legal handbooks of Byzantium?[8]

To study the care of orphans, it is also necessary to examine the educational system of the Byzantine world. All the East Roman orphanages about which detailed information has survived emphasized education as the cornerstone of their program of child care. In the fourth century, Basil of Caesarea, one of the most influential writers of the Greek-speaking church, laid out specific rules for educating homeless children as well as those with living parents. He devoted "Question Fifteen" of his famous *Long Rules* for his monks to describing how monasteries should organize their schools for both boys and girls. Basil laid down regulations for discipline and recommended methods of instruction including academic contests for the children.[9] In the centuries that followed, orphan schools, supported by both bishops and monastic communities, closely followed Basil's suggestions. By the twelfth century, the biggest orphan home in the empire, the Orphanotropheion of Constantinople, had become famous as an educational institution that employed some of the leading intellectuals of the day to teach its students. The Orphanotropheion also sponsored contests for its children, just as Basil had recommended.

Education clearly shaped the routine of daily life in Byzantine orphanages, but primary sources also show that successful guardians considered education as one of their first obligations. When the future monastic leader Plato of Sakkoudion lost both his parents in the middle of the eighth century, his uncle accepted the boy into his home and gave him excellent training in accounting and bookkeeping, training that gained Plato a lucrative government post as his uncle's assistant.[10] In the early fourteenth century, Athanasios, the future leader of the Meteora monasteries, also received an excellent education under his

---

8. See the articles in *Law,* esp. the "Preface," pp. vii–ix.
9. Basil, *Interrogatio XV* (PG, 31: 952–58).
10. *Oratio XI* (PG, 99: 808).

uncle's tutelage.[11] Many other sources stress the same point: a conscientious guardian secured a good education for his ward.

A careful study of orphan care in the Byzantine Empire, therefore, must examine what sort of education orphans in fact received. With regard to guardians, the sources do not reveal any clear pattern. In some cases the guardians personally tutored their wards, but in other cases they sent them away to schools. The few surviving sources we have regarding group homes, however, do describe many common elements in orphan schools. Some of these common practices derived from the guidelines that Basil of Caesarea had set down in his "Question Fifteen" while others the orphanages had inherited from the pre-Christian schools of Hellenistic and Roman times.

A monograph on how the Byzantine Empire cared for its orphans therefore must address many issues beyond those directly related to child care. It must discuss how the empire's orphan care program fit in with other social welfare programs such as the medical hospitals. With regard to guardianship, it must examine many legal issues arising from the Roman law tradition of *tutores* (legal guardians). Finally, it must explore the wider area of Byzantine education and instructional methods to understand how these orphan homes functioned. Moreover, in pursuing these goals, this study will focus on those elements of East Roman society that historians had ignored until the 1950s: the people beyond the circle of the imperial family and the key policymakers in church and state. The sources that we shall examine describe some children from the very poorest classes, many from the middle layers of society, and only a few, such as the nephews of Patriarch Keroularios, who came from the leading aristocratic families.

In studying Byzantine orphan care, it is also useful to address several issues beyond the scope of East Roman history proper. Since Byzantine civilization did not evolve in a vacuum but interacted on many levels with Christian society in the West, the methods the East Roman Empire used to care for homeless children both influenced Western in-

11. *Vita Athanasii (Meteora)*, pp. 239–41.

stitutions and in turn were effected by Latin developments. One cannot accurately trace the history of medieval orphan care in Western Europe nor account for the apparently sudden changes that appeared during the early Italian Renaissance without considering developments in the Byzantine Empire.

In the past fifteen years, medievalists have focused attention on a particular category of orphan children in Western Europe: abandoned infants. In 1989, John Boswell published a sweeping study of infant abandonment from pre-Christian Roman times to the Italian Renaissance. Boswell maintained that the practice of abandonment in ancient society usually did not end in the abandoned infant's death, but rather functioned as an informal adoption system. The christianizing of the Mediterranean basin made only minor changes in this ancient system, which continued until the late medieval period. At that time, many Italian towns decided to establish orphan asylums in order to prevent infant abandonment by providing a safe place to leave babies whom the natural parents were either unable or unwilling to keep. Boswell then showed that these asylums did not save the babies, but rather hastened their death. By a cruel irony, the well-intentioned establishment of infant asylums such as the Ospedale degli Innocenti in Florence or the Orphanage of the Holy Spirit in Rome did not save the lives of unwanted babies, but instead encouraged the abandonment of infants at an ever-increasing rate, a process that eventually led to severe overcrowding and eventually to the death of thousands in these chronically underfinanced charitable foundations.[12]

After the appearance of Boswell's controversial book, the École Française de Rome published a massive collection of articles on abandoned children in Italy and southern Europe from the fifteenth to the nineteenth century. The detailed research presented in these articles was based in most cases on careful statistical evidence; these studies prove that Boswell was wrong in claiming a high death rate for abandoned babies in such orphanages during the fifteenth century, but he was correct in maintaining that these institutions encouraged abandonment by offering the poor or the proud an easy and relatively guilt-

12. Boswell, *Kindness*, pp. 397–427.

less way of getting rid of unwanted infants.[13] As the number of babies kept increasing and eventually surpassed the capacity of such institutions to supervise the infants in their charge, death rates did indeed soar. By the middle of the eighteenth century, death rates at the Milan asylum and in the newer infant orphanages in Paris and Vienna were approaching 80 percent of the babies left in their care.[14]

The studies sponsored by the École Française de Rome, as well as several articles by Volker Hunecke in other publications, have emphasized the sudden appearance of these foundling orphanages in fifteenth-century Europe. Florence began construction of the Innocenti in 1419; Venice had a full-scale foundling home called the Pietà by the mid-fifteenth century; and Pope Sixtus IV redesigned a section of the Hospital of the Holy Spirit to accept abandoned infants and orphans in the 1470s. Hunecke stressed the fact that these foundling homes opened only in Italy during the 1400s and did not spread to other countries of Europe before the sixteenth century. Both Hunecke and Boswell reject the notion that the foundling hospitals of Renaissance Italy had developed out of earlier medieval traditions.[15]

Among the historians studying these Italian foundling homes, only Boswell took any interest in Byzantine sources. He briefly discussed the problems of infant abandonment in the Greek-speaking provinces of the Roman Empire and noticed in a footnote the Greek term *brephotropheion* (asylum for infants). Boswell claimed that Byzantine records fell silent concerning social conditions after the seventh century and therefore merited no further investigation. He then turned his gaze to the medieval West.[16]

As we shall see, specialized orphanages for abandoned infants, the *brephotropheia*, did indeed exist in the Byzantine Empire. Moreover, there is ample evidence to show that some episcopal and monastic schools were capable of accepting infants, finding them wet nurses,

13. See *Enfance abandonnée*, the large collection of articles by the École Française de Rome. See also the article by Hunecke, "Findelkinder," pp. 123–53.

14. Hunecke, "Abandonment," pp. 117–35.

15. For the origins of foundling homes in Italy, see Hunecke, "Findelkinder," pp. 142–48. With regard to the medieval origins of foundling homes, see Boswell, *Kindness*, p. 225, and Hunecke, "Abandonment," p. 119.

16. Boswell, *Kindness*, pp. 196–98, and note 63.

and eventually educating them. Anna Komnena even referred to wet nurses feeding babies at the Orphanotropheion of Constantinople, the only indication we have that some of the children at the great orphan school of the capital were abandoned infants.[17]

In sum, no complete study of orphan care in general or of abandoned infants in particular should ignore the thousand-year history of Byzantine welfare institutions. Especially when historians are considering medieval and Renaissance Italy, they need always to bear in mind the uninterrupted contact between Constantinople and the major cities of Italy. Social historians and other scholars should not forget that the Venetians chose to pattern San Marco on Justinian's famous five-domed Church of the Holy Apostles in the Byzantine capital. They should also recall that the Abbey of Grottaferrata near Rome maintained a continuous tradition of Greek asceticism from its foundation in 1003 through the time of Cardinal Bessarion (1403–1472) to the present. Moreover, Salerno, the southern Italian medical center, also remained in contact with the Byzantine world. Salernitan physicians translated many Byzantine medical texts, and some of these Western doctors even journeyed to Constantinople to study.[18] Finally, these historians should remember the Council of Ferrara-Florence (1438–1445) and the tremendous impact that this meeting of Latin and Greek bishops exercised on the subsequent course of the Italian Renaissance.

Especially in investigating social welfare institutions, historians should view Western philanthropic programs in light of developments in the East Roman provinces, an area that established highly specialized charitable facilities far earlier than did the West. From Constantine's conversion circa 312 to the early seventh century, many cities of the Greek-speaking provinces grew steadily in population. As these urban centers expanded, the local city governments and the Christian Church had to deal with ever more pressing social problems: homeless migrants from overpopulated villages, the aged without living relatives

17. Anna Komnena, *Alexiad*, 15.7.6 (3: 216).
18. For the Byzantine influence on Salerno, see Browning, "Greek Influence," pp. 189–94. For Salernitan doctors studying in Constantinople, see Magdalino, *Empire*, p. 363, and note 162.

to care for them, sick people too poor to afford medicines or doctors, and, of course, orphans and abandoned infants.

Such social problems arose not because of an impoverishment of the Eastern Empire, as earlier scholars had supposed, but because of a large population growth and a concomitant expansion of urban areas. The precapitalist economy of the East Roman Empire was unable to expand enough to integrate the new urban dwellers into manufacturing or commerce. As a result, the Christian bishops of large Eastern towns, such as Constantinople, Alexandria, Antioch, and Ephesus, opened many new philanthropic institutions to meet the varied needs of these people.[19]

During these same years the Latin provinces of the Late Roman Empire did not experience the same population boom nor the same expansion of urban populations. In the largely rural West, people remained in their village communities and were able to depend on extended family and local community networks for assistance. Thus, the Western bishops were less active in founding philanthropic institutions in their sees than were their Eastern brethren. Only in Italy did a few urban communities remain large enough to need specialized welfare institutions.

By the seventh century, Rome had shrunk greatly in population since its years of prosperity in the second century. The ancient capital, however, still retained some importance as a Byzantine military stronghold in Italy and as an ecclesiastical center with close ties to Constantinople. During the same years, despite deteriorating circumstances, the seaport town of Naples experienced some growth as a commercial center trading with cities of the Byzantine Empire. It is revealing that in the same seventh century, both Naples and Rome opened charitable institutions, called *diakoniai,* to provide food and access to bathing facilities for the poor. It is of even greater significance that these *diakoniai* were modeled on institutions that had first appeared almost a century earlier in the great Eastern cities of Antioch and Constantinople.[20]

Later, during the High Middle Ages, cities throughout Italy and oth-

---

19. Miller, *Birth,* pp. 68–88; Patlagean, *Pauvreté,* pp. 156–81.
20. Marrou, "L'origine orientale," pp. 95–142.

er areas of Latin Europe began to grow more rapidly. As a result, they too experienced the kind of social dislocation that had plagued the cities of the Greek East during the fifth and sixth centuries. To assist the growing number of homeless poor in Western towns of the twelfth century, the Knights of Saint John, a crusading order with close ties to the Byzantine world, established a network of philanthropic services throughout Western Europe, a network that helped to stimulate the foundation of many other charitable institutions.[21] These Western philanthropic facilities resembled in many ways the Byzantine foundations established five hundred years earlier during the reign of the emperor Justinian (527–565).

Any scholar who studies both Byzantine and Latin primary sources will soon see how many links existed between Eastern and Western charitable institutions. I do not maintain that all innovations in welfare services came from the Byzantine Empire. Certainly, some aspects of Western charitable programs developed spontaneously to meet immediate needs. For example, the Knights of Saint John organized their widespread network of hospitals and hospices to provide assistance to Western pilgrims and crusaders journeying to and from the Holy Land. Although the Knights borrowed some features of their medical services from Byzantine *xenones,* they developed a centralized administration of their charitable facilities that was distinctly Western. Moreover, there is evidence that some Western innovations in philanthropic care passed from west to east, especially during the thirteenth and fourteenth centuries.[22]

Given the many points of contact between the Byzantine Empire and Western Christendom, especially in the area of social welfare, one would expect that medieval Greek and Latin societies would also have shared many approaches to the problem of proper care for orphans. As a result, social historians should not be surprised that orphanages in Italy such as the Innocenti in Florence, the Hospital of the Holy Spirit in Rome, or the Pietà in Venice resembled earlier Byzantine institutions. These Western orphanages did not emerge ex nihilo as both

---

21. Miller, "Knights," pp. 709–33.

22. See the reference to centralized supervision of hospitals in fifteenth-century Constantinople in the account of Nicholas of Cusa (*Nicolai de Cusa cribratio Alkorani,* pp. 5–6).

Boswell and Hunecke have maintained, but had inherited a long institutional tradition with roots both in the Roman West and in the Byzantine East. A major goal of this study is to bring these Greek roots to the attention of a wider circle of scholars and laymen.

An understanding of how the East Roman Empire developed its system of orphan care and improved it through the years from 312 to 1453 also offers important insights on modern child welfare problems. A major mistake for today's welfare experts and social planners is to ignore the experiences of the past. Local, state, and federal agencies in the United States spend millions of dollars on expensive research projects involving wide-ranging surveys regarding homeless boys and girls, on costly psychological testing of children in foster care, and on follow-up studies to determine what happens to modern orphans—usually children ignored by negligent single mothers or removed from abusive homes. Private foundations also pour money into expensive research on the problems of today's foster children. Few government programs, private foundations, or even academic public policy centers, however, have supported historical research on how earlier societies handled social problems including the care of homeless children.

In developing solutions for society's most difficult problems, modern experts have condemned themselves to working in a historical vacuum. Very few people in child welfare work have displayed any interest in examining how ancient or medieval societies met the needs of orphaned or abandoned children. In such a delicate area of social planning, where well-intentioned reforms can so easily generate harmful unintended effects, politicians, social workers, and child care experts proceed with no knowledge of the many experiments conducted in the past. In such an atmosphere, it is no wonder that so often we are forced to reinvent the wheel again and again.

As an example, one need only consider the debate that Newt Gingrich, former Speaker of the U.S. House of Representatives, stirred up in 1994 when he suggested that Americans should consider reopening orphanages for some of the children currently trapped in the system of foster-care homes. Gingrich's suggestions triggered an avalanche of opposition to orphanages, largely based on a vague sense that orphanages had failed in the past to meet the needs of homeless children. In making their arguments, orphanage opponents often referred to the dismal asylum depicted by Charles Dickens's novel, *Oliver Twist*, published in 1840. On the other side of the argument, Gingrich appealed to a movie he had seen about the founding of Boys' Town in 1925.[23] Neither side in this debate had any accurate knowledge of the fourteen-hundred-year history of orphanages, of their successes and failures, of their role as educational centers and music schools, and occasionally of their use to eliminate unwanted children.

Neither Gingrich nor his opponents realized that their debate over the proper approach to orphan care—that is, orphanages or foster homes—had a long history. Immediately after World War II, England, the United States, and the other Allied Powers sponsored limited research on children who had been in group homes during the conflict. A generation earlier, following World War I, Germany had debated whether orphanages provided the proper environment for homeless children. Surprisingly, a great dispute over orphanages had also raged in Germany during the eighteenth century. German disciples of Jean Jacques Rousseau had condemned orphan asylums because they robbed children of a natural environment. According to these critics, children in orphanages not only lacked fathers and mothers, but they also missed the opportunity of living in a normal society and learning the natural lessons of hard work and financial responsibility, lessons that only a good foster home could provide.[24]

Other Enlightenment thinkers, however, argued that orphan schools offered the best environment to shape perfect citizens in the manner of the ancient Spartan schools. This concept eventually led the Jacobin Party of revolutionary France to sponsor orphanages as the ideal institutions to nurture true children of the *Patrie,* again on the model of the Spartan schools. The subsequent wars of the French Republic, however, prevented the Jacobins from building their utopian state orphanages.[25]

In short, the debate Gingrich's comments sparked in 1994 has a long

23. London, "1994 Orphanage Debate," pp. 79–102.

24. See the excellent but rarely cited essay by Jacobs, *Waisenhausstreit,* on arguments for and against orphanages in eighteenth-century Germany.

25. Forrest, *French Revolution,* pp. 116–33.

history stretching back to the Enlightenment and possibly even earlier. Those in charge of the Holy Spirit Hospital in seventeenth-century Rome conducted some interesting statistical studies that suggest that they too were considering the advantages of foster care over institutionalization. Very few people making decisions about homeless children in the United States, however, even suspect that a seventeenth-century Roman orphanage under the direct control of the pope might have discovered some important facts about institutionalized child care over three hundred years ago.[26]

From liberal and conservative politicians, to psychologists, social workers, and progressive social planners, almost no one considers the past as a source of practical experience recording successes and failures, brilliant reforms and costly setbacks. As we enter the twenty-first century, it seems imperative not to ignore the vast fund of information that the past has to offer concerning social problems, and no ancient or medieval state was more inventive in the field of social welfare than the Christian Empire of Byzantium.

SOURCES

Before beginning this study, it is useful to discuss briefly the extant primary sources that describe orphan care in the Byzantine Empire. Since the legal institution of guardianship formed the key element in the Byzantine child welfare system, collections of imperial legislation and manuals summarizing principles of East Roman law offer perhaps the most basic information. To understand how Byzantine society selected guardians and protected orphans from abuses by these same adult custodians, one must carefully examine the many relevant imperial laws that have been preserved in law codes from the fifth-century *Codex Theodosianus* to the last Byzantine legal manual, the fourteenth-century *Hexabiblos* of Constantine Harmenopoulos. Most of these legal texts either reproduce or summarize specific laws of the emperors, but a few, such as the eleventh-century *Peira*, include records of individual cases involving orphans and their guardians. The most fascinating collection of case law, however, comes not from a codex of imperial

26. Schiavoni, "Gli infanti esposti," pp. 1031–37.

laws or a legal manual, but from a private collection of court cases decided by the thirteenth-century archbishop of Ohrid, Demetrios Chomatianos. Of the one hundred and ten cases in this collection that involve issues of private law, thirteen deal directly with guardianship disputes and preserve invaluable information on how courts actually applied the regulations governing this institution.[27]

With regard to group homes, we have already discussed two of the principal sources, Anna Komnena's *Alexiad* and Basil of Cappadocia's "Question Fifteen." In addition to outlining the three methods of assisting orphans that Anna's father activated in 1116, the *Alexiad* offers the most complete description of the Orphanotropheion of Constantinople that has so far been found among the records of the Byzantine period. Basil's "Question Fifteen," on the other hand, influenced the educational organization both of the Constantinopolitan Orphanotropheion and of the many smaller provincial orphanages from the fourth to the fourteenth century.[28]

In addition to these two sources, several letters of the ninth-century monastic leader Theodore of Stoudios offer important details on the size of provincial orphanages.[29] Finally, the thirteenth-century letters of John Apokaukos vividly depict the difficult discipline problems that the directors of orphanages confronted in dealing with individual children in their care.[30]

Most Byzantine sources describing orphans either in the care of guardians or in group homes assumed that these children had lost both parents. Anna Komnena stated explicitly that the orphans whom her father brought back from Asia Minor had no living parents and therefore needed guardians or the discipline of a Constantinopolitan orphanage. In fact, Byzantine writers used the Greek term *orphanos* much as contemporary speakers of English employ the modern word "orphan." Today's English dictionaries list the primary meaning of *orphan* as "a child whose father and mother have died." A common second meaning, however, is a child who has lost only one of its two par-

27. Chomatianos, nos. 24, 32, 42, 59, 63, 81, 82, 83, 84, 85, 90, 91, and 95.

28. Basil, *Interrogatio XV* (PG, 31: 952–58); Anna Komnena, *Alexiad*, 15.7.1–9 (3: 213–18).

29. Theodore of Stoudios, *Ep.* 211 (pp. 333–34).

30. Apokaukos, *Epistolai*, Ep. 27 (pp. 85–88); Ep. 100 (pp. 150–52), and Ep. 101 (p. 52).

ents. Byzantine sources reflect the same ambiguity. For example, the letters of a tenth-century mother referred to her son as an orphan because his father had recently died.[31] The Byzantine term *orphanos* and its modern derivatives have inherited this ambiguity from the world of classical antiquity.

Both the Greeks and the Romans of the pre-Christian period considered an orphan to be a child without a living father. For the Greeks of Periclean Athens, Hector's son Astyanax from Book 22 of the *Iliad* symbolized the hardships suffered by all orphans, but especially those of powerful families. Although Astyanax still had his mother, Andromache, he had lost his father, Hector, and the protection that only a male parent could provide in a society of warriors (*Iliad,* 22.484–506).

Ancient Rome also defined an orphan as a child who had lost its father. According to Roman law, a woman could not physically protect her children. Therefore, if her husband died, the mother's children were classed as orphans and needed a male guardian, even if the mother was willing to care for them herself and had the financial resources to raise them. A mother might continue to nurture her children, but she needed the approval of a male guardian for major decisions regarding the children's education, marriage, or property.[32]

The story of how mothers came to exercise the rights of guardianship over their own children represents a key element in the unfolding of the Byzantine approach to child welfare. It also forms part of the process whereby the Christian emperors removed one by one the legal liabilities that women had suffered under the classical Roman legal system and the earlier laws of the individual Greek *poleis*. Moreover, it explains how, during the early Byzantine period, the term *orphanos* came to mean primarily children who had lost both parents.

In examining the issue of mothers and their role as legal guardians, I shall naturally include specific cases of children who had lost only their fathers and therefore fell under the protection of their mothers. This study as a whole, however, will focus on what the Byzantines from the time of the emperor Justinian (527–565) judged to be true orphans, that is, children who had lost both parents.

31. Symeon Magistros, no. 31 (pp. 120–21).   32. See Chapter Two.

As in most areas of history before the fifteenth century, not enough information from the Byzantine period survives to provide statistical certainty concerning any question about orphans and the care they received. From the vast span of years beginning with the foundation of Constantinople in 326 and stretching to the conquest of this city by the Turks in 1453, I have found biographical information concerning seventy-seven orphaned children. These seventy-seven cases represent the only data base for this study. Although this sample is too small to offer any statistical certainty, with respect to some key questions the careful study of these cases does provide significant information, especially when other kinds of evidence confirm conclusions based on an analysis of these seventy-seven children. The Appendix lists these seventy-seven cases in chronological order.

With regard to the orphans of ancient Athens, Lysias, Demosthenes, and the other Attic rhetoricians have preserved in their orations most of the details regarding the lives of children who had lost a father or perhaps both parents. Since these speeches formed part of the litigation concerning guardianships, however, they leave an inaccurate impression that most orphans of classical Greece suffered at the hands of unscrupulous adult protectors. The information regarding the seventy-seven Byzantine orphans, on the other hand, comes from a wider range of sources. Only fifteen of the seventy-seven cases are preserved in court records. As one would expect, all of these children had major legal problems resulting from their status as orphans. In eleven of these disputes the guardians had caused these legal difficulties; in three other cases someone else had defrauded the children.

The greatest number of orphan biographies from Byzantine times, however, derive not from forensic orations or court records, but from hagiographical sources—thirty-four, or almost half, of the seventy-seven cases. Unlike court cases which by their very nature described only children involved in legal conflicts, these biographies recounted the lives of orphans who had led holy lives, whether or not they had suffered injustices during their childhood years. Saints' lives, therefore, provide a more representative sample of how orphans fared in Byzantine times. Of the thirty-four children described in these hagiographical sources, twenty had good experiences, thirteen had bad experiences, and in one case the biography did not include enough information to evaluate the orphan's early life.

In addition to hagiography and court records, several other categories of historical records describe the lives of orphans. Specifically, detailed biographical information on children without parents comes from eight letters, six Egyptian papyrus documents (not court cases), four nonforensic speeches, two narrative histories, one poem, one imperial novel, and four monastic *typika* (the foundation charters of individual Byzantine monasteries). Like the saints' lives, these sources better reflect how Byzantine orphans were treated than do the court records.

Compared to the evidence from classical Athens, therefore, the seventy-seven Byzantine cases provide a more balanced picture of how in fact society treated its orphans. Again, the number of examples is not sufficient for statistical certainty, but with respect to a few key questions these Byzantine sources do offer conclusive answers.

Besides these seventy-seven cases, we have available a different category of evidence based on detailed tax surveys. Although the vast fiscal records of the Byzantine state have all vanished, a few monastic documents of the thirteenth and fourteenth centuries preserve private copies of government tax surveys that include detailed information concerning the composition of each taxable family. For example, the Limbiotissa monastery, located in the vicinity of Smyrna, saved a thirteenth-century tax assessment from the nearby village of Baré. The contemporary Christodoulos monastery on Patmos possessed similar records from two villages on a neighboring island, probably Lernos. The records from these three villages list fifty-one families; of these households only four families included nephews or younger siblings who were probably orphans living with uncle or brother guardians. Thus, from this sample of fifty-one families in three different villages, 7.8 percent of the households appear to have been caring for children who had lost both parents.[33]

The monastery of Iveron on Mount Athos saved a similar tax record dated 1301 from six villages near Thessalonike. This survey listed 167

33. MM, 4: 13–14 (anno 1235) and MM, 6: 215–16 (anno 1263).

families, of which 43 households included relatives or adopted children most of whom were either orphaned or abandoned, that is, 25.6 percent of the families. That more orphans or abandoned children were living with relatives or foster parents in fourteenth-century Macedonia than had been living with uncles or older brothers fifty years earlier in the Aegean basin should not cause surprise. This disparity probably resulted from increased political and military instability in the southern Balkans following the death of Emperor Michael VIII in 1282.[34]

In considering these figures, one should recall, first, that the number of true orphans residing with guardian relatives was no doubt somewhat lower than these numbers indicate since not all the younger brothers and sisters living with older siblings were minors at the time of the survey. If some had reached adulthood, they would no longer have been classed as orphans though they continued to live in the households of their older siblings. Second, the disparity in the number of orphans between these two distinct areas and times vividly portrays how the number of orphans could oscillate from decade to decade and from place to place. It shows, moreover, that these oscillations were closely tied to political, military, and social problems.

As Anna recounted in the *Alexiad*, the Turkish invasions and subsequent warfare between Byzantine forces and Moslem armies greatly elevated the number of orphans in Asia Minor and led to the emperor Alexios's rescue efforts of 1116. As we shall see in the study that follows, warfare, but especially an endemic state of guerrilla conflict, could create a larger number of homeless children and necessitate the opening of many new orphanages.

One must also bear in mind that these tax records come only from rural areas. The statistics regarding orphans might differ in tax records from the great city of Constantinople or even from more modest towns such as Smyrna or Nicaea.

In sum, these tax records cannot offer any reliable evidence as to how common orphans were at any one time throughout the extensive and varied Byzantine lands. They do not even provide maximum and minimum statistics for the frequency of *orphania*. Fortunately, it is pos-

---

34. Dölger, *Aus den Schatzkammern*, pp. 35–51.

sible to make a few comparisons with other societies to place the Byzantine situation in perspective.

In a recent study of orphans during the Roman period, Jens-Uwe Krause calculated the number of orphans in Roman Egypt based on a series of papyrus documents: marriage arrangements, apprentice contracts, and applications for admission to the roles of young adults *(ephebate)*. Basing his calculations on a limited number of these documents, mostly from the first and second centuries, A.D., Krause concluded that about 40–45 percent of the children were orphans by the time they reached their teens. Since Krause was studying pre-Byzantine Egypt, he classed children whose fathers had died and were represented by their mothers as orphans. Krause then compared this percentage with records from rural England in the seventeenth century, where 35.4 percent of the children were either true orphans or had only one parent still living.[35]

By including families headed by widows together with the households caring for true orphans, we can obtain comparable statistics from the Byzantine tax records. Of the fifty-one families from the thirteenth century, 25.5 percent of the homes were either headed by widows or had true orphans under their roof; of the 167 families from Macedonia, 44 percent had widows as their heads or maintained true orphans in their care. The Macedonian statistics thus fit in at the higher end of Krause's reckoning for Roman Egypt, while those from the Aegean basin are considerably lower.

From the above considerations, one can easily see that such tax records cannot be used to determine how many Byzantine families were caring for orphans. These documents, however, do offer important information that can be used to corroborate the results of studies based on the seventy-seven cases. For example, classifying the seventy-seven cases shows clearly that uncles and adult brothers served as guardians for orphans far more frequently than did any other family relatives, a conclusion confirmed by a careful analysis of the tax records.

35. Krause, *Rechtliche und soziale Stellung*, pp. 6–10.

II THE ANCIENT WORLD

 Classical Greco-Roman civilization underlay many facets of East Roman society. Ancient Greece and Rome inspired Byzantine political concepts, literary tastes, ideas about the material universe, and philosophical systems, as well as the more mundane aspects of life such as games, foods, festivals, and superstitions. It is not surprising, therefore, that the Greco-Roman world also helped to shape the ideas the Byzantines held about orphans and the methods they adopted to assist these children.

We have already noted that the Byzantine Empire as the later phase of the Roman state continued to uphold the Roman law in the eastern Mediterranean and thus maintained the Roman rules regarding guardianship—the most common method of protecting, nurturing, and educating Byzantine orphans. East Roman society, however, was built not only on Roman legal and governmental institutions; it rested also on the incomparable heritage of Hellenic civilization and on the religious traditions of Judaism as Christianity interpreted them. To comprehend how Byzantine society cared for its orphans, one must first examine how these three earlier civilizations—Greek, Roman, and Jewish—treated children who had lost their parents.[1] Such a study is especially necessary because these three civilizations in some instances differed dramatically in the way they viewed *orphania*.

---

1. Ostrogorsky, *History*, p. 27: "Roman political concepts, Greek culture, and Christian faith were the main elements which determined Byzantine development. Without all three the Byzantine way of life would have been inconceivable."

ANCIENT GREECE

Although Roman civilization directly shaped the Byzantine state and its legal system, ancient Hellas perhaps exercised an even greater influence on East Roman society. First, the Byzantine capital and the provinces it governed lay in the Greek-speaking half of the former Roman Empire. The subjects of the Byzantine emperor were either descendants of the ancient Greeks or of the peoples hellenized in the wake of Alexander's conquests. Second, the official language of the Byzantine Empire was in fact ancient Greek. After the mid-sixth century, the government used Greek for all its decrees and legal proceedings, and the Byzantine Church had inherited Greek from the Christian communities of apostolic times. Third, educated Byzantines had far easier access to ancient Greek literature than they did to Latin works.[2] It is therefore essential to study how the ancient Hellenes considered the plight of orphans and the steps they took to aid them.

To comprehend the Roman influence on Byzantine orphan care, one can focus almost exclusively on studying legal texts that define Roman rules of guardianship, but to understand how ancient Greece shaped this care, one must turn to a wider selection of Hellenic literature—epic poetry, drama, rhetoric, political philosophy, and historiography—the classical texts that exercised such a powerful hold on the imaginations of the Byzantine elite.

After the Bible, the Homeric poems occupied the premier place in the Byzantine hierarchy of literature. As we saw in Chapter One, the *Iliad* preserved at the close of Book 22 the passage best known among educated Byzantines as the *typos* of an orphan's suffering. Achilles had just slain Hector and the Greeks were dragging the body of the fallen Trojan hero back to their ships. As Hector's wife, Andromache, watched from the walls of Troy, she lamented the fate of their orphaned son, Astyanax, and presented a vivid picture of the injustices and humiliations he would endure as a fatherless child (*Iliad*, 22.484–506).

---

2. Wilson, *Scholars*, esp. pp. 1–27, and Hunger, *Reich*, pp. 299–369.

Both modern and Byzantine commentators on the *Iliad* have classi-fied Andromache's speech as a later interpolation since her words here do not fit the context. The Greeks and the Romans of pre-Christian times considered an orphan a child without a living father or grandfa-ther. Astyanax had lost his own father, Hector, but Astyanax still had a powerful grandfather, Priam, who as ruler of Troy could easily have protected the boy. The twelfth-century Byzantine commentator Eu-stathios claimed that these lines, spoken by Andromache, applied not to the life of a prince such as Astyanax, whose grandfather still reigned, but to the suffering of orphans without powerful male guardians.[3] Modern critical opinion also holds that these lines were added after the *Iliad* was composed circa 800 B.C. and describe the fate of the typical or-phan from an aristocratic family in Archaic Greece (700–500 B.C.).[4]

According to Andromache's speech, such an orphan could expect other aristocratic families to seize his patrimonial lands. Without friends he would wander about downcast and alone. Even his father's companions *(hetairoi)* would reject the boy and refuse him a seat at their festive meals. Worst of all, one of the *amphithaleis* (children with both parents still living) would come forward to eject him from his banquet seat. Striking the boy and hurling insults, the brazen *am-phithales* would send the poor orphan crying back to his helpless moth-er (*Iliad*, 22.496–98).

This passage shows that a living mother provided no help for an or-phan in Archaic Greek society. Without a father alive, or a grandfather, the boy had no protection. At this period in its social development, Greece had apparently not yet devised the concept of a legal guardian *(epitropos)*. Moreover, the passage reveals that an *amphithales* drove away the orphan with no protest from the father's *hetairoi*. Archaic and Classical (500–336 B.C.) Greek culture allotted a special place of honor to these *amphithaleis*. Children or youth with both parents living were comparatively rare in Archaic Greece both because life expectancy in general was short and, more specifically, because female deaths in

3. Eustathios, *Commentarii*, pp. 661–62.
4. The famous Alexandrian scholar Aristarchus (second century B.C.) considered these lines spurious. See the standard school text of the *Iliad* and the commentary in Monro, *Homer*, p. 395 (for *Iliad* 22.487).

childbirth occurred frequently. Thus, children with a living mother and father were considered blessed by fortune and especially favored by the gods.

At Athens these *amphithaleis* performed special rites in honor of Apollo. They also participated at several stages in the traditional wedding ceremonies. They formed part of both the bride's and the groom's procession, and, crowned with acorn wreaths, they circulated among the guests during the matrimonial festivities distributing bread from a special basket. Athenians believed that their presence at such ceremonies brought good fortune to the newly wedded couple.[5]

Following ancient Greek and Hellenistic customs, the emperor Augustus instituted a choir of *amphithaleis* in 17 B.C. to sing on the Capitoline Hill as part of the emperor's Secular celebration. A hymn of Horace survives that the poet composed for these *amphithaleis* to perform.[6] The very prominence of these favored *amphithaleis* highlighted the deprivation of the orphans. As a Byzantine commentator noted, the visibility of the *amphithaleis* brought obscurity to those who had lost their parents.[7]

The *Ajax* of Sophocles, written sometime in the mid-fifth century, presents another portrait of the perils of *orphania*. As the Greek hero Ajax prepared to kill himself, his wife, Tecmessa, tried to dissuade him by describing how his son, Eurysakes, would suffer if Ajax should succeed in suicide. After Ajax's death, the other Achaian chiefs would either enslave Eurysakes or hand him over to unloving *orphanistai*, apparently officials selected in some fashion to supervise orphans. In her speech to Ajax, Tecmessa also revealed that she herself had lost both her parents. After Ajax had conquered her fatherland, she had lost everything—mother, father, patrimony, and homeland—and had become a slave. Ajax alone rescued her from her plight by sharing his bed with her and making her the mother of his son (vv. 485–524). Tecmessa's story unveils another aspect of *orphania;* both in the ancient world and in later Byzantine times, female orphans often escaped the depriva-

---

5. Golden, *Childhood*, pp. 30 and 44; see also Stengel, "Ἀμφιθαλεῖς παῖδες," *RE*, 1: 1958–59.

6. Weidemann, *Adults*, p.182. See Horace, *Carmen saeculare.*

7. *Archaia Scholia*, p. 127.

tion of their predicament through some sort of sexual activity. Some fortunate ones found husbands, others such as Tecmessa became concubines, and still others survived through prostitution.

To allay Tecmessa's fears regarding her son, Ajax told her that he had provided for Eurysakes' protection by leaving him a guardian, the renowned warrior Teucer, who would both nurture and defend the boy until the fighting at Troy had ceased (vv. 545–82). In a warrior society such as that of Homeric and Archaic Greece, a woman like Tecmessa could not protect her son because she could not fight. In fact, she herself needed protection. Ajax's words clearly indicated that Teucer's prowess in combat would guarantee not only Eurysakes' safety, but also that of Tecmessa.

Sophocles' dialogue thus revealed the emergence of a new legal institution sometime before the mid-fifth century, guardianship, an institution that offered some protection for orphaned children. Anticipating his own death, a father could designate a trusted friend such as Teucer or a relative to serve as a guardian *(epitropos)* and defend the interests of the children after the father's death. By the Classical age Athenian law enabled a father in his written will or testament to designate a man or several men to protect his children and see to their sustenance and education.[8] Sophocles' dialogue also explains why ancient Greek law—as well as ancient Roman law—not only refused to allow women to function as guardians for their own children, but required even competent adult women to have their own male guardians: women were unable to wield the sword in their own defense or that of their children.

Though this system of testamentary guardianship offered some security to orphans, it did not always guarantee justice. The most famous rhetorician of Athens, Demosthenes, began his career as an orator trying to obtain the property his guardians had stolen from him. Before Demosthenes' father died, he had appointed three guardians to manage his property and protect his family: one nephew as guardian for his wife, another nephew as guardian for his daughter, and a close

---

8. For a summary of the ancient Greek laws of guardianship, see F. Wilberg, "Ὀρφανοί," *RE,* 18.1: 1198–1200. For the most complete account of Athenian laws of guardianship, see Schulthess, *Vormundschaft.*

friend for his seven-year-old son Demosthenes. According to Demosthenes' accusations, after his father's demise, these men deprived him of his patrimonial estates, gave away his farm buildings, stripped his dwelling place of its furnishings, led away his slaves, destroyed his wine vat, and even tore off the door of his home. His mother's guardian finally migrated to the neighboring city-state of Megara to avoid repaying Demosthenes.[9] As a result of his guardians' crimes, Demosthenes had been too poor to pay his teacher and was therefore unable to complete his education. Despite his efforts to recover his father's property, Demosthenes succeeded in regaining only a fraction of what was rightfully his. His biographer Plutarch emphasized, however, that the difficulties of his *orphania* no doubt spurred Demosthenes to the study of rhetoric and offered him repeated opportunities to speak before the law courts at a young age.[10]

Another oration, composed by the famous sophist Lysias, described an uncle who served as guardian for his deceased brother's wife and her three children. The uncle provided for the children's food, shelter, and education, but when they came of age he apparently refused to surrender to them all their father's estates. In the formal accusation prepared by Lysias, the children accused their uncle of squandering their paternal inheritance on the children from his second marriage and of undertaking the expensive liturgy of *triarch* (the maintenance of a warship for the Athenian navy) with their money.[11]

Clearly the system of guardianship did not solve all the problems for orphans. It depended totally on the character of the guardian. If he were indeed a fair-minded man, he could provide his ward with the necessary material security and even in some cases with the affection of a father, but if he viewed his position as an opportunity to enrich himself and his own children, then the unfortunate ward suffered a fate not much better than that of the despoiled and rejected orphan boy depicted in Andromache's speech. Indeed, Plato used the despicable con-

---

9. Most of the details about Demosthenes' guardians are found in *Oratio 27*. *Orationes* 28 and 29 contain information about the damage the guardians wrought to Demosthenes' estate. See also the commentary by Murray, *Demosthenes 4*, pp. 2–5.

10. Plutarch, *Demosthenes*, 4.2–6.2.

11. Lysias 32 *(In Diogitonem)*, 4–5.

duct of unjust guardians to exemplify how lust for wealth destroyed moral behavior in society. Plato selected the actions of such guardians because he knew that fourth-century Athenians would easily recognize the problem (*Rep.*, 554 A–C).

It is probable that guardianship began as a strictly family matter. Male relatives assumed responsibility for an orphan to protect the child's person and, perhaps of greater concern to the extended family, to preserve the minor's property. As disputes over guardianship grew in number and complexity, the *polis* intervened by establishing guidelines for the proper conduct of *epitropoi* and judicial procedures for resolving conflicts arising from guardianship situations. When Sophocles mentioned the *orphanistai*, he was probably referring to public officials who oversaw the appointment of guardians and the proper fulfillment of their duties (*Ajax*, v. 512). By the early fourth century Athens allowed disgruntled wards such as Demosthenes and the client of Lysias to sue their former guardians before the popular law courts.

According to the *Constitution of Athens*, an invaluable study on Athenian political institutions attributed to Aristotle, the leading magistrate among the nine archons of Athens included among his many duties the supervision of orphans and their guardians. The eponymous archon, as this magistrate was called, handled actions regarding the ill treatment of orphans by their *epitropoi*, confirmed appointments of guardians, determined among rival candidates for the office of guardian, and in general, protected both male and female orphans and their property. The eponymous archon also forced tight-fisted guardians to release the necessary money for the suitable support of their wards.[12] As the speeches of Demosthenes and Lysias show, the eponymous archon did not actually judge disputes of fact regarding guardian issues. Rather, in these cases he performed administrative and policing functions and submitted the determination of guilt or innocence to popular juries *(dikasteria)*.[13]

While the eponymous archon supervised the Athenian orphans, the *polemarch* (the archon of war) oversaw guardianship cases with regard to *metics* (resident aliens of Athens).[14]

---

12. Aristotle, Ἀθηναίων πολιτεία, 56.6–7.   13. Demosthenes, 27.4; Lysias, 32.1.
14. Aristotle, Ἀθηναίων πολιτεία, 58.

The *Constitution of Athens* demonstrates how great a role the Athenian *polis* assumed in supervising guardianship. Perhaps this public concern to ensure justice for orphans began with Solon's reforms. Certainly these measures were in place under the constitution of Cleisthenes.[15]

The Athenian *polis* not only tried to regulate the conduct of individual *epitropoi*, it also assumed the guardian responsibility for particular orphans: those whose fathers had died in battle in the city's defense. Apparently, Solon began the practice of Athen's assuming financial responsibility for raising children of fallen heroes.[16] As Plato expressed it, the city took the place of their fathers and served as their guardians.[17] When the orphans reached seventeen, the *polis* provided them with arms for battle and presented these youths to the people at the Great Dionysia. Following this presentation ceremony, the *polis* assigned these orphans seats of honor in the theater.[18]

The Athenians strictly limited the orphans they supported by admitting only the children of citizens. The offspring of heroic *metics* were excluded from any benefits. After 403, Athens refused to support the orphans of mixed families or of those who had received honorary citizenship.[19]

Although Athens did not continue supporting the minor children of fallen heroes beyond the mid-fourth century, Aristotle testified that other Greek cities had adopted the practice. As early as the fifth century, Hippodamos of Miletos, a city planner and political philosopher, had recommended the Athenian program of public support as part of an ideal city constitution.[20] In early Hellenistic times (305 B.C.), Rhodes

15. The ancient historian Harpokration (an Alexandrian historian of uncertain date) stated that Solon had required that Athens nourish its widows and orphans. See *Suda,,* 4: 369.

16. Stroud, "Greek Inscriptions," p. 288.

17. Plato, *Menexenus,* 249 A.

18. Goldhill, "Great Dionysia," pp. 58–76, describes this ceremony in great detail and places it in its wider civic context.

19. Stroud, "Greek Inscriptions," pp. 280–301.

20. Among the primary sources, Aeschines, *In Ctesiphontem,* 154, provides the most complete description of the Dionysian ceremony (see Goldhill, "Great Dionysia," pp. 63–64). Aeschines clearly indicates that the presentation of orphans no longer took place c. 330 B.C. For Hippodamos of Miletos, see Aristotle, *Politica,* 1267a–1268b.

established the Athenian system of orphan assistance to encourage citizens to risk their lives for the liberty of their *polis*.[21]

Almost fifteen hundred years later, the Byzantine emperor Alexios, the same emperor who had brought back the war orphans to Constantinople in 1116, organized a unit of soldiers that resembled the ancient Athenian orphan warriors, ceremonially armed by the state. Alexios, however, did not recruit the surviving children of all soldiers who had died in battle, but only those of fallen officers. These young men the emperor equipped and trained to form a new corps called the *archontopouloi,* a unit of soldiers who soon proved themselves to be some of the empire's best troops. Alexios's biographer, his daughter Anna, compared her father's *archontopouloi* to a Spartan institution, but the better documented Athenian program to aid the children of deceased warriors probably inspired the emperor in creating his new fighting force.[22]

Beyond the *archontopouloi* of Alexios, ancient Greek institutions do not appear to have directly influenced Byzantine orphan care. Under the Roman Empire, the guardianship laws of Rome gradually supplanted the local customs of Athens and the other Hellenic *poleis.* Nevertheless, that the governments of Greek city-states expanded their responsibilities to include the protection of orphan citizens shows clearly that state concern for the care of children without parents predated the Christianization of the fourth century A.D. and even the spread of Roman power in the eastern Mediterranean basin (199–131 B.C.).

ROME

Despite the importance of its legions, the Roman state never developed any welfare program for the orphans of its fallen soldiers as Athens and some of the other Greek cities had done. A few historians

---

21. Diodorus Siculus, *Bibliotheca historica,* 20.84.

22. Anna Komnena, *Alexiad,* 7.7.1 (2: 108). See also *De scientia politica dialogus,* caps. 71–72 (p. 13), which recommends that the Byzantine state provide for widows and orphans of its soldiers. The *De scientia politica dialogus (Περὶ πολιτικῆς ἐπιστήμης)* was written sometime in the reign of Justinian. Its author is unknown. In dialogue form it discusses how the Byzantine Empire should be reorganized to strengthen its military and to draw more successfully on the talents of its subjects. The author even proposes a method of electing the emperor. This text exemplifies how Byzantine writers carefully studied ancient Greek texts and tried to apply what they learned to solve contemporary problems.

have cited the well-documented *alimenta* programs, initiated by the emperor Trajan (98–117), as evidence of state care for fatherless children. Recent research, however, has shown that the *alimenta* were schemes to aid families from Italian towns in raising their children. Certainly, some of these boys and girls were orphans in the homes of their guardians or widowed mothers, but most had living fathers. Trajan designed his *alimenta* systems not to aid orphans, but to encourage Roman citizens of the Italian homeland to have more children. Trajan and his immediate successors wanted Italian communities to produce more Roman citizens for the empire's vast army. The *alimenta* programs formed part of a wider imperial initiative to promote higher birth rates among Roman families. Once the Roman Empire lost its sense of ethnic identity by the beginning of the third century A.D. and granted Roman citizenship to all free persons of its vast Mediterranean possessions, the government suspended the *alimenta* programs.[23]

Although Rome never devised public support systems for any group of orphans, it did take great interest in promoting and regulating the institution of guardianship. As early as the XII Tables (circa 450 B.C.), Roman law required that an adult male protect the person and property of minor children who had lost their fathers.[24] Gradually, the norms governing the appointment of guardians, the sphere of their functions, and the standard of behavior which they had to observe in overseeing their wards grew in scope and complexity. By the third century A.D., the law of guardianship (Latin *tutela*) formed a substantial section of the Roman legal tradition. The classical jurists of the third century A.D.—Paulus, Papinian, Ulpian, Modestinus, and several others—devoted much effort to rationalizing the *tutela* rules.[25]

Since the Byzantine emperors considered Roman jurisprudence as the foundation of their legal system, they naturally accepted Roman rules of guardianship. Through the thousand-year history of the Eastern Empire, the Byzantine institution of guardianship remained

23. Duncan-Jones, "Purpose," pp. 123–46; Weidemann, *Adults*, pp. 38–39.
24. Käser, *Das römische Privatrecht*, I: 352–54; Jolowicz, *Historical Introduction*, pp. 121–22.
25. For a summary of the Roman law of *tutela*, see Käser, *Das römische Privatrecht*, I: 352–69. See also the shorter English account in Käser, *Roman Private Law*, pp. 316–24.

remarkably faithful to Roman ideas about *tutela.* Even when Byzantine emperors introduced radically new elements into the guardianship rules, they made every effort to mold their innovations to fit as much as possible the larger framework of the Roman legal tradition.

Classical Roman law, the system enshrined both for the Byzantines and for us in Justinian's *Digest* and *Institutes,* distinguished three types of guardianship: *tutela legitima, tutela testamentaria,* and what Justinian called *tutela Atiliana.*[26] The oldest of these types was the *tutela legitima.* This system of guardianship recognized the right of the extended family to protect the person and the property of orphans within its fold. The *tutela legitima* followed closely the Roman rules regarding inheritance. If a man died leaving orphan children, and if he were survived by his father (the children's grandfather), the old man naturally protected the orphans. In this case Roman law did not classify the grandfather as a guardian; he, in fact, had been the father of the family *(pater familias)* and was legally responsible for his grandchildren before their father had died, and he continued to bear this responsibility after their father's death. Ancient Roman law vested all power over the persons of the family and its property in the oldest living male (father, grandfather, great grandfather). In fact, only such a *pater familias* existed as a legal person in the eyes of ancient Roman law.[27] Recent research regarding life expectancies, however, indicates that grandfather *patres familiarum* were not very common in antiquity.[28]

If the minor children had no surviving grandfather, then their eldest brother, if he were no longer a minor, became their guardian; if no adult brother, then their paternal uncle; if no paternal uncle, then adult paternal cousins. If no male relatives existed on the father's side (agnatic relatives), then the ancient Roman clan unit, the *gens,* selected one of its male members to serve as guardian.

According to the rules of *tutela legitima,* only Roman citizens could serve as guardians. Thus, if a freed person died leaving children, he

26. *Inst,* 1.14, 1.15, and 1.20.
27. Käser, *Roman Private Law,* pp. 304–14.
28. Saller, "Men's Age," pp. 21–34; Saller, *"Patria Potestas,"* pp. 7–22.

had no citizen relatives. In his case, his patron, the Roman who had liberated him from slavery, assumed the guardianship of the freedman's minor children.[29]

Although the *tutela legitima* was no doubt the oldest form of guardianship in Rome, as early as the XII Tables most citizens used the *tutela testamentaria*. Before a man died, he wrote a testament or will in which he established his heir or heirs and made specific benefactions to other friends, relatives, or municipal governments by way of legacies. The testator also named a specific person, a male relative or trusted friend, to serve as guardian of any minor children who survived him. The *tutela testamentaria* was not restricted to Roman citizens; the testator could appoint anyone as guardian.[30]

As the speeches of Demosthenes and Lysias show, Athenian law also recognized the right of individuals to nominate guardians for their children, but the testamentary system appeared at an earlier stage of social and economic development at Rome and became the dominant mode of guardianship sooner there than in Greece. Its precocious development reflected the strength of individual rights in the Roman legal system against the demands of family and *gens*, expressed under the *tutela legitima*.[31]

The Roman law developed the third class of guardianship, the *tutela Atiliana* (sometimes called the *tutela dativa*), comparatively late. Whereas the XII Tables regulated both the *tutela legitima* and the *tutela testamentaria*, a law of circa 210 B.C., the *Lex Atilia*, established the *tutela dativa*. In cases where the deceased father had left no will and the orphans had no living paternal male relative, the *praetor urbanus*, together with the ten tribunes, appointed a respectable person to serve as guardian. A separate law gave this same power to provincial governors. Modern historians of Rome consider the introduction of this new class of guardians as strong evidence that the ancient *gentes* had ceased functioning. In place of these old clans, the power of the state, exercised in

29. For the *tutela legitima*, see Käser, *Das römische Privatrecht*, I: 356. For the intestate order of succession, see Käser, *Roman Private Law*, pp. 337–43.

30. Käser, *Das römische Privatrecht*, I: 354–56.

31. Jolowicz, *Historical Introduction*, pp. 126–27.

Rome by the urban praetor and in the provinces by the governors, found guardians for orphans without male agnatic relatives.[32]

In early Roman law guardians were primarily concerned with preserving orphans' property and protecting their persons from attack. As time went on, this protection did not mean defending them from physical attack so much as representing them in court. Initially, the guardians were free to deal with orphans' property with no restrictions. By the Classical Roman period (second and early third century, A.D.), however, both legislation and juristic interpretation had vastly curtailed the freedom of guardians to manage wards' property as they wished. They were not to alienate property by gift or sale, except under extraordinary circumstances, nor were they to use the wards' property to secure loans of any kind.[33]

As early as the XII Tables, Roman law provided adult orphans a legal remedy against their former guardians if the orphans thought they had been defrauded of their property. They could sue their former guardians just as Demosthenes had done with regard to his *epitropoi* at Athens. By the early first century B.C., however, wards were permitted to sue their former guardians not only for criminal fraud and theft, but also for mismanagement, for any actions not done in good faith *(bona fide)*.[34]

Guardian problems became so numerous under the emperors that Marcus Aurelius (160–180 A.D.) created a special magistrate, the *praetor tutelarius,* to examine only cases involving guardianship. This new magistrate was to make all appointments in cases of *tutela dativa,* but he was also to examine accusations concerning improper conduct of guardians. These praetors gradually defined ever higher standards of management for guardians.[35] By the third century the rules governing the proper conduct of *tutela* had become so complex that the law strongly encouraged guardians to prepare a detailed inventory of their wards' properties before they assumed their responsibilities. Such an

---

32. Käser, *Das römische Privatrecht,* 1: 357–59; Jolowicz, *Historical Introduction,* p. 239.

33. Käser, *Das römische Privatrecht,* 1: 360–62.

34. Ibid., 1: 361–67; Käser, *Roman Private Law,* pp. 322–24.

35. *Vita Marci Antonini philosophi,* 10.11, in *Scriptores historiae Augustae;* Käser, *Das römische Privatrecht,* 1: 360–61.

inventory would help to protect a guardian from future problems if his former ward decided to sue him for mismanagement of the estate.[36]

Roman law clearly revealed that guardians supervised orphans' property, but did they actually care for the children? If the mother was still living, she usually continued to raise the children and limited the guardian's role to managing the property. Paulus, however, stated that guardians had to govern not only the property of their wards, but also their behavior *(mores)* which implied that they oversaw educating the children.[37] With regard to children who had lost both parents, one would suppose that they remained in the custody of guardians, and many no doubt did. In the Classical legal texts, however, there are a few passages that suggest that the *praetor tutelarius* sometimes assigned the orphans to the custody of others. In a rescript the emperor Septimius Severus (193–211 A.D.) ordered that, when the testator required that his surviving children be raised by the adult who would inherit all the orphans' property if the children died (that is, he was the substitute heir), the praetor should examine the situation carefully together with the children's other relatives before confirming this arrangement.[38] Any guardian according to the *tutela legitima* system would have been such a substitute heir, and so were many guardians appointed by testament. Moreover, Ulpian mentioned that the *praetor tutelarius* frequently heard requests to examine the custodians of orphans, many of whom were no doubt also the legal guardians.[39]

The Romans seem in general to have harbored fears about the personal safety of wards under the care of guardians, if such guardians might gain materially by the early death of their wards. When the future emperor Galba (68–69 A.D.) was serving as governor in southern Spain, he condemned to death by crucifixion a guardian who had poi-

36. *Dig*, 26.7.7, where Ulpian maintains that a guardian who does not prepare an inventory might be suspected of fraud. The inventory did not become a legal requirement until 396 (*CodTheo*, 3.30.6).

37. *Dig*, 26.7.12.3.

38. *Dig*, 27.2.1 (Ulpian). See also Krause, *Rechtliche und soziale Stellung*, pp. 12–15, who stresses that the Roman law of the Late Republic and the Early Empire did not expect the guardian personally to care for the child. The guardian's concern was almost exclusively the orphan's property.

39. Ibid.

soned his ward. Galba wanted to set a powerful example to deter other evil men from such schemes. When the condemned man objected that the governor could not legally crucify him since he was a Roman citizen, Galba raised the cross higher, painted it white, and crucified the man on this more distinguished instrument of execution.[40]

At the time of the XII Tables, guardianship only lasted until an orphan reached the age of fourteen. Thereafter, young men were considered competent adults. Girls of the same age, on the other hand, did not gain their freedom. In fact, they remained under the supervision of male guardians throughout their entire lives.[41]

Fourteen-year-old males, however, often proved incapable of managing estates properly or of representing themselves adequately before the magistrates. Gradually, the custom evolved that orphans fourteen years or over could request the praetor to appoint a curator to help them with their affairs; on occasion, the praetor appointed a curator to assist an orphan in a particularly difficult court case, even when the orphan had not sought such help. Finally, circa 200 B.C., the Romans passed the *Lex Laetoria,* which established as a regular institution the curatorship of minors, who were now defined as young males from fourteen to twenty-five years of age.[42]

These curators differed from guardians (Latin *tutores*) in that they had to be established by a magistrate and their scope of authority was limited to a specific case—for example, a particular law suit or a specific sale of land. The emperor Marcus Aurelius extended the more general legal responsibilities of *tutores* also to curators and thereby began a process that gradually merged the two offices so that an orphan did not normally gain independence from legal supervision until he reached twenty-five.[43] The Classical Roman law, however, continued to distinguish *tutores* (guardians) from curators and to require a magisterial appointment of a curator at the close of guardianship. Thus, when

---

40. Suetonius, *De vita Caesarum* (Galba), 9. On this whole issue of untrustworthy guardians, see Jolowicz, "Wicked Guardian," pp. 82–90.

41. Käser, *Das römische Privatrecht,* 1: 367–69.

42. Ibid., 1: 369–71.

43. Callistratus maintained that curators were to be held to the same standards of good management as *tutores* were (*Dig,* 26.7.33.1). See also note 45, below.

a boy reached fourteen, his guardian ceased to function as tutor until the *praetor tutelarius* or a provincial governor confirmed him as the orphan's curator. It was also possible for the orphan or magistrate to find another person to serve as curator.

The Roman distinction between guardian and curator proved remarkably tenacious through the many centuries of later Roman and Byzantine rule despite the tendency of imperial legislation to unite the two offices.[44] Even in the fourteenth century some Byzantine landowners still conceived of curators as distinct from guardians *(epitropoi)*. In 1349 a young woman named Philippa wished to sell a share of her property to the monastery of Xèropotamou. Her guardian had died, but she had not yet reached the age of legal maturity: by the Byzantine period women became legally responsible at twenty-five, just as men did (see below). Philippa approached the magistrate in Thessalonike and asked him to appoint a curator to confirm the sale of her land. The magistrate she dealt with happened to be the renowned fourteenth-century jurist Constantine Harmenopoulos. He duly appointed as her curator Peter Hadrianos, a man who was one of the emperor's intimates *(oikeioi)* and Philippa's relative.[45]

It is important to notice that Philippa followed the ancient Roman rule of seeking a curator for a specific transaction and of requesting this appointment directly from a state official.[46] Despite the legislation of Marcus Aurelius and the decrees of subsequent Byzantine emperors that equated guardians with curators, some East Roman subjects or their lawyers seem to have been aware of the Late Republican and Early Imperial period ideas about curatorship.

Under the law of the XII Tables Roman women faced many of the same liabilities with regard to guardianship that Athenian women had suffered under Attic law. Not only did the ancient Roman law prevent them from serving as guardians for their own children, it also required that they themselves have male guardians. Just as Ajax had appointed Teucer to protect both Tecmessa and their little boy, so too in preparing their testaments Roman men established *tutores* not only for their

44. Käser, *Das römische Privatrecht*, 2: 223–24.
45. *Actes de Xèropotamou*, no. 26 (pp. 193–96).
46. Käser, *Das römische Privatrecht*, 1: 369–70. See also the rule as stated in *Inst*, 1.23.1.

minor children, but also for their wives and adult daughters. In both primitive Rome and Archaic Greece, women needed the guarding strength of a male warrior to keep them safe.[47]

As Roman society grew more sophisticated and as guardians came to protect their wards more in court than in combat, adult women did not necessarily need the assistance of a guardian. By the first century B.C., adult women had liberated themselves from the direct control of their male *tutores* and were able to manage their own property freely, though the technicalities of the law still required that they have male guardians. Even in the third century A.D., a woman with no living father or husband needed a male tutor. Not until the reign of Diocletian or possibly the early years of Constantine's rule did Roman law finally abolish the *tutela* of adult women. During the Byzantine era orphan girls were subject to guardians until they reached puberty, which the law defined as twelve (compared with fourteen for boys). Thereafter, they received curators who supervised their affairs until they reached adulthood at twenty-five (the same age required for males).[48]

Although during the Late Republic and the Early Empire women won increasing freedom in many areas of marriage and inheritance law, they never managed to break completely free of the guardianship rules until the early fourth century. As a result, the Roman legal tradition continued to exclude them from holding the office of guardianship over others since they were technically still under the supervision of male *tutores*. Roman law refused to allow them to function as guardians even for their own children.

The Classical jurists strongly rejected the concept of women as guardians. Papinian stated emphatically that, if in his will a father designated as guardian the mother of his children, his wish had no effect. Moreover, if provincial officials had ruled in favor of such appoint-

---

47. Sophocles, *Ajax*, vv. 545–82; cf. Crook, *Law*, pp. 113–15, and Käser, *Das römische Privatrecht*, 1: 367–69.

48. Käser, *Das römische Privatrecht*, 2: 222, and note 3. Käser cites Constantine's rules for ending curatorship before age twenty-five (*CodTheo*, 2.17.1) as evidence that the *tutela* of adult women was no longer in force. Käser also mentions a law of Diocletian that implies that an adult woman no longer needed a tutor. Apparently no law has survived that formally abrogated the institution of *tutela mulierum*.

ments, their decisions contravened the law and should not be followed by future provincial magistrates.[49]

Papinian's opinions indicate that the tendency to appoint mothers as guardians came from the provinces, and, in fact, Egyptian papyri of the Roman Imperial period reveal that Greeks of the former Ptolemaic kingdom often made female relatives *epitropoi*. A first-century testament appointed an adult sister as coguardian with her adult brothers for her underage brother. Another will made a grandmother guardian of her grandchildren; a third from the second century A.D. appointed an aunt *epitropos* of her nieces and nephews. Under the influence of Hellenistic Egyptian custom, Romans resident in Egypt developed new terms for women who aided the Roman law *tutores* in supervising the orphaned children. Thus, a will executed in 172–173 A.D. established a grandmother as *epakolouthetria* (attendant or supervisor) to assist the legal guardians in raising the children.[50]

The desire to appoint mothers as guardians of their own flesh and blood affected even Roman citizens who remained firmly within the legal tradition of their city-state. According to Ulpian, Roman men of the third century A.D. had devised a way to make their wives de facto *tutores* of their common children by exploiting the great freedom the law gave *patres familiarum* in disposing of their own property through their written testaments. Because the Roman rules of guardianship blocked them from appointing their wives as guardians, these husbands disinherited all their children and made their wives sole heirs with the instructions to surrender specific portions of the estate as the children reached the age of twenty-five. This sort of will successfully circumvented the rule requiring male guardians.[51]

Despite the wish of many Roman husbands to establish the mothers of their children as guardians and the example of the Greek customs followed in Hellenistic Egypt, the Roman law clung tenaciously to the principle that only men could serve as guardians. As late as 294 A.D., the emperor Diocletian reiterated this view: "To take up the de-

49. *Dig*, 26.2.26 pr.

50. Taubenschlag, *Law of Greco-Roman Egypt*, pp. 157–60.

51. *Dig*, 28.2.18. See the discussion in Gardner, *Women*, p. 153.

fense of another is a man's task and beyond the female sex; if your son is a minor, get a tutor [male] for him."[52]

It is impossible to assess whether or not the Roman law of guardianship succeeded in finding competent guardians for most orphans. Moreover, it is difficult to know how far down the social and economic ladder the rules of guardianship had effect. In general, the Roman state shaped its private law to regulate the relationships among society's elite.[53] With respect to guardianship, one of the sanctions the law prescribed for criminous *tutores* was to ban them from holding public office, a punishment only effective against the landowning aristocrats.[54] Possibly under the emperors some less privileged families benefitted from the guardianship laws, but as late as the third century A.D., the jurist Ulpian asserted that fathers of poor families did not normally bother to appoint guardians for their children.[55] Evidence from the Byzantine epoch, on the other hand, reveals that at least some rural and urban midlevel families tried to appoint *epitropoi* according to the strict rules of the Roman law.

Despite Byzantine changes in the regulations and in the court structure, many lower-class families during later centuries probably designed ad hoc arrangements for nurturing the orphans in their midst without ever consulting the rules of *tutela legitima* or bothering to draft a proper testament. Many of the poor would have lacked the economic resources to hire a lawyer or notary to prepare a legal will or the education to write or even dictate one on their own.

The Romans did not design their laws of guardianship to address the problem of providing food, shelter, and care for homeless waifs. During the years from 14 to 235 A.D., many displaced persons congregated in the great cities of the empire such as Rome, Alexandria, and Antioch; among these people were old men, the disabled, the chronically ill, widows, and orphans. Roman governors or local city magistrates had no interest in finding guardians for these children since they had no property and were rarely Roman citizens or even citizens of the large Greek cities of the East where they often begged. The Chris-

52. *JCod*, 2.12.18.   53. Crook, *Law*, pp. 9–13.
54. Ibid., p. 66.   55. *Dig*, 38.17. 27.

tian philosopher Clement of Alexandria vividly portrayed the indifference of the empire's elite by describing the lives of wealthy pagan women at the beginning of the third century. They ignored the widows they saw, but turned to pamper their Melitaian puppies; they avoided the orphans along the streets, but wasted time in feeding pet parrots and plovers.[56] Clement wanted to portray the corruption of pagan society and perhaps exaggerated his account, but he did identify a weakness of the classical world: its inability to empathize with the rootless people who had no city-state identity, a group that grew as the Roman Empire became more cosmopolitan in the second and third centuries.[57] For the orphan children of these people the Roman laws of guardianship offered no protection.

JUDAISM AND CHRISTIANITY

The Jewish conception of *orphania* differed radically from that of both Greeks and Romans. Whereas classical civilization conceived of the *amphithaleis* as especially favored by the heavenly powers, the God of Abraham chose to bless with his protection widows, orphans, and strangers (Deut 10:18). If anyone of the Hebrews tried to harm an orphan, the God of Abraham promised to punish the evil doer with death by the sword (Exod 22:21–24). The Psalmist expressed God's special love for orphans by describing the Divine Being as Father of orphans (Ps 68:5). The Jews of the Diaspora preserved the notion that God loved orphans and hearkened to their prayers (Sirac 32:12–14).

The Prophets branded injustice toward orphans and widows as one of the signs of a truly corrupt society. Isaiah condemned the magistrates of Judah who did not judge in favor of fatherless children (1:23); Jeremiah accused the sinful rich in Jerusalem of despoiling the property of orphans (5:27–28). If the people of Judah truly would repent, if they would cease oppressing orphans and widows, God would restore them to the promised land (Jer 7:5–7).

The Mosaic law established several specific customs to benefit orphans, widows, and strangers. First, the law required that each year the

---

56. Clement, *Paedagogus*, 3.4.30 (p.253).
57. Miller, *Birth*, pp. 69–70.

Hebrews surrender a tenth of their harvest for God and the priests. Every third year the laws of Deuteronomy required that a portion of these tithes be used to assist orphans and widows (Deut 14:22–29). This custom continued among the Jews at least until the Second Temple period, circa 300 b.c. (Tob 1:8). Second, the law mandated that orphans should share in the communal meals celebrating the Pentecost (Deut 16:11), a law which contrasts sharply with the Homeric image of the fallen Hector's boy ejected from the festival meals of his father's former companions (*Iliad*, 22.496–98). Third, the Mosaic law allowed orphans to glean the fields after the harvest; they had the right to shafts of wheat left in the fields or to olives and grapes still on the branches (Deut 24:19–24).

In addition to these strict requirements of the law, Judaism encouraged individual acts of charity toward orphans by ranking these as paramount examples of virtue. In depicting his righteous life, Job stressed that he had always tried to assist the fatherless in their distress (29:11–12). As part of the path to true wisdom, Ben Sirach exhorted his son always to be a father for the fatherless (Sirac 4:10).

The rules and moral exhortations of the Law, the Prophets, and the wisdom literature would have accomplished little to assist orphans if no responsible adult had assumed the burden of feeding, sheltering, and educating these children. It is therefore surprising that the Old Testament says absolutely nothing about legal guardians. The concept of guardianship first appears in the Mishnah (circa 200 a.d.), where in fact the text employs the Greek term *epitropos* in place of a Hebrew word.[58] Apparently, ancient Jewish society did not know the institution of legal guardianship. Scholars have suggested that extended family ties and wider clan organization were so strong that Jewish society did not need to devise legal rules to obligate certain relatives or friends. Just as the primitive Roman *gens* assigned the role of guardian without fixed rules, so too the Jewish clan selected specific persons to care for orphans among its ranks. Such seems to have occurred in the family of Tobit sometime after the restoration of Jerusalem (circa 537 b.c.). As a young boy Tobit had lost his father, but his paternal grandmother had

---

58. Cohn, "Jüdisches Waisenrecht," p. 437.

taken charge of feeding him and instructing him in the laws of God (Tob 1:6–9).

Jewish society only worked out formal rules of guardianship after the Diaspora in the wake of Alexander's conquests. Greater mobility during the Hellenistic centuries eroded the tighter extended family and clan ties and made it necessary for Jewish law to define more exactly which relative bore the responsibility of raising children who had lost one or both parents.[59]

By Hellenistic times, the Jews had developed another practice to assist orphans. According to 2 Maccabees, when Onasias was high priest of Jerusalem, one of his enemies stirred up trouble by revealing to Seleucus IV (187–175 B.C.) of Syria that the Temple treasury contained a great hoard of gold and silver. Since the temple state of Judah now lay within his territory, Seleucus dispatched an official named Heliodoros to inventory the Temple's treasury. The high priest explained to Heliodoros that much of the gold and silver in the Temple belonged to orphans and widows who had intrusted their movable wealth to this sacred place for protection. Heliodoros nevertheless ordered that the Temple priests surrender the treasure to the government of Seleucus. Heliodoros's request shocked the people of Jerusalem and the Temple priesthood. They poured forth their anger in prayer to God who miraculously defended the property of these orphans and widows by striking Heliodoros with a sudden disease.[60]

This story reveals that wealthy orphans of early-second-century Judah could choose to store their liquid assets in the Temple treasury to protect them from theft, embezzlement, or mismanagement. The account does not provide any indication when this custom had begun.

As a sect of Judaism, early Christianity inherited the moral perspective of the Old Testament. Although Jesus himself did not specifically mention orphans in his Last Judgment sermon (Matt 25) or in his other exhortations to active charity, the writings of the apostles and of the early Church fathers considered care of orphans as especially virtuous. In portraying the life of the active believer who put into practice the

---

59. Ibid., pp. 435–37.
60. 2 Macc 3: 1–36. To set these events in a wider context, see Peters, *Harvest*, pp. 240–60.

words of God, the Epistle of Saint James presented only one example: the pure devotion of those who helped orphans and widows (James 1:27).

The apostle Paul described the care of orphans indirectly in his instructions concerning Christian widows. He insisted that widows first care for their own orphaned children and grandchildren. If these women had proven virtuous in raising their children, receiving strangers, and assisting those persecuted for the faith, and if they had reached the age of sixty, then the Christian community should enroll them as widows (1 Tim 5:3–12). Paul's ordinances provide the first evidence of an order of widows in the early Church, not simply poor widows in need of sustenance, but older women who have accepted a special ministry after demonstrating lives of piety and charity.[61]

Paul's words also help to explain why both the Jewish and Christian Scriptures always linked widows and orphans. Apparently, Jewish custom assumed that widows naturally undertook the care of their children at the death of their husbands. Moreover, both the Book of Tobit as well as Paul's words in 1 Timothy 5:4 indicate that grandmothers sometimes supervised grandchildren who had lost both parents. In encouraging mothers and grandmothers to accept the primary responsibility for nurturing orphans, the Jewish and early Christian tradition differed markedly from the Athenian and Roman rules that insisted upon only male guardians.

The *Shepherd of Hermes*, a Christian apocalyptic text from early-second-century Rome, reveals that Christian communities had some form of communal organization for widows and orphans beyond the family relationships. The author of the *Shepherd* mentions a woman named Grapte who had the responsibility of teaching the widows and orphans of the Roman church. It is probable that she was herself a widow.[62] No other early Christian text describes a widow entrusted with instructing a group of orphan children, but the *Pantokrator Typikon* from twelfth-century Constantinople provided salaries for old-

---

61. Thurston, *Widows*, pp. 36–55, presents a detailed study of the references to widows in this letter and also clearly points out that most scholars now consider 1 Tim to date from postapostolic times. Its writer, therefore, was not Paul, but one of his disciples.

62. *Shepherd of Hermes*, visio, 2.4 (p. 7). See also Thurston, *Widows*, pp. 71–72.

er women whom the text referred to as *graptai*. According to this monastic *typikon*, these women were to supervise a group of orphan acolytes who served the Pantokrator monastery's public church.[63] Here the word *grapte* is used as the title of an office, not as a proper name in the manner that the *Shepherd* employs it.

From the time of the *Shepherd* to the twelfth-century *Pantokrator Typikon* over one thousand years elapsed. During these many years, neither Greek patristic texts nor later Byzantine ecclesiastical sources referred to widowed women, known as *graptai*, who cared for groups of homeless children. It is therefore impossible to prove the continuous existence of such a ministry in the East Roman Church. Nevertheless, the presence of these *graptai* at the Pantokrator monastery at least raises the possibility that widows, enrolled by churches in the manner Paul described, had been instructing orphans in small Christian schools for centuries.

During the course of the second century, the office of bishop rapidly grew in importance until it dominated almost all aspects of local Christian life. Thus, it is not surprising to find the bishop emerging as the central figure in administering aid to orphans. According to Justin Martyr (circa 165), the Christians of mid-second-century Rome brought their voluntary contributions to the Sunday assembly of worship and presented these gifts to the bishop. He in turn supervised the distribution of this food or money to the orphans, widows, and others in need.[64]

The *Didascalia Apostolorum*, a code compiled in early-third-century Syria, described the bishop at the head of a far more elaborate program to aid orphans. According to this Syrian code, the bishop oversaw the care of orphan girls until they reached marriageable age, at which time he was to find them husbands from among the Christian families of his community. He also was to nurture the orphan boys until they had mastered a trade and were able to support themselves. Apparently, these orphans had no widowed mothers to care for them and no relatives willing to serve as guardians, either informally or according to

---

63. *Typikon Pantokrator*, p. 77, ll. 790–94; p. 77, ll. 807–8.
64. Justin, *Apologia (Prima)*, p. 67.

strict Roman law rules. To house these boys and girls, give them some education, and, in the case of the boys, train them in a craft, the bishop had organized some sort of boarding school. The *Didascalia Apostolorum* makes clear that the local Christian community met the expenses of this group home.[65]

In addition to describing the duties of the bishop, the *Didascalia Apostolorum* urged Christian couples with no children to adopt orphan boys. It also recommended that those families with sons of the proper age require these young men to choose wives from among the orphan girls. Finally, it warned wealthy Christians of the local church that they had an obligation to assist the boys and girls without families by sharing their abundance with these unfortunate children.[66]

By the mid-fourth century, the Church of Alexandria had established a highly sophisticated program to assist both orphans and widows. Its bishop maintained special houses *(oikiai)* both to provide shelter for these women and children and to store their food supplies. Although the evidence for these orphan houses comes from the time of the Arian bishop George of Cappadocia (361), these buildings and the organized institutional care they reflected might have been established some time earlier.[67]

As early as the second century the Christian sect had grown large enough and its orphan care program sufficiently prominent to make an impression on the wider Greco-Roman world. The satirist Lucian (120–180) not only made fun of common pagan practices, but he also ridiculed the gullibility of Christians. In portraying the strange life of Proteus, a man he considered a charlatan, Lucian described a period of Proteus's life when he had belonged to a Christian community of Palestine. After his conversion, Proteus became so famous among the

---

65. *Didascalia Apostolorum*, 4.1–2 (pp. 218–21). It is impossible to restore the original Greek text of the *Didascalia Apostolorum*, but its sense can be reconstructed from the *Constitutiones Apostolorum* (a fourth-century Greek text) and from Latin and Syriac translations of the original third-century *Didascalia Apostolorum*. See the detailed study on the *Constitutiones Apostolorum* by Marcel Metzger which includes an explanation of the *Didascalia Apostolorum* (*Constitutiones Apostolorum*, pp. 13–62, esp. pp. 15–16). See also Connolly, *Didascalia Apostolorum*, pp. xi–xxi.

66. *Didascalia Apostolorum*, 4.1 (pp. 218–19).

67. Sokrates, 2.28 (p. 137).

Palestinian Christians that the Roman governor of Syria ordered him arrested. While in prison, elderly Christian widows and orphans waited outside his cell, probably in prayer; the sect leaders (bishops and elders) also stayed with Proteus, read to him from the Scriptures, and secured him the best food.[68]

Even a non-Christian skeptic such as Lucian noticed the significance of the Christian program involving widows and orphans. From his account one cannot determine whether these were orphans appearing together with their widowed mothers or a group of homeless orphans under the guidance of widow ministers. That Lucian stressed the advanced age of these widows, however, provides an indication that he was describing an orphan school under the supervision of the enrolled widows of at least sixty years, elderly women such as the Roman lady named Grapte whom the *Shepherd of Hermes* described.

Neither the Old Testament nor any other ancient sources provide evidence that traditional Jewish communities in Palestine or in the Diaspora supported group homes for orphans such as those described in early Christian texts. Evidence is mounting, however, that the Jewish separatist sect known as the Essenes maintained some form of group care for orphans similar to that of Christian communities. The first-century Jewish historian Josephus mentioned that the Essenes adopted the children of other men to train them in the doctrines of their sect. In the present state of research, however, it is not possible to determine what sort of influence Essene institutions exercised on the development of Christianity.[69]

In 312 Constantine entered Rome after his stunning victory over Maxentius at the Battle of Milvian Bridge. Constantine now ruled the entire western half of the empire from his original territory in Britain to Illyricum and North Africa. Not only did the Battle of Milvian Bridge represent an important turning point in Constantine's military and political career, but it also signaled a profound shift in the spiritual direction of the entire Mediterranean basin. Scholars still dispute the exact chronology of Constantine's conversion to Christianity, but they

68. Lucianus, *De morte Peregrini*, 11–12.

69. Flavius Josephus, *De bello Judaico*, 2.120. For a description of Essene philanthropic practices, see Kippenberg, pp. 263–65.

do not doubt that he continually drew closer to the cult of Christ and eventually rejected the ancient gods. Milvian Bridge marked an important stage in this transition. One year after this victory, Constantine and his coemperor Licinius in the East granted the Christian churches the status of legal corporations.

Eusebios of Caesarea, Constantine's Christian biographer, considered Milvian Bridge the key event in Constantine's conversion. To illustrate the fervent Christian faith of the victor, Eusebios described conspicuously Christian acts of the emperor following his triumphant entry into Rome. After erecting a monument to commemorate his victory and restoring all of Maxentius's political enemies to their property and legal rights—both traditional acts of civil war victors—Constantine summoned Christian bishops to his court and kept them closely by his side as advisors. He also reconstructed Christian church buildings and provided food and shelter for beggars in the forum. Finally, Eusebios stated that Constantine took the place of a father for those who suffered *orphania* and offered protection to the widows.[70] Eusebios also mentioned that after Constantine had conquered the East (323) and had selected the old Byzantium for his new capital, he instituted a relief program for the poor and orphan children in many of the Greek cities as well.[71]

Constantine's reign began the process of Christianizing the Roman state. His death in 337 saw the division of the empire into separate Greek-speaking eastern and Latin-speaking western halves. In these Greek provinces, the synthesis of Greek, Roman, and Jewish-Christian ideas and institutions that took place during the next hundred and sixty years (312–472) would create a new Byzantine civilization. The following chapter will examine how the care of orphans changed in this Christian empire of the east.

70. Eusebios, *Vita Constantini*, 1.39–43.
71. Ibid., 4.28.1.

III   THE NEW JERUSALEM

Toward the end of his reign, the emperor John II Komnenos (†1143) appointed Alexios Aristenos head of Constantinople's great orphanage for the second time in Aristenos's public career. The famous twelfth-century poet and rhetorician Theodore Prodromos dedicated an encomium to celebrate Aristenos's appointment and praise his past virtue as an administrator. In the course of his speech Prodromos referred to the Orphanotropheion as "Sion" and to the needy people including the orphans as "the assembly of the first-born, enrolled in heaven."[1]

In describing the Orphanotropheion as Sion, Prodromos may well have known about 2 Maccabees 3:10–11, the passage describing how the Jews of the Hellenistic period stored the movable wealth of orphans in the Temple treasury on Mount Sion. Prodromos's earlier references to Aristenos as the Ark of the Covenant, the tablets of the Law, and the seven-branched candelabra, lit by the gifts of the Holy Spirit, suggest, however, that the orator was speaking metaphorically, not historically.[2] God's law of love, made manifest by the just and charitable Aristenos, would take up its abode in the new temple of the Orphanotropheion, a great philanthropic institution built on the acropolis of Constantinople, the New Jerusalem.

During the years from 312 to 472 the Greco-Roman world experienced many momentous changes: the capital of the empire moved

---

1. Prodromos, *Eisiterios* (PG, 133: cols. 1269–71). Cf. Heb 12: 22–23.
2. Prodromos, *Eisiterios* (PG, 133: col. 1269).

from Old Rome to Constantinople, the New Rome; the emperors became Christian, as did many from the upper classes, especially in the
East; and the cities of the Greek-speaking provinces experienced un-
usual demographic pressures. In many ways the new capital of Constantinople came to symbolize the empire's changes. Its location reflected the growing economic and political prominence of the East. Its
exploding population resulted, at least in part, from an urban migra-
tion pattern observable in many areas of the East. Finally, its Christian
character, which grew more pronounced as the fourth century progressed, revealed a general shift of religious orientation throughout
the eastern provinces.[3] By the end of the fifth century, Constantinople
was called not only the New Rome, but also the New Jerusalem.[4]

This chapter will examine how these profound changes in ancient
society reshaped the nature of orphan care during the period from 312
to 472 and set new standards for assisting children without fathers or
mothers, standards that would last through the entire Byzantine era.
First, it will be essential to study the Orphanotropheion, founded during the period 312–472. This philanthropic institution came to symbolize the importance of orphan care in Byzantine society. Indeed, by the
twelfth century, Prodromos conceived of this charitable facility as the
very center of the New Jerusalem. Second, it will be necessary to discuss the effects that rapid Christianization had upon the philanthropic
deeds of leading citizens of the ancient empire, including the emperors themselves. Finally, it will be essential to review the legislation of
fourth- and fifth-century emperors regarding the Roman rules of
guardianship to learn what changes Christian attitudes brought to the
traditional system of Roman *tutela,* outlined in the previous chapter.
In the process, we shall also examine how these innovations in
guardianship began to effect the Orphanotropheion of Constantinople
and smaller orphan asylums sponsored by the Christian Church.

---

3. See Miller, *Birth,* pp. 68–76, which summarizes the evidence for these changes.

4. *Vita Danielis Stylitae (Epitome),* cap. 1 (p. 95). See also Alexander "Strength of Empire,"
pp. 346–47, where the author illustrates how the Byzantines began to compare themselves
in many ways to the ancient kingdom of Israel. See also later references to Constantinople
as the New Jerusalem in Fenster, *Laudes,* p. 121.

THE ORPHANOTROPHEION

Sometime between Constantine's dedication of his new capital in 330 and the patriarchate of Gennadios (458–471), the Christians of Constantinople established the Orphanotropheion, an institution that soon became the premier philanthropic foundation of the Eastern Empire. In view of this facility's significance throughout Byzantium's long history, we need to determine exactly where the Orphanage was located and discover when and by whom it was first established. Answering these questions will also uncover additional information concerning the circumstances of the institution's origins and early development.

Byzantine sources place the Orphanotropheion on the eastern-most hill of Constantinople, where as Anna Komnena says "the access to the sea opens up."[5] The tenth-century historian Joseph Genesios stated that the orphanage stood on the city's acropolis, and, as we have seen, Theodore Prodromos referred to its location as Sion.[6] Although the ridge that Constantine selected for his Church of the Holy Apostles was higher, the Orphanotropheion occupied the citadel of ancient Byzantium, the hill that travelers by sea would first see as they approached Constantinople.[7]

On the northern side of this acropolis archaeologists have discovered complex ruins and near these remains a capital with the inscription "Of Demetrios the *orphanotrophos.*" Moreover, the ruins of these buildings show signs of renovation under the Comnenian emperors.[8] The *Alexiad* and other twelfth-century sources state that the emperor Alexios (1081–1118) had refurbished the orphanage on a grand scale.[9] These ruins therefore provide archaeological evidence regarding the precise location of the Orphanotropheion, but to date no systematic

---

5. Anna Komnena, *Alexiad*, 15.7.4 (3: 214–15).

6. Genesios, 1.9 (pp. 8–9). Prodromos, *Eisiterios* (PG, 133: col. 1271).

7. See Müller-Wiener, *Bildlexikon,* p. 495, for the Orphanotropheion, and pp. 405–6, for the Holy Apostles. The Church of the Holy Apostles no longer exists. In its place stands the Fatih Camii where Sultan Mehmet II, the conqueror of Constantinople in 1453, is buried.

8. For archaeological traces of the Orphanotropheion, see Mango, *Développement,* pp. 33–34, and note 66.

9. Anna Komnena, *Alexiad*, 15.7.3–6 (3: 214–16); Zonaras, pp. 744–45.

study of the site has been undertaken, a study that might in the future shed light on how the Orphanage was laid out.

Byzantine sources also reveal who founded the Orphanotropheion. The oldest evidence comes from a law issued by the emperor Leo I in 472. This decree granted specific rights and privileges to the *orphanotrophos* Nikon, who at that time directed the orphanage, and to all those who would hold that post in the future, an office that "Zotikos of blessed memory is said to have established."[10] In a later law of the early seventh century, the emperor Herakleios referred specifically to the orphanage as "the Orphanotropheion of Zotikos."[11] In subsequent centuries the name of Zotikos was always associated with the office of *orphanotrophos*. The Church of Jerusalem came to celebrate the memory of Saint Zotikos on 31 December. The Georgian version of the Jerusalem lectionary, dating from the eighth century, identified Zotikos as the sustainer of orphans. The several tenth- and eleventh-century redactions of the *synaxarion* of the Great Church of Constantinople also refer to Zotikos as priest and *orphanotrophos*.[12]

Only one source, a fragment preserved by a tenth-century version (version 3) of the *Patria Constantinopolis*, attributed the founding of the Orphanotropheion to anyone else, and even in this account Zotikos played a part. According to this fragment's account, the emperor Justin II (565–578) and his pious wife, Sophia, established the Orphanotropheion as well as a leprosarium named after Zotikos. Having founded these institutions, the imperial couple appointed an official, also named Zotikos, to supervise them.[13] The reliable ninth-century historian Theophanes, however, provided a different and more consistent account; he stated that Justin had built a church dedicated to the apostles Peter and Paul within the precincts of the Orphanotropheion, which obviously had been founded earlier.[14] Apparently, the later com-

---

10. *JCod*, 1.3.34 (35): rebus . . . ad curam Niconis viri religiosissimi presbyteri et orphanotrophi vel ad eos, qui post eum loco eius successerint, pertinentibus ad similitudinem Zotici beatissimae memoriae, qui prius huiusmodi pietatis officium invenisse dicitur, . . .

11. Novel 4 (Herakleios), RP, 5: 240.

12. Aubineau, "Zoticos," pp. 92–95, provides a detailed discussion of the *typika* and *synaxaria* that refer to Saint Zotikos.

13. *Patria Constantinopolis III*, 47 (Preger, 2: 235).

14. Theophanes, 1: 244.

piler of the *Patria* (version 3) or his source had confused this information and attributed the building of the entire orphanage to Justin II.[15]

Extant Byzantine sources thus reveal that a man named Zotikos played the key role in establishing Constantinople's orphanage, but when did he accomplish this and under what circumstances? Answering these questions is much more difficult. Leo's constitution of 472 proves that Zotikos had died before that law was issued. Moreover, the law stated that previous emperors had granted the Orphanotropheion and its dependent institutions various privileges.[16] Since the text of the law referred to more than one previous emperor, the Orphanotropheion must have existed at least from the reign of Theodosius II (408–450)—Leo's immediate predecessor was Marcian (450–457). It is possible, however, that it had been founded under an earlier predecessor, perhaps Theodosius I (379–395) or Constantius II (337–361).

One family of sources—the three versions of the *Vita Zotici*—provides more precise information regarding Zotikos and his life in Constantinople. According to these sources, Zotikos worked in the Byzantine capital under the emperors Constantine and Constantius and was executed by the Arian ruler Constantius (that is, he died before that emperor's death in 361). Unfortunately, all three versions of this legend date from the middle Byzantine period, probably from the eleventh century.[17] Moreover, none of them link Zotikos with founding the Orphanage, but rather with establishing a leprosarium outside the city walls on a hill across from Constantinople, on the north shore of the Golden Horn (an area later generations called Pera). All versions of the *vita* as well as other sources refer to the exact location of the leprosarium as Elaiones (The Olive Trees).[18]

The three *vitae* of Saint Zotikos obviously contain many fictitious elements. First, a story in the *vitae* concerning Constantine's contracting leprosy was derived from the Pope Sylvester legend, a tale invented

15. For a thorough study of the versions of the *Patria Constantinopolis*, see Dagron, *Constantinople Imaginaire*.

16. *JCod*, 1.3.34 (35).

17. For the three versions of the *Vita Zotici* and their dates, see Miller, "Legend," pp. 339–45, and Aubineau, "Zoticos," p. 67 and pp. 92–93.

18. Miller, "Legend," p. 371.

in sixth-century Rome and passed to Byzantium before the ninth century. No part of the Pope Sylvester legend has any basis in fact.[19] Second, the Zotikos *vitae* describe how, after his cure, Constantine and his officials tried to execute all lepers to halt the spread of this contagious disease. This also is pure fabrication. Third, the *vitae* recount how a daughter of the emperor Constantius contracted leprosy, was marked for death by her own father, but saved by Zotikos who "accepted her as his daughter in Christ." No other historical sources support this tale. Finally, all three versions of the *vitae* close by portraying Zotikos's painful death by Constantius's order, the miraculous talking mules who revealed to Zotikos's executioners where the saint should be buried, and Constantius's sudden repentance made manifest by his decision to rebuild Zotikos's leper asylum and to endow it with state revenues and rich imperial estates.[20]

How much of the story about Zotikos's martyrdom is true? No other source refers to Zotikos as a martyr. The 472 law of Leo I did not indicate in any way that Zotikos had died for the faith, but only called him a predecessor "of happy memory."[21] The oldest surviving lectionary (the Georgian version from Jerusalem) referred to Zotikos only as a sustainer of orphans. The Constantinopolitan *typika* also did not once give him the title of martyr.[22] It is probable, therefore, that the story about Zotikos's martyrdom is another fabrication, as was the tale about Constantine's leprosy. But are the *Vitae Zotici* at least correct in maintaining that Zotikos lived under Constantius and established his philanthropic institutions before that emperor's death in 361?

This study has so far demonstrated that later Byzantine sources associated Zotikos with two philanthropic institutions: the Orphanotropheion on the acropolis of Constantinople and a leprosarium at Elaiones in Pera. Although the *Vitae Zotici* describe only the leprosarium, one version does mention an administrative connection between the leper asylum and the Orphanage. According to this account, the

19. Ibid., pp. 369–70. Regarding the origin of the Silvester legend, see Kazhdan, "Constantin Imaginaire," p. 239.
20. Aubineau, "Zoticos," chap. II (pp. 80–83).
21. *JCod*, 1.3.34 (35).
22. Aubineau, "Zoticos," pp. 92–95.

emperor Justin II (565–571) required that the Orphanotropheion make regular payment to the leprosarium to help sustain its patients.[23] A later law of Leo VI (886–912) confirmed this story by referring to Justin's special monetary gift to the Orphanage.[24] By the reign of Justin II, therefore, the Orphanotropheion and the leprosarium were linked administratively.

The ninth-century *Kletorologion of Philotheos* indicated this relationship more clearly by listing the Orphanage and the leper asylum as two separate administrative divisions under the *orphanotrophos*'s supervision.[25] Moreover, a tenth-century version of the *typikon* of the Great Church stipulated that Zotikos was to be commemorated on two different days: on 31 December in the Orphanotropheion and on 8 January at the leprosarium.[26] Leo I's law of 472 indicated that Zotikos and his successors as *orphanotrophoi* supervised not only the Orphanage, but several other philanthropic institutions and ascetic communities in the city. Our study of the *Vitae Zotici* confirms that one of these charitable institutions was the leprosarium at Elaiones.

Leo I's law of 472 proves that Zotikos had established the Orphanotropheion no later than the reign of Theodosius II and possibly earlier.[27] With regard to the leprosarium, the church historian Sokrates demonstrated that this asylum had gained renown by the time of the episcopal election of 425. When the patriarch Attikos died in that year, the people of Constantinople demanded that Sisinnios be their new bishop. He had been serving as a priest not at a church within Constantinople, but rather at the leprosarium at Elaiones. He had become so well known for his piety and care for the poor that the people demanded him as their new shepherd. Sisinnios was subsequently elected as bishop and held the office for two years.

In this same passage, Sokrates stated that the people of Constantinople were accustomed to cross the Golden Horn to celebrate the feast of the Ascension at Elaiones.[28] It is well known that after Theodo-

23. Ibid., chap. 12 (p. 82).   24. Leo VI, *Novel*, pp. 377–78.
25. *Kletorologion of Philotheos*, p. 123.
26. Mateos, ed., 31 Dec. (p. 168) and 8 Jan. (p. 190).
27. *JCod*, 1.3.34 (35).
28. Sokrates, 7.26 (p. 375).

sius I restored Nicaean Christians to the see of Constantinople in 380, he forced the Arians under their bishop Demophilos to withdraw from the city and settle their communities in churches beyond the walls.[29] At these suburban sanctuaries the Arians organized elaborate liturgical celebrations for Sundays and feasts such as the Ascension. Even during the episcopate of John Chrysostom (398–404), Arian groups were staging nocturnal processions within Constantinople with singing, lanterns, and candles to lure the people to venture outside the walls where they would celebrate Sunday liturgies and those of great holy days in Arian sanctuaries.[30] It is therefore likely that Elaiones became a popular place for commemorating Jesus' ascension because of a well-orchestrated Arian liturgical program centered there. On the basis of Sokrates' description, Zotikos seems to have been associated with an Arian party in Constantinople. Such a conclusion concurs with the statement of the three *Vitae Zotici* that this holy man had lived during the reign of Constantius II when Arian bishops—Eusebios of Nikomedeia (341–342), Makedonios (342–348 and 350–360), and Eudoxios (360–369)—ruled the church of Constantinople.

Byzantine lectionaries as well as the manuscript titles of the *Vitae Zotici* identify Zotikos as a priest serving the church of Constantinople, but one version of the *vita* also describes him as an ascetic who had embraced a life of celibacy and of the greatest humility in the service of the poor.[31] According to this version, although Zotikos chose to live as a monk, he remained in Constantinople to rescue abandoned orphans and lepers. The earliest monks of Syria, Palestine, and Egypt, however, had totally rejected urban life and sought out the desert wastes or the mountain wilderness for solitude and spiritual peace. On the other hand, another form of monasticism propagated an ascetic life of celibacy and self-denial, a life lived not in the desert, but in or very close to the cities where these monks could serve the poor in a fashion similar to Zotikos's ministry as described in his *vitae*. This form of monasticism had originated in fourth-century Asia Mi-

---

29. Sokrates, 5.7 (pp. 278–79); Sozomenos, 7.5.5–7 (pp. 306–7). See also Miller, *Birth*, pp. 82–85.

30. Sozomenos, 8.8.1–6 (pp. 360–61); Sokrates, 6.8 (p. 325).

31. Aubineau, "Zoticos," chap. 1, pp. 71–72.

nor and reached Constantinople sometime before the mid-350s through the efforts of Eustathios, later bishop of Sebasteia.[32] An influential deacon of the Constantinopolitan clergy, Marathonios, became an avid disciple of Eustathios and helped establish this new ascetic tradition in the capital. He also convinced his bishop, Makedonios, not only to allow these monks to work in and around Constantinople, but to identify his episcopacy with these ascetics and the philanthropic labors they performed.[33]

By encouraging the urban monks and their charitable activities, Bishop Makedonios not only followed Christ's mandate to assist those in distress, but he also gained much-needed support among the humble classes of Constantinople. Makedonios's position in the capital had always been precarious. His opponent within the clergy, Paul, had challenged Makedonios's right to occupy the episcopal office in 340. At that time, the emperor Constantius decided to reject both Paul and Makedonios and to appoint as bishop his own spiritual advisor, Eusebios of Nikomedeia, who died soon after in 342. The emperor eventually and half-heartedly allowed Makedonios to become bishop of Constantinople. Constantius deposed him once in 348, restored him in 350, and finally removed him from office permanently in 360.[34] To offset his poor standing at the imperial court, Makedonios desperately needed to build a power base within the urban populace. The philanthropic program of Marathonios and Eustathios gave him this opportunity.

Makedonios's campaign to win the affections of the lower classes in Constantinople apparently succeeded. When the emperor Constantius forced him to leave the city in 360, a crowd of humble people followed him outside the walls cheering him as a friend of the poor (philoptochos).[35] Even his ecclesiastical opponent, the strong Nicaean Gregory of Nazianzos, recognized that many of Makedonios's supporters led holy lives. In and around Constantinople they had become renowned for their asceticism, their love of the poor, and their beautiful chanting.[36]

32. For the urban monastic movement, see Dagron, "Moines e la ville," pp. 229–76, and Miller, Birth, pp. 76–85 and pp. 118–40.

33. Miller, Birth, pp. 79–80.   34. Dagron, Naissance, pp. 440–41.

35. "Vie des saints Notaires," AB 64 (1946): 170.

36. Gregory of Nazianzos, Oratio XLI: In Pentecosten (PG, 36: col. 440).

Gregory's admiration for the Macedonians is remarkable when one considers that the group had bitterly attacked him when the emperor Theodosius I made Gregory bishop of Constantinople in 380.[37]

In sum, a comparison of what the *Vitae Zotici* reveals about Zotikos's ascetic life in Constantinople and what other sources say concerning Marathonios's movement therefore indicates a relationship between Zotikos's philanthropic program and the larger monastic movement supported by Bishop Makedonios.

The sources of the fourth and fifth centuries offer some additional evidence that Zotikos and his orphanage were linked to Makedonios and the urban monks of Marathonios. About one hundred years after Makedonios had served as bishop of the capital, while Gennadios was patriarch of Constantinople, a priest named Akakios held the office of *orphanotrophos* at Zotikos's orphanage. After Gennadios's death in 471, Akakios became the next patriarch, an indication that both the *orphanotrophos* and the institution he directed had gained great prestige in the capital. While Akakios had administered the orphanage, his brother, Timokletos, a gifted composer, used to write hymns to be performed at Akakios's institution. In those days, the people of Constantinople enjoyed visiting the Orphanotropheion to hear a choir, probably composed of orphans, chant Timokletos's songs.[38]

It is possible that this choral tradition at the Orphanotropheion originated with Zotikos. Other sources clearly show that the urban ascetics of Makedonios's party had emphasized choral singing as part of their religious life. As head of the Nicaean community in Constantinople, Gregory of Nazianzos had noticed that Makedonios's urban monks were fond of singing.[39] Even in the fifth century when the Macedonians had become an isolated sect in the rural areas outside Constantinople, they continued their musical tradition. Influenced by his Macedonian uncle and a Bithynian community of Macedonian nuns, Saint Auxentios (early fifth century) developed a love of choral music and all-night vigils.[40] Had Zotikos instituted a music pro-

---

37. Gregory of Nazianzos, *Ep. 77* (pp. 66–68).

38. Zachariah of Mitylene, 4.11 (pp. 79–80). For Zachariah of Mitylene, see the entry "Zacharias of Mytilene," in *ODB*, 3: 2218.

39. Gregory of Nazianzos, *Oratio XLI: In Pentecosten* (PG, 36: col. 440).

40. Sozomenos, 7.21.6–8 (p. 334); *Vita Sancti Auxentii* (PG, 114: col. 1380).

gram at the Orphanotropheion under the influence of the urban
monks of Constantinople or had the choir evolved for some other reason, perhaps as part of the educational system established for the
homeless children? Chapter Eight will explore this question more
fully.[41]

As a final indication that Zotikos opened his orphanage and leprosarium during the reign of Constantius, one should consider what
has been discovered concerning the development of Christian *xenones*
(medical hospitals) and *xenodocheia* (hospices) during these years. The
proliferation of hospices and their evolution into philanthropic medical
hospitals took place in East Roman cities during the years of the Arian
controversy. The complex rivalries among ecclesiastical factions that
rocked the Greek-speaking provinces after the Council of Nicaea (325)
over the term *homoousios* (of the same substance) used in the creed
quickly destroyed any dreams that the end of persecution by the Roman state would bring lasting peace to Christianity. These same rivalries, however, spurred some church leaders to remarkably creative activities in developing new modes of worship and of philanthropic
service to the community. We have already seen how the Arians, once
expelled from Constantinople by Theodosius, organized beautiful liturgical processions and hymnody to attract the people of the city.[42] Some
of the richness of Byzantine liturgy no doubt descends from these Arian efforts.

This period of creative strife also stimulated the development of the
first Christian philanthropic institutions dedicated to providing medicines and the services of paid, professional physicians for the sick
among the homeless poor. It would not be surprising, therefore, to discover that the same period witnessed a new charitable institution to assist orphans in the capital city during the reign of the Arian emperor
Constantius II.[43]

When one considers all the evidence regarding Zotikos and his
orphanage—(1) that the law of Leo I clearly stated that Zotikos had
served as *orphanotrophos* under an earlier emperor; (2) that one of his
foundations, the leprosarium, had been associated with Arians; (3) that

41. See Chapter 2, note 6.   42. See note 30 above.
43. Miller, *Birth*, pp. 68–88.

many aspects of his life paralleled the philanthropic ministries of the Macedonian ascetics; and (4) that the period of the Arian crisis in the eastern Mediterranean (325–380) stimulated the foundation of numerous philanthropic institutions—it seems reasonable to accept the account of the *Vitae Zotici* that this saint lived and worked during the reign of Constantius II.

Additional evidence, again from Leo I's law of 472, clearly links Zotikos's Orphanotropheion with the episcopal church of Hagia Sophia. According to Leo's legislation, the Orphanage and all its dependent institutions such as the leprosarium at Elaiones were to enjoy all the rights and privileges of Hagia Sophia.[44] The emperor Justinian confirmed this special status in 545.[45] Moreover, the Orphanotropheion was located not far from the Great Church, and was even closer to Saint Irene, the episcopal church of Constantinople before Constantius dedicated the new Hagia Sophia in 360. That Zotikos's foundation shared the legal privileges of the cathedral church and was located very close to Hagia Sophia and to Saint Irene indicate that the saint had established his orphanage as part of a charitable program directly under the bishop's control.

As the *Didascalia Apostolorum* made clear, many Eastern bishops of the third century maintained orphans and provided some schooling for them.[46] When George of Cappadocia arrived in Alexandria in 357, he found that the church provided both food and housing for widows and orphans.[47] When Constantius II dedicated Hagia Sophia three years later in 360, he gave gifts to the clergy of the capital, to the virgins and widows, to the *xenodocheia,* and to the poor. He also provided money to the orphans for their protection. The account of this dedication describes these orphans, widows, indigent, and clergy as attached in some way to the bishop's church.[48] These orphans were likely those for whom Zotikos, as a priest of the Constantinopolitan church, estab-

---

44. *JCod,* 1.3.34 (35).

45. *JNov,* 131.15.

46. *Didascalia Apostolorum,* 4.1–3 (pp. 218–21); see also Connolly, chap. 17 (pp. 152–56).

47. Sokrates, 2.28 (pp. 137–38).

48. Fragment of an Arian historian published as Anhang VII, in Philostorgios, pp. 202–41. For the relevant passage, see p. 225. For a discussion of this substantial fragment of Arian history, see the introduction in Philostorgios, pp. cli–clvii.

lished the Orphanotropheion and endowed it with his own patrimony and with gifts from the emperor Constantius.[49]

Earlier bishops of Byzantium had no doubt offered some program to shelter orphans, as biblical and early Christian texts exhorted. When Constantine vastly expanded provincial Byzantium to form his new capital and the city's population began to grow with astonishing rapidity, the number of poor and needy increased as well. Zotikos surely played a key role in expanding the church of Constantinople's facilities so that it could care for larger numbers of orphans as well as lepers, a role that included finding new resources to sustain these facilities.[50]

The Orphanotropheion of Zotikos was not the only place in Constantinople where Christians cared for children with no parents. Just as the official church centered at Saint Irene / Hagia Sophia sheltered orphans at Zotikos's orphanage, other Christian communities in the capital provided similar services. When Gregory of Nazianzos took over as shepherd of the small Nicaean community of Constantinople in 380, he found at the congregation's Anastasia Church groups of ascetic men, wandering monks, infirm poor persons, and, apparently, a choir of orphans and widows.[51] In fact, the picture Gregory drew of the Nicaean community assembled at the Anastasia resembles closely Philostorgios's description of the orphans and other needy people who gathered in Hagia Sophia for that church's dedication in 360. The Nicaeans no doubt built some facility close to the Anastasia Church or their bishop's residence, an *oikia* resembling those George of Cappadocia saw in Alexandria, to shelter the homeless children. It is possible that other splinter Christian communities of Constantinople such

49. Cf. Aubineau, "Zoticos," chap. 11 (pp. 80–83), and Miller, "Legend," chap. 15 (pp. 362–65).

50. For the rapid expansion of Constantinople in the fourth century, see Hunger, *Reich*, p. 47, who presents estimates for the size of Constantinople's population in 350 and also in 450, but finally concludes "Ausser Zweifel steht jedoch der ungewöhnlich schnelle Anstieg der Bevölkerungszahl Konstantinopels in den ersten Jahren nach der Einweihung der neuen Metropole." See also Durliat, *De la ville antique*, pp. 249–65, who discusses the growth of Constantinople's population based on estimates of the amount of wheat the imperial government had to supply the city from the time of Constantine to the reign of Justinian (527–565).

51. Gregory of Nazianzos, *Poemata de seipso* (PG, 37: 1260).

as the Novatians and the extreme Arians (the Anomoians) also had facilities for orphans, although these have left no record in the sources.

Beyond such general references to the presence of orphans or orphan choirs only one source exists from any period of Byzantine history that expressly mentions an orphanage in Constantinople other than the Orphanotropheion of Zotikos, and that source is a sermon delivered by Patriarch Proklos (434–447), described below.[52] It is clear, however, that other orphanages existed. The eighth-century legal code, the *Ecloga*, required that orphans of the capital without any extended family be given care in the Orphanotropheion or in the other pious houses (*euageis oikoi*—presumably monasteries) and well-known churches.[53] It is possible that some of these well-known churches had been founded much earlier by heretical or schismatic groups such as the Nicaean community prior to 380. Justinian's Novel 43 (issued in 536) stated specifically that a number of the capital's philanthropic institutions had originally belonged to heretical sects.[54] This is further testimony to the creativity of the Arian conflict in Constantinople, a time of competition among contending sects that not only produced Zotikos's Orphanotropheion, but smaller philanthropic services such as the orphan program at the Anastasia Church of the Nicaean community.

CHARITY AS PERSONAL VIRTUE

The Christian churches of the first three centuries organized the relief of orphans around the office of bishop. Justin described how members of the Roman Church gave their voluntary gifts to the bishop, who distributed these to the orphans, widows, and those in need.[55] The third-century *Didascalia Apostolorum* also placed the major responsibility for assisting children without parents upon the bishop.[56] On the other hand, there were also individual Christians who personally aided orphan children. Seleukos, a Roman soldier from Cappadocia who was martyred under Diocletian for his fervent faith, had won renown for aiding orphans as though he were their father.[57] Gregory of

---

52. Proklos, *Homélie 26*, pp. 174–83.   53. *Ecloga*, tit. 7 (p. 198).
54. *JNov*, 43 (praef.).   55. Justin, *Apologia (Prima)*, 67.
56. *Didascalia Apostolorum*, 4.1–3 (pp. 218–21); Connolly, chap. 17 (pp. 152–56).
57. Eusebios, *De martyribus Palaestinae*, 11.20–24 (pp. 942–43).

Nazianzos (fourth century) described his pious mother as a friend of the clergy and as a support of orphans.[58] Gregory of Nyssa also praised Placilla, the wife of Theodosius I (379–395), for her great charity toward orphans.[59]

Constantine's acceptance of Christianity meant that individual Christians who chose to aid children without parents came from ever higher social strata—by the end of the fourth century from the imperial family itself—but it also brought a new freedom for individual benefactors to donate larger amounts of property for philanthropic purposes, to specify precisely how this property should be used, and to have the legal means of enforcing the conditions they had set for their gifts.[60] It is possible that the Orphanotropheion itself began with a large private donation that Zotikos made from his patrimonial property to support both the orphans near Saint Irene / Hagia Sophia and the lepers at Elaiones. According to the *Vitae Zotici*, the emperor Constantius later added substantially to this initial gift.[61]

A short sermon of Patriarch Proklos (434–447) provides evidence that there were also some small, privately endowed orphanages in Constantinople that were independent of the Orphanotropheion and apparently not associated with sectarian facilities such as the one that the Nicaean community had maintained at the Anastasia before 380. According to Proklos, a wealthy Christian widow of Constantinople had established a church and orphan asylum dedicated to the Holy Innocents. By sheltering these orphans the widow had gained "tiny children of the Lord." Her generosity had formed for her a new family without the impurities of intercourse and had erected a lasting monument to her generosity.[62]

Proklos consciously used words from the vocabulary of classical civic virtue to describe the widow's generosity in constructing this home for children. She had shown herself a person of *megalopsychia* (greatness of soul), Aristotle's term for the virtue of beneficence to-

58. Gregory of Nazianzos, *Oratio XVIII: Funebris in patrem* (PG, 36: 996).
59. Gregory of Nyssa, *Oratio funebris de Placilla* (PG, 46: 884).
60. See the discussion in Hagemann, *Stellung der Piae Causae*, pp. 59–61.
61. Aubineau, "Zoticos," chap. 11 (pp. 80–81).
62. Proklos, *Homélie 26*, chap. 6 (pp. 182–83).

ward one's *polis*. Moreover, Proklos claimed that the widow's actions had won her fame surpassing even the glory of the consulship, the highest city magistracy at Rome and Constantinople.[63]

By the fifth century Christian aristocrats had ceased to pay for traditional pagan buildings such as theaters, amphitheaters, or gymnasia and were supporting instead churches and Christian philanthropic institutions. At about the same time that this wealthy widow opened her orphanage, Paulinos, a prominent court official of Theodosius II, constructed a church, monastery, and hospital dedicated to Saints Cosmas and Damian just beyond the walls of Constantinople.[64] During these same years, a wealthy citizen of Ephesus named Bassianos provided the resources to build a *ptocheion* with seventy beds to assist the indigent of his city.[65]

During the fifth and sixth centuries many local aristocrats built hospitals and hospices throughout the empire. Even after the momentous changes that overwhelmed the empire in the seventh century, wealthy individuals continued to endow philanthropic hospitals and almshouses in Constantinople, and even in some provincial towns such as Thessalonike and Philadelphia in Asia Minor.[66] On the other hand, there are extremely few references to privately endowed orphanages anywhere in the empire at any period. The *vita* of Saint Clement of Ankyra, however, does describe a privately funded orphan asylum in central Asia Minor.[67]

According to this *vita*, Clement was born in Ankyra during the reign of Valerian and suffered a martyr's death under Diocletian (284–305). While Clement was still a baby, he had lost his father; before reaching maturity (circa 280), he also lost his mother. Thereupon, a wealthy woman named Sophia adopted him and continued his spiritu-

---

63. Ibid., chap. 6 (p. 183): θαύμασον μεγαλοψυχίαν, τὴν τοῦ οἴκου βλέπων εὐπρέπειαν, καὶ βλέπε χήρας φιλοτιμίαν, πᾶσαν ὑπερβαίνουσαν ὑπατείαν.

64. For the example of Paulinos's hospital and monastery, see Miller, *Birth*, pp. 124–25.

65. *ACO*, 2.1.3: 405.

66. For a *xenon* in twelfth-century Thessalonike, see Eustathios, *Espugnazione*, p. 146. For a xenon in thirteenth-century Philadelphia (Asia Minor), see Theodore Laskaris, Ep. 118 (pp. 164–65).

67. This *Vita Clementis Ancyrani et sociorum* was recast from earlier versions by Symeon Metaphrastes, the late-tenth-century hagiographer. For a summary of the information regarding Symeon Metaphrastes, see *ODB*, 3: 1983–84. The text is found in PG, 114: 815–94.

al education. When a deadly pestilence struck Galatia, Clement and Sophia collected infants whose non-Christian parents had died because of the plague and also those whom poor parents had abandoned along the roads. Sophia donated large sums of money for Clement to set up an institution where he could provide these children with food, shelter, clothing, and instruction. Clement strove zealously to lead as many of these orphans as possible to God. As a result of endowing this orphanage, Sophia, a woman who for years had desired children without success, now had many offspring.[68]

Eventually, the people of Ankyra asked that Clement become a deacon and then a priest of their church. After two years serving the Christian community of Ankyra, Clement was elected by the people to be their new bishop. In this high office, Clement continued to care for his orphans, but he now expanded the service he provided and integrated his asylum into the local church structure. When the more pious orphans reached sufficient age, he was able to introduce them into the minor orders of the Christian clergy.[69]

One cannot accept the *Vita Clementis* as a truly historical account. Clement was indeed martyred under Diocletian, but many of the details of the *vita* story are anachronistic. For example, women could not formally adopt children under Roman law until Leo VI issued his Novel 27 at the end of the ninth century, although informal adoptions by Christian women occurred as early as the fourth century.[70] Moreover, the elaborate private orphanage that Sophia and Clement organized would probably have been impossible in the third century. The details of the *vita* correspond more closely to the conditions of the fourth and fifth centuries when private Christian foundations were becoming common in Asia Minor, though one should not rule out completely a third-century orphan asylum.[71]

The *Vita Clementis* thus does not prove that Sophia used her wealth

---

68. *Vita Clementis* (PG, 114: 816–24).

69. Ibid., 824–25.

70. Leo VI, *Novel*, 27 (pp. 105–11). Palladius, *Lausiaca*, chap. 6 (pp. 30–36), recounts the story of a woman in the fourth century who adopts (τεκνοποιεῖται), the daughter of her sister. At that time women could neither adopt nor serve as guardians according to Roman law.

71. There are also indications that Symeon Metaphrastes used two different archetypes in composing his version of the *Vita Clementis*. For example, see *Vita Clementis* (PG, 114: 821),

to establish an orphanage for Clement to supervise, but it does demonstrate that such institutions were familiar, if not in the third century, then in the fourth or fifth century when the original version of the *Vita Clementis* was probably composed. In addition, both Proklos's sermon and the *Vita Clementis* illustrated the good fortune of generous widows by emphasizing how these women had formerly desired children without success, but once they had established their orphanages they obtained many offspring.[72] Such a sentiment probably became a standard mode of praising widows who had chosen to found private orphanages or provide money for already existing orphanages. Indeed, it is possible that as the enrolled widows (see Chapter Two) lost their official status in the church and ceased to function in any formal capacity as teachers of orphans, wealthy Christian matrons whose husbands had died began to set up private asylums for homeless children.

The *Vita Clementis* also provides a possible solution to the puzzle of why Byzantine sources so often describe independent *xenones* and *xenodocheia*, but rarely mention independent orphanages. Early Christian texts frequently stressed that bishops were responsible for orphan care. The third-century *Didascalia Apostolorum* implied that such care ranked first among the philanthropic duties of the bishop and his community.[73] When a private person such as Sophia established an orphanage and provided it with an endowment, the local bishop soon assumed responsibility over the institution, especially since the bishop and the episcopal church could use the services of the older orphans as acolytes, lectors, or singers in a children's choir. The fifth-century *Vita Sancti Euthymii* has preserved a detailed description of such an episcopal school for boys including orphans.

According to this *vita*, Bishop Otreios of the city of Melitene in northern Syria accepted the task of caring for young Euthymios after the boy's father had died. Otreios first baptized Euthymios and then tonsured him as a lector, one of the lowest ranks of the Christian cler-

---

where the narrative records that Clement became a monk. There is no further indication in the Metaphrastic version that Clement formally embraced monasticism.

72. Proklos, *Homélie 26*, chap. 6 (p. 182); cf. *Vita Clementis* (PG, 114: 824).

73. *Didascalia Apostolorum*, 4.2 (p. 219).

gy. When Euthymios was old enough, Otreios handed the boy over to the teachers of the Holy Scripture for more formal training. As Euthymios progressed in his studies, the bishop ordained him to higher ranks of the clergy until he reached the order of the priesthood. The *vita* mentioned other boys with Euthymios who also served as lectors and studied with the young saint.[74]

The *Vita Sancti Euthymii* described a school directly under the care of Melitene's bishop. It functioned both as a seminary to train clergy for the city's Christian community and as an orphanage to care for boys such as Euthymios. This was exactly the sort of institution described in the *Vita Sancti Clementis*.[75] The stories of Euthymios and Clement clearly illustrate how easily bishops could integrate *philanthropia* toward orphans into the routines of their episcopal churches.

Just like orphanages, medical hospitals and hospices had emerged as new Christian institutions in the fourth century. Hospitals and the Hellenic medicine they provided their patients, however, occasionally aroused opposition among some Christians who did not believe that the Bible sanctioned the use of pagan science. Moreover, hospitals with their professional physicians as well as hospices with their constantly shifting group of poor residents did not harmonize as easily with the liturgical routines and obligations of the bishop and his cathedral staff as did the orphans of the episcopal school. As a result, one should not be surprised to find many independent, self-governing *xenones* and *xenodocheia* functioning in the Byzantine Empire, but very few independent orphanages. Such private orphan asylums had easily merged with the bishop's own orphan school, if he already had one. In Constantinople, some of these private orphanages merged with local parish churches or even monasteries, which also could easily adapt an orphan school to their liturgical needs. Thus, the eighth-century *Ecloga* mentioned well-known churches and *euageis oikoi* (in this case monasteries) which took in children with no parents, and Anna Komnena also referred to twelfth-century monasteries that maintained orphanages.[76]

Most Byzantine medical hospitals and hospices therefore developed

---

74. *Vita Euthymii*, pp. 8–11.
75. Ibid., pp. 10–13.
76. *Ecloga*, tit. 7 (p. 198); Anna Komnena, *Alexiad*, 15.7.3 (3: 214).

into philanthropic institutions that were in fact completely independent of the local bishop. Despite Canons 8 and 10 of the Council of Chalcedon (451), Justinian's novels allowed many *xenones* and *xenodocheia* total freedom from the bishop in managing their resources. During later centuries, private founders were able to exclude all ecclesiastical officials from playing any supervisory role in the functioning of their charities. As a result, these hospitals and hospices frequently appear in the surviving sources as distinct charitable institutions. Most orphanages, on the other hand, disappeared from written records since they functioned as integral parts of the local episcopal organization.[77]

Constantine's conversion not only encouraged wealthy individuals to provide assistance for orphans, but it also meant that the emperor himself began to interest himself in the care of children without families. Eusebios described how Constantine aided orphans as soon as he had gained control of Rome and later in the East after he defeated Licinius.[78] By the reign of Theodosius I, even traditional pagans such as Themistios, the court orator, included kindness to orphans as a mark of the ideal ruler. In a speech praising the emperor Theodosius's many beneficent deeds, Themistios especially focused on the assistance the emperor rendered to boys and girls deprived not only of their fathers and mothers, but also of their patrimonies. Themistios painted a dismal picture of children, born into the best of families, whom *orphania* drove penniless into the streets of the capital. To these unfortunates the emperor became a father, restoring their property and thus rescuing them from their destitution. He did this, according to Themistios, not by simply confiscating their lost patrimonies from the unscrupulous persons who had seized these properties, but by purchasing back these estates with gold. Thus, Theodosius had found a way to return their rightful inheritances to the orphans without destroying those who had defrauded them.[79]

Themistios's speech praised Theodosius not for having founded a

77. By the eleventh century, private founders of hospitals excluded from their institutions any interference by the local bishop, the metropolitan, or the patriarch of Constantinople (Miller, *Birth*, pp. 100–17). Concerning private ecclesiastical foundations in the Byzantine Empire, see Thomas, *Private Religious Foundations*.

78. Eusebios, *Vita Constantini*, 1.39–43 and 4.28.1.

79. Themistios, *Oratio 34*, para. 461–62 (pp. 74–76).

new orphanage nor for offering additional revenues to Zotikos's Orphanotropheion, but for assisting children who had lost property to dishonest guardians. Despite the growth of Christian orphan asylums during the fourth century, most children whose parents had died received care from their nearest male relative *(tutela legitima)* or from a relative or friend whom their father had chosen for them *(tutela testamentaria)*. How did the Christianizing of the East Roman world during the fourth and fifth century affect the nature of guardianship?

GUARDIANSHIP

To build the New Jerusalem Byzantine emperors had to alter the ancient Roman legal traditions that they had inherited from the pagan past, but they pursued this goal with caution because they and their advisors were well aware that the Roman legal tradition was one of the great achievements of their civilization. To change it haphazardly might destroy its delicate balance of clarity and elasticity. Thus, the Christianization of the Roman legal tradition proceeded slowly in almost every area of law. With regard to the rules governing guardianship, however, the Byzantine emperors of the fourth and early fifth century moved more rapidly to offer increased protection against unscrupulous guardians.

On 26 March 314, two years after his victory over Maxentius, Constantine issued a law that profoundly altered the nature of guardianship. Constantine placed a lien (in Roman law, a *hypotheca*) on all property belonging to the guardian to guarantee his proper management of the orphan's property and legal affairs. This *hypotheca* applied to both classes of guardians, *tutores* and *curatores*. According to Constantine's law, the property of the guardian remained under the *hypotheca* until the competent official conducted an audit of the orphan's property and confirmed that the guardian had performed his duties honestly. Since this audit only took place when the orphan reached age twenty-five, the lien could remain in effect many years. Moreover, Constantine gave this *hypotheca* on behalf of the ward priority over all other liens on the guardian's property, even if these other liens had originated prior to the beginning of the *tutela* or *cura*.[80]

80. *CodTheo*, 3.30.1 (anno 314). For the Late Roman law of pledge including the general

By providing the ward with such a privileged lien on his guardian's property, Constantine inadvertently made it very difficult for a tutor or curator to borrow money until he had successfully completed his service as guardian. With such a *hypotheca* over his property, a guardian possessed no unencumbered real estate, money, or movable goods with which to secure a loan.[81]

As we noted in the previous chapter, Roman law had been increasingly protecting orphans from their guardians since the Late Republic. By the time of the Classical jurists, *tutores* were advised to take inventory of their wards' properties and keep careful records of their management both to protect their wards and also to provide themselves a defense if their wards were to sue them in the future, but Constantine's *hypotheca* offered additional protection to the orphan. According to Classical Roman law, the former ward had the responsibility of initiating an action against his guardian for a crime the guardian had committed, for an act in bad faith, or for grossly negligent behavior. By introducing the general *hypotheca,* Constantine placed the responsibility on the guardian to remove the lien on his property by demonstrating at the end of his service that he had competently carried out the duties of the *tutela.*

With this *hypotheca,* Constantine completed a process of transforming the office of guardian from a form of public office into a public burden *(munus).* In a similar fashion the emperor Diocletian (284–305) had altered the nature of service as a municipal magistrate or as a member of the governing *polis* council *(curia)* from a privilege to a burden by placing a lien on the property of all such officeholders to ensure the collection of the *annona* tax. Diocletian's financial reforms made curial service in provincial cities increasingly unpleasant for local aristocrats and encouraged them to find immunities from holding such public offices. During the fourth century, subsequent emperors had to force local notables to undertake municipal offices, positions

---

hypotheca, see Käser, *Das römische Privatrecht,* 2: 312–21. Sargenti, *Diritto privato,* pp. 168–69, argues that this general *hypotheca* was placed over the property of a guardian not by Constantine, but by a later fourth-century emperor. Käser (2: 234), however, accepts the accuracy of the *CodTheo* in this case.

81. Käser, *Das römische Privatrecht,* 2: 316–17.

that their ancestors of the second century had avidly desired.[82] So, also, as a result of Constantine's law, people throughout the empire became increasingly unwilling to serve as *tutores* or *curatores* even for close relatives. By 384, the emperors Theodosius I and Valintinian II had noticed that many orphans were unable to find either *tutores legitimi* or *tutores testamentarii* and had to introduce new procedures that applied when magistrates appointed guardians (Justinian's *tutela Atiliana*).[83]

In 316 Constantine decreed that if a tutor or a curator failed to carry out the terms of legacies or gifts made to the orphan in his care, and if the child thereby suffered any loss, the law would require the guardian to make good from his own resources what his negligence had cost the ward.[84] In 326 Constantine forbad a tutor or a curator to sell any property—agricultural land, urban real estate, or slaves—belonging to the ward unless the guardian first obtained a special *decretum* from the urban prefect or from the provincial governor authorizing such a sale.[85] In 195 A.D. the emperor Septimius Severus had forbidden the sale of any of the ward's agricultural property by a guardian; Constantine now widened this restriction to include every conceivable kind of property, movable as well as immovable.[86] The emperor stressed that a guardian was not to sell the ward's slaves since they were usually loyal to their old master and often helped to monitor the actions of the tutor or curator in administering the orphan's estate.

Also in 326 Constantine issued his most draconian measure to protect orphans, in this case to defend only female children. According to this new regulation, if a girl orphan lost her virginity while under the protection of her guardian (that is, before she reached age twenty-five), the competent magistrate was to hold the tutor legally responsible and punish him with banishment and confiscation of his property. In short,

---

82. The decline in the status of local curial service is a very complex issue. The Severan emperors had already placed a general *hypotheca* over the property of all debtors to the *fiscus* (Käser, *Das römische Privatrecht*, 2: 316). Jones, *Later Roman Empire*, discusses Diocletian's systemization of the *annona* levy (1: 61–68), and describes the role of *curiales* in collecting the *annona* (1: 456–59).

83. *CodTheo*, 3.17.3 (anno 384?).

84. *CodTheo*, 3.30.2 (anno 316 or perhaps 323).

85. *CodTheo*, 3.30.3 (15 March 326).

86. Käser, *Roman Private Law*, p. 321.

the law punished the guardian as though he had committed rape. The law did not require that the guardian had acted negligently. If the female ward could not prove her virginity before her first wedding, then her guardian suffered the severe punishments that Constantine's law demanded.[87]

In 331 Constantine issued a law regulating the minimum age of city councillors (curiales). To fill the seats of these councils (curiae), some cities had been requiring minor children to assume the responsibility if their father had died without leaving an adult male heir. This is another sign of how burdensome local notables considered service on the curial councils after Diocletian secured the collection of the annona by placing a lien on all land of curiales. Constantine required that a boy be at least seventeen before he could serve on a city council. One should notice that Constantine did not require the full adult age of twenty-five, an indication that in this law he had to balance his strong wish to protect orphans with the necessity of filling the seats on polis councils.[88]

A letter of Basil of Cappadocia, written circa 372, however, indicates that not all city councils were observing Constantine's regulation. In this letter Basil complained to the governor that a city had drafted an orphan boy of four to serve on its curia. Since the child was so young, his elderly grandfather was legally responsible for him and would therefore have to carry out the actual obligations of curial service. In attempting to release the boy from his obligation, Basil did not mention Constantine's law, but only the advanced age of the boy's grandfather and the imperial decree the old man had received earlier to exempt him from further service to his polis.[89]

In 333 Constantine legislated that, if a tutor or curator mismanaged lands leased from the imperial estates (res privata) in the name of the orphan, he had to make good the losses to his ward's account from his own resources.[90] Finally, in 334 Constantine protected both orphans and their guardians from third-party suits. If a third party should sue

87. CodTheo, 9.8.1.
88. CodTheo, 12.1.19 (anno 331). See comments in Weidemann, Adults, p. 137.
89. Basil, Ep. 84 (2: 103–8).
90. CodTheo 3.30.5 (18 April 333).

the orphan before the emperor's high court, the orphan did not need to journey beyond the province where he lived to defend himself. The orphan with his guardian could present his defense before the governor without the pain and expense of a long journey to the imperial court.[91]

Constantine's panegyricist, Eusebios of Caesarea, emphasized how the emperor had pursued a vigorous policy of Christianizing the Roman laws by banning pagan sacrifices and gladiatorial games and removing Augustus's laws that penalized chastity, a virtue Christianity held in high esteem. Some modern scholars have claimed, instead, that Constantine's reforms simply completed trends already evident in the Classical period of Roman law.[92] This is especially clear with regard to Constantine's laws in defense of orphans. In most of his legislation, he expanded or made more specific the rules already contained in Classical law. Even his most radical step, the *hypotheca* placed on all of a guardian's property, had a strong precedent in earlier liens placed on the property of *curiales* to guarantee their performance of government services, a system expanded by Diocletian to cover the collection of the *annona* levy. That Constantine framed his laws on behalf of orphans in terms of earlier Roman law, however, does not preclude his having acted in the spirit of Saint James's dictum that a pure faith seeks to assist the orphan and the widow in their distress (James 1:27).

Whatever Constantine's motivation, his legislation did not have the desired effect. According to the orator Themistios, the emperor Theodosius (379–395) had to intervene personally to restore property unlawfully taken from orphans by their callous guardians.[93] In addition to individual acts of philanthropy to protect orphans, Theodosius also issued several general laws to assist them, laws that were designed in part to correct problems Constantine's laws had introduced.

In 384 Theodosius I and his coemperor in the West, Valentinian II, restructured the procedure to appoint guardians where no testamen-

---

91. *CodTheo*, 1.22.2 (17 June 334).

92. Eusebios, *Vita Constantini*, 4.25. See also the general discussion of Christianity's influence on Constantine's legislation in Vogt, "Christlicher Einfluss," pp. 118–48. See also Hunger, *Reich*, pp. 143–49, esp. 143, where Hunger discusses the controversy over the extent of Christian influence on Constantine's legislation.

93. Themistios, *Oratio 34*, 462 (p. 76).

tary or legitimate guardians could be found. Since the time of Marcus Aurelius the *praetor tutelarius* had performed this task at Rome. Now the emperors transferred this responsibility to the urban prefects, the principal imperial bureaucrats at Rome and Constantinople. In the provinces, the governors, assisted by important men from the curial councils, would now make these appointments.[94] This law also indicated that orphaned children were experiencing difficulty in finding *tutores* and *curatores* because many of their relatives were claiming exemptions, such as the size of their own families, their important official duties, or the distance of their residence from that of their potential ward.[95] As a result of Constantine's many regulations concerning guardians, especially his *hypotheca* over their property, and the severe punishments for negligent guardians of orphan girls, potential testamentary and legitimate guardians were trying to avoid their appointments just as local aristocrats during the fourth century were striving to obtain exemptions from curial service.

Theodosius I and Valentinian II issued another important law regarding guardianship in 390. The emperors finally removed the traditional legal barrier against women serving as guardians. In a case where no testamentary or legitimate tutor or curator could be found, the orphan's mother could assume the duties of legal guardianship provided that she signed a statement that she would not remarry. Even if she did remarry, however, she still could remain the child's guardian, but Constantine's general *hypotheca* that attached to any of the mother's personal property now extended to include the whole estate of the second husband.[96] It would be interesting to know if such a guardian widow had more difficulty in finding a new mate than did a woman who would not encumber her second husband with a privileged lien on all his property.

That Theodosius I and Valentinian II broke with the strong Roman law tradition that only men were fit to serve as guardians and that they were also willing to make exceptions for mother guardians who decided to break their written promises not to marry a second time suggest

---

94. *CodTheo*, 3.17.3 (anno 384?). Regarding the *praetor tutelarius*, see Chapter 2, note 34.
95. Käser, *Das Römische Privatrecht*, 1: 358–59; 2: 228; Crifò, *Rapporti*, pp. 66–78.
96. *CodTheo*, 3.17.4 (anno 390).

that in issuing this law the two emperors were trying to deal with the growing shortage of men willing to assume the burden of guardianship.

In 472, seventy-seven years after the death of Theodosius I, the emperor Leo I provided additional evidence that Constantine's *hypotheca* and other Byzantine changes in the law of guardianship had made it increasingly difficult for orphans to find blood relatives or even trusted family friends who would accept the burdens and liabilities of guardianship. Leo decreed that the *orphanotrophos* of the Zotikos orphanage and the directors of other asylums for homeless children in Constantinople were to act as though they were *tutores* and *curatores* of the boys or girls entrusted to the institutions they administered. They were to defend these orphans in legal proceedings and assist them in their business dealings. The *orphanotrophoi* were to prepare an inventory of the property of each orphan subject to them and accept the supervision of the property in the presence of agents representing the urban prefect of Constantinople.[97]

Leo's law clearly demonstrates that by the second half of the fifth century not all the children sheltered at Zotikos's Orphanotropheion or in other orphan homes of the capital were destitute children of the streets or infants abandoned by their hopelessly indigent parents. Although such were the orphans Zotikos had initially intended to shelter in his orphanage, by 472 some of the children at the Orphanotropheion owned enough property to require written inventories or had business interests of some sort. They had inherited estates sufficiently complex to involve some of them in potential legal conflicts. Why would orphans of such means be nurtured at Zotikos's Orphanotropheion? Some might have lost both mother and father, been left without a testamentary guardian by negligent parents, and have had no living agnatic relatives (paternal male relatives). Others, however, might have been left with a testamentary guardian who found a way to excuse himself from service, or with an agnatic relative who also claimed an exemption from *tutela* duties, or even a mother who preferred not to limit her prospects for remarriage by presenting her potential sec-

97. *JCod*, 1.3.31 (32).

ond husband with a *hypotheca* over all his property, a lien of such a kind that it would be almost impossible for him to borrow money in the future.

By trying to restructure the Roman law of guardianship to protect orphans, the Christian emperors from Constantine to Theodosius I made it increasingly difficult for children who had lost one or both parents to find guardians. On the other hand, the institutions supported by the organized church and by wealthy Christians were able to assist at least some children of property who could find no relatives or friends willing to accept the financial and legal responsibility of caring for them and their estates. Did the influx of wealthy orphans into Zotikos's Orphanotropheion or smaller institutions significantly limit the places available for indigent orphans? No evidence exists that answers this question. It is clear, however, that the presence of prosperous orphans at the Orphanotropheion guaranteed that the care and especially the education of the children raised there was of a high quality. As we shall see in Chapter Eight, the Orphanotropheion developed into one of the major educational institutions of Constantinople.

From 312 to 472 the late Roman emperors, bishops, and pious laymen and laywomen tried to reshape the society of the Roman world according to the mandates of the new religion that the emperors themselves and a growing number of the empire's population had accepted. The capital city of Constantinople came to symbolize this change as it gradually assumed its role as the center of the Christian Empire. Part of this process involved new methods of caring for orphans, a class of people Christianity considered especially worthy of loving care. Zotikos's Orphanotropheion, standing on the new capital's acropolis, provided a potent symbol of the change from ancient Rome to the New Jerusalem. As we have seen, by the time of Akakios's election as patriarch in 471, it had become one of the most prominent charitable institutions of the capital city.

The Byzantine emperors were far less successful in reshaping the legal code of the new Christian Empire. In attempting to protect orphans, they ultimately made it far more difficult for orphans to find protection through the system of legal guardianship and drove some of these children into the Orphanotropheion or other group homes for orphans. In altering the Roman law rules of guardianship, however, the Christian emperors had made one beneficial innovation. They had opened the office of legal guardian to the orphan's surviving mother. As the eighteenth-century political and legal philosopher Montesquieu observed, "The laws which gave the right of tutelage to the mother were most attentive to the preservation of the infant's person."[98] Theodosius I and Valentinian II still restricted the mother's rights of guardianship to cases where the departed father had appointed no tutor by will and where no male relative on the father's side came forward to accept the guardianship, but these two emperors opened the door to further advances in maternal rights to serve as their children's *tutores*, a process we shall examine in the next chapter.

98. Montesquieu, *Esprit des lois*, 19.24 (pp. 305–6).

IV   BYZANTINE GUARDIANSHIP

 During the eleven hundred years of its existence, the Byzantine state preserved many of the rules and definitions of Roman guardianship, but, as we have seen, the Christian emperors began to alter substantially certain aspects of the Roman system as early as the reign of Constantine. This chapter will examine Late Roman and Byzantine guardianship to determine which principles of the Roman *tutela* Byzantine rulers and their legal advisors chose to retain and which aspects they changed or discarded completely. At the same time that we are pursuing these two questions, it will be valuable to consider evidence for the application of these rules—whether descended directly from the definitions of Classical Roman law or from the novels of Byzantine emperors. In other words, is it possible to find evidence that Roman rules of *tutela* and subsequent Byzantine innovations were actually followed by the emperor's subjects, and, if these rules were transgressed, whether Byzantine courts stood ready to enforce these norms by punishing those who violated them?

In order to understand the Byzantine system of orphan care and eventually to evaluate its effectiveness, this chapter will also indicate any cases where changes in the Roman law of guardianship produced unintended effects. Constantine's legislation to protect orphans had, in fact, made it more difficult for some children to find guardians. Were there other such instances of unintended effects in the history of Byzantine guardianship law?

CONTINUITY

According to Justinian's *Corpus Juris Civilis*, a legal expert of Cicero's time, Servius Sulpicius Rufus, provided a binding definition of guardianship. Servius had described it as a protective power over a free person (that is, over someone not a slave and no longer under the power of his father), a person still too young to protect himself. The Roman civil law granted this *tutela* (guardianship) to specific persons called *tutores* (guardians).[1]

Paulus included Servius's definition in his commentary on the Praetor's Edict. In the sixth century, the emperor Justinian incorporated the same formula in the *Digest* and also quoted it word for word in his student manual of Roman law, the *Institutes*.[2] From the Justinianic corpus, it passed directly into several key summaries of Byzantine law. When the emperor Basil I (867–886) and his legal advisors prepared a new legal handbook called the *Prochiron*, they placed a paraphrase of Servius's definition at the beginning of the title on guardianship.[3] Some manuscripts of the *Synopsis Basilicorum*, an alphabetical guide to Basil I's Greek version of the Justinianic corpus, included a word-for-word translation of the same definition.[4] Finally, the *Hexabiblos*, the last comprehensive summary of Byzantine law, prepared by Constantine Harmenopoulos circa 1345, also employed Servius's words to introduce its section on the protection of orphans.[5]

The Roman conception of guardianship thus passed directly through the many centuries of Byzantine rule without alteration. The Christian Church did not need to change a single word of Servius Sulpicius's definition to accept *tutela* as a useful rule of law. The thirteenth-century legal expert and archbishop of Ohrid Demetrios Chomatianos considered guardianship as a special gift, created by the Roman law, to assist orphans in their constant battle against the ill winds of fortune, the schemes of rapacious relatives, and the attacks of evil-minded outsiders.[6]

---

1. *Dig*, 26.1.1.
2. *Dig*, 26.1.1; *Inst*, 1.13.1–3.
3. *Prochiron*, 36 (*JGR*, 2: 204).
4. *SynBas*, E.38.1 (*JGR*, 5: 296 note a).
5. *Hexabiblos*, 5.12.1 (p. 708).
6. Chomatianos, no. 84 (p. 369).

Chomatianos not only referred to the definition of guardianship in the abstract, he applied it on at least two specific occasions to render decisions in defense of orphans. In the first case, a man named John Achyraites appeared before Chomatianos's court to seek the return of his patrimonial property.[7] John explained that he and his two older brothers, Leo and Constantine, had first lost their father, and then a few years later, when John was nine, they had lost their mother. Before she had died, their mother had designated the eldest sibling Constantine as guardian for both John and the middle brother, Leo, since Constantine had reached the age of maturity. She even left Constantine a legacy (a share of property, separated from the general inheritance) as payment for his labors in supervising the children.

After their mother's death, Constantine chose to ignore his brothers' interests, and even decided to abandon John and Leo by joining the Byzantine army and squandering their wealth. John managed to find another protector named Basil, the husband of a female cousin. Subsequently, Basil also took control of Leo's property and forced the older boy out of the house to seek support from others.[8] Basil then exploited his position of authority over John to deprive the boy of the remainder of his movable and immovable property while at the same time using John as an agent in his agricultural business operations. During the years he worked for Basil, John claimed that his guardian had not even fed him properly.

Having heard John's sorrowful story of abuse and neglect and the counterarguments of the defendants, the former guardians Constantine and Basil, Archbishop Demetrios Chomatianos rejected all the claims that the guardians presented and ruled that they had violated the basic duty of *tutores,* which, according to Servius Sulpicius's definition, was to defend and protect orphans in their care.

In the second case, four brothers told Chomatianos that their legal guardian, an adult half-brother named Ganadaios, had taken every bit of their paternal property. Ganadaios argued that the time limit for reclaiming the property had passed and therefore that Chomatianos

---

7. Chomatianos, no. 84 (pp. 369–78).
8. Chomatianos, no. 84 (p. 371).

should reject the four brothers' request that their patrimonial property be returned to them. Chomatianos, however, used the Roman definition of guardianship as the obligation of protecting underage orphans to overturn Ganadaios's legal arguments based on technical time limits.[9]

As we saw in Chapter Two, Classical Roman law recognized three types of guardians: those who were appointed by testament *(tutela testamentaria),* those who assumed the *tutela* based on their family relationship to the orphan *(tutela legitima),* and those who were appointed by magistrates *(tutela Atiliana;* also known as *tutela dativa).* Byzantine law retained these distinctions in practice to the end of the empire, with the exception of the period of Iconoclastic law (741–867). In fact, Justinian's *Institutes* (circa 533) preserved the clearest description of the three types of guardianship to survive from Classical, Postclassical, or Byzantine times.[10]

Although in the *Institutes* Justinian described all three forms of Roman guardianship in the traditional way, eleven years later he introduced a major change in the *tutela legitima.* His Novel 118 clearly broke with the old Roman rule that only agnatic relatives (those related through the father's family) could serve as guardians. From now on, all relatives, both through the father's line and the mother's line (cognates), bore the obligation to act as guardians. Justinian's Novel 118 represented a true Byzantine innovation on Roman guardianship laws, but, just as with other early Byzantine changes of *tutela* rules, this too had precedents in the pre-Christian period. As early as the first century A.D., the emperor Claudius had tried to supplant agnatic ties with a system based on blood relationships including cognate relatives, but his legislation did not remain in force, and by Constantine's reign the traditional *tutela legitima* was fully restored.[11] Justinian's liberal predecessor, the emperor Anastasios (491–518), had begun to alter the agnatic system, but Justinian's Novel 118 clearly realigned the *tutela legitima* on

9. Chomatianos, no. 83 (pp. 365–68).
10. *Inst,* 1.14–20.
11. Käser, *Das römische Privatrecht,* 2: 225, and note 9. A law of Leo I *(JCod,* 5.30.3), issued in 472, claimed that Constantine was the emperor who abrogated the rules of Claudius and reestablished the traditional agnatic system.

the basis of blood relationship.[12] "We decree that each person enters upon the liturgy [civic duty] of guardianship according to degree and rank . . . with no distinction between the rights of agnates and cognates."[13]

In the eighth century, the Iconoclastic emperor Leo III (717–741) totally revised Byzantine legal institutions when he issued his *Ecloga,* an innovative summary of Roman law that introduced changes in many aspects of the empire's laws and customs.[14] In its section on guardianship, the *Ecloga* broke with the previous system of three types of *tutela* and recognized only guardians appointed by testament. If parents died without drafting a will or failed to nominate a tutor in their testaments, the Orphanotropheion of Constantinople was to assume the care of their children, or if not the great Orphanage, then one of the monasteries *(euageis oikoi)* or well-known churches in the city (see Chapter Three). In the provinces, the local episcopal authorities or other monasteries or churches were to assume the guardianship of such children. Leo justified this change by citing how many lay guardians, assigned this task by the old Roman law system, had in fact despoiled the children under their supervision. He believed that the pious administrators of philanthropic houses, such as the Orphanotropheion, or the devout officers of monasteries and provincial bishoprics, would manage the affairs of orphans entrusted to them with greater justice.[15]

It is unlikely, however, that Leo III's program was ever widely practiced. In the reign of Constantine V (741–775), when the *Ecloga* was still in full force, Sergios and Euphemia, the maternal grandparents of Saint Theodore of Stoudios, died suddenly on the very same day as the result of a vicious pestilence that had gripped Constantinople. They left one son named Plato and two daughters, one of whom later became Theodore's mother. After his parents' sudden death, Plato was cared for by some of his blood relatives. Eventually one of his uncles assumed sole responsibility for the boy and apparently became his guardian. From Theodore of Stoudios's brief account of his uncle Pla-

---

12. *JCod,* 5.30.4 (anno 498).   13. *JNov,* 118.5.
14. Vasiliev, *History,* 1: 240-44.   15. *Ecloga,* 7 (p. 198).

to's *orphania,* it appears that the parents had not had time to draft a will before their untimely deaths. Without a guardian assigned by testament, Plato should have been taken in by the Orphanotropheion or by some other philanthropic institution in Constantinople, but this did not occur. Instead, Plato's relatives accepted responsibility for him as one would expect according to the Roman rules of *tutela legitima.* In this case there is no evidence of recourse to the *Ecloga's* system of institutional care.[16]

The ninth-century *Ecloga privata aucta,* an expanded version of Emperor Leo's manual, provides evidence that the *Ecloga* system of guardianship was soon altered.[17] According to this second version of the *Ecloga,* orphans whose parents had died without designating a *tutor testamentarius* were not entrusted to the care of the Orphanotropheion of Constantinople. Rather the director of that institution, assisted by an official called the *scriba,* assigned guardians for the orphaned children of the capital, while in the provinces the local bishop or the *defensor* of the town (a Late Roman municipal official) assumed this responsibility.[18] In other words, this later version of Iconoclastic law reestablished the *tutela Atiliana,* but now on a much wider scale and administered by the *orphanotrophos* and the provincial bishops.

When the emperor Basil I seized the throne in 867, he initiated a policy to restore the Byzantine law to its original Roman foundations. As a result, his first legal publication, the *Prochiron,* reestablished the old Roman system of three types of guardianship.[19] The tenth-century *Synopsis Basilicorum* presented an even clearer outline of the Classical Roman system.[20] The eleventh-century private treatise by the lawyer Michael Attaleiates, on the other hand, acknowledged only two forms of guardianship: the *tutela testamentaria* and the *tutela legitima.* At-

16. *Sancti Theodori Studitae oratio XI: Laudatio S. Platonis Hegumeni* (PG, 99: 804–8). The Roman law did make special provisions to simplify the making of wills in time of plague (see Käser, *Roman Private Law,* p. 347), but the fact that several relatives assumed responsibility for Plato indicates that no specific person had been appointed by testament.

17. Pieler, "Rechtsliteratur," pp. 458–59.

18. *Ecloga privata aucta,* 8.2 (*JGR,* 6: 28–29).

19. *Prochiron,* 36.6–7 (*JGR,* 2: 204) restored the *tutela Atiliana,* but it did not use that term, and *Prochiron* 36.9 (*JGR,* 2: 204) restored the *tutela legitima.* The *Prochiron* did not mention the *tutela testimentaria,* but iconoclastic law had never abrogated that form of guardianship.

20. *SynBas,* E.38.1a (*JGR,* 5: 295–96).

taleiates defined *tutela legitima,* however, not as the right and duty of relatives to assume the guardianship, but as the power of magistrates to appoint *tutores.*[21] Apparently, by the eleventh century, the importance of the magisterial confirmation of guardians summoned because of their blood relationship had become the key factor in creating the power of *tutela,* and therefore jurists conflated the *tutela legitima* with the old *tutela Atiliana.* Both of the fourteenth-century legal summaries, the *Prochiron auctum* and the *Hexabiblos,* repeated Attaleiates' definition.[22]

How much evidence survives to demonstrate that these three forms of *tutela* were actually employed by the subjects of the empire? Several sources prove that Byzantines of every epoch of the empire's long history used wills to appoint guardians. One of the longest extant papyrus documents preserves the testament of a chief physician *(archiatros)* named Flavius Phoibammon from the Egyptian city of Antinoopolis.[23] Drafting this will in 570, Phoibammon established his legitimate sons as his heirs. Since these boys were still underage— Phoibammon described his younger sons as infants—he appointed as their guardian the superior of the monastery of Jeremiah. This monk was to protect the children according to the laws and to recall that God, the father of orphans, would demand a careful reckoning of the superior's conduct as tutor and curator of these children before his awesome seat of judgment.[24]

Another case from late-eleventh-century Constantinople proves that well-educated Byzantine subjects usually prepared testaments and that they used these as instruments to create guardians. According to a novel issued by the emperor Alexios I (1081–1118), the *sebastos* Constantine, the brother of the patriarch Michael Keroularios (1043–1058), had managed almost all things well during his life. He had, however, made one serious error: he had failed to draft a properly phrased testament before he died. Instead, he had written up some short notes that instructed Constantine's eldest son, Michael, to manage the family prop-

21. Attaleiates, *Ponema,* 25.3 (*JGR,* 7: 446).
22. *Prochiron auctum,* 36.14–15 (*JGR,* 7: 257–58); *Hexabiblos,* 5.12.2–3 (p. 709).
23. Maspero, no. 67151 (2: 88–100).
24. Ibid., p. 98.

erty for his younger brothers. Since Constantine had neglected to employ the proper form in establishing the elder brother as tutor of the younger children, Michael was plagued by fears that his younger siblings might sue him later. He therefore sought approval for his role as guardian from the emperor Nikephoros III (1078–1081) and later from Alexios I.[25]

A decision of Archbishop Demetrios Chomatianos demonstrated the use of testaments to create guardians in the thirteenth century. A man named Apergios Barouses had lost his father at the tender age of two. Fortunately, his father had established by testament the husband of Apergios's older sister as the young child's guardian.[26]

While it is possible to find specific references to the *tutela testamentaria,* it is far more difficult to distinguish clear examples where the rules of the *tutela legitima* were put into practice. The seventy-seven cases introduced in Chapter One, however, clearly indicate that Byzantine magistrates continued to enforce the family obligation. In fifteen of these cases, the sources either indicate that the orphans never received guardians or fail to mention the family relationship of the tutor. In eighteen cases, the orphans were raised in group homes, administered by monasteries, bishops, or private philanthropists. The forty-four remaining cases describe individual guardians; of these, seventeen (slightly more than a third) were uncles, seven were older brothers, six were grandparents, and the others were either sisters, relatives by marriage, or foster parents from outside the family. Granted shorter life expectancies for grandparents, these figures concur with the results one would expect from applying the rules of the *tutela legitima*. It is also possible, however, that in some of these cases the dying parent(s) had appointed these relatives by testament.[27]

One specific case, the *orphania* of Saint George Chozebites, does present a clear example of the *tutela legitima*. George was born on

25. Novel 19 (Alexios I), *JGR*, 1: 292–96.

26. Chomatianos, no. 82 (pp. 363–65). In this case the term διαθήκη is not used, but it is clear from the court record that the guardian (the brother-in-law) was made guardian by will of the father and that the father left detailed instructions regarding the property of his son. Only a written testament could have contained such instructions.

27. These figures were assembled in the course of preparing the present study. See Chapter One.

Cyprus in the late sixth century. According to his biographer, his older brother Herakleides left home to live as a hermit along the River Jordan. Sometime later, both George's parents died. One of George's uncles subsequently accepted the supervision of the boy and his property. When this uncle tried to force George into marriage, the young saint fled to another uncle, the brother of George's guardian. This second uncle also served as the superior of a monastery on Cyprus and supported George's desire to remain celibate. The first uncle eventually traced George to the monastery and then began to argue with his brother over who should have charge of the boy. While the two uncles were wrestling with this issue, George escaped again. This time he fled to his brother in Palestine. George was still too young to join the monastery, but his brother gave him over to the monk in charge of a school for children attached to his ascetic community.[28]

Had George's parents specified in a testament which uncle was to assume the *tutela*, it is unlikely that a quarrel between the two brothers over control of George would have been possible. The *tutela legitima*, however, granted equal guardianship rights to all family members of the same degree, and George's two uncles were both related to him in the third degree. By fleeing to his brother, however, George blocked the claims of both his uncles because as a brother Herakleides was related to George in the second degree.[29]

It is also difficult to find specific cases of the *tutela Atiliana* with regard to *tutores*, but two extant sources describe the magisterial appointment of *curatores*. At the end of the fourth century, Olympias, who later became a supporter of John Chrysostom, lost her parents before she reached adulthood. She then married the urban prefect Nebridius, who died one year later and left Olympias a widow. The emperor Theodosius, her relative, assumed her curatorship and subsequently delegated this power to the new urban prefect Clementinus. He in turn tried to force Olympias to marry, most likely in an attempt to find her a new curator.[30]

28. *Vita Georgii Chozebitae*, pp. 97–100.

29. Käser, *Das römische Privatrecht*, I: 356; regarding degrees of relationship, see Käser, *Roman Private Law*, p. 76.

30. *Vita Olympiadis*, pp. 409–13.

Perhaps a better example of the magisterial appointment is the case involving Philippa Asen, which comes from the mid-fourteenth century. Since she was still under twenty-five, she sought the appointment of a curator from Constantine Harmenopoulos, who at that time (1349) was serving as an agent of the public treasury in Thessalonike.[31]

There also exists evidence that some orphans who, for whatever reason, were unable to find friends or relatives to serve as their guardians were not always given them by the local magistrates. According to one of the stories in the *Pratum Spirituale,* the pagan parents of an Alexandrian girl died in the mid-sixth century leaving their only daughter a great fortune, but establishing no guardian to protect her. One day the orphan girl met a man preparing to commit suicide because of his many debts. To help him in his need, she gave him all her property and ended up penniless. She eventually turned to prostitution to support herself, but before she died she conceived a desire to become a Christian.[32] When her Christian neighbors refused to sponsor her baptism, the Lord sent angels to assist her at her Christian initiation. While this story is probably apocryphal, to make its point, the background information regarding the girl's *orphania* and her lack of guardians had to be believable. By the mid-sixth century, apparently some children of wealthy families could end up without guardians. Is it significant that this girl was a pagan and that by the sixth century bishops often appointed *tutores Atiliani?*

Which magistrates would have appointed guardians during the Byzantine period and would have supervised the conduct of all types of *tutores* in administering their wards' affairs? In second- and third-century Rome, the *praetor tutelarius* had designated guardians for children with no testamentary or legitimate guardian and adjudicated disputes arising from any type of *tutela.* In the provinces the Roman governors had performed these services.[33] As we saw in Chapter Three, the Christian emperors Theodosius I and Valentinian II transferred this responsibility in the capital cities of Rome and Constantinople to the urban prefect, but in the provinces they reconfirmed the governors' role in

31. *Actes de Xèropotamou,* no. 26 (pp. 193–96).
32. John Moschos, *Pratum Spirituale,* 207 (PG, 87.3: 3097–3100).
33. Käser, *Das römische Privatrecht,* 1: 357.

guardianship cases.[34] The *orphanotrophos* assumed the urban prefect's power to appoint guardians in Constantinople sometime after Leo III issued the *Ecloga* (721). An official called the *scriba* assisted the orphanage director in this capacity.[35] By the reign of Basil I (867–886), however, the urban prefect was again supervising all cases involving orphans in the capital.[36]

In the sixth century, the emperor Justinian introduced a major innovation in magisterial appointments of some guardians in the provinces. In those cases where the orphan children inherited estates valued at less than 500 *solidi*, the *defensor* of the local city together with the bishop or other municipal officials was to establish guardians. If the bishop took part, the records of appointment, which included an inventory of the property, were to be filed in the church archives. At Constantinople, Justinian entrusted these smaller cases to the *praetor tutelarius*, whose role in guardianship cases had previously been eclipsed by the expanding power of the urban prefect.[37]

Justinian's legislation reestablishing the jurisdiction of the *praetor tutelarius* had no long-range effect; in fact, subsequent records ceased to mention this official. On the other hand, the new role Justinian assigned to provincial bishops in guardianship cases expanded greatly in later centuries. Leo III's major revision of Roman law made local bishops the actual guardians of all orphans without *tutores testamentarii*.[38] Later changes in the regulations of the *Ecloga* established these bishops as the principal magistrates in designating guardians.[39] Basil I's return to Justinianic law did not restrict the jurisdiction of bishops over guardianship cases. The extant record of decisions rendered by Archbishop Demetrios Chomatianos in the thirteenth century includes thirteen cases involving guardianship issues.[40] In one case that Chomatianos reviewed on appeal, he instructed the bishop who had first heard the charges to designate a tutor for an infant boy whose father had apparently murdered the baby's mother.[41] Chomatianos's instruc-

---

34. *CodTheo*, 3.17.3 (anno 384?).
35. *Ecloga privata aucta*, 8.2 (JGR, 6: 28–29).
36. *Epanagoge*, 4 (JGR, 2: 243–44).   37. *JCod*, 1.4.30 (anno 531).
38. *Ecloga*, 7 (p. 198).   39. *Ecloga privata aucta*, 8.2 (JGR, 6: 28–29).
40. Chomatianos, nos. 24, 32, 42, 59, 63, 81, 82, 83, 84, 85, 90, 91, and 95.
41. Chomatianos, no. 27 (pp. 119–24).

tions in this case also offer strong evidence that Byzantine magistrates continued to use the *tutela Atiliana,* at least in exceptional situations such as this.

While the bishops assumed almost total responsibility for orphan cases in the provinces, at Constantinople the urban prefect retained his authority over guardians until the emperor Leo VI (886–912) gave the quaestor supervision over wills.[42] As a result of this legislation, the quaestor soon assumed control over most guardian and orphan issues. In the eleventh century, the renowned jurist Eustathios Rhomaios described the quaestor as both appointing guardians and supervising the sale of orphans' property to pay inherited debts.[43] By the Palaeologan era, however, the growth of episcopal jurisdiction in the provinces came to affect the administration of justice in the capital as well. The patriarch of Constantinople emerged as one of the principal magistrates in adjudicating guardianship cases and appointing tutors.[44]

Although these magistrates continued to supervise guardianship cases and to confirm relatives as *tutores legitimi,* it is unlikely that they appointed many *tutores Atiliani.* One must recall that there are few examples of such appointments in the Byzantine period. In fact, the term *tutela Atiliana* vanished from legal manuals after the sixth century, and, as we saw above, by the eleventh century jurisconsults were applying the concept of magisterial appointment to describe the confirmation process of a *tutor legitimus.*[45] Moreover, when Anna Komnena described her father Alexios's program to assist orphans among the refugees from Asia Minor, she mentioned his finding relatives to serve as guardians as his first approach to the problem (this is additional strong evidence that the *tutela legitima* of Roman law continued to function). She did not, however, refer to his appointing guardians for children without relatives or confiding this task to the quaestor, the urban prefect, or other competent magistrate (the *tutela Atiliana*). Instead, according to Anna's account, Alexios entrusted these orphans to monastic orphanages or to the Orphanotropheion.[46]

By the twelfth century, then, the *tutela Atiliana* had become rare. In

42. Leo VI, *Novel,* no. 44 (pp. 177–79).   43. *Peira,* 16.20; 17.11 (*JGR,* 4: 60 and 63).
44. MM, 2: 406.   45. Attaleiates, *Ponema,* 25.3 (*JGR,* 7: 446).
46. Anna Komnena, *Alexiad,* 15.7.3 (3: 214).

most cases where parents had died without establishing guardians by testament and where magistrates could not locate suitable relatives, the state normally handed the children over to the orphanages maintained by the Christian Church. As we saw above, however, Chomatianos instructed a bishop to find a guardian in the thirteenth century, a case that demonstrates that the *tutela Atiliana* had not disappeared completely.

Just as Byzantine law preserved the Classical Roman definition of guardianship and most of its system of *tutela* classifications, so too it accepted the age limits assigned by the Classical jurists to the two stages of guardianship, *tutela* and *cura*. Justinian's *Institutes* clearly restated the Roman ages for the sixth-century Byzantine Empire. Tutors supervised boys until they reached the age of fourteen, girls until they reached the age of twelve. Thereafter, curators oversaw youths of both sexes until their wards turned twenty-five.[47]

As in other aspects of the legal system, Leo III's *Ecloga* radically altered the Roman regulations regarding age. Leo's law code eliminated the distinction between tutor and curator; it also set the end of guardianship at twenty for both sexes or at whatever age the ward entered marriage.[48] Later revisions of the *Ecloga* repeated the twenty-year rule, but then added a second paragraph that set the end of *tutela* at fifteen for boys and thirteen for girls (a year more for both boys and girls than the Classical Roman system had required), but restored the traditional age of twenty-five as the end of *cura*.[49] Apparently, the innovations of the *Ecloga* and the disorganized attempts to return to pure Roman law had created some confusion among jurists, or the manuscript copyists, about the age limits governing guardianship.

When Basil I issued his *Prochiron* as part of his effort to restore Justinianic law, the title on guardianship did not include a section on ages. The tenth-century *Synopsis Basilicorum* also did not include a definition of age limits, but a law of Romanos I (920–944) confirmed the age of twenty-five as ending any legal restriction on a young adult, and the eleventh-century jurist Eustathios Rhomaios defined the two

---

47. *Inst*, 1.22–23.
48. *Ecloga*, 7 (p. 198).
49. *Ecloga privata aucta*, cf. 8.1 and 8.2 (*JGR*, 6: 28–29).

stages of *tutela* and *cura* in the same terms as Justinian had used in the *Institutes*.[50]

A curious clause found in the Typikon of the Monastery of Kosmosoteira, on the other hand, raises some doubts about whether testators could alter these time limits. When Isaak Komnenos, brother of the emperor John II (1118–1143), composed his will circa 1152, he donated many of his estates to build and sustain a monastery near the Thracian town of Ainos. After carefully presenting in this testament the rule the monks of the community were to observe, Isaak entrusted his ward, a boy named Konstitzes, to the care of the monastic community. The monks were to hand over to Konstitzes the money and clothes Isaak had set aside for him when the boy reached eighteen. They were to give him control of his land when he reached age twenty-four or entered into marriage.[51] These age limits do not reflect exactly the Roman-Byzantine rules. Could any testator set his own time limits, or only a powerful member of the ruling Comnenian family who had received from the emperor special powers over the many lands assigned to him? Or is twenty-four simply another scribal error for completing the traditional age of twenty-five?

As part of his duty to protect his ward, the Roman guardian also had to preserve the orphan's property. In fact, the Archaic Roman law considered the supervision of the property to be more important than the care of the ward's person. Although jurists of the Classical age emphasized the guardian's obligation to secure the orphan's personal welfare, still they too demanded careful management of the property. In an effort to guarantee responsible stewardship by guardians, the Classical jurists introduced an inventory; before a guardian assumed control of an orphan's property he was to draw up an accurate list of all the

50. *Novelles des empereurs Macédoniens*, 2.5 (p. 64); *Peira*, 17.14 (*JGR*, 4: 64). According to Byzantine law it was also possible for minors to be given the full rights of adulthood before they reached age twenty-five. Constantine (*JCod*, 2.44.2) stated that the emperor could grant full adult rights to males who had reached twenty and females who had reached eighteen if, after careful investigation, he found these young people to be especially competent. The emperor Leo VI (Leo VI, *Novel*, no. 28, pp. 111–15) allowed any magistrate (that would have included bishops by the late ninth century) to waive the normal age limit of twenty-five and grant full adult rights *(venia aetatis)* at an earlier age (twenty for men, eighteen for women).

51. *Typikon Kosmosoteira*, cap. 117 (p. 74).

child's movable and immovable property. Ulpian maintained that, without extenuating circumstances, failure to prepare such an inventory implied deceit on the part of the guardian.[52]

Byzantine emperors made this inventory a requirement of law. In 396 Arcadius, the son of Theodosius I, ordered that guardians of whatever type—*testamentarii, legitimi,* or *Atiliani*—prepare an inventory of all the orphan's property in the presence of the local city's chief citizens, the *defensor,* and other public officials.[53] In 472, the emperor Leo I exempted the *orphanotrophos* of the Zotikos Orphanage from undergoing an audit for his management of the property belonging to orphans in his institution, but not from the obligation to draw up a proper inventory of their property.[54] In 530 Justinian threatened tutors or curators who failed to make an inventory with removal from their offices as guardians and with the punishment of infamy, a legal mark on their reputations that would bar them from any municipal, provincial, or imperial office.[55]

Despite these stringent requirements that guardians carefully inventory property, not all Byzantine tutors or curators did so. It is difficult to imagine that, when George Chozebites fled his first guardian uncle to seek protection from his other uncle, his new guardian had time to prepare an inventory of the property.[56] Moreover, a papyrus of Aphrodito, dated 567, preserved a lengthy record of a complex guardianship case in which the guardian seemed to have kept no records.

According to the papyrus, first the mother and then, some years later, the father had died. They had designated their oldest son, Psates, guardian for his two sisters and two younger brothers. Psates stated that he had discharged many of his father's debts, repaired the family houses, paid for his youngest brother's wet nurse, and provided dowries for his sisters. Phoibammon, the husband of one of Psates' sisters, however, claimed that he himself had never received his wife's dowry from Psates and therefore was representing his wife in this suit against her brother and former guardian. The lengthy court record—

52. *Dig,* 26.7.7.
54. *JCod,* 1.3.31 (32).
56. *Vita Georgii Chozebitae,* pp. 97–100.

53. *CodTheo,* 3.30.6.
55. *JCod,* 5.51.13.

one of the longest papyrus documents to survive from the Byzantine era—reveals that Psates had made no inventory of family property, had kept no record of the repairs he had made to the houses, and had saved no receipts of the debts he had paid. He did keep a list of household items he was to give to his sister's husband as part of the marriage gift, but in the course of the case Psates acknowledged that he had not, in fact, handed over the items he had enumerated. The magistrate, whose rank is not mentioned (according to sixth-century law, it should have been the *defensor* of Aphrodito), had to order a detailed investigation to establish the disbursements that Psates had actually made from the property of his wards. The magistrate, however, did not punish the careless guardian with infamy as Justinian's law of 530 required. In fact, Psates' failure to present an inventory or other accurate records does not seem to have affected the magistrate's final determination.[57]

As an additional measure to protect the property of orphans from either the carelessness or the malevolence of guardians, Constantine legislated in 326 that any sale of orphan property for any reason had to be approved by a magistrate who was to issue a *decretum* authorizing the sale.[58] Justinian added that, even when the guardian accepted payment of debts to his ward, he ought to have this confirmed by a magisterial *decretum*.[59] Later Byzantine legal handbooks repeated these laws.[60] The fourteenth-century *Hexabiblos* included two chapters stressing the need for the magistrate to approve any alienation of orphans' property.[61]

The thirteenth-century records of Archbishop Demetrios Chomatianos's judicial decisions prove that well-educated bishops in the late period of the empire continued to enforce Constantine's law of 326. According to Chomatianos's records, a Jewish boy named Manuel had first lost his father and then his mother. Before her death, however, Manuel's mother married a second husband named Moses. She designated him as guardian. After Manuel's mother died, his stepfather took no thought of the boy and sold all of the orphan's property. Now a

---

57. *PLond*, no. 1708.   58. *CodTheo*, 3.30.3.

59. *JCod*, 5.37.25; *Inst*, 2.8.2.

60. Cf. *Ecloga ad Prochiron mutata*, 9.2 (*JGR*, 6: 249–50); *SynBas*, E.38.59–60 (*JGR*, 5: 303–4).

61. *Hexabiblos*, 5.12.45 (p. 718).

teenager, Manuel fled his stepfather's house and wandered aimlessly for several years. Manuel eventually learned the art of cooking, and after gaining some financial security and a renewed sense of self-confidence, he returned to reclaim his patrimony. He brought his case against Moses before the bishop of Kastoria, who found for Manuel. Apparently, Moses appealed this verdict to the archbishop of Ohrid, Chomatianos. The archbishop confirmed the lower court's decision and rejected Moses' argument that Manuel had waited too long to claim his father's estates. Chomatianos justified his decision against Moses and Manuel's mother by stressing that both of them had sold sections of Manuel's patrimony without a *decretum* from a magistrate.[62]

Were there cases in which guardians were able to alienate property without obtaining a magisterial *decretum?* The *Vita Sancti Abramii,* composed originally in fifth-century Syria, provides an interesting example of a guardian's alienating property, in this case by gift, apparently without a *decretum.* Abramios lived as a recluse in a village not far from Edessa. When Abramios's brother died, he left a daughter, Maria, only seven years old. Those who knew her brought the little girl to Abramios, who accepted responsibility for her. (Abramios's brother had apparently left no will; therefore, this is another example of Byzantine *tutela legitima.*) Abramios built a separate cell for little Maria, and through a window in the wall separating their two living quarters he instructed his niece in the ascetic way of life. Maria had inherited much property from her parents, but, in order to free her from worldly cares, Abramios ordered his ward to give all her wealth to the poor.[63] There is no reference here to Abramios obtaining the written permission of a magistrate for these gifts. Although most Byzantine judges would have regarded such philanthropic gifts sympathetically,

---

62. Chomatianos, no. 85 (pp. 377–82).

63. *Vita Abramii,* pp. 932–37, is the Greek version of the *vita,* but it does not include any reference to where Abramios lived. The commentary by Kislinger, "Taverne," p. 84, implies that Abramios had lived in western Asia Minor during the sixth century. Brock and Harvey, *Holy Women,* pp. 27–29, however, have shown that the Abramios legend originated in Syria in the fifth century. Wherever Abramios came from, the *Vita Abramii* clearly shows that monks who read this story did not expect that an orphan's guardian would obtain a magisterial *decretum* before alienating his ward's property for charitable purposes.

some might have found Abramios's order in conflict with the spirit of Constantine's legislation to preserve the property of orphans until they reached age twenty-five and were fully competent to make such decisions on their own.

Through the Byzantine centuries magistrates gradually expanded their supervision of tutors and guardians. From the time of the emperor Septimius Severus (193–211), judges joined with family members in selecting suitable husbands for orphan girls. In the fifth century, the emperors Honorius and Theodosius II ordained that the appropriate magistrate should take the leading role in making such decisions. In the eleventh century, the competent magistrates—bishops in the provinces and presumably the quaestor in Constantinople—were still participating in the process of finding suitable husbands for girls without living parents.[64] Together with the relatives, a civil judge or bishop was to examine the prospective husband's property and mode of life before sanctioning the girl's marriage. In ancient Greece or Rome only family members would normally have participated in making such decisions.

CHANGE

So far this chapter has discussed aspects of Byzantine guardianship that the Christian Empire accepted without change from Classical Roman law or altered without a major break with ancient tradition. Only Leo III, through his *Ecloga*, tried to transform the very nature of Romano-Byzantine guardianship by shifting the responsibility for orphan care from the extended family to philanthropic institutions. His reforms were short-lived, however, and later editions of the *Ecloga* reintroduced the traditional Roman approach, a process brought to completion under Basil I. Having demonstrated the continuity between Classical Roman rules of guardianship and the Byzantine system, this study will now present specific aspects of Byzantine law that broke with the Roman tradition. The most striking of these trends was the opening of guardianship to women.

The first step in this process we discussed in Chapter Three. Proba-

64. Krause, *Rechtliche und soziale Stellung*, pp. 168 ff.; *Peira*, 25.50 (*JGR*, 4: 104).

bly in response to difficulties in finding male guardians, the emperors Theodosius I and Valentinian II allowed the surviving mother to assume the *tutela* of her children, if it were not possible to find any other male relative willing to accept the office.[65] This law of 390 broke a strong tradition of Roman law, restated as recently as the late third century, that women were too weak to serve as guardians, doubtless a statement reflecting the Archaic Greek and Roman concept that the guardian might have to defend his ward in battle.[66]

In a series of novels issued during the first twenty years of his reign (527–547), the emperor Justinian introduced a number of major innovations in the law of guardianship. Although two of these novels did not directly deal with women's capacity to serve as guardians, the combined effect of this legislation was to remove all legal barriers to the appointment of female *tutores* and curators. Moreover, Justinian's laws finally broke with the ancient Roman tradition of recognizing family relations only through agnatic relationships.

Beginning in 530, Justinian expanded the law of Theodosius I and Valentinian II concerning female guardians to include mothers of illegitimate children. If the natural fathers failed to appoint guardians for such boys and girls, then their mothers could become their guardians, especially since the paternal relatives of these children might be unwilling to accept any burden on their behalf.[67]

In 538 Justinian issued another edict to protect all orphans from the machinations of unscrupulous guardians, a law that indirectly expanded women's guardianship rights. The emperor observed that some guardians used their offices to take money from wards under the pretext that the children's estates owed them money. Other guardians who owed their wards money employed the powers of guardianship to remove any record of their debts without actually repaying the cash. To prevent such abuses, Justinian ordered that no person, whether appointed by testament or by the regulations of the *tutela legitima*, was to serve as tutor or curator for any child to whom that potential guardian owed money or from whom he claimed money. In

65. *CodTheo*, 3.17.4.
67. *JCod*, 5.35.3.

66. *JCod*, 5.35.1; 2.12.18.

other words, the guardian of an orphan could no longer be a debtor or a creditor of the child he was to protect.[68]

In banning creditors and debtors from serving as guardians, Justinian affected a substantial innovation in Roman law. A number of later Byzantine legal summaries repeated Justinian's ban, but no sources survive that demonstrate conclusively that magistrates enforced this edict in specific cases.

A year after issuing this law, Justinian published a second constitution that exempted mothers from the ban on debtors and creditors. If a mother owed money to her children or claimed any money from their estate—claims that would have arisen usually through the complicated rules governing dowries and the husband's counterpayment, the marriage gift—she could still serve as a tutor or a curator, because, as Justinian phrased it, "mothers could in no way be compared with others."[69]

When Justinian initially banned creditors and debtors from serving as guardians, he inadvertently made it more difficult for orphans to find competent tutors or curators because relatives frequently loaned money to or borrowed money from one another. The emperor quickly saw the unintended harmful effects of his law and moved to remedy the problem by exempting mothers from the requirements of the new law. Justinian and his advisors seem to have perceived the negative effects of overregulating guardianship relatively quickly. Two centuries earlier, on the other hand, Constantine and his jurists appear never to have comprehended the problems that arose after they had enacted their stringent innovations to improve the conduct of tutors and curators (see Chapter Three).

Justinian issued his most sweeping reform of the Roman guardianship system in 543. In that year, he published Novel 118 that broke definitively with the old agnatic system of reckoning the *tutela legitima* and replaced it with one based on degrees of relationship calculated through both the male line and the female line. As part of this new law, Justinian also established that in cases where a father died without es-

68. *JNov*, 72.
69. *JNov*, 94.

tablishing a guardian by testament, the mother had the first claim to serve as tutor or curator. If there was no surviving mother, then one of the grandmothers ought to assume this responsibility. As a result of this novel, the Byzantine rules of *tutela legitima* offered the guardianship to women in preference to any male relative. Only when the father expressly designated a male relative or friend in his testament were men now preferred to mothers or grandmothers.[70]

Leo III's *Ecloga* strengthened the claim of the mother even further. The *Ecloga*'s title on guardianship stated that, when both mother and father died, their instructions, either written in a formal testament or given orally, were to be respected in finding a guardian. The *Ecloga*'s words implied that, when only one parent died, whether the father or the mother, the survivor naturally assumed control of the orphan's person and of the property. Leo's law did not even consider a mother as a guardian; rather she continued in her role as head of the household, a role she had shared jointly with her husband while he was alive, but which she exercised alone now that he had passed from this life. Only when both parents were dead did true guardianship arise.[71]

When one considers that women, if they survive their childbearing years, usually live longer than men and that until recently women normally married men considerably older than themselves, one would expect that, after Justinian's legislation, mothers became the normal guardians of their children. Unless a father specifically barred his wife from guardianship and named another person as the legal protector of his children, the mother naturally assumed the task. It is impossible to prove that women outnumbered men as guardians after 543 because no detailed census survives from the Byzantine era, but the extant tax records, described in Chapter One, surviving from the thirteenth and fourteenth centuries support this conclusion.

When, in 1235, Byzantine tax officials surveyed a section of property belonging to the monastery of Lembos in western Asia Minor, they listed heads of households together with the other family members. Of the twenty-one households listed, widows headed five families

---

70. *JNov,* 118.5
71. *Ecloga,* 7 (p. 198).

with children (23.8 percent of the households). Only one family seemed to have had a nephew living with his uncle, probably a case of guardianship.[72] In a similar tax survey of the Macedonian village Hieryssos, carried out in 1301, widows headed ten of the thirty-six households with children (27.7 percent), compared with five households where younger siblings were living with their elder brother (13.3 percent).[73] Only in two surveys of *proasteia* (large estates with tenant peasants), conducted in 1263, were fewer than 10 percent of the households under the care of widows.[74] In all the tax surveys listed in Chapter One, mother guardians far outnumbered the next most common relatives to serve as guardians: uncles and older brothers.[75]

A few specific cases should suffice to demonstrate widowed mothers acting as guardians of their children. The most dramatic example occurred in the reign of the emperor Theophilos (829–843), after a governor's injustice forced the widow of a brave soldier from Asia Minor and his two orphan children into poverty. The widow's warrior husband had fought in many battles, but he had always escaped without serious injury thanks to his wonderful horse. Unfortunately, the soldier's commander, the *strategos* (military governor) of the province, conceived a desire to possess this horse, but the soldier tenaciously clung to his beloved animal. When the emperor Theophilos sought a new mount suitable to the imperial office, the *strategos* saw an opportunity to confiscate the soldier's steed under the pretext of obeying the emperor.

After the *strategos* had sent this horse to Constantinople, the soldier was killed in battle because he no longer had his trusty animal to speed him away to safety. His death plunged his widow and children into poverty. To find assistance for herself and the soldier's orphans, the widow decided to journey to Constantinople.

When she arrived in the capital, she saw the emperor leaving the Blachernai palace upon her husband's noble steed. She ran out from the crowd, seized the reins of the horse, accused the emperor of com-

72. MM, 4: 13–14.
73. Dölger, *Aus den Schatzkammern*, pp. 40–41.
74. MM, 6: 215–16.
75. See Chapter One, pp. 19–20.

plicity in her husband's death, and claimed his mount as her property. The emperor was amazed by her boldness and agreed to hear her case. Subsequently, she explained how the *strategos* had unjustly seized her husband's horse, an act that led to his death and the impoverishment of her family. The emperor summoned the *strategos,* who began his defense by denying everything, but under the scathing gaze of the widow he finally admitted the truth. Renowned for justice, Theophilos restored the horse to the rightful owners, the widow and her orphan children, and removed the *strategos* from office. The historian of Theophilos's reign placed this story in his narrative to demonstrate the emperor's love of justice and accessibility to his subjects, but he also revealed how effective widowed mothers could be in protecting their children's patrimony.[76]

The tenth-century high official Symeon Magistros tried to aid two widows who had sought his assistance in protecting their children and their property. In the first case, a wealthy widow complained to Symeon that soldiers of the Byzantine army were lodged on her estate and were consuming the revenues of these lands that she and her orphan children needed for their sustenance.[77] The second widow asked that Symeon try to rescue her son from army service. Even though her son's inheritance was military land (subject to the obligation to serve in the province's army), the widow sought his release from military duty on the grounds that she could not afford to equip him with adequate arms, nor could she survive on the estate without his help at home.[78]

The sources also provide evidence that grandmothers served as guardians. In the early eleventh century, Maria Kastorissa arranged a marriage for her grandson and even signed the marriage contract in his name. The young man was able to void the agreement later because his grandmother had not obtained his signature on the contract.[79] In the fourteenth century the maternal grandmother of Philippa Asen assumed the *tutela* for the young girl and tried to protect

76. Theophanes Continuatus, 3.7 (pp. 92–94).
77. Symeon Magistros, no. 31 (pp. 120–21).
78. Ibid., no. 50 (pp. 130–31).
79. *Peira*, 17.19 (*JGR*, 4: 67).

her lands from the claims lodged by the Athos monastery of Xèropota-mou.[80]

The 390 law of Theodosius I and Valentinian II permitting mothers to assume the guardianship as well as Justinian's novel of 543 preferring mothers and grandmothers as tutors and curators tried to dissuade these women from marrying a second time. Before they could become guardians, mothers were supposed to renounce any thought of finding a new husband. If they later did marry a second time, the law placed a *hypotheca* over the property of the new husband to guarantee that his wife would continue to protect the interests of the children of her first marriage.[81] The Church Fathers had long been discouraging second marriages. About the time Theodosius I and Valentinian II issued their law of 390, John Chrysostom wrote a short tract on second marriages in which he vividly portrayed the sufferings that the children of the first husband experienced when they were forced to see their mother in the arms of another man and when they saw their half brothers and sisters depriving them of their mother's love and in some cases of their father's property.[82]

The misgivings of church leaders and secular legislators concerning second marriages seem to have been at least partially justified. The emperor Justinian described a specific case that had occurred sometime prior to 533 to illustrate the dangers of second marriages. After promising not to marry again, a woman named Auxentia assumed the guardianship of her daughter, Martha. A few years later, however, Auxentia took a second husband with whom she had two male children. Before her marriage, she had found a new guardian for Martha named Paul, but after the birth of her boys she hatched a plan to deprive her daughter of her patrimony. When Martha reached age twelve, Auxentia told her to dismiss Paul as her tutor and select a new person to serve as curator. Auxentia then insisted that Martha sign an agreement renouncing any claim to audit her new curator's conduct when Martha reached age twenty-five. With time, Martha realized that she was being cheated of her father's property and eventually got the emperor Justin-

---

80. *Actes de Xèropotamou*, no. 26 (pp. 193–96).
81. *CodTheo*, 3.17.4 (anno 390).
82. John Chrysostom, *De non iterando conjugio* (PG, 48: 609–20).

ian to render a verdict against her mother and the false curator. Had Martha not belonged to a high-ranking family and been able to appeal to the emperor, could she have defended her interests so successfully?[83]

In the thirteenth century Demetrius Chomatianos reviewed the case of Manuel, the Jewish boy whose mother married a second time shortly after Manuel's father had died. Manuel's mother and her new husband, Moses, sold the vineyard Manuel's father had given him to provide for the boy's later needs. After the mother's death, Manuel's stepfather seized all the rest of his property and neglected the boy to such an extent that Manuel fled his home, not to return for many years.[84]

There is some evidence that Byzantine custom allowed women greater scope to serve as guardians than the letter of the law dictated. Although Novel 118 preferred mothers and grandmothers as tutors or curators over all male relatives, it specifically banned all other female relatives from becoming guardians of children.[85] The *vita* of Neilos of Rossano, however, offers an example of a boy raised by his older sister.

Neilos was born in the south Italian town of Rossano, still part of the Byzantine Empire in the tenth century. Both his parents died while Neilos was a young boy. His older sister decided to raise him and made every effort to instruct him in piety. She had no husband and was apparently living as a single celibate, which is perhaps why the *vita* describes her as a God-loving person. When Neilos reached his teens, however, the *vita* claimed that he entered the bloom of youth without someone to apply the reins of reason (that is, he had no strong male role model in the phraseology of modern social science). Moreover, no bishop or priest took an interest in his case. As a result, Neilos began to lust after women and quickly married the most beautiful one he was able to find. They had a little girl, but Neilos, haunted now by the fear of death, deserted his family and eventually became a monk.[86]

It is tempting to dismiss Neilos's sister as an exceptional case, but

83. *JNov*, 155 (anno 533).

84. Chomatianos, no. 85 (p. 377); see also no. 41 (pp. 177–84) for another case demonstrating the problems posed by a second marriage.

85. *JNov*, 118.5.

86. *Vita Nili*, p. 263.

the fourteenth-century tax records from the Athonite monasteries reveal that in Macedonian villages younger brothers or sisters often lived
with older sisters, most likely after the death of their parents. In 1301
three of the forty-nine households of the village of Gomatos included
siblings of the wife as part of the family. One peasant named Basil had
a family consisting of two sons, two daughters, and four of his wife's
siblings.[87] It is possible that in these cases the parents had designated as
guardian not their eldest daughter, but her husband. In the thirteenth
century, Archbishop Demetrios Chomatianos adjudicated just such a
case where the orphan's brother-in-law had served as *tutor testamentarius*.[88] In the fourteenth-century village of Hieryssos, however, widows
without second husbands headed two households that included their
brothers among their dependents. These women were responsible for
their brothers with respect to the tax collection.[89] Were they also functioning as guardians for these brothers as Neilos's sister had cared for
him?

Chomatianos adjudicated a second case that provides additional evidence that older sisters, in this example an older half sister, could serve
as guardians. After two powerful men of Skopje in present-day Macedonia had unlawfully seized his property, George Litoboes brought a
suit before Chomatianos's court. George explained that his father had
married a second time and had two boys by the new wife, George himself and a younger son, Melas. Sometime later both George's father
and mother died, but his father had designated his daughter Helen by
his first wife (that is, George's half sister) to care for George and Melas.
Unfortunately, Helen died before the boys reached adulthood, and this
gave the two powerful men of Skopje the opportunity to seize
George's family property.

Chomatianos restored George's property to him because George
was able to prove with documents the validity of his claim, while his
opponents had no testaments or sales records to prove their rights of
ownership. Nowhere in deciding the case did Chomatianos mention
that older sisters could not serve as guardians. On the other hand, the

87. Dölger, *Aus den Schatzkammern*, pp. 37–39.
88. Chomatianos, no. 82 (pp. 363–64).
89. Dölger, *Aus den Schatzkammern*, pp. 40–41.

archbishop also did not confirm such an appointment as legally correct. Since the issue in this case never involved the validity of a legal action performed by Helen, it does not confirm that Byzantine courts accepted sisters or half sisters as tutors or curators, but it does provide additional evidence that sisters served as informal protectors of their orphan siblings.[90]

When Byzantine legislators made major changes in the Roman system of guardianship, they were usually striving to provide greater advantages for orphans. Several laws issued by the emperor Alexios I (1081–1118), however, were designed to limit some of the privileges orphans had gained over the centuries. Alexios's Novel 19 ordered that judges should not restore orphans to their property, if these children, acting with their curators' permission, had sold, purchased, or exchanged property after they had reached their fourteenth year and had taken an oath not to overturn their actions in the future. Alexios insisted that the law should hold a minor over fourteen to his oath, unless the orphan had been deceived or coerced.[91]

In a second novel Alexios ordered that, where orphans had been defrauded of less than 10 percent of their estates, they could initiate actions against their guardians, but they could no longer sue the third party who had actually purchased properties from, or sold properties to, the orphans. From now on, such agreements would stand. Where more than 10 percent of their properties was involved, orphans could pursue either their guardians or the third parties who had benefitted from the juristic acts.[92] There is also evidence that Alexios issued yet a third novel that reduced the time limits within which orphans could reclaim property that they thought had been unjustly taken from them while they had been under the care of guardians. Before Alexios's legislation, orphans could wait in some cases up to thirty years after they had turned fourteen to initiate actions for the return of their property. Alexios's law reduced the period under certain circumstances to just one year after an orphan reached age twenty-five.[93]

---

90. Chomatianos, no. 59 (pp. 261–67).   91. Novel 19 (Alexios I), *JGR*, 1: 292–96.

92. Novel 44 (Alexios I), *JGR*, 1: 361–62.

93. This novel is preserved only in a marginal note to the text of the *Hexabiblos*. See *Hexabiblos*, 1.12.66 (pp. 154–56), and also the comments of Zachariä von Lingenthal, *Geschichte*, p. 126.

One should notice that Alexios, the only Byzantine emperor who dared to restrict the legal rights of orphans, was the same emperor who had restored the Orphanotropheion of Zotikos, an act that not only the emperor's daughter praised, but also the famous twelfth-century ascetic, Cyril Phileotes.[94] In defense of Alexios's policy there is evidence that some wealthy orphans were abusing the legal privileges available to them.

In the early eleventh century, another Komnenos, perhaps a relative of Alexios, had tried to exploit his situation as an orphan to break an engagement contract he had signed to marry the daughter of the *protospatharios* Helias. In fact, this young Komnenos had made two separate contracts and agreed to two penalty payments in case he failed to complete the marriage. As it turned out, he finally decided not to wed Helias's daughter and tried to avoid making the penalty payments by claiming that he had been only eighteen when he had signed the contracts. The judge rejected his argument since minors could make contracts with the approval of their curators, and apparently the young Komnenos's curator had given his consent. The judge did, however, partially accept the youth's argument in that he freed Komnenos from the first contract he had signed and held him only to a single penalty payment, based on the second agreement. It is clear from the record of this case, however, that both the judge, Eustathios Rhomaios, and the reigning emperor himself considered that the young Komnenos was abusing his legal privileges as an orphan.[95]

In view of the above case, it is possible that Alexios Komnenos had begun to perceive unintended effects of earlier Byzantine legislation to protect orphans. His laws to limit the legal privileges of orphans in certain cases might represent an attempt to trim back such unintended effects so as to make guardianship laws just and fair for both wards and tutors.

To build the Christian Empire Byzantine rulers promoted major realignments in the ancient society of the Greco-Roman world they had inherited. The most striking was to shift the empire's capital from the

---

94. Anna Komnena, *Alexiad*, 15.7.4–8 (3: 214–18); *Vie de Cyrille le Philéote*, p. 230.
95. *Peira*, 17.14 (*JGR*, 4: 63–65).

banks of the Tiber to Constantinople in the East where Christianity had deeper roots. As part of this process of realignment, the Byzantine emperors took special interest in orphans, because the Christian God, the Lord of the universe, offered divine assistance to children without parents and required that all who worshiped him succor the orphans in their midst. In response to this ethical demand, however, the Byzantine state chose not to change radically the ancient Roman system of guardianship. The Christian emperors were always willing to innovate in attempting to find more dependable, and if possible, more loving guardians—hence the opening of *tutela* and *cura* to mothers and grandmothers—but with the exception of Leo III's radical rejection of the *tutela legitima*, they remained remarkably close to the Roman law principles of guardianship. Even Chomatianos rendered his decisions in cases involving orphans with few direct appeals to Christian texts. He simply applied the rules of Roman *tutela* and *cura* as modified by Byzantine emperors and found these sufficient to shield the children.

The emperor Justinian was one of the few Byzantine sovereigns to introduce overtly Christian references or practices into the guardianship laws. In his Novel 72, he reminded all guardians that God was watching their behavior as protectors of the orphans in their care.[96] Justinian also required new guardians to swear on the Holy Scriptures that they would manage the property of their wards as though it were their own.[97]

This study has reviewed the history of Byzantine guardianship laws and attempted to illustrate both continuity and innovation in the system. On the other hand, it has avoided addressing perhaps the most important questions about East Roman guardianship. Did the changes in Byzantine law secure better tutors and curators than the ancient Roman system had? Were Byzantine guardians more attentive in caring for the person and the property of their wards than ancient Roman tutors had been? These are questions which, given the nature of Byzantine sources, the historian cannot answer in a satisfying manner. Chapter Nine will return to these questions, however, and try to reach some

---

96. *JNov,* 72.8 (anno 538).
97. *JNov,* 72.8.

conclusions about the success of Byzantine guardianship laws in obtaining good tutors and curators for orphans of all social classes.

In order to supplement the guardianship system the Byzantine state also supported institutional care for orphans. As we saw in Chapter Three, the Byzantine Church had developed philanthropic institutions to assist children who for whatever reason were unable to find guardians. The emperor Leo III considered these Christian orphanages so successful that he preferred them to family guardians except for mothers or, in the cases where both parents had died, tutors designated by testament.[98] The next chapter will explore the role of the Byzantine Church in the care of orphans and will devote special attention to examining the nature of these church orphanages.

98. *Ecloga*, 7 (p. 198).

V THE BYZANTINE CHURCH

Byzantine laws of guardianship developed from the Roman legal system of *tutela* and *cura*. Although Christian concepts of God's special love for orphans probably inspired Constantine to legislate greater protection for such children and surely led Justinian to insist that guardians swear an oath on the Sacred Scriptures to guarantee their proper conduct, the emperors were scrupulously careful to use the terms and concepts of traditional Roman jurisprudence as they altered the institution of guardianship. Christianity, however, did have a more direct impact on the empire's system of orphan care in cases where it was not possible to find a guardian.

Classical Roman law provided only one remedy for children whose parents had failed to appoint a guardian by testament and who had no relatives willing to assume the *tutela legitima*. In such cases Roman magistrates could appoint any competent person to serve as a guardian for the child (the *tutela Atiliana*).[1] But how many children won the attention of Roman magistrates or of their Byzantine successors? In the early third century, Clement of Alexandria harshly criticized the Greco-Roman society of his day for ignoring the needy orphans on the streets of Egypt's capital.[2] We have already seen that in Byzantine times a wealthy pagan girl was left without any guardian in sixth-century Alexandria, and no magistrate, whether the provincial

1. *Inst*, 1.20.
2. Clement, Paedagogus, 3.4.30 (p. 253).

governor or by that time the bishop of the city, intervened to appoint a guardian.[3]

After the sixth century the legal sources cease to mention the *tutela Atiliana*, and later juristic manuals emphasize that the power of magistrates to appoint guardians referred to confirming tutors who were summoned to this duty because of their blood relationship to the orphans, not to designating people from outside the family to assist children without living relatives.[4] By the twelfth century the *tutela Atiliana* seems to have vanished, at least in Constantinople. Anna Komnena's description of orphan care did not refer to any magisterial appointment of guardians. Instead, she stressed that the emperor Alexios entrusted orphans without relatives to monastic orphanages in Constantinople or to the Orphanotropheion—in other words, to various types of Christian philanthropic institutions that functioned as group homes for the children.[5]

Following the dictates of the Old Testament and the advice of James's epistle, the Christian Church began to organize some form of group care for orphans without any family guardians as early as the second century. We examined evidence for that care in Chapter Two. After the conversion of Constantine, however, the Church was forced to expand its orphan-care system to meet the needs of many more children since the population of the fourth century was increasing, especially in urban areas of the eastern Byzantine provinces, and the number of Christian children was expanding even more rapidly because of the many conversions after the emperors publicly acknowledged the new God.[6] This chapter will examine these Christian orphanages in detail to determine how they nurtured and educated the children in their care.

In addition to examining the history of these orphan schools, this chapter will explore other ways the Byzantine Church affected the care of orphans, especially in encouraging laymen to build new orphanages or to provide other kinds of assistance. Finally, this chapter will study

---

3. John Moschos, *Pratum Spirituale*, 207 (PG, 87.3: 3097–3100). See also Chapter Four, note 32.

4. See Chapter Four, p. 84.   5. Anna Komnena, *Alexiad*, 15.7.3 (3: 214).

6. Miller, *Birth*, pp. 68–74, esp. note 8.

the role that individual bishops, priests, or monks assumed in acting as guardians for orphans. In this case the Byzantine state attempted to limit the role of clergy and ascetics in caring for orphans by trying to ban them from serving as tutors or curators for the children of relatives or friends. Ultimately, this attempt failed since many Byzantine subjects preferred to designate priests or monks, even from outside the family circle, to serve as guardians for their children in place of blood relatives who were laymen.

THE BISHOPS

As we saw in Chapter Two, bishops emerged as the key figures in every aspect of Christian life. When Justin described the Roman church in the mid-second century, its bishop supervised all the community's philanthropic activity, including the care of orphans and widows.[7] After Constantine's conversion, bishops tended to involve themselves in many new activities, especially of a political nature. They gradually began to exercise more power in their local *polis* governments. For example, in 328 Bishop Athanasios of Alexandria was able to threaten a dockworkers strike in his city to block the *annona* shipment of wheat to Constantinople.[8] Bishops also began to mix in court politics in efforts to benefit their home cities or increasingly to influence the emperors' decisions regarding doctrinal controversies.

At the Council of Sardica, called by the emperor Constantius II in 343 to resolve the many conflicts that erupted following the Council of Nicaea (325), the elderly bishop Hosius of Cordova expressed his irritation over the new political activities his fellow bishops were engaging in. Hosius believed that bishops should return to their more traditional duties of protecting widows and preventing the unjust from dispossessing orphans.[9]

Despite their far greater responsibilities both in local and in imperial affairs, conscientious bishops of the fourth century continued to support the care of orphans. The famous bishop of Caesarea in Cappadocia, Basil the Great, gained renown for his program to benefit or-

7. Justin, *Apologia (prima)*, 67.   8. Sokrates, 1.35.2–3 (p. 85).
9. *Can. 3 Synodi Sardic.*, in Mansi, 3: 12.

phans.[10] When John Chrysostom became bishop of Constantinople in 398, he drastically reduced the time and money his predecessor had spent on entertaining the powerful of the capital so that he could devote more of his efforts to prayer and to the bishop's social duties, which included the care of orphans.[11]

From the fourth century to the conquest of Constantinople by the Turks, bishops continued to look after homeless children. In the eleventh century, the provincial aristocrat Kekaumenos considered feeding orphans a prime duty of the patriarch of Constantinople.[12] When the saintly Athanasios I became patriarch of the Byzantine capital at the end of the thirteenth century, he developed a policy to help all the poor of the city, but especially the orphans.[13]

A superficial review of East Roman sources leaves no doubt that bishops were expected to take care of children who had lost their parents and had no relatives or friends willing to serve as guardians. But how did Byzantine bishops provide this care? What sort of institutions did they create to house these orphans and provide them nourishment? Finally, what sort of schools did they establish to educate or train these children?

In its early years the Christian Church probably assigned the actual supervising and training of orphans to the inscribed widows described in 1 Timothy 5:4, but by the end of the fourth century such widows no longer seemed to have overseen any kind of organized orphan school or group home. When John Chrysostom wrote a commentary on 1 Timothy 5:4, he emphasized the duty of these enrolled widows to nurture orphans, but his words clearly meant that they were to care for orphans within their own families. In fact, Chrysostom's commentary strongly advocated that these widows assume responsibility to protect their own children or grandchildren.[14] Since at that time (circa 387), Roman law still excluded any woman from assuming legal guardianship,

10. Gregory of Nazianzos, *In laudem Basilii*, 81 (p. 228).

11. Palladios, *Dialogos*, 13 (1: 264).   12. Kekaumenos, *Strategikon*, cap. 122.

13. *Theoctisti vita Sancti Athanasii*, p. 24.

14. *Vidua elegatur* (PG, 51: 323–32). See esp. col. 332 where Chrysostom contrasts the *xenoi* (strangers) the widows are to assist with the children they care for. These children are the widows' own children or grandchildren.

Chrysostom might have been lobbying in this commentary for a change in Roman law to permit widowed mothers and grandmothers to assume the office of *tutela*. One should recall that three years later in 390 Theodosius I and Valentinian II in fact granted mothers the right to become tutors and curators for their own children.[15] Chrysostom, however, did not mention any orphan group home or school under the supervision of these inscribed widows.

Despite Chrysostom's silence, however, at least one early Byzantine source indicated that some widows continued to care for orphans or abandoned children. According to a fifth-century *vita*, a married woman of Constantinople named Matrona so desired to lead a strict ascetic life that she left her husband and decided to entrust the care of her little daughter, Theodotes, to a woman named Susanna. The *vita* described Susanna as belonging to the order of widows since her youth. Had she, in fact, lost her husband when she was young, or does this passage employ the term *widow* to indicate a consecrated virgin? As one of these widows, Susanna had a place to live in the stoa outside the Holy Apostles, the church in which she regularly participated in all-night vigils.[16]

The *Vita Sanctae Matronae* did not indicate whether Matrona asked Susanna to assume custody of her child because Susanna was inscribed in the order of widows or if she asked her because of a spiritual friendship between the two women. It is interesting, nevertheless, that a woman described as belonging to the order of widows accepted a young girl abandoned by her mother. In this context one should recall also that as late as the twelfth century, women described as *graptai* (widows) exercised a supervisory role over the orphan acolytes at the Church of the Pantokrator in Constantinople.[17]

The *Vita Sanctae Matronae* and the later evidence from the Pantokrator Typikon thus suggest the continued existence of widows who had a special calling to work with orphans. Since the *Vita Sanctae Matronae* described Susanna as having embraced virginity early in life and

15. *CodTheo*, 3.17.4.

16. *Vita Matronae*, pp. 790–93. As early as the time of Ignatios of Antioch, virgins were enrolled in the list of widows. See Ignatios of Antioch, *Ad Smyrnaeos*, 13.1.

17. *Typikon Pantokrator*, pp. 75–79.

as participating with other women in the all-night vigils at the Church of the Holy Apostles, it is likely that she belonged to a community of ascetics similar to the loosely organized communities of Marathonian monks founded in Constantinople one hundred years earlier during the episcopacy of Makedonios. The word widow *(chera)* apparently evolved into a term that referred to a particular kind of ascetic. We will return to the subject of monastic care for orphans later.[18]

Although pious widows and nuns often served as caretakers for homeless children, Christian bishops played the principal role in organizing institutional care for orphans. Five sources describe in detail orphan schools, administered by local bishops, schools in widely scattered provinces of the empire: Syria, Cappadocia, and mainland Greece. These five texts date from as early as the fourth century to as late as the thirteenth century. Nevertheless, the schools they mention shared many common characteristics. Indeed, the evidence points to a common pattern of school organization that Byzantine bishops used to provide orphans in their care with food, shelter, discipline, and an education. References to orphan schools run by monasteries reinforce this general pattern, as do the few glimpses the sources provide regarding the Orphanotropheion in Constantinople. Moreover, the orphan school described in the legendary *Vita Sancti Clementis* resembles in many ways these episcopal schools and provides additional evidence that there existed a well-established system for organizing Christian orphanages.

THE SCHOOLS

The first of these five sources, the *Apostolic Constitutions,* probably describes a number of episcopal orphan schools, not just one, since this text was initially designed as a rule book for all the bishops dependent on the see of Antioch. The compilers of the *Apostolic Constitutions* issued these regulations in 380, but in preparing the section on orphans they copied many of the regulations found in the third-century *Didascalia Apostolorum.*[19] According to the *Apostolic Constitutions,* Syrian bish-

---

18. See Chapter Two, notes 61, 62, and 63. Regarding the confusion of the terms *widow* and *virgin* in Christian asceticism, see Elm, *Virgins,* pp. 44–46.

19. With regard to the complex history of the *Apostolic Constitutions,* see Metzger's explanation in *Constitutiones Apostolorum,* 1: 13–62.

ops of the fourth century were to care for both male and female orphans. With regard to the girls, bishops were to find them suitable husbands who were Christians. To preserve the girls' virginity bishops surely maintained separate group homes with women supervisors, perhaps the inscribed widows. The *Apostolic Constitutions,* however, provided no information regarding any female supervisors. For the boys, bishops were to ensure adequate training in a trade so that these male orphans would eventually be able to support themselves and no longer burden the resources of the churches, a requirement taken directly from the *Didascalia Apostolorum.*[20]

The *Apostolic Constitutions* recommended that bishops use harsh discipline in raising the orphans. A bishop or any father should not hesitate to strike the children, for as Proverbs 13:24 states, "A father who spares the rod hates his son." The bishop also was to instruct the orphans in the Holy Scriptures and in other godly literature. Finally, bishops were to keep the boys from drinking parties and any other activities that could lead to *porneia.*[21]

One cannot determine whether the *Apostolic Constitutions* intended to limit the children of the bishop's orphanage to Christians. These rules did require that Christian families adopt only Christian orphans, but this does not necessarily mean that pagan orphans were excluded from the school. The *Vita Sancti Clementis* stressed that Clement and Sophia had cared for both Christian and pagan children at their orphanage at Ankyra. Such orphan schools no doubt played a role in Christian proselytism.[22]

The second Byzantine school that we know accepted orphans operated in late-fourth-century Caesarea in Cappadocia. The city's talented bishop (and guiding theologian of the Eastern Church), Basil the Great, described this school that he supported as part of his monastic community, located just outside the walls of Caesarea. Since Basil placed his description in his *Long Rules (Regulae fusius tractatae),* which he intended as a set of guidelines for his ascetic community in Caesarea and for similar communities throughout Asia Minor, he clearly

20. *Constitutiones Apostolorum,* 4.1–2 (2: 170–72).
21. Ibid., 4.11 (2: 188–90).
22. Ibid., 4.1 (2: 170); cf. *Vita Clementis,* 10 (PG, 114: 824).

expected that monks would run this orphan school. On the other hand, Basil also served as bishop of Caesarea and firmly believed that monks should be subject to the local bishop. When Basil established a number of monastic charities by the gates of Caesarea, including this school, a hospital, and a hospice, he desired not only to provide his monks with an opportunity to practice the saving work of charity, but he also sought to fulfill his obligation as bishop to minister to the needy of his flock. As a result, Basil's school at Caesarea served as a model both for subsequent monastic orphanages and for those run by bishops.[23]

Basil designed his school not exclusively for orphans. The monks were first to accept homeless children so that they, like Job, could become fathers of orphans, but they were also to accept boys and girls brought to the school by their parents.[24] Basil clearly intended his school to provide a training program for future monks. The children would remain in the institution until they were old enough to choose freely whether they wished to join the monastery or return to the secular world. Basil stressed that the youths were to make this choice freely when they had reached the full age of reason, that is, when a just judge would hold them legally responsible for crimes or wrongful acts they might have committed. Basil's legal reference might refer to the age of puberty. According to Roman law, children who reached puberty (fourteen for boys, twelve for girls) were held responsible for any crimes or wrongful acts they had committed. Moreover, at this age orphan children moved from the protection of a tutor to that of a curator. It is more likely, however, that Basil meant the seventeenth or eighteenth year when, according to Roman custom, boys became men, the age when male children assumed civic responsibility.[25] This later age also fit the ancient Hellenistic pattern of education that required boys to attend the gymnasium (the secondary school) until they reached young adulthood (seventeen to twenty) and were ready to join the *polis* community.[26]

---

23. Mazza, "Monachesimo Basiliano," pp. 79–91; Miller, *Birth*, pp. 85–88.
24. Basil, *Interrogatio XV* (PG, 31: 952).
25. Ibid., col. 956. For the various stages of life and their legal consequences, see Käser, *Roman Private Law*, pp. 81–83, and Wiedemann, *Adults*, pp. 113–16.
26. Marrou, *History*, pp. 147–59.

Basil recommended that the monastery accept children as soon as they reached the first age, sometime between five and seven.[27] His school apparently did not accept infants and very small children. It is conceivable, however, that Basil simply outlined in this section the functioning of the school and left out any description of how his monastery nurtured infants and small children. Pre-Christian educational theorists had also avoided discussing these early years as irrelevant to a child's subsequent intellectual development.[28] Moreover, the care of very small children would have involved obtaining and supervising wet nurses, an activity Basil might have left to another department of his monastic charities, distinct from the school.

Christian institutions to nurture infants did exist. The *Vita Sancti Clementis* clearly described its hero collecting abandoned infants along the roads of central Asia Minor.[29] Moreover, several novels of Justinian and the records of the Fifth Ecumenical Council (553) referred to *brephotropheia* in sixth-century Constantinople, institutions designed for the care of infants.[30] Christian philanthropic foundations to nourish babies therefore existed, but they were probably organized separately from schools for older children (see Chapter Six).

Basil required that the monks house the children in facilities isolated from the monastery proper. He also stipulated that the monks were to provide separate buildings and daily routines for female children. This is the only passage in Basil's rules for the school where he specifically referred to girls.[31] Basil described in far greater detail how to keep older and younger male children apart. The school should house the older boys separately from the younger, wake them at different hours of the morning, provide their meals at varying times, and teach them in separate classes. Basil clearly had in mind a lower and an upper school. The lower school taught the students the basics of reading and writing; the upper school instructed them in the rules of Greek grammar and introduced them to the Holy Scriptures and to both Christian and pagan Greek literature.[32]

27. Basil, *Interrogatio XV* (PG, 31: 952).   28. Marrou, *History*, p. 147.

29. *Vita Clementis*, 10 (PG, 114: 824).

30. See Janin, *Églises*, p. 569. Cf. *JNov*, 7 proem.

31. Basil, *Interrogatio XV* (PG, 31: 952).

32. Ibid., cols. 952–53.

Since early Hellenistic times, Greek city-states had maintained a two-tiered educational system. At six or seven, children entered primary school. When they reached puberty, they advanced to the gymnasium which, earlier in the fifth century (B.C.), had focused primarily on athletics, but during the Hellenistic period evolved into general schools teaching Greek literature, grammar, and music.[33] In designing his Christian school, Basil simply adopted the traditional Greek educational structure and altered it slightly to fit the monastic community he had founded. He left out athletics, but evidence from other Late Roman sources suggests that sports training had been declining throughout the Greco-Roman world for centuries. In the same way the Hellenistic gymnasium readied boys to enter the *polis* at eighteen, Basil's monastic school prepared orphans and the students with families to make the decision either to enter the monastic community or to return to the world.

Although Basil laid great stress on keeping the older children completely separate from the younger, he made two exceptions. First, the students should come together for common prayer so that the older students could serve as examples in contrition for the younger students and the younger could inspire the older by their simple fervor. Second, the school staff should appoint the best among the older students— those who had displayed the greatest patience—to act as leaders *(epistatountes)* for small groups of younger students. These group leaders were to guide the younger children with a father's feeling and with sound reason. If the younger children misbehaved, these *epistatountes* were to impose fitting punishments.[34]

Basil listed some specific punishments the group leaders were to apply. If one student showed anger toward another, the group leader was to force the angry child to wait on the object of his ill temper and serve him at table. If a student took food at the wrong time, he was to go without dinner. If a boy lied or gave verbal offence, he was to keep total silence and fast. Basil emphasized that each punishment should fit the transgression as a kind of opposite that would function as a corrective to the soul's disorder.[35] Since Basil had studied Greek medicine, he

33. Marrou, *History*, pp. 147–59 and pp. 223–24.
34. Basil, *Interrogatio XV* (PG, 31: 953).
35. Ibid., col. 953.

was no doubt referring in this passage to the principle of opposites in the Galenic system of drug therapy.[36]

Basil also wanted these group leaders to frequently interrogate the younger students about what they were thinking at a precise moment. These younger children would guilelessly answer and thereby reveal their inner-most thoughts. If these thoughts were shameful or silly, the children would feel disgrace and learn to shun such idle thoughts in the future. Basil emphasized that the proper daily routine would help to form the malleable souls of the young. By inculcating good habits, the school prepared the children to make the right moral choices once they had acquired the ability to make decisions on their own.[37]

In explaining why he so firmly insisted on separating older students from their younger colleagues, Basil made no reference to possible sexual temptations as did some monastic writers. He emphasized instead that certain routines that benefitted older boys were not suitable for the younger boys. He also thought that if the younger students saw the older ones punished for various offenses, they would lose heart and think that proper conduct was impossible to achieve.[38]

Basil revealed little about the content of the courses the orphans and other children pursued at his school. He did specify, however, that their grammar lessons should use names and places drawn from the Sacred Scriptures and that they should study the marvelous deeds of the Bible, not those of the ancient Greek myths. He added that the students should especially study the maxims in the Book of Proverbs. As a stimulus to learning, Basil also recommended that the teachers institute contests for the students to test their memory regarding names and events. He believed that children loved such competitions and that they would study with greater diligence if they were also enjoying themselves.[39]

Basil's emphasis on competitions no doubt sprang from the ancient

---

36. See Gregory of Nazianzos, *In laudem Basilii*, chaps. 23.6 (p. 108) and 63.5–6 (p. 190).

37. Basil, *Interrogatio XV* (PG, 31: 956).

38. Ibid., cols. 952–53; cf. *Vita Euthymii*, pp. 25–26, where Euthymios (fifth century) did not want to allow three young monks to join his *lavra* because of their age. It is clear from the account that Euthymios was concerned about sexual temptations.

39. Basil, *Interrogatio XV* (PG, 31: 953).

Greek concept of contests as an integral part of education. Contests such as the Olympic Games had played a central role in Hellenic athletic training. Later, during the Hellenistic period, *poleis* adapted such competitions to purely academic subjects by sponsoring contests in reading, grammar, oratory, and music. At Teos in the second and first century B.C., secondary-school children competed in reading passages of Homer. Many other cities sponsored similar competitions.[40] By recommending such contests as effective teaching tools, Basil ensured their survival in the Byzantine educational system. We shall see that similar contests formed an important part of the instructional program at the Orphanotropheion of Constantinople.

In describing the school's curriculum, Basil seems to favor banning classical Greek literature from his school. He stated that the students ought not to learn the pagan myths, a requirement that would have removed the Homeric poems from the curriculum. We know, however, from another of Basil's tracts that he, in fact, encouraged students to study the great works of Greek literature, including Homer, provided that the children approached these sometimes seductively beautiful poems with caution, and according to Basil's vivid image, select from this literature only what was truly valuable, as bees extract honey from the flowers of the fields.[41]

Basil's school obviously provided an academic training for the students, including the orphans. The *Apostolic Constitutions,* on the other hand, had required bishops to provide the orphans in their care only with schooling in some craft or trade. Basil, however, realized that some of the children in his monastery school might possess special talent for a particular craft. Moreover, to learn many manual skills well, boys needed to begin training early in life. Basil therefore provided the opportunity for some children to leave the academic school during the day to learn a trade from master craftsmen, but these students were to return in the evening to dine with their fellows and spend the night. Although Basil made no reference to the social background of the boys who pursued these trades, such apprentices probably came from

40. See Marrou, *History,* pp. 166–67, for sports contests, and pp. 230–31, for contests in reciting or singing Homer and the lyric poets.

41. *Ad adulescentes de legendis libris gentilium,* Basil, *Ep,* 4: 390.

among the orphans in the student population. Wealthy parents who had committed their children to the monastic school would have rejected any practical training as totally inappropriate for their own children. As the *Apostolic Constitutions* stated, a useful trade was especially appropriate for orphans who needed to acquire a skill in order to support themselves.[42]

The third Byzantine school was located at Melitene in Syria. As we saw in Chapter Three, the fifth-century *Vita Sancti Euthymii* described this school as it was operating at the end of the fourth century, between 382 and approximately 400. According to the *vita*, Saint Euthymios was born to an aristocratic couple of Melitene, Paul and Dionysia. Three years after his birth, however, Euthymios's father, Paul, died. With the assistance of her brother, Dionysia convinced Otreios, the bishop of Melitene, to accept the little boy into the *episkopeion*, the bishop's palace. After baptizing the boy, Otreios, according to the words of the *vita*, "in a fashion adopted" Euthymios and accepted the duty of raising him. The bishop then tonsured the boy and enrolled him among the lectors of the local church. At the same time, Otreios ordained Euthymios's mother as a deaconess.[43]

According to the *vita*, Dionysia had decided to hand over Euthymios to Otreios because of a vow she had made to God at the boy's birth, a promise that she would dedicate him to the Lord. It is curious, though, that she had not baptized Euthymios before she entrusted him to the bishop as one would have expected, if she had immediately dedicated him to God's service. The *vita*'s account thus arouses the suspicion that, in fact, Dionysia's brother, Euthymios's maternal uncle, was not in a position to assume the guardianship of the little boy and that it was better for all involved to let the bishop accept responsibility for the child.[44]

As soon as Euthymios was old enough (probably when he reached Basil's first age) Otreios handed him over to the teachers of sacred letters. In addition, the bishop assigned supervision of Euthymios to two older boys among the lectors, Akakios and Synodios. These two

---

42. Basil, *Interrogatio XV* (PG, 31: 956–57); cf. *Constitutiones Apostolorum* 4.2 (2: 172).
43. *Vita Euthymii*, pp. 8–11.
44. Ibid., pp. 8–10.

helped to train the boy in piety and, as Euthymios himself acknowledged, took over the duties of raising him.[45]

As Euthymios grew in age and grace, he was promoted to higher ranks of the clergy. Eventually, the bishop ordained him a priest and assigned him to supervise the monasteries in Melitene. Euthymios had clearly been attending a kind of seminary which the bishops of Melitene had organized at their *episkopeion*.[46] The youngest students were immediately ordained as lectors and, as they grew older and received more education, they moved up the order of ministries; some eventually became deacons, priests, and even bishops—Euthymios's student mentor Akakios succeeded Otreios as bishop of Melitene.[47] These students apparently lived together; the older ones exercised authority over the younger ones and shared some of the duties of raising them. The school of Melitene thus employed student monitors similar to Basil's *epistatountes,* the officers at Caesarea who bore some responsibility for disciplining the younger boys and helping in their moral training.[48]

Although this seminary at Melitene was designed primarily to train young boys for the clergy, it could also serve to nurture and educate orphans, as it did in the case of Euthymios. The legendary *Vita Sancti Clementis* provides additional evidence that such seminaries often provided care for orphans during the fourth and fifth centuries. According to the legend, once Clement was made bishop of Ankyra, he began enrolling into the ranks of the clergy the worthy among the orphans he had been nurturing.[49] What Clement had initially established as a simple orphanage rapidly developed into a school for training orphans and perhaps other children for the Christian clergy.

The school at Melitene, and the one described in the *Vita Sancti Clementis* were totally controlled by the local bishop. No monastic community seems to have played any role in caring for or teaching the boys at Melitene. In fact, the Melitene school resembled the episcopal orphanage described in the *Apostolic Constitutions* from Antioch more

45. Ibid., p. 11.   46. Ibid., p. 13.
47. Ibid., p. 32.
48. Ibid., p. 11; cf. *Interrogatio XV* (PG. 31: 953).
49. *Vita Clementis,* 13 (PG, 114: 824–25).

than the monastic educational foundation that Basil established at Caesarea.

In one aspect, however, the earlier school of the *Apostolic Constitutions* seems to have differed from the institution at Melitene. According
to the *Apostolic Constitutions,* the bishop was to provide the orphans
with practical training in some craft or trade, while at the Melitene
school the *Vita Sancti Euthymii* only portrayed the students receiving a
strictly academic education, based on the Sacred Scriptures and some
secular education, a curriculum designed to train future clergy of the
Christian Church.[50] Since the *Apostolic Constitutions* incorporated the
rules regarding the orphan school from the *Didascalia Apostolorum* of
the early third century, the type of institution that the *Constitutions*
was describing surely represented an earlier stage in the development
of these group homes, before they had begun the process of evolving
into seminaries.[51]

The fourth orphan school was located in Argos in the Peloponnesus. The tenth-century *Vita Sancti Petri Argivorum* includes some
valuable details regarding this institution, details that place the school
firmly in the tradition of Byzantine episcopal orphanages that we have
been tracing. According to this *vita,* Peter's family lived in Constantinople. Unfortunately, his mother and father both died while Peter
and his younger brother, Plato, were still very young. Both of them
entered a monastery where they received care and an education. The
vita does not mention the name of the ascetic community that accepted the two boys, but it was probably located in Constantinople.[52]

When the patriarch Nicholas Mystikos (901–907 and 912–925) made
Peter's older brother, Paul, bishop of Corinth, Peter followed Paul to
this new location and joined a monastic community outside the city.
When the bishop of nearby Argos died, the people there selected Peter
as their new shepherd.[53]

As soon as Peter assumed the episcopacy of Argos, he initiated a
generous philanthropic program, especially to assist the victims of

50. Cf. *Constitutiones Apostolorum,* 4.2 (2: 172).
51. See the "Introduction" by Metzger, *Constitutiones Apostolorum,* 1: 14–17.
52. *Vita Petri Argivorum,* pp. 1–5.
53. Ibid., pp. 5–6.

Arab pirate raids—at that time Arabs were launching raids against the Greek peninsula and the islands from their bases on Crete. For the orphans among these displaced people, Peter provided an orphan school.[54] Some of these orphans received training at this school designed to prepare them for the clergy, and one of them, the author of this *vita*, became a priest and eventually succeeded Peter as bishop of Argos. In fact, this man wrote Peter's biography as a work of thanksgiving for the care and moral guidance he had received while growing up at this institution.[55]

Other orphans who displayed a talent for a particular craft Peter sent out to work with master craftsmen. If these students had to move to another city for their lessons or to a country estate, Peter gave them the necessary money for their maintenance outside the orphanage. He also paid for any tools they might need.

In sum, the orphanage Peter maintained at Argos continued the traditions we found in fourth-century Cappadocia and Syria. The episcopal office supported a school that provided orphans with food, shelter, and an education. At Argos this education included both training for the clergy and special arrangements for learning practical crafts.[56]

The fifth orphan school John Apokaukos, bishop of Naupaktos from 1199 to 1232, described in several of his fascinating letters. Apokaukos's references to the orphanage under his supervision not only confirm the institutional structures we have already seen in the previous four descriptions, but they also add valuable details on the behavior of the children raised in these orphan schools.[57]

In his Letter 27, addressed to the bishop of Dyrrachium, Apokaukos claimed that God had especially blessed him by entrusting many orphans to his care. Unfortunately, Apokaukos did not mention a precise number so that one cannot establish the size of his orphan school. Apokaukos also described how the church of Naupaktos inscribed

54. Ibid., pp. 7–8.
55. Ibid., pp. 1 and 17; Basil, *Interrogatio XV* (PG, 31: 956–57).
56. *Vita Petri Argivorum*, p. 8.
57. For a brief discussion of Apokaukos's letters and legal *responsa* and for bibliographical references, see Laiou, "Contribution," pp. 276–79, esp. note 4. See also the article by Magdalino, "Literary Perception," pp. 28–38.

these children as lectors, just as the school at Melitene had immediately ordained Euthymios a lector in the late fourth century. In fact, Apokaukos expressly stated that the orphan school was designed to prepare these children to serve as clergy for the church of Naupaktos.[58]

In addition to learning to read and write and studying Greek grammar, the orphans also received lessons in choral singing so that they could chant the psalms. Apokaukos's words imply that such choral singing was normal practice for church lectors. The bishop understood the duties of a lector to include singing sacred songs at church services. None of the four earlier descriptions of orphan schools specifically mentioned singing as training for students, but, as we shall see in Chapter Eight, choral practice represented a major component of the educational system used at the Zotikos Orphanotropheion in Constantinople.[59] Moreover, in view of the significant role singing played in the traditions of Anatolian asceticism, Basil probably included singing as part of his school's educational program, although he did not specifically refer to it in his *Long Rules*.[60]

Like Peter of Argos, Apokaukos sent some of his orphans to other towns for specialized training. In one case, he dispatched a youth to the town of Vonditza to study accounting and calligraphy because no skilled teachers of these professions lived in Naupaktos. Apokaukos paid the living expenses of these orphans from his church's resources, a practice Peter also had followed in tenth-century Argos.[61]

Apokaukos's letters, however, do not describe a smoothly running orphanage completely free from problems. The bishop candidly admitted that the boys hated him. In fact, some of them had fled the orphanage to find an easier life. One of these escapees named Theodore finally returned and sought Apokaukos's forgiveness with tearful entreaties, but others clearly never came back. Apokaukos asked his friend, the bishop of Dyrrachium, to pray that the orphans would be

58. Apokaukos, *Epistolai*, Ep. 27 (pp. 85–86), esp. p. 85.

59. Akokaukos, *Epistolai*, Ep. 27 (p. 85) and Ep. 100 (pp. 151–52); cf. Miller, "Orphanotropheion," pp. 90–92.

60. Miller, "Orphanotropheion," pp. 88–89.

61. Apokaukos, *Epistolai*, Ep. 100 (pp. 150–52).

better disposed toward him so that when Apokaukos died, some of the students would still remain with him as priests and deacons of the church at Naupaktos to provide him with a proper burial.[62]

Apokaukos described in considerable detail a boy named John, one of the orphans at the school. The bishop had accepted John while the boy was still in his mother's womb. Apokaukos had promised John's mother while she was pregnant that he would care for the baby if it were a boy. Apparently, the church of Naupaktos did not have the facilities to nurture and educate girls. One should be cautious in generalizing from the single example of Naupaktos, but when one considers that these episcopal orphanages had been developing into seminaries since the late fourth century and that women were excluded from the Orthodox clergy, it seems likely that most, if not all, orphan schools supervised by bishops accepted only males. As we shall see, female monastic communities and some private orphanages bore the responsibility of caring for girls.[63]

Since Apokaukos accepted John as a newborn infant, he must have had some arrangement to provide the baby with a wet nurse. Apokaukos baptized the infant and gave him his own first name, John. According to the bishop's letters, he especially loved John, personally taught the boy grammar, and, because of his affection for the boy, hesitated to send him away from Naupaktos for advanced training.[64]

Apokaukos admitted, however, that John did not always behave well. The other boys in the orphanage nicknamed him *kleptes* (thief). Apokaukos tried to explain that the boy had gained this sobriquet because of his quick-wittedness and his skill in grammar exercises, but when Apokaukos later described how John stole eggs from an aviary for Easter games with the other children, it seems apparent that the boy had won his nickname because he stole things.[65]

Apokaukos also mentioned that John had a problem following instructions properly. The bishop praised the boy's intelligence but pointed out that John often was in such a hurry to perform the tasks assigned him that he failed to listen properly to all he was supposed to

62. Ibid., Ep. 27 (pp. 85–86).
64. Ibid., Ep. 100 (pp. 150–52).
63. Ibid., Ep. 100 (pp. 150–52).
65. Ibid., Ep. 100 (p. 151).

do. In addition, Apokaukos claimed that John sometimes wandered off on his own. In his letter presenting John to Nicholas, bishop of Vonditza, Apokaukos warned the bishop that he would have to supervise the boy very carefully and not hesitate to whip him if he shirked his duties or displayed any other of his character flaws.[66]

Apokaukos firmly supported harsh punishments. Those who had charge of the boys should not hesitate to scold them, whip them, and even beat them with the rod. In supporting physical punishments, the bishop was following a fundamental rule of discipline recommended by the Book of Proverbs (13:24) and repeated in the fourth-century *Apostolic Constitutions*. On the other hand, Apokaukos's penchant for harsh discipline probably accounted for the hatred the orphans felt toward him and explained why some of them fled his school.[67]

From the one thousand years of Byzantine history, the surviving sources provide details concerning only these five orphan schools run by bishops. The sixth-century *Vita Sancti Alypii* also refers to an episcopal orphanage at Adrianople in Paphlagonia, but without describing it in any detail. How many others were there? Did every episcopal see in the empire maintain such a school to prepare children for the clergy as well as to provide group care for orphan boys? Justinian's Novel 120 referred to *orphanotrophoi* outside Constantinople who were subject to their local bishop or metropolitan. The same emperor's Novel 131 described *orphanotrophoi* who received property belonging to orphans in their care in the presence of the provincial governor or the *ekdikos* of the local *polis*. These *orphanotrophoi* probably supervised the episcopal orphan schools and seminaries.[68]

After the sixth century Byzantine sources contain very few references to either orphanages or their directors outside of Constantinople. An eleventh-century inscription from the Athenian agora records the grave of a local *orphanotrophos*, and a seal from the same century refers to an *orphanotropheion* in the city of Ionopolis.[69] Moreover, as

66. Ibid., Ep. 100 (pp. 151–52).
67. Ibid., Ep. 100 (pp. 151–52) and Ep. 101 (p. 152); cf. Ep. 27 (p. 85).
68. *Vita Alypii*, p. 149; *JNov*, 120.6, and *JNov*, 131.15.
69. For Athens, see Orlandos, *Charagmata*, no. 168 (pp. 134–35); for Ionopolis, see Athenagoras, "Thesmos," p. 26.

late as the fourteenth century, the bishop of Thessalonike appointed one of his priests to the post of *orphanotrophos*, presumably to supervise the care of homeless children in the second city of the empire.[70] The scarcity of such references, however, does not necessarily indicate that facilities to care for orphans were rare outside the capital. Probably the terms *orpanotropheion* and *orphanotrophos* were used less frequently as local episcopal schools focused increasingly on preparing boys for the ranks of the clergy and ceased to be exclusively *orphanotropheia*. The author of the *Vita Sancti Petri Argivorum* never once referred to Peter's school as an *orphanotropheion*, although Bishop Peter clearly designed his institution primarily to nurture and educate orphans.[71]

As we saw in Chapter Three, bishops had been able to adapt the routines of housing, feeding, and educating orphan children to the needs of their churches more easily than they could the services of hospitals, old-age homes *(gerokomeia)*, or almshouses *(ptocheia)*. Apparently, many episcopal sees supported such orphan schools because in the eighth century, a very difficult period in the history of the Byzantine state, the emperor Leo III assumed that provincial bishops were maintaining group homes large enough to care for and educate all the local children whose parents had left them without guardians.[72]

MONASTIC SCHOOLS

In addition to episcopal orphan schools, the Christian Church also supported monastic orphan schools. Basil's *Long Rules* were in fact designed to provide guidance for ascetic communities, and the institution he described not only sheltered orphans, but also served to prepare future monks.[73] Basil's school influenced development of subsequent episcopal schools such as Peter's orphanage in Argos with its system for supporting apprentice artisans and Apokaukos's institution at Naupaktos, but it also helped to shape later monastic schools. When Theophanes, a superior of the Stoudite monastery in Constantinople during the tenth century, added a school building for the children, he followed

70. *Encomium Gregorii Palamae auctore Philotheo* (PG, 151: 614 and 619).
71. *Vita Petri Argivorum*, passim.
72. *Ecloga*, 7 (p. 198).
73. See Basil, *Interrogatio XV* (PG, 31: 952–58).

Basil's advice by placing the structure far enough away from the adult monks that the boys would not disturb the men's ascetic routines.[74] At the thirteenth-century monastery of Emathia, Blemmydes employed Basil's system of questioning the children about their hidden thoughts to assist them in driving silly or lustful images from their minds.[75]

Just as some monastic schools followed Basil's recommendations concerning where to place school buildings and the routines they should use in educating the boys, they also followed his command to imitate Job and become fathers of orphans. We have already seen that in the early tenth century when Peter of Argos and his younger brother Plato lost their parents, they received care and an education in a monastery school. Here, the teachers not only instructed Peter in the Scriptures, as Basil suggested, but they also introduced the students to secular learning—that is, Hellenic literature—although Peter's *vita* emphasized that the saintly boy did not highly prize it. The monastery school also allowed the boys time to play games.[76]

According to the *Ecloga* of Leo III, the monasteries of Constantinople shared with the Orphanotropheion the tasks of caring for orphans whose parents had failed to designate a guardian; moreover, these ascetic communities were obliged to accept the responsibility of serving as tutors for these children. In the provinces Leo III assigned these obligations to the episcopal sees (*episkopeia* in the words of the text) and to monasteries, a clear indication that throughout the empire monasteries played a significant role, alongside the episcopal schools, in providing care for orphans without *tutores testimentarii*.[77]

As we saw at the beginning of this chapter, Alexios Komnenos continued to make use of monastic schools in the twelfth century as part of his program to assist orphan refugees from Asia Minor. For those children who had no family members in Constantinople, he found ascetic communities in Constantinople that were able to provide shelter and an education for these orphans.[78]

By the twelfth century, then, many monasteries of Constantinople were sheltering orphans in some manner. As an example of such a

---

74. *Vita Sancti Nicolae Studitae* (PG, 105: 868–69).

75. *Typikon Blemmydes*, p. 94.   76. *Vita Petri Argivorum*, pp. 4–5.

77. *Ecloga*, 7 (p. 198).   78. Anna Komnena, *Alexiad*, 15.7.3 (3: 214).

monastic community one should consider the Pantokrator foundation of the emperor John Komnenos. According to its *typikon* (rule), the Pantokrator monastery was to provide paid positions for twelve orphans. Eight of these children were to serve the monastery's public church as acolytes for specific services, while the other four filled auxiliary positions with the prospect of eventually becoming permanent acolytes. The Pantokrator also paid four older women, called *graptai* (see Chapter Two), to supervise these children. This *typikon* provided no instructions regarding a school for these orphans. Perhaps they were hired from nearby monasteries with orphan schools. It is also possible, however, that the care of orphan children and their use as minor clerics beyond the cloistered sections of monastic communities had become so much a part of the fabric of ascetic life that the *typikon* omitted any precise instructions.[79]

The *typikon* of the monastery of Saint John on Patmos, composed a few years before Alexios assigned the Christian orphans to monasteries in Constantinople, also referred to homeless children in the care of the ascetic community. This rule mentioned a certain number of children whom the monastery of Saint John had been feeding and training from the time these boys had been infants. These same children apparently performed menial tasks for the monks. Like the Pantokrator rules, this *typikon* also provided no guidelines regarding the schooling, disciplining, or living arrangements of these children.[80] Perhaps the orphans on Patmos received care similar to that which Basil had designed for the orphans of fourth-century Cappadocia. On the other hand, the monks might have maintained the boys merely to perform labor services for the community.

Monastic communities for women assumed a major role in the Byzantine system of orphan care because most episcopal schools preferred to accept only boys. Among the five episcopal schools we examined above, only the earliest two included any reference to care for female orphans.[81] As the episcopal orphanages increasingly concentrated on preparing boys to be deacons and priests, they eventually excluded

---

79. *Typikon Pantokrator,* pp. 75–79.
80. MM, 6: 83 and 86.
81. See *Constitutiones Apostolorum,* 4.2 (2: 172), and Basil, *Interrogatio XV* (PG, 31: 952).

female orphans from their care. Monasteries for women, however, continued to serve as refuges for homeless girls.

When Basil mentioned facilities for girls in his *Long Rules,* he was probably referring to a school run by women ascetics living under his authority in or around Caesarea. Other sources have revealed that Anatolian monasticism maintained a strong tradition of women as equal partners in the quest to attain the angelic lifestyle.[82] Basil assumed that nuns within his see would take care of orphan girls, just as the monks accepted boys.

From the earliest days of the Christian monastic movement, the evidence suggests that nuns bore the responsibility of caring for female orphans without families. The *Vita Febroniae monachae,* written in the fourth century, recorded in gory detail the torture and execution of a nun from a monastery in eastern Syria, located near the Persian border, an execution carried out during the reign of Diocletian (284–305). This *vita* contains fascinating details about the prayer life of these nuns. For example, they held their principal services on Fridays.[83]

According to the *vita,* Febronia had lost her parents while still an infant. Her aunt, Bryene, superior of a nearby monastery, had accepted the duty of raising her. Bryene found a wet nurse to suckle the baby, but when Febronia reached age two Bryene received her back into the ascetic community and raised her to join the monastery. One might explain Bryene's accepting Febronia as fulfilling the obligation of the *tutela legitima,* and no doubt Bryene recognized a moral obligation to care for Febronia, although Roman law did not grant any females the right to serve as tutors at this time. Febronia's aunt, however, also was caring for a second orphan named Prota whom the *vita* did not identify as a relative.[84]

The *Vita Sancti Antonii,* written in the mid-fourth century by the bishop of Alexandria, Athanasios, recorded how the most celebrated of early monks, Antony of Egypt, lost both his parents when he was about eighteen years old. After their deaths, Antony had to manage his

82. For the history of Anatolian monasticism in the fourth century, see Dagron, "Moines et la ville," pp. 229–76.

83. *Vita Febroniae,* p. 17.

84. Ibid., pp. 17–18.

family's property and care for a much younger sister. After some thought and, as Athanasios portrayed the events, divine direction, Antony handed his little sister over to the care of well-known and faithful virgins so that they could raise her in their community. Antony then left to pursue his ascetic goals. In this case, the female ascetics accepted an orphan who was not a relative of the community's superior.[85]

In fifth-century Herakleia, the future Saint Elizabeth lost both her parents by the time she had reached fifteen. She decided to liberate her family's slaves and give away all her inherited wealth. Her biography does not refer to her having obtained the approval of any guardian to make these donations. Thereupon, she went to Constantinople and joined the monastery of Saint George where her paternal aunt served as superior. When her aunt died, Elizabeth succeeded her as the new superior. Elizabeth's aunt apparently had accepted the duty of caring for Elizabeth, her blood relative, but as an individual she could not have become a legal tutor or curator for the girl because in the fifth century Roman law prevented women, except the mother, from accepting the duty of guardianship. As in the case of Febronia, so also at this Constantinopolitan monastery, the Christian duty to care for orphans offered to the community's female head the opportunity to perform a family obligation otherwise forbidden to women. Also from fifth-century Constantinople comes the example of the widow Susanna who belonged to a community of women at the Church of the Holy Apostles. She agreed to care for the daughter of Matrona so that the latter could pursue a life of extreme asceticism.[86]

In the ninth century a community of nuns raised the orphan girl Theoktiste. According to a short account of her life, her parents had died when Theoktiste was still very young. She had living relatives, but they decided not to raise her themselves, but rather to hand her over to a community of female ascetics.[87]

Only one surviving *typikon* specifically refers to the obligation of

---

85. *Vita Antonii*, 1–5 (PG, 26: 840–48). For a discussion of the Latin and English translations of this *vita*, see Elm, *Virgins*, p. 227, note 1.

86. *Vita Elisabethae*, pp. 251–58, and *Vita Matronae*, pp. 790–93.

87. *Vita Theoctistis*, pp. 228–29.

nuns to undertake the care of homeless orphans. In 1118 Irene Doukas, wife of the emperor Alexios, established the monastery of Kecharitomene. In describing the number of nuns the community was to include, Irene added that the monastery was always to nourish, rear, and educate two orphan girls and prepare them for tonsure at the proper time. This number is exceedingly low, but the ascetic community itself consisted of only twenty-four nuns. Byzantine monasteries for women tended to be small, but numerous. If every women's community accepted a small number of orphans, would this have met the need for supporting girls with no living relatives willing to undertake the obligation of *tutela*?[88]

The early-ninth-century letters of Theodore of Stoudios provide evidence that a private orphanage, not connected to a monastic community or a bishop's see, sheltered a larger number of girls, sometimes as many as forty. Such private orphanages may have played a substantial role in supplementing episcopal and monastic facilities, especially with respect to girls. We shall examine more fully these private orphan asylums in the following section entitled "Personal Charity."

The Christian Church thus maintained within the Byzantine Empire a system of institutional care for orphans without guardians, a system consisting of episcopal schools and orphanages associated with monastic communities of both men and women. This network of orphan schools probably was unable to care for all children without guardians throughout the entire empire. One should recall, though, that the emperor Leo III thought that it was sufficiently large to provide care for all orphans whose parents failed to make a written or oral will designating a guardian, a group significantly larger than the children for whom absolutely no guardians could have been found.[89]

PERSONAL CHARITY

In addition to maintaining orphanages, the Christian Church also supplemented the Roman guardianship laws by encouraging individ-

88. *Typikon Kecharitomene,* chap. 5 (p. 41).
89. *Ecloga,* 7 (p. 198).

ual believers to contribute some of their wealth to assist orphans. The *Apostolic Constitutions* assumed that the gifts of lay Christians would help sustain the children in the bishop's care as well as support the other philanthropic activities of the local church.[90] Sermons throughout the Byzantine period constantly exhorted the faithful to aid widows, orphans, the poor, and wandering strangers. The seventh-century monk and theologian Maximos the Confessor praised the prefect of Africa for the steps he had taken to sustain orphans and other persons in need.[91] But exactly how did lay Christians, especially wealthy and powerful individuals, offer their help to orphans?

Some wealthy individuals apparently founded small orphanages in association with private chapels that they had constructed. We have already examined the case of the wealthy widow who had lived in Constantinople in the early fifth century and had established some sort of an institution for homeless children in connection with her private church.[92] Extant sources testify to the existence of two other such private orphanages, one in Bithynia and the other in the Peloponnesus.

In the early ninth century, the famous monastic leader and defender of icons Theodore of Stoudios addressed four letters to a pious aristocrat named Moschos and his two sisters. This family lived together on an estate just outside the Bythinian town of Prousa. Theodore praised all three for their generosity toward the poor, but in his four letters he especially commented on their care for orphans. In Letter 211, he stated specifically that Moschos supported forty orphans and that his two sisters, Irene and Kale, supervised an additional forty. To house and feed eighty children would have required organizing a sizable institution. Theodore did not allude to schooling as part of this group home, but he did emphasize how Moschos and his sisters provided an inheritance for each boy orphan and a dowry for each one of the girls.[93]

Until the discovery of Theodore's Letter 211, Irene Doukas's *typikon* was the only extant source to specify a precise number of children in any one orphan program, two girls at the monastery of Kecharito-

---

90. *Constitutiones Apostolorum*, 4.5–8 (2: 176–84).
91. Maximos, Ep. 44 (PG, 91: 645 and 648).
92. Proklos, *Homélie 26*, pp. 174–83.
93. Theodore of Stoudios, Ep. 211 (pp. 333–34).

mene. Theodore's letter thus presents solid evidence that the Byzantines sometimes organized orphanages that could hold many more children. Moreover, in none of Theodore's letters did he imply that Moschos's asylum at Prousa represented an exceptionally large institution. From the sources, we have no way of knowing how many other orphanages equaled or surpassed Moschos's *orphanotropheion*, but given that this was a privately financed institution and located on the outskirts of a modest provincial town, it is possible that the episcopal schools of larger cities such as Thessalonike or Smyrna took in a much greater number of orphans.

Since Moschos provided dowries, we know that some of the orphans in his institution were girls. Theodore's letters do not mention precisely how the girls were housed in this *orphanotropheion*, but in Letter 211 he did state that Moschos himself had cared for forty children while his sisters, Irene and Kale, had cared for an additional forty. It seems reasonable to assume that the sisters were in charge of a separate section for girls. In any case, Theodore's letters provide valuable evidence that some private orphanages accepted girls and helped to supplement the system of orphan care provided by female monasteries.

A collection of edifying tales, compiled in tenth-century Monembasia, included a story about a second private orphanage located somewhere in the Peloponnesus. According to this tale, in the reign of the emperor Leo VI and his brother Alexander (889–912), a Peloponnesian magnate purchased a Scythian slave (perhaps a Khazar or Pecheneg of the Russian steppes) and entrusted him to the priest in charge of the church attached to the great man's estates. The priest was to teach the boy to read, to write, and to comprehend the Scriptures. When the boy reached age twelve, the magnate asked him if the Scythians had accepted Christianity. In the course of the conversation, the boy revealed not only that the Scythians were not Christian, but that he himself had never been baptized. He had been regularly receiving communion because all the other boys had done so. These children apparently served the church and worked about the magnate's estate while they completed their elementary education in a school under the supervision of the priest. The story does not reveal whether all the boys were slaves, or why the magnate was training them. Did he want to have literate slaves working for him in positions requiring more skill, or did he simply desire more valuable commodities to sell? On the other hand, it is possible that he was financing a philanthropic service to buy young children, provide them with an education and proper care, and then liberate them as free adults.[94]

The boys at this school lived and studied in close connection with the magnate's private church. Perhaps Leo III was referring to such private orphanages in his legislation to reform guardianship laws. Among Christian orphanages in the provinces, Leo listed first the *episkopeia*, second monasteries, and third simply *ekklesiai* (churches). In this last category, Leo was probably including the private churches on the estates of landed magnates, private churches that maintained the kind of school alluded to in this Peloponnesian tale of the tenth century.[95] In sum, the evidence regarding both these private orphanages, but especially Moschos's asylum at Prousa, suggests that such foundations helped to supplement the services of episcopal schools and monastic orphanages in providing care for children without parents or loving relatives.

Christian laymen also aided orphans by naming them as beneficiaries in their testaments. The eleventh-century magnate Eustathios Boilas of Cappadocia left such a legacy in his will. His son and his wife having died earlier, Eustathios established his two daughters as the joint heirs of his estate. From his property Eustathios designated two villages as a legacy for three people, two brothers named Christopher and George and their cousin. Eustathios gave them these villages because, as he phrased it, "they are poor and orphans." The testament did not indicate whether these orphans had reached maturity, or were still in the care of a guardian, nor did it reveal whether they belonged to Eustathios's extended family. The document only stated that Eustathios had made this grant to assist three orphans who, according to his last will and testament, lived in poverty.[96]

---

94. *Récits de Paul,* tale 9, pp. 76–78.
95. *Ecloga,* 7 (p. 198).
96. "Testament d'Eustathios Boilas," pp. 22–23. See also Vryonis, "Will of Eustathios Boilas," pp. 265–66, for an English translation.

In the twelfth century Isaak Komnenos left a legacy to an orphan whom he had adopted in some fashion. In his will, Isaak provided precise instructions as to the care of the boy and designated one village as a legacy for him. Isaak also selected the superior of the monastery of Kosmosoteira and two of his own retainers as guardians to preserve the boy's property and provide him with an education.[97]

A law of Manuel I (1143–1180) indicated that testators frequently granted legacies to benefit orphans. Manuel issued this constitution to ensure that heirs or executors immediately fulfilled the pious works that the deceased had instructed them to perform. As an example of such a pious work, Manuel first mentioned money left for rearing orphans, and second, funds for feeding the poor. If the heirs or executors failed to provide the legacy to the amount stated for the orphans, the poor, or other needy persons, the emperor, or in his absence the urban prefect, was to find other persons to supervise the administration of the testament.[98]

CLERGY AND MONKS AS GUARDIANS

The Christian Church, on the one hand, sought to provide group homes for orphans without guardians and encouraged laymen and laywomen to help finance such institutions, to found their own private group homes, or to leave legacies to aid specific children. On the other hand, it discouraged both clergy and monks from accepting guardianships. Canon 3 of the Council of Chalcedon (451) forbade bishops, clerics, and monks from managing the property of others unless the laws summoned them to assume the guardianship of orphans. In effect, this canon mandated that clerics and monks accept only guardianships that fell to them by the rules of the *tutela legitima*, but not those cases where testators appointed them in their wills.[99] In 546 the emperor Justinian greatly expanded this restriction, presumably with the support of Church leaders. In his Novel 123, he banned bishops and monks from accepting any guardianship for any reason whatsoever; he al-

---

97. *Typikon Kosmosoteira*, no. 69 (pp. 52–53), no. 107 (p. 70), and no. 117 (p. 74).
98. The *prostagma* is paraphrased by Balsamon, *Commentarius ad Nomocanonum*, RP, 1: 82–85.
99. *ACO*, 2.1.2 (pp. 158–59).

lowed priests, deacons, and subdeacons to assume the burden of guardianship only when it fell to them by the rules of the *tutela legitima*.[100]

Leo VI (886–912) issued a revision, or rather a clarification, of this law. In converting Roman legal terms into Greek, jurists had chosen *epitropos* to translate both the Latin term *tutor* (guardian) and *executor* (an individual named to carry out the terms of a testament in place of the actual heir). Leo VI stated that bishops, clerics, and monks could accept the duty of executor of a testament, but not the obligation of guarding minor children, a duty Leo thought was too burdensome for clergy and would pull them away from their sacred duties. Leo therefore upheld Justinian's total ban against bishops or monks serving as tutors or curators.[101]

Later legal textbooks continued to state the traditional ban. The eleventh-century *Peira* specified that monks could not assume guardianship of minors.[102] The famous twelfth-century canonists Theodore Balsamon and Alexios Aristenos confirmed Justinian's prohibition.[103] Finally, Constantine Harmenopoulos's *Hexabiblos* (circa 1345) repeated the rule that bishops and monks could not become *epitropoi* of orphans.[104]

Despite the strong legal tradition against bishops or monks accepting guardianships, Byzantine sources prove that, in fact, bishops and monks often served as guardians. When Saint Abramios's brother died sometime during the fifth century, friends and neighbors did not hesitate to entrust the deceased brother's seven-year-old daughter to her uncle Abramios, even though he had been practicing the ascetic life for years.[105] One could argue that Abramios simply assumed the care of his niece in an informal capacity. Had a legal issue developed, perhaps the courts would have constrained him to find another legal guardian.

In a will dated 570, however, the Egyptian physician Phoibammon

---

100. *JNov*, 123.5. For a thorough discussion of the legal issues involved with this novel, see Crifò, *Rapporti*, pp. 29–89.

101. Leo VI, *Novel*, no. 68 (pp. 247–49).

102. *Peira*, 16.3 (p. 55).

103. *Commentarii ad canonem III. Synodi Calcedonensis*, RP, 2: 220–25.

104. *Hexabiblos*, 5.12.23 (p. 714).

105. *Vita Abramii*, p. 935.

appointed the superior of the monastery of Saint Jeremiah as the legal guardian of his young children. Since Phoibammon was concerned that his wife not have any claim to his property beyond the legacy he gave her and clearly did not want her to serve as tutor—an office that by the sixth century she could have claimed as a mother, if the testament were invalid—he surely thought that the courts would not object to his appointing a monastic superior. Did Phoibammon not know of Justinian's ban issued in 546, or did he realize that local courts in Egypt either were unaware of the new rule or failed to enforce it?[106]

In eleventh-century Bari, the monk Basil left a testament in which he revealed that he had been administering the property of his cousin Blasios who had died earlier and left Basil in charge of these lands on behalf of Blasios's two underage orphans. The testament avoided the term *epitropos,* but the text clearly indicated that Basil had been performing the duties of that office.[107]

In one of his encomia, the famous scholar, rhetorician, and legal expert Michael Psellos praised the patriarch Michael Keroularios for accepting the responsibility of raising his deceased elder brother's two sons. According to Psellos, Keroularios did not allow the obligations of his high ecclesiastical office to blind him toward his family duty to provide for these orphans. Psellos's description implied that Keroularios not only provided the boys legal protection, but he personally raised them. The rhetorician never mentioned that the law formally banned Keroularios from serving as a guardian, but it is perhaps significant that Psellos, an expert in Byzantine law, avoided using the technical legal terms *epitropos* and *kourator* for guardian and selected instead a literary term for caring to describe the patriarch's loving concern for his nephews.[108]

John, metropolitan of Herakleia (Pontos) in the early fourteenth century, had been a monk before he was selected as the city's bishop. As a result, the Justinianic law, confirmed by the novel of Leo VI,

106. Maspero, no. 67151 (2: 88–100); for the establishment of the superior as guardian, see esp. p. 98, ll. 228–34.

107. "Cartulary of Saint Elias," doc. 2 (pp. 139–41).

108. Psellos, *Encomium ad Cerullarium,* pp. 351–52. See also the commentary by Volk, *Der medizinische Inhalt,* p. 223.

banned him from guardianship on two counts: as both a monk and a bishop. Nevertheless, four years after he ascended the episcopal throne of Herakleia, he accepted his young nephew, Nikephoros Gregoras, as his ward. John paid especial attention to Gregoras's education to ensure that the boy had proper training in classical Greek. John also introduced his ward to Platonic studies. It is possible that the bishop simply entrusted the boy to the episcopal school and orphanage, but Gregoras's account did not refer to any group home and indicated instead that John had personally raised him from early childhood.[109]

These examples should suffice to show that in practice Byzantine society allowed bishops and monks to accept the care of orphan children despite the prohibition of Justinian's Novel 123. Indeed, the Church itself acknowledged problems with a total ban, because it recognized the special obligation of clergy to assist orphans while at the same time it tried to keep its clergy free from worldly cares.

The twelfth-century legal expert and canonist Theodore Balsamon was well aware of the glaring contrast between the law and popular practice regarding bishops and monks serving as guardians. Balsamon attempted to solve the dichotomy by introducing the issue of intention. According to Balsamon's interpretation, Justinian's Novel 123 did not ban bishops and monks from all guardianships; it forbad their seeking after such duties or being constrained to assume them by force of law. If, however, they chose to accept a guardianship because of a general moral obligation to watch over orphan children, then the law did not apply. No other prominent legal expert so directly confronted this problem as Balsamon did. His comments, however, should be sufficient to prove that the Byzantine courts had in practice been ignoring the Justinianic rule for generations.[110]

The Christian Church thus assumed a major portion of society's responsibility to assist orphans. First, the schools maintained by Christian bishops and monastic communities provided group-home care and an

---

109. Gregoras, "La vie de Jean," pp. 33–34 and 55–63.
110. For Balsamon's opinion, see *Commentarii ad canonem III. Synodi Calcedonensis*, RP, 2: 223–24; cf. the views of Aristenos, *RP*, 2: 225.

education for orphans who had no relatives or family friends ready to take up their *tutela*. Second, Christian exhortations to care for orphans and the frequent references in sermons and religious tracts to God's special concern for orphans motivated lay believers to contribute to existing orphan schools, to found new ones, or to establish legacies for boys and girls who had lost their parents. Finally, Christian bishops, priests, deacons, and monks sometimes accepted the burden of guardianship for the children of relatives or friends. Moreover, they were willing to assume this difficult task even though both the canons of the Church and the laws of the state provided them an easy exemption from those burdens.

Among those orphans without any family members or family friends willing to assist them, those in the most desperate plight were surely the infants abandoned along the roads and byways of the Byzantine Empire. They represented a special category of orphans with specific needs. In addressing the issue of abandoned babies and young children, Byzantine society had to make some major alterations in the fabric of classical Greco-Roman traditions. In the following chapter we will examine the issue of abandoned children and also the Byzantine practices of adoption, based on an ancient Roman legal institution. Adoption proved valuable in providing new fathers and mothers for orphans in general, but especially for infants whose birth parents had rejected them.

VI   ABANDONMENT AND ADOPTION

Regarding abandonment and adoption in the Byzantine Empire, one can formulate the key issues with two simple questions: Did the people of East Rome abandon as many babies as their pre-Christian ancestors had? And, second, were devout Christians willing to adopt the exposed infants they happened to find? Answering these two questions would provide valuable information not only about the society of the Byzantine Empire but also about the efficacy of Christianity in reshaping deep-rooted customs and instilling respect for human life in its most helpless form. In sum, answering these two questions would help us gage how much success the Byzantine Church and Byzantine state achieved in their effort to create the New Jerusalem.

Unfortunately, sufficient evidence has not survived to enable modern historians of Byzantium to answer either of these questions precisely. Historians of the ancient world have to date failed to establish exactly how often infant abandonment occurred in pre-Christian Greco-Roman society, or what happened to most of these babies. Scholars have been debating for decades how often and for what reasons Greeks and Romans exposed their infant children. Was it a widespread phenomenon practiced by all classes to limit family size? Was it only a desperate strategy of the poor to avoid starvation? Or was it a method to restrict the number of females a family had to support? Historians have so far failed to answer any of these questions definitively, although they

now agree that the pre-Christian Greeks and Romans did expose babies for all three of the above reasons.[1]

Granted that we cannot succeed if we try to calculate the rate of
abandonment in the Byzantine Empire or compare that percentage
with the ancient rate in general, which has in fact never been established (and probably never can be established), what can we discover
about infant exposure in the East Roman state? Did the Byzantine Empire make a concerted effort to discourage abandonment? Did the East
Roman state and church develop effective methods to assist foundlings
or older abandoned children? Finally, can we demonstrate any link between abandonment and the practice of adoption? Although the surviving evidence does not provide any precise statistics about the frequency of abandonment and the chances of subsequent death or
adoption, it does provide enough information to trace changes in legal
and religious institutions regarding both infant exposure and adoption,
changes that did alter ancient customs and attitudes. Before we begin
examining the Byzantine period, however, it is useful to summarize
what ancient sources reveal about abandonment and adoption in the
Greco-Roman world.

THE ANCIENT WORLD

At some time in the one hundred years before the reign of Constantine (306–337), a Greek apparently from the Isle of Lesbos wrote a
popular prose novel entitled *Daphnis and Chloe*.[2] The plot of this pastoral romance revolved around abandonment and adoption.

The tale begins when a Lesbian goatherd named Lamo followed
one of his straying she-goats and discovered that she had been secretly
nursing a beautiful baby boy, abandoned in an oak grove together with
three valuable tokens: a purple cloak, a golden broach, and a silver
dagger. At first, Lamo thought to seize the precious tokens and leave
the baby, but when he pondered the she-goat's actions, he was
ashamed at his own lack of human affection (*philanthropia* in the text)
and decided to take the infant home to his wife. Since they had no chil-

1. Weidemann, *Adults*, pp. 36–41; *RE*, "Aussetzung," 2: 2588–89; Patterson, "Not Worth
the Rearing," pp. 103–23, see esp. p. 103, note 2; Cameron, "Exposure," pp. 105–14.
2. Reeve, "Praefatio," pp. v–vii.

dren of their own, Lamo and his wife decided to adopt the baby. They named him Daphnis. When the boy was old enough, they put him to work guarding the family's herd of goats.

Two years later, their neighbor, the shepherd Dryas, followed one of his female sheep into a nearby cave, which served as a shrine to the Nymphs. Here Dryas found the sheep nursing a newborn girl, also abandoned with valuable tokens. After some initial hesitation, Dryas also took the baby home. He and his wife adopted her and gave her the name Chloe. When she reached sufficient age, she took over Dryas's shepherding duties.[3]

As it turned out, Daphnis and Chloe grew up together, and when they reached youth they fell in love with each other as they guarded their flocks. After many exciting adventures interspersed with innocent kisses, they eventually learned who their natural parents were: aristocrats from the Lesbian capital of Mitylene. Daphnis's true father confessed that he had decided to abandon him as a newborn because he already had three children, and a fourth would have been too many. Chloe's father had abandoned her because he had just performed two expensive civic liturgies for Mitylene and was for the time being too poor to support her.[4] Daphnis's father frankly stated that he had expected his boy to die; the tokens were meant not to facilitate later recognition, but to serve as burial ornaments.[5]

How much of *Daphnis and Chloe* was literary invention and how much reflected reality? Some ancient historians have rejected as evidence of widespread abandonment both this pastoral romance and the plots of several earlier Greek and Roman new comedies; but for a literary work such as *Daphnis and Chloe* to have had any impact, at the least readers would have had to accept the plausibility of infant exposure for the reasons stated by both fathers.[6] That the babies were nursed by animals, were soon found by humans, were subsequently adopted by caring peasant families, and eventually were reunited with their true parents of high status required divine intervention, but the initial abandonment represented a harsh fact of contemporary reality.

3. *Daphnis and Chloe*, 1.2–6.   4. Ibid., 4.19–35.
5. Ibid., 4.24.
6. See Boswell, *Kindness*, pp. 3–49, esp. pp. 6–7.

Other evidence confirms such a reading of *Daphnis and Chloe*. During the Classical period, Athenian authors assumed that parents often abandoned their infants. In his play *The Clouds* (circa 428 B.C.), Aristophanes confessed that he had abandoned his earlier comedy, *The Banqueters*, to another author, just as a young unmarried maiden might abandon her child for others to raise.[7] Several decades later, in one of his dialogues, Plato depicted the old philosopher Socrates examining a new idea for possible defects. Socrates declared that if this newborn idea were discovered deformed, its parents would have to abandon it.[8] Both Aristophanes and Plato used the abandonment of infants as metaphors: in the first case for giving up authorship of a comedy and in the second for rejecting a bad idea. Neither Aristophanes nor Plato would have considered abandonment an effective metaphor if it were not a familiar practice to contemporary Athenians.

Although the literature of Classical Greece contains many passages such as these, no reference provides any basis for establishing how frequently the Athenians or the Greeks of other city-states abandoned their infants. Since the Spartans required by law that citizens expose deformed or sickly babies, one would suppose that in this *polis* citizens abandoned more children than in other Greek cities.[9]

More abundant evidence, however, survives from the Greek-speaking provinces of the second-century Roman Empire. While serving as governor of Bithynia, Pliny the Younger addressed many letters to his superior in Rome, the emperor Trajan (98–117 A.D.). In one of these letters, Pliny indicated that a substantial number of free persons were abandoning their babies and that others were picking them up and raising them as slaves. Pliny asked Trajan whether the law should consider such children free or slave. The emperor responded that, if such former foundlings could prove that their birth parents had been free persons, they were to regain their liberty without having to repay their masters for the expense of rearing them. In his letter Pliny also mentioned that the Greek language employed a special term, *threptos*, for such abandoned babies reared in the homes of strangers.[10]

7. Aristophanes, *Nubes*, vv. 518–35.   8. Plato, *Theaetetus*, 160E–161A.
9. Plutarch, *Lycurgus*, 16.   10. Pliny the Younger, *Epistulae*, 10.65–66.

From the reign of Marcus Aurelius (160–180), a detailed list of spe-cial taxes and levies survives from the immense province of Egypt, a list kept current by one of the imperial financial bureaus, the *Idiologos*. This list included two regulations that required that provincials who adopted abandoned babies leave a quarter of their estates at their death to the office of the *Idiologos*. The provincial government did not en-force this levy as a penalty for adoption, but rather as a method to en-sure that the *Idiologos* did not lose revenue because of such adoptions. In Egypt, when a provincial died without heirs, the *Idiologos* had tradi-tionally claimed a fourth of his estate. Apparently, enough couples without children were adopting abandoned infants that it would have reduced the revenues from this source if the bureau had not intro-duced these new rules.[11]

In addition to such literary and documentary sources, archaeolo-gists have discovered many inscriptions that mention *threptoi*. The Ital-ian scholar Theresa Nani catalogued 230 such inscriptions, primarily from the Greek-speaking provinces of the Roman Empire. According to Nani's careful analysis, some of those who commissioned these in-scriptions had purchased very young children or had taken them as ba-bies from slave mothers already in their possession. Nani also found, however, that many of the *threptoi* had in fact been exposed and subse-quently rescued.[12]

The evidence we have considered so far clearly shows that the an-cients abandoned their children, and that by the second century A.D. they were exposing a significant number of children, at least in Bithy-nia and Egypt. But how many of the babies abandoned actually died and how many survived? In *Daphnis and Chloe*, Daphnis's father expect-ed that abandoning his infant boy would result in his death.[13] When Plato and Aristotle recommended that the state should require parents to expose deformed babies, they wanted to eliminate these children.[14] We have seen from the many inscriptions, however, that a significant number of abandoned children were in fact discovered and taken in by

11. *BGU* V, 1210. See the commentary by Maroi, "Intorno all' adozione," pp. 378–406.
12. Nani, "Threptoi," pp. 60–63.
13. *Daphnis and Chloe*, 4.24.
14. Plato, *Respublica*, 460C; Aristotle, *Politica*, 1335b.

others.[15] Whether an exposed infant was likely to live or die depended on where the natural parents left the child. When in the *Republic* Plato wanted to dispose of deformed infants, he stipulated that they should be left in hidden, secret places.[16] When Daphnis's father abandoned his infant to die, he left him in a deep oak grove.[17] On the other hand, parents who wanted their babies to live left them along roads or in other heavily traveled places. According to the rules of the *Idiologos,* Egyptian parents were abandoning infants at the town refuse heap, a place that many people visited everyday.[18]

Among those abandoned children who were rescued many were raised as slaves. The author of the early Christian apocalyptic text *The Shepherd of Hermes* revealed that he had begun his life as a *threptos* slave.[19] Among the 230 inscriptions collected by Nani, the overwhelming majority refer to children raised as slaves. Only eleven of the 230 commemorate free *threptoi,* that is, children who had been legally adopted.[20] On the other hand, the evidence from the Egyptian *Idiologos* indicated that in that province at least many people who rescued exposed infants chose to raise them as free heirs.[21]

In the final analysis, the ancient sources do not permit us to establish what percentage of abandoned children survived or how many of these ended up as slaves. In the same way, the surviving evidence does not provide enough information to know why most ancient Greeks and Romans exposed their offspring. Although some literary sources mention reasons for abandonment—deformity in the baby, too many children, lack of money, the unmarried status of the mother—the many inscriptions referring to *threptoi* provide no such information. As a result, historians have been unable to establish a primary reason for the widespread practice of infant exposure in the ancient world.

The early Christian writers strongly condemned the practice of infant abandonment, no matter what reasons parents might allege. In

---

15. Nani, "Threptoi," pp. 50–58.   16. Plato, *Respublica,* 460C.
17. *Daphnis and Chloe,* 1.3 and 4.24.
18. Boswell, *Kindness,* pp. 110–11; Maroi, "Intorno all' adozione," pp. 392–94.
19. *Shepherd of Hermes,* 1.1–3.
20. Nani, "Threptoi," pp. 60–63, and notes 6, 7, and 8.
21. Maroi, "Intorno all' adozione," pp. 377–79.

expressing their opposition to exposure, Christian authors also offered additional information on the fate of abandoned children. To demonstrate Christians' respect for human life, the second-century apologist Athenagoras claimed that the followers of Christ avoided gladiatorial games, did not attend executions, refused to have abortions, and never abandoned their infants. Athenagoras categorically condemned exposure as the murder of children.[22]

About 160 A.D. the Christian philosopher Justin Martyr asserted that the faithful had been taught never to abandon their children. Justin demonstrated the evil of exposure and the general corruption of pagan Roman society by describing men who abandoned their infants and then later in life unknowingly fornicated with these same children when they visited local brothels.[23] Although it is impossible to say how often such incest in fact took place, Justin's statements provide additional testimony to the widespread practice of exposure and they also allude to one of the reasons why people were willing to assume the expense and labor of raising abandoned children. They would be able eventually to employ these children as prostitutes or sell them to others who already owned brothels. Justin claimed that such evil businessmen were willing to purchase both boys and girls to work in their sordid establishments.[24]

At the beginning of the third century, Clement of Alexandria also condemned pagan society for its many vices. He described wealthy women who, on the one hand, rescued baby birds that had fallen from their nests, but, on the other hand, who exposed their own children and those born to members of their household.[25] Echoing Justin, Clement described fathers who frequently abandoned their offspring, fathers whose lustful ways subsequently led them unknowingly to commit incest with their own children in the brothels of the Egyptian capital.[26]

Following the teachings of these early Christian writers, the fourth-century bishop Basil of Cappadocia also condemned exposure. Using animal imagery to illustrate his views, he compared those who aban-

22. Athenagoras, *Legatio*, 35.1.
24. Ibid., 27.
26. Ibid., 3.3 (21.1–22.2) [p. 249].
23. Justin, *Apologia (Prima)*, 27.
25. Clement, *Paedagogus*, 3.4 (30) [p. 253].

doned their offspring to eagles, heartless birds that expelled one of their hatchlings to concentrate their attentions on the other baby. The eagles were unjust, unlike the *phenai*, birds that rescued the rejected eaglets and raised them with their own young. In this essay, Basil stressed that the poor abandoned their babies because of their inability to provide for their children, while the rich, imitating the eagles, did so because of their desire to avoid splitting their property into too many shares.[27]

In the ancient world, Christians were not the only group to condemn exposure. As early as the fourth century B.C., Aristotle mentioned Greek communities where the *polis* government forbad abandonment as a method of population control.[28] Gradually, Stoic philosophers came to oppose exposing infants. Teaching Stoic philosophy at Rome in the reign of Nero (54–68 A.D.), Musonius Rufus censured the rich who refused to raise all their children in order to guarantee more wealth for their firstborn.[29] Teachers like Musonius might have influenced later Christian writers such as Basil of Caesarea, who also criticized the rich for such behavior. With regard to many questions of morality, Christians propounded views that the Stoics and other philosophical and religious groups also upheld, a convergence that facilitated the ultimate victory of the new religion in the cities of the Mediterranean.

BYZANTINE LEGISLATION

As we saw in Chapter Three, the Christian emperors of the fourth century began to construct the New Jerusalem by supporting orphanages and by altering the laws governing guardianship. As part of this program to restructure society, they also set in place a program to discourage the abandonment of infants, a program that may have been more successful in rescuing babies than the laws they enacted to regulate the behavior of guardians.

In 315, even before he moved the imperial capital to Byzantium, the

27. Basil, *Homiliae in hexaemeron, sermo* 8.6 (pp. 458–60).
28. Aristotle, *Politica*, 1335b.
29. Regarding Musonius Rufus, see Cameron, "Exposure," pp. 109–11.

first Christian emperor, Constantine, ordered the praetorian prefect Ablavius to make payments both from the regular treasury and from the revenues of the *res privata* (the private estates of the emperor) to any parents who could not afford to raise their children. In the law Constantine stated explicitly that he wished to prevent parents from killing their children *(parricidium)*, an expression that included murder in general, but given the scope of the problem implied by the law, the term in this context referred primarily to exposing infants.[30] As we saw, Athenagoras had not shrunk from labeling abandonment as murder, a view that the first Christian emperor apparently shared.[31] Constantine's law applied only to Italy, but in 322 he issued a similar directive for the province of Africa.[32]

It is unclear whether this welfare program for families ever applied to the whole empire. We have no indication that Eastern governors ever received similar orders, nor do we have any evidence that such a program was functioning in the East during the reigns of later emperors. The many and varied documents issued by the emperor Justinian (527–565) contain no mention of such payments. Moreover, no sources from later Byzantine centuries refer to such a comprehensive assistance plan. Apparently, Constantine's system proved too expensive or too difficult to monitor since it seems to have ceased functioning within a few years of its inception. It clearly demonstrates, however, that the first Christian emperor desired to stop the practice of exposure and that he recognized that economic factors played a key role in the decision of many parents to abandon their offspring.

One should also notice that Constantine did not forbid exposure. Enforcing such an order would have proved to be an extremely difficult policing problem.[33] It is also possible that Constantine did not wish to jeopardize his popularity or that of his new religion by trying to eradicate such a deeply rooted practice, an attempt that would have involved tracking down and punishing many poor persons who could not afford to feed and clothe all their children.

In 331, Constantine adopted another method. Rather than the ex-

---

30. *CodTheo*, 11.27.1 (anno 315).
32. *CodTheo*, 11.27.2 (anno 322).

31. Athenagoras, *Legatio*, 35.1.
33. Hunger, *Reich*, pp. 146–47.

pensive aid program he had initiated in 315, the emperor decided to
break with Trajan's ruling regarding the legal status of a *threptos* (that
is, whether a former foundling was free or slave). As we saw above,
Trajan declared that a *threptos*'s liberty depended on whether his natural parents were free, not on the will of the person who had found and
reared him.[34] Constantine's new law permitted the person who took in
the foundling to raise that child in any way he chose, either to adopt
him as a free person or to hold him as a slave. The birth parents would
no longer have any right to the *threptos* or have any effect on the child's
status.[35] Had Daphnis and Chloe lived after 331 (and had their foster
parents not been slaves), their adopting fathers, Lamo and Dryas,
could have blocked their return to their aristocratic birth parents in
Mitylene.[36]

Why did Constantine initiate this change? At least one scholar has
suggested that, in the spirit of his predecessor Diocletian, the first
Christian emperor wanted to establish quickly and securely the family
identity of these *threptoi* for taxing purposes and military recruit-
ment.[37] Other researchers, however, have maintained that Constantine
framed this law to discourage abandonment.[38] Under the new rule, a
father who abandoned his own child or forced one of his slaves to expose his child would lose any future claim to the abandoned person if
someone happened to find the baby and raised it to maturity. Moreover, the law rewarded those who were willing to take in abandoned
children by giving them a clear right to authority over these foundlings
with no fear of later claims by the birth parents. Thus, Constantine's
law both penalized those who abandoned babies and rewarded those
who accepted such babies into their households, and it did so at no
cost to the state. On the other hand, it may well have encouraged an
increase of enslaved *theptoi*, although it is impossible to attain any statistical evidence of this.

34. Pliny the Younger, *Epistulae*, 10.66.

35. *CodTheo*, 5.9.1 (anno 331).

36. Since Lamo and Dryas were the slaves of the Mytilenean aristocrats, Dionyso-
phanes and Megakles, they had no legal rights to use against their masters. See *Daphnis and
Chloe*, 4.33–40.

37. Boswell, *Kindness*, pp. 71–72.

38. Hunger, *Reich*, pp. 146–47.

Subsequent emperors renewed Constantine's law with a few minor changes. In 374 Valentinian I and Valens rephrased Constantine's original decree in such a way as to leave no doubt that they intended the law to discourage parents or masters of slaves from abandoning infants born in their power.[39] In 412 the emperor Theodosius II added a requirement that the people who took in abandoned babies should register this action with the local bishops to ensure their rights over the children.[40]

The innovative emperor Justinian completely revised the laws regarding exposed infants for a second time. In 529 he issued an edict that retained Constantine's rule that parents or slave owners who exposed infants of their household lost any claim to them, but Justinian denied that the persons who took in foundlings had a right to enslave such children. As Justinian conceived of the issue, these people should not be allowed to overshadow the virtue they had displayed in rescuing the *threptoi* by the heartless act of enslaving them.[41]

In another law issued in 541, Justinian stressed that those who exposed their infants even in public places such as churches committed murders.[42] Moreover, the final version of the *Digest*, Justinian's vast summary of earlier treatises on the Roman law, cited the third-century jurist Paulus as having classified exposure as a form of murder. This passage probably represents an interpolation by Justinian's editors; if not, it was surely a minority opinion that Roman courts did not enforce before the sixth century.[43]

From the time of Justinian, however, it seems clear that the government now classed abandonment with other serious crimes. A later Byzantine legal manual, the early-tenth-century *Epanagoge Aucta*, placed Paulus's definition of abandonment as murder at the head of its title on abandonment, an indication that judges were to consider this principle first when dealing with cases of infant exposure. The *Synopsis Basilicorum*, the widely disseminated legal handbook of the tenth century, also defined abandonment as murder.[44]

39. *JCod*, 8.51.2 (anno 374).   40. *CodTheo*, 5.9.2 (anno 412).

41. *JCod*, 8.51.3 (anno 529).   42. *JNov*, 153 (anno 541).

43. *Dig*, 25.3.4.

44. *Epanagoge aucta*, 47.1; *SynBas*, N. 3 (p. 441). For the popularity of the *SynBas*, see *ODB*, 3: 1995.

The legal sources thus reveal that the Byzantine emperors pursued a consistent policy to discourage exposing infants and that by the sixth century they condemned the practice as murder. It is more difficult to establish the effectiveness of this policy in preventing infant abandonment. A treatise written by Gregory of Nyssa in the late fourth century still considered exposure a common cause of death among infants of Asia Minor.[45] Moreover, the repeated legislation to stop abandonment from the time of Constantine to that of Justinian provides additional evidence that parents continued to expose babies. Finally, Justinian's novel of 541 revealed that people in Thessalonike were regularly abandoning infants in the churches of the city, a practice that the emperor condemned as worse than barbaric.[46] After the sixth century, however, the sources rarely mentioned abandoned infants directly. One should consider, though, that an eighth-century hagiographical text described how Anthousa, the daughter of the emperor Constantine V, searched for children exposed in the streets of Constantinople. Moreover, the eleventh-century *Peira* included two legal opinions regarding the abandonment of female babies, opinions that assumed that exposing girl infants was not rare.[47]

Beyond these explicit references to abandoned infants, there have survived a number of sources that mention programs established by local churches and especially by monasteries to care for abandoned infants—additional proof that abandonment continued throughout the Byzantine period. These passages are especially valuable in supplementing the lack of information regarding exposure in the years after 600. We shall present this evidence not only to confirm that abandonment continued throughout Byzantine times, but also to explore some of the institutions the Christian Church evolved to provide care for the victims of exposure.

CHRISTIANITY AND INSTITUTIONAL CARE

Justinian's Novel 153, issued in 541, reveals a basic shift in the practice of abandonment. Whereas the ancient Greeks and Romans had

---

45. Gregory of Nyssa, *De infantibus qui praemature abripiuntur ad Hierium*, PG, 46: 161–68.
46. *JNov*, 153 (anno 541).
47. *Menologium Basilii Porphyrogeniti*, PG, 117: 409; *Peira*, 49.7 and 8 (*JGR*, 4: 200).

exposed children along roads, or in the case of Egypt, near city dumps, where people might find them, the people of Byzantine Thessalonike were leaving their unwanted offspring in or near Christian churches. As a result of Christianity's triumph in the eastern Mediterranean and its claim to be the protector of orphans, people now considered churches as the most suitable places to leave unwanted infants. Churches offered the spiritual protection of Christ and the saints. Moreover, since Theodosius II's law of 412 required those who were willing to take in foundlings to register the infants with the local bishop, abandoning babies in churches made this administrative procedure easier for the finders.[48] In addition, as we saw in Chapter Five, Christian bishops had been developing institutions to receive orphans and provide them with an education. These orphan schools could also offer shelter and sustenance to abandoned children. A careful reading of two hagiographical texts will show examples of this.

When only a boy of three, Saint Euthymios lost his father circa 400. As we saw in Chapter Five, neither Euthymios's mother nor his uncle wanted to care for the boy. Instead, they convinced the bishop of Melitene to receive Euthymios and place him in the episcopal school for his education.[49] A second case comes from sixth-century Paphlagonia. Saint Alypios lost his father before he reached age three. His mother did not want to marry a second husband to provide for little Alypios, but desired instead to join a monastic community. Knowing that God was the best guardian of orphans, she dedicated Alypios to God, like a second Samuel, and placed the boy in the arms of Theodore, bishop of Paphlagonian Adrianople.[50]

The mothers of both Euthymios and Alypios were in fact "abandoning" their young children, but in a safe manner. By dedicating them to God and leaving them with the local bishop, they avoided a serious sin by committing the virtuous act of dedicating their children to God's Church, a good work that in later years the Christians of the medieval Latin West would call "oblation." In fact, when the author of Alypios's *vita* compared the little saint to the Old Testament Samuel, he was em-

48. *CodTheo*, 5.9.2 (anno 412).   49. *Vita Euthymii*, pp. 10–11.
50. *Vita Alypii*, 2–7 (pp. 148–52).

ploying the same biblical allusion Latin texts would use to describe oblates in Western monasteries.[51]

Although the *Vita Sancti Alypii* described Bishop Theodore as nursing the young Alypios with spiritual milk, the narrative stressed that the boy had already been weaned; it is also unlikely that the three-year-old Euthymios still fed at the breast.[52] These two examples therefore provide no evidence that bishops were able to take in infants who still required breast-feeding. Sixth-century sources do, however, refer to charitable institutions called *brephotropheia,* a term derived from the Greek word *brephos* (infant). To care for such *brephe,* these institutions surely had to have maintained some system to find nursing mothers.

Justinian frequently listed these *brephotropheia* with other types of philanthropic institutions. His laws referred to *brephotropheia* in provincial cities where they were under the authority of the local bishop, and in the capital where the patriarch had some supervisory power over them.[53] In listing officials of local churches who enjoyed clerical privileges, Justinian placed the directors of infant asylums ahead of hospital and hospice managers.[54] When in 536 Patriarch Menas summoned a synod of Constantinopolitan clergy, he included a priest named Anastasios who was connected with a *brephotropheion* in the capital.[55]

These sixth-century *brephotropheia* were among the many philanthropic institutions—*euageis oikoi* in the terminology of Justinian's novels—that the Christian churches of the empire supported and supervised. Some were directly under the bishop and were probably closely connected to the orphan schools we described in Chapter Five. Others had private endowments supervised by their own directors, but over these too the local bishop exercised some authority.[56] What differentiated the work of these *brephotropheia* from orphan asylums, stud-

---

51. Boswell, *Kindness,* pp. 228–31.

52. *Vita Alypii,* 3 (p. 149); cf. *Vita Euthymii,* pp. 10–11.

53. *JNov,* 7, refers to *brephotropheia* in the provinces; *JNov,* 43 (anno 536), refers to those in Constantinople. *JNov,* 120 (anno 544), guaranteed the local bishops' rights to supervise all charitable foundations within their dioceses, even those with endowments independent of the local church.

54. *JCod,* 1.3.0: "De episcopis et clericis et orphanotrophis et brephotrophis et xenodochis. . . ."

55. *ACO,* 3: 128–29.

56. *JNov* 120.6 (anno 544).

ied in Chapter Five, would have been the payment and supervision of wet nurses. Probably, in smaller towns, bishops organized *brephotropheia* as departments of a larger orphan school as Apokaukos apparently did in thirteenth-century Naupaktos.[57]

After the sixth century, these *brephotropheia* vanish from the records of Byzantium. Neither Leo III nor the Macedonian emperors Basil I and Leo VI referred to them in their legislation. Moreover, the *vita* of Saint Anthousa implies that the sixth-century *brephotropheia* were no longer functioning in eighth-century Constantinople.

According to this short hagiographical text, Anthousa, the daughter of the emperor Constantine V, refused to marry and devoted her life to Christian *philanthropia*. She offered money to repair churches and monasteries, she ransomed prisoners of war, and she rescued orphans from the streets of Constantinople. In the words of the *vita:*

She [Anthousa] became the mother of many orphans for she gathered up the children thrown away [*riptoumena*], fed them, and educated them. Those who died she sent to God, and those who lived she enrolled in the old-age homes [*gerokomeia*].[58]

This account no doubt referred to exposed infants. *Ripto* was a standard verb used since classical times to describe exposing an infant.[59] That some of these children died also indicates that they were still babies since infants suffered a high death rate when they were abandoned before they were weaned.[60]

This brief *vita* made no mention of existing *brephotropheia* to which Anthousa could entrust the infants she saved. Apparently, the sixth-century foundling homes were no longer functioning. The emperor's daughter had to initiate some sort of new program to take care of an increase of foundlings, perhaps due to the many plagues that befell Constantinople during these years or to the hardships of wars. Unfortunately, her *vita* does not explain how Anthousa organized her

---

57. See below, note 64.

58. *Menologium Basilii Porphyrogeniti*, PG, 117: 409.

59. E.g., the fourth-century *Vita Macrinae*, 26 (p. 232): (Makrina) ἃς ἐν τῷ τῆς σιτοδείας καιρῷ κατὰ τὰς ὁδοὺς ἐρριμμένας ἀνελομένη ἐτιθηνήσατό τε καὶ ἀνεθρέψατο. . . .

60. Gavitt, *Charity*, pp. 216–26.

foundling program. Since she eventually became a nun, she might have placed the babies in the care of women's monasteries.[61]

Why Anthousa enrolled the children in the old-age homes is puzzling. Perhaps she enrolled them so that, when they grew older, they could assist the elderly in these *gerokomeia*. Three centuries later, in 1116, Anna Komnena depicted the many different philanthropic institutions that formed part of the Orphanotropheion in Constantinople. In addition to the orphan school, Anna mentioned a residence for the poor and facilities for aged and maimed persons. Here Anna described an old woman helped by a young person, a blind person by one who could see, and a handicapped man by one in good health.[62] It seems reasonable to assume that in a similar fashion Anthousa assigned her former foundlings to assist the invalids in the *gerokomeia* of eighth-century Constantinople.

Anna Komnena's description of the twelfth-century Orphanotropheion, an institution we will study in detail in Chapters Seven and Eight, also includes the only explicit reference to wet nurses in a Byzantine asylum for abandoned children. As an example of the mutual aid given and received by the residents of the great Orphanage, she mentioned not only the crippled led by the healthy and the old served by the young, but also babies nursed by other mothers.[63] By 1100, therefore, the Orphanotropheion of the capital included a section that provided wet nurses for abandoned babies.

The thirteenth-century correspondence of John Apokaukos provides another example of an episcopal orphanage that occasionally admitted infants. As we saw in Chapter Five, Apokaukos, bishop of Naupaktos, accepted the responsibility for one of his favorite orphans, John the Thief, even before the boy was born. While pregnant with John, the mother had asked Apokaukos to take care of her baby, if it were a boy. As in the case of the sixth-century Alypios, John's mother entrusted her infant to the local bishop and to the service of the local church instead of abandoning him. Bishop Apokaukos stated that he

61. *Menologium Basilii Prophyrogeniti*, PG, 117: 409.
62. Anna Komnena, *Alexiad*, 15.7.6 (3: 216).
63. Ibid.

had taken John, not when the boy had reached the age of two or three, apparently the usual age for entering the church orphanage, but indeed from the womb. Apokaukos provided baby John with special care which naturally included finding him a wet nurse.[64]

These brief accounts of infant care provided by episcopal schools such as the one that received Saint Alypios or the one at Naupaktos that took in the infant John and the scattered references to *brephotropheia* in Constantinople are extremely scarce as well as being spread over many centuries. There exists, however, additional evidence of institutional care for abandoned babies provided by the Christian Church. Just as in the case of older orphans, so too with regard to foundlings, monastic communities supplemented the assistance offered by the bishops. As early as the late fourth century evidence has survived that monks and nuns accepted abandoned babies.

In writing the *vita* of his sister, Makrina, Gregory of Nyssa closed his narrative with a moving account of Makrina's death in the company of her nuns. Besides the cries of the women in her monastery, Gregory heard the laments of those whom Makrina had taken in, the former infants abandoned along the roads of Cappadocia during time of famine. Makrina and her nuns had accepted these babies, nursed them, and raised them through their formative years. Gregory's emotional account implied that all of these former foundlings chose to remain in Makrina's community as nuns. If this statement is accurate, then Makrina received only girl babies at her monastery.[65]

The *vita* of Saint Makrina stated that the nuns had nursed the babies. To have accomplished this, the monastery needed to find nursing mothers outside the ascetic community to breast-feed the infants. An early fourth-century *vita* recounted how Saint Febronia, while still an infant, lost her parents. Febronia's aunt, a monastic superior, received the infant at her Syrian monastery, but the abbess had to find a nursing mother who was willing to accept Febronia and feed her at the breast until the little girl was two years old.[66] Febronia was not a foundling,

64. Apokaukos, *Epistolai*, ep. 100 (pp. 150–52).
65. *Vita Macrinae*, 26 (p. 232).
66. *Vita Febroniae*, pp. 17–18.

but Makrina's monastery in Cappadocia no doubt used a system similar to that employed by Febronia's aunt to locate women willing to nourish abandoned babies.

According to a fifth-century story about the Egyptian abbot Gelasios, his monastery had received at least one child described as a *threptos*. As Theresa Nani has shown, *threptos* usually referred to an infant, abandoned by his or her parents, who was subsequently found and nursed in the house of another. It is probable, therefore, that Gelasios's monastery had secured a wet nurse for this boy when he had first come to the community, although the *vita* does not state this explicitly.[67]

From sixth-century Antioch comes more explicit evidence that even monasteries for men took in exposed infants and found wet nurses for them. According to his *vita*, Saint Symeon the Younger once took mercy on a common criminal and prayed for his deliverance from prison because that otherwise sinful man had carried out several acts of mercy. In performing one of his virtuous acts, this criminal had rescued a baby abandoned by its mother and had brought it to a nearby ascetic community of men, whom he hoped would find a wet nurse for the baby. The brothers were soon able to locate such a woman, and the criminal provided the money to pay the fee for her nursing the infant.[68] Although one modern scholar has suggested that this story indicates the presence of women at a male monastery, it would seem to prove instead that everyone around Antioch including career criminals knew that monasteries accepted abandoned babies for whom they were usually able to find wet nurses.[69]

As we saw in Chapter Four, George Chozebites was orphaned as a young boy and then ran away from his two uncle guardians to the tutelage of his brother Michael at a monastery near Jerusalem. Michael's community did not accept any children or youths, but the brother located a nearby monastery that did maintain some kind of a home for children, an institution that took in runaways such as

67. *Apophthegmata patrum, Apendix ad Palladium*, PG, 65: 148–49. See also Nani, "Threptoi," pp. 48–84, regarding *threptoi* in general.

68. *Vie de Syméon*, 165 (pp. 146–47).

69. Boswell, *Kindness*, p. 195.

George, but probably accepted abandoned children as well.[70] This story, however, includes no evidence that this monastery could find nursing mothers for infants. Scattered references from the *typika* of later
centuries, however, reveal that monasteries often accepted responsibility for infants who would have required breast feeding.

At the end of the eleventh century, the renowned ascetic Christodoulos wrote a *typikon* for the ancient monastery of Saint John on Patmos. In this rule, Christodoulos listed those whom he considered
members of the monastery. First, he wrote down the monastic officers
by name, then he added the ordinary monks who belonged to the
community, and finally he listed the children, "as many children as I
have raised for God from their infancy."[71] The monastery had accepted
the infants at a very young age and had nurtured and trained them to
join the ascetic community.

The *typikon* of the Mamas monastery, drafted in 1159, confirms that
such "monastic infants" might remain in ascetic communities all their
lives. The author of the Mamas Typikon, Athanasios, revealed that he
had grown up in the monastery of Christ Philanthropos. The brothers
of that community had taken him in while he was still an infant, raised
him, educated him, tonsured him as a monk, and finally selected him
to serve as *oikonomos* (steward) of the Philanthropos community, before he was chosen as superior of the Mamas monastery.[72] Another
twelfth-century *typikon* from Sicily stated that the founder of the
monastery of Saint Philip chose as his successor one of his own disciples named Blasios, who had been raised from his infancy in the
monastery.[73]

These later sources do not indicate precisely how these babies came
to the monasteries. We do not know whether their mothers or fathers
abandoned them in the ancient manner along roads where the monks
subsequently found the infants, or deposited them at monastery gates,

70. *Vita Georgii Chozebitae*, p. 99. The text here uses the word νεοκήπιον to describe
this facility for the children. I have found no other place where this term appears. Is it possible to translate this term as "kindergarten"?

71. *Typikon Christodoulos*, p. 83.

72. *Typikon Mamas*, p. 259. See also Thomas, *Private Foundations*, p. 212.

73. *Typikon of St. Philip*, pp. 200–201.

or left them in the public churches, as the sixth-century Thessalonians had done.[74] Or did their parents present these children to the monasteries as oblates, just as Saint Alypios's mother had handed him over to the bishop of Paphlagonian Adrianople?

A speech by the fourteenth-century patriarch Philotheos, however, recorded an example of a baby not presented to the monastery as an oblate, but abandoned outright. According to Philotheos, one of the women at the monastery of Saint Theodora in Thessalonike rescued a baby girl whose mother had exposed her. Unfortunately, Philotheos did not indicate where the baby had been found. The nun decided to nurture the infant in the hope that the girl would remain a servant of the monastery. So far in my research regarding orphan care, this is the only specific case I have found of infant abandonment in the later Byzantine period.[75]

In her excellent study concerning philanthropic institutions in Venetian Crete, however, Anastasia Papadia-Lala states that both Greek and Latin mothers frequently abandoned infants in front of private houses and churches in the suburbs of Candia. Since Crete under the Venetians enjoyed prosperity until the seventeenth century, the evidence of infant abandonment on the island is probably due to the survival of records, not to particularly harsh conditions.[76] The case of Crete suggests that families abandoned babies in Byzantine territory as well, but the records of these children have vanished save for Patriarch Philotheos's description of the little girl in Thessalonike.

Reviewing Byzantine sources has demonstrated, first, that parents continued to abandon infants after the reign of Constantine the Great. The sources do not provide enough information, however, to determine whether in fact Byzantine parents exposed infants to the elements in the same way the fathers of Daphnis and Chloe had left their offspring in the Lesbian countryside. Second, it has revealed that Christianity evolved new ways of caring for abandoned infants. As early as the fourth century monastic communities were accepting abandoned infants, finding them wet nurses, and assuming responsibility

74. *JNov,* 153 (anno 541).
75. Philotheos, *Encomium Gregorii Palamae,* PG, 151: 629.
76. Papadia-Lala, p. 116.

for their subsequent education. Local bishops provided similar services by taking in unwanted babies and eventually enrolling them in their orphan schools. There were no antecedents in the Greco-Roman world for such institutional care. Finally, this investigation has found that the practice of dedicating children to God substituted the virtuous act of oblation for the dreadful sin of abandonment.

As a result of these two innovations, that is, the development of institutional care in monasteries and episcopal schools and the Christian concept of oblation, we would expect to find a significant reduction in the number of babies exposed along highways and byways during the Byzantine centuries, and in fact, references to infants exposed to the elements in the ancient manner *are* rarer after 330 and almost disappear from the sources after 600.

With regard to the decrease in reference to abandoned children after 600, one should also bear in mind that demographic pressures eased during the seventh century. Whereas the populations of Byzantine provinces in Syria, Palestine, Egypt, and Asia Minor grew continually from the fourth through the mid-sixth century, they began to decline in these same areas sometime after 550. Archaeological evidence from western Asia Minor shows conclusively that Ephesus, Pergamon, Miletos, and even Nicaea decreased in population after 600. In this less densely populated world, it is likely that poor families felt less economic pressure to abandon their children than had their ancestors in the crowded towns of Justinian's reign.[77] The evidence from Venetian Crete, however, demonstrates that Christianity did not succeed in totally surpressing infant exposure.

ADOPTION

In the ancient world adoption provided the surest way to a happy life for abandoned babies. Lamo and Dryas had in effect adopted Daphnis and Chloe, and the second-century rules of the *Idiologos* described many Egyptians adopting exposed infants.[78] Most of the inscriptions

77. See Browning, *Byzantine Empire*, pp. 70–72. See also Lilie, *Byzantinische Reaktion*, pp. 201–54, who argues on the basis of grain supplies for Constantinople and of government-sponsored population migrations that both the urban and rural populations of the Byzantine Empire declined in the seventh century.

78. *Daphnis and Chloe*, 1.3–6; Maroi, "Intorno all' adozione," pp. 377–79.

catalogued by Theresa Nani refer to abandoned children who were raised as slaves, but a few mention *threptoi* adopted by their foster fathers.[79] According to Justinian's Novel 153, pious persons were assuming the care of abandoned babies in sixth-century Thessalonike. As we have seen above, in 529 Justinian had forbidden those who took in abandoned children to enslave them.[80] Since the emperor referred to those who took in the foundlings of Thessalonike as pious, they were probably adopting the abandoned infants, just as good people had been doing for centuries in the classical world.

Adoption therefore had provided families for many abandoned infants of the ancient world, and it no doubt continued to do so into the Byzantine era, but so far I have discovered very few specific cases after 330 of couples who adopted exposed infants. There are no such examples even in the huge corpus of Byzantine hagiographical texts. Because after circa 350 institutional care became an option in rescuing abandoned babies, it is possible that adoption gradually came to play a lesser role in providing nurture for such infants than it had in the pre-Christian empire.

Although sources after 330 do not mention adoptions of abandoned babies, they do occasionally describe situations where couples adopted orphaned children or children whose parents could no longer support them and sought adoption as a means of avoiding the pain of abandoning their offspring. Since adoption therefore formed a part of the Byzantine program to assist all types of orphans, including those who had been abandoned, it is useful to examine the few specific cases of adoptions during the Byzantine era concerning which we have sufficient information and also to discuss some of the changes which Byzantine emperors introduced into the Roman law rules regarding legal adoptions.

With regard to adoption and its legal ramifications concerning family rights and duties, the Byzantines accepted the Roman law, just as they accepted the basic Roman principles and definitions regarding guardianship *(tutela* and *cura)*. According to the Roman legal tradition, there were two distinct methods of adoption. Regarding children still in the power of a living father or grandfather, a magistrate could authorize their transfer to the authority of another family. For children who had lost their fathers or grandfathers (that is, who belonged to no family), only the emperor could approve an adoption.[81] Roman law strictly forbad the arrangement of an adoption by private contract.[82]

Roman law also distinguished strictly between guardianship and adoption. A person who served as tutor or curator could not adopt his ward for two reasons. First, by becoming the adopted father, the tutor would avoid the obligation of undergoing an audit concerning how he administered his ward's property; and second, by adopting the minor in his care the tutor gained total control over his ward's property and could abrogate the testament of the orphan child's natural father.[83]

These Roman law rules clearly had in mind orphans of the senatorial and equestrian class and of wealthy families in the provinces. They had not been framed to offer protection to exposed infants or to poor children who had lost their parents.[84]

Justinian reiterated these principles of Roman adoption in his legal textbook, the *Institutes,* as did many of the subsequent Roman law handbooks including the latest summary compiled by Harmenopoulos in the mid-fourteenth century.[85]

In practice, however, these rules seemed to have had little effect, at least in the case of humble people from the provinces. A papyrus doczument dated 335 preserves a contract from the Egyptian city of Oxyrhynchos. According to this text, a couple gave their two-year-old boy to another family to adopt as the new parents' legitimate heir. The adopting father pledged never to reject the boy or reduce him to slavery, and the natural parents promised never to reclaim him.[86] It is important to notice that contemporary imperial legislation regarding abandoned children dealt with the same two issues, namely, possible enslavement by the foster parents and eventual reclamation by the natural parents.[87]

81. *Inst,* 1.11.1.   82. Kurylowicz, "Adoption," pp. 61–75.
83. *Dig,* 1.7.17.   84. Crook, *Law and Life,* pp. 111–12.
85. *Inst,* 1.11; *SynBas,* Y.3 (pp. 537–39); *Epanagoge aucta,* 44 (pp. 187–89); *Prochiron auctum,* 26 (pp. 164–69); *Hexabiblos,* 2.8 (pp. 316–18).
86. *POxy,* 1206.
87. Cf. *CodTheo,* 5.9.1, and *JCod,* 8.51.3.

The document closed by indicating that the two parties had used the Roman law form of stipulation (oral question and response) before witnesses. Since Republican days, the Romans had required a verbal stipulation to make legally binding contracts. On the other hand, Roman law did not allow adoptions by contract. In 335 adoptions were supposed to take place in a formal ceremony before the emperor or a magistrate. Only forty-five years earlier Diocletian had expressly banned the use of private contracts to carry out adoptions.[88]

A papyrus dated 381 preserves another adoption contract, this one signed in the Egyptian city of Hermoupolis. According to this text, a woman named Aurelia Teus had borne two sons, Papnouthios and Silvanos. The older son, Papnouthios, had died, leaving an orphan boy ten years old. Aurelia Teus made this contract with her second son, Silvanos, a contract in which Silvanos promised to adopt his brother's boy, to manage all the orphan's property, and in addition to give by testament all his own property to the boy when he, Silvanos, died.[89] This contract not only ignored the rule against adoptions by contract, it also violated the Roman law principle that a guardian should never adopt his ward, because Silvanos, as paternal uncle, would have received the office of tutor unless the boy's grandfather, the husband of Aurelia Teus, were still alive.[90]

Another puzzling issue in this contract is the role of the grandmother, Aurelia Teus. Before the legislation of Justinian, grandmothers had no guardianship rights over their grandchildren, yet here the grandmother seems to have exercised great authority.[91] Perhaps she was acting as the representative of her husband, the still living grandfather, who would have had *patria potestas* over the boy. If the grandfather were still living, this might explain how the uncle, Silvanos, could adopt, since in such a situation he would not have been the tutor.

A third adoption contract, again from Oxyrhynchos, was signed in

88. *JCod,* 8.47.4 (anno 290).

89. *PLips,* 28.

90. For the rules of guardianship, see Chapter Four.

91. Even in the years before Constantine, grandmothers and other women relatives seem to have exercised greater powers over orphans in Egypt than in other provinces. See Taubenschlag, *Law of Greco-Roman Egypt,* pp. 157–59.

554, in the reign of Justinian. In this text a widowed mother handed over her nine-year-old daughter to a couple on condition that they adopt her as their own child. The widow stated explicitly that she could not afford to take care of her girl. The contract did not specifically require that the adopting couple establish the girl as their heir.[92]

In his thorough study of these contracts, Marek Kurylowicz has suggested that their principal purpose was to ensure that the adopted children attain the position of heirs in the testaments of their adopting parents.[93] Certainly the first two contracts emphasized the hereditary rights of the adopted children, but in the third contract the poor widow only wished to guarantee that the new family provide for her little daughter. In this case, the adoption probably substituted for abandonment.

In the same article, Kurylowicz claimed that these contract adoptions rested on *Volksrecht* at variance with traditional Roman law *(Reichsrecht)*.[94] Kurylowicz no doubt has correctly analyzed these Egyptian documents, but the custom of contract adoptions was far more widespread than he has indicated. Five centuries later, similar contracts were being used in southern Italy. Two Greek documents from former Byzantine territory near Naples, one dated 1146 and the other dated 1170, reveal that the adopting parents promised to accept the children as their legitimate heirs.[95] Of greater significance, a collection of legal forms from the mid-fourteenth century included two separate model contracts for adoptions, one for adopting parents without children and the other for adopting parents who already had legitimate heirs. In both these forms, the foster parents swore that they would establish the adopted child as a legitimate heir and that no relative would block the adopted child from entering upon his inheritance.[96]

The compiler of these forms intended them to serve as models for real contracts in Constantinople and the few remaining provinces of the empire.[97] By the fourteenth century, then, contract adoptions had moved from the outer provinces such as Egypt and southern Italy to

92. *POxy*, 1895.
93. Kurylowicz, "Adoption," p. 70.
94. Ibid., p. 75.
95. Christophilopoulos, pp. 81–82.
96. Sathas, 6: 628–31 (nos. 18 and 19).
97. Pieler, "Rechtsliteratur," p. 475.

the core of the Byzantine Empire. Apparently, without imperial legislation, contract adoption had become *Reichsrecht*.

It is possible that as early as the sixth century the official imperial law began to recognize these contracts. In 530, the emperor Justinian issued a novel that vastly streamlined the legal adoption procedure by eliminating the repeated emancipations and manumissions required to transfer a child from the *patria potestas* of one father to that of another. In place of these antiquated rituals from the Early Roman Republic, Justinian substituted simple statements of intention to adopt and of willingness to be adopted, statements pronounced before a magistrate and supported by written documentation.[98] These written declarations of intention might well have evolved into the contracts preserved in the fourteenth-century collection of forms, an evolution accelerated by the widespread use of contracts in Egypt and other provinces.

The fourteenth-century legal forms were clearly designed for adopting babies. The adoption formula for parents who already had legitimate children referred to the adopted child as an infant still in swaddling clothes, and the formula for childless mothers and fathers twice described the adoptee as resting in the arms of the new parents.[99] Such formulae could easily have been used for babies whose parents opted to offer them for adoption rather than to abandon them in the ancient manner.

The gradual acceptance of these contracts surely benefitted abandoned babies or destitute orphans since these agreements helped to ensure that blood relatives of the adopting parents did not dispossess the adopted children after the foster parents died. As we saw with regard to the rules of guardianship, the Roman law originally aimed at protecting property, not at securing a good home for orphans or foundlings. Thus, the ancient Roman rules governing adoption did not give adopted children unambiguous claims either on the property of their natural parents or on that of their adopting parents. In fact, some birth fathers had used adoption laws to unload extra children on wealthier families and thereby avoid having to provide their unwanted

---

98. *JCod*, 8.47.11 (anno 530). See commentary by Nardi, "Giustiniano," pp. 47–63.
99. Sathas, 6: 630 (no.19); and 6: 629 (no. 18).

legitimate offspring with shares of the family estate.[100] In effect, offering a child for adoption could serve as another form of abandonment for upper-class families.

To stop such legal, but according to Christian morality, unethical practices, Justinian decreed in 530 that adoption did not break the obligation of the natural parents to provide the legal share of an inheritance to the child whom they had surrendered to the care of others. On the other hand, Justinian ruled that adopting parents were under no obligation to leave any property to the children they adopted.[101] Although these changes probably assisted some children of wealthy families by discouraging their birth parents from handing them over to wealthier friends or patrons, they destroyed any rights adopted orphans or foundlings could claim over the property of their foster parents. When one contemplates the effects of Justinian's legislation, it is clear that the adoption contracts provided essential protection for children who, because of abandonment, had no knowledge of the birth parents other than that they had been desperately poor. Such children needed a confirmation of their inheritance rights regarding the property of their foster families.

In addition to introducing adoption contracts, Byzantine law made three other significant changes in the Roman rules of adoption, all three changes legislated by the late-ninth-century emperor Leo VI. The first innovation concerned women. Because Roman law had not permitted women of any age to exercise *patria potestas*, it did not allow them to adopt. Jurists supported this ban with a logical argument. Roman law naturally defined *patria potestas* as a male prerogative; since the law defined adoption as the creation of an artificial *patria patestas*, women could not assume that power.[102]

In the late third century, the emperor Diocletian mitigated this ban by allowing women who had lost their own children to adopt a foster child for their own comfort and support.[103] Although the great legisla-

---

100. *JCod*, 8.47.10 (anno 530).
101. Ibid.
102. The emperor Diocletian expressed this principle clearly and succinctly in his constitution of 291 (*JCod*, 8.47.5).
103. *JCod*, 8.47.5.

tor Justinian made many changes to the Roman rules of guardianship, he accepted the traditional Roman concept that women were normally unable to adopt. The emperor Leo VI, however, finally broke completely with Roman tradition by granting all women the capacity to adopt.[104] In his regulations, Leo included both married women who could not bear children and those who opted to remain virgins. Leo stated that his law would encourage women to remain virgins since they would be able to satisfy the high-minded desire for children without submitting to the sexual duties of marriage.[105]

Leo saw the principal social benefit of his legislation not in the help it offered to children—whether orphans, foundlings, or children of families with too many mouths to feed—but rather in the assistance it offered to childless women in their old age, since the adopted children would be able to assist their elderly benefactresses.[106]

It is interesting to notice that subsequent legal handbooks continued to repeat the traditional rule banning women from adopting without mentioning Leo's novel. Neither the tenth-century *Synopsis Basilicorum major* nor the thirteenth-century *Prochiron auctum* referred to Leo's changes, although both of these lengthy compendia included substantial sections on adoption. The fourteenth-century *Hexabiblos* did record Leo's novel, but it also included the ancient rule forbidding women to adopt.[107]

Although the legal handbooks clung tenaciously to the Roman principle of women's incapacity to adopt, Byzantine practice immediately recognized their power to become foster parents. A document of the Lavra monastery on Mount Athos, dated 952, recorded that a donor named David gave to this ascetic community property that he had received from his mother, property she in turn had taken as a dowry from the woman who had adopted her. Since this document was drawn up in 952, the adoption had taken place much earlier, probably around 900, while Leo VI was still governing the empire.[108]

---

104. *Inst*, 1.11.10; Leo VI, *Novel*, no. 27 (pp. 105–11).
105. Leo VI, *Novel*, no. 27 (p. 109).
106. Ibid., p. 107.
107. See Christophilopoulos, p. 83, and notes 3 and 4. See esp. *Hexabiblos*, 2.8.3 and 2.8.4.
108. *Actes de Lavra*, doc. 4 (1: 101–2).

Patriarchal documents from later centuries prove that women continued to exercise the right to adopt at least through the fourteenth century.[109]

None of these cases concerned abandoned infants or orphan boys or girls, but one source, the *Chronicle* of George Sphrantzes, did record the story of a woman, the mother of Nicholas Kabasilas, who adopted an orphan girl named Thomais. The little girl's relatives, presumably those who should have stepped forward as her guardians, brought her to Constantinople and entrusted her to the mother of Kabasilas. This saintly woman adopted Thomais, gave her a good education, and when she died left the girl half of her property. In this case, a woman adopted an orphan girl, in a sense abandoned by her guardians.[110]

There can be no doubt that by allowing women to adopt, Byzantine law expanded the pool of potential foster parents who could offer care and shelter to orphans of all categories including foundlings and other abandoned children. It also gave women a way to circumvent Byzantine guardianship laws that excluded all but mothers and grandmothers from the office of tutor. By adopting an orphan relative, a woman could become a de facto guardian.[111]

The second change in Byzantine law allowed eunuchs to adopt. Traditional Roman law banned *castrati* from adopting since, as the legal experts expressed it, the law should not grant a power, in this case, the power to have children, that nature denied. Justinian's *Institutes* stated that sterile persons could adopt, but true eunuchs—those who had been castrated—could not.[112] As in the case of women, so too with regard to eunuchs the great innovator was Leo VI. He broke with the old Roman law and allowed all eunuchs to adopt. Leo argued that many eunuchs had not chosen castration: it had been forced upon them. Why should they be punished twice, once by suffering castration and again by loosing forever the solace of children. As in the case of his novel concerning women, Leo wished to grant eunuchs the capacity to

---

109. For the document dated 1315–1319, see MM, 1: 17–18; for the document dated 1360, see MM, 1: 391–97.

110. *Chronicon Sphrantzae,* 18.1–3 (pp. 46–48).

111. See Chapter Four.

112. *Bas,* 33.1.59; *Inst,* 1.11.9.

adopt, not to provide for abandoned children or orphans, but to guarantee some care for the aging *castrati*.[113]

After several years of research, I have found no references to eunuchs who adopted orphans or foundlings. In the fourteenth century, John, the metropolitan of Herakleia in Pontos, assumed the care of his orphaned nephew, Nikephoros Gregoras. As we saw in Chapter Five, John did an excellent job in providing both spiritual and intellectual guidance for the ten-year-old Gregoras. In addition to being a bishop, John was a eunuch. Because he was Gregoras's uncle, however, he probably assumed care of John under guardianship laws rather than under adoption rules.[114]

The extant sources perhaps do provide one significant statement regarding eunuchs and the care of abandoned or orphaned children. The eleventh-century intellectual and eunuch Theophylaktos of Ohrid, wrote a fascinating tract defending *castrati* from the many calumnies spoken against them by society at large. In this tract Theophylaktos did not hesitate to criticize the laws of the most famous imperial legislators. As an example of the moral superiority of eunuchs, Theophylaktos described how they protected widows and often nurtured and educated orphans. According to Theophylaktos, eunuchs became "to such as these [widows and orphans] the words and deeds of philanthropy and of personal service." Theophilaktos compared these charitable eunuchs to those not castrated who often seized the property of orphans and sometimes even killed them; they violated virgins and widows and counted such deeds as triumphs.[115]

It is difficult to determine exactly what service Theophylaktos was referring to in this rhetorical passage. Were the eunuchs whom he described as caring for widows and orphans workers in philanthropic institutions? Or were they assuming personal responsibility for defenseless people, in the case of orphans adopting them or assuming guardianship duties on their behalf? Whatever the exact meaning, Theophylaktos chose the care of orphans as one of the most visible

113. Leo VI, *Novel*, no. 26 (pp. 101–3).

114. Gregoras, "Vie de Jean," pp. 53–55; John as eunuch, ibid., p. 34.

115. Theophylaktos of Ohrid, *Apologie de l'eunuchisme*, p. 317.

examples of eunuchs' virtuous behavior in the service of others. It is possible that Leo's novel had played a significant role in providing new opportunities for eunuchs to practice this conspicuous *philanthropia* on behalf of orphans by giving them the capacity to adopt such children.

The last legal change, sponsored by the emperor Leo VI, introduced a formal Christian blessing of adoption, performed in a church by a priest. This custom developed gradually. The first reference to it appeared in a late-ninth-century marginal comment to the text of the *Epanagoge*. This ceremony included solemn prayers and the imposition of the priest's hands.[116] A few years later, the emperor Leo VI recognized this ecclesiastical blessing as an essential part of adoption.[117] It is impossible to calculate what effect such a ceremony had on assisting orphans. To the extent that a religious ceremony inspired the foster parents to commit themselves more fully to the responsibilities of raising an adopted child, it obviously helped these children.

Besides legal adoptions or the formal assumption of guardianship, the Byzantines used less legally binding methods of providing care for abandoned or orphaned children, methods that did not raise the complicating issues of inheritance as both adoption and guardianship did. In his testament signed 570, Phoibammon from the Egyptian city of Antinoopolis provided a legacy consisting of an annual revenue for a boy whom he had raised with his own family. Phoibammon had received this child from the boy's mother, Epiphania, who had apparently been unable to care for him and entrusted him to a substantial citizen, namely, Phoibammon, who worked as a physician in Antinoopolis. This document makes no reference to adoption.[118]

A tenth-century story preserved by the monk Paul of Monembasia describes a virtuous *archon* (leading citizen) from the city of Larissa in northern Greece. This *archon* accepted into his household a poor girl of his community who had lost both her parents. He raised and educated her as his own daughter, and when she reached a sufficient age, he

---

116. Christophilopoulos, pp. 80–81, discusses the evidence regarding this ecclesiastical adoption ceremony.

117. Leo VI, *Novel*, no. 24 (pp. 93–95).

118. Maspero, no. 67151, l. 294.

married the orphan girl to his only son.[119] Earlier Roman law would have permitted a marriage between an adopted daughter and a legitimate son; the fourth-century *Apostolic Constitutions* even recommended that Christians assist orphan girls by adopting them and subsequently wedding them to their foster brothers.[120] Under the influence of increasingly strict Christian moral views, however, Leo VI forbad such practices.[121] It is therefore unlikely that this *archon* of the tenth century formally adopted the orphan girl; he probably kept her as a simple *threpte,* neither a slave nor a legitimate daughter, until she was old enough to become his daughter-in-law.

In his twelfth-century testament, which served also as a *typikon* for his monastery, Isaak Komnenos actually used the term *anathreptos,* derived from the ancient term *threptos,* to describe a child he had raised almost from the boy's infancy. This *threptos* was the nephew of one of Isaak's household officials. The *typikon* did not explain why Isaak had assumed responsibility for the child, but it did specify a legacy for the boy and the care he was to receive if Isaak died before the child reached twenty-four years of age (see Chapter Four regarding ages).[122]

The two biographies of the tenth-century monastic reformer Athanasios the Athonite *(Vita A* and *Vita B)* offer the most interesting example of an informal adoption. According to *Vita A,* Athanasios had already lost his father before he was born. His mother died a short while later while she was still nursing her baby. Athanasios was in a situation almost as desperate as an exposed infant.

A woman among the leading citizens of Trebizond, the city in which Athanasios was born, assumed care of the baby boy and, in the words of *Vita A,* she accepted him "with a mother's love." She also provided for his education. She raised Athanasios together with a number of other children who were apparently not her own. The young saint developed a close bond with one of these children, a girl who later left to marry a high official in Constantinople. Some years

---

119. *Récits de Paul,* tale 12 (pp. 96–98).

120. Leo VI, *Novel,* no. 24 (pp. 93–95); *Constitutiones Apostolorum,* 4.1.1 (2: 170).

121. Leo VI, *Novel,* no. 24 (pp. 93–95).

122. *Typikon Kosmosoteira,* no. 69 (pp. 52–53), no. 107 (p. 70), and no. 117 (p. 74).

later, this childhood companion of Athanasios helped him find a teacher when the saint came to the capital in search of a higher education.[123]

A careful reading of the two *vitae* gives the impression that the woman who rescued Athanasios had organized a kind of group home. She was apparently able to locate a wet nurse for Athanasios and to provide for other children as well. Perhaps she had founded a private orphanage or *brephotropheion* similar to the asylum that the wealthy woman, described by Patriarch Proklos, opened in fifth-century Constantinople, or the school that the local magnate maintained in the Peloponnesus during the tenth century.[124] The shorter *Vita B* depicted the woman of Trebizond as a wealthy citizen who had donned the monastic habit.[125] If in fact she had become an ascetic and had accepted the care of orphaned and abandoned children as part of her monastic vocation, she was pursuing an ancient calling of Anatolian monasticism, going back at least to the fourth century and the community of Makrina.

Having examined the Byzantine sources dealing with abandonment and adoption, let us return to some of the questions posed at the beginning of this chapter. First, did the Byzantine Empire make a concerted effort to stop abandonment? The answer to this question is clearly yes. Almost as soon as Constantine gained control of the Western half of the Roman Empire, he began a program to discourage abandonment, first through payments to poor families, and later by penalizing parents who exposed their babies by depriving these fathers and mothers of any future rights over these children. Subsequent emperors expanded Constantine's program until Justinian finally defined exposure as a form of murder.

Second, did the Byzantine Empire develop effective methods to assist foundlings and older abandoned children? Again the answer is yes. Both the bishops and monastic communities supported institutions that accepted infants, found them wet nurses, and later educated them

---

123. *Vitae duae antiquae, Vita A,* nos. 7–11 (pp. 5–8); *Vita B,* no. 2 (p. 128).
124. Proklos, *Homélie 26,* pp. 175–83; *Récits de Paul,* tale 9 (pp. 76–78).
125. *Vitae duae antiquae, Vita B,* nos. 2–3 (pp. 128–29).

in orphan schools. Hand in hand with these institutions, the Byzantine Church evolved the concept of oblation, which offered parents a far better alternative than exposure to solve the problem of unwanted babies. These two Christian institutions—*brephotropheia* and oblation—did not stop abandonment, but they significantly decreased the practice of exposure in the ancient fashion, that is, as it was portrayed in *Daphnis and Chloe.*

Third, can we demonstrate any link between abandonment and adoption? To this question the response is negative. No source after Justinian's Novel 153, from 541, refers to the adoption of abandoned babies. The Byzantines continued to practice adoption, and in fact made a number of changes in the Roman law to facilitate the adoption of poor children and orphans, changes that would have benefitted abandoned infants as well.[126] Perhaps no sources record the adoption of an abandoned infant because the Byzantine state and the Byzantine Church had been so successful in discouraging exposure. Parents who could not raise a child or who did not want to could place the baby in the local episcopal school or monastery as a gift to God, or they could try to locate persons willing and legally qualified to adopt their baby, a pool of people that was much larger after Leo VI allowed barren women, unmarried virgins, and even eunuchs to assume the care of unwanted children.

With regard to the frequency of adoptions, Byzantine sources provide absolutely no indication. As a result of this lack of information, it is also impossible to guess at how many of these adoptions involved abandoned infants or older orphan children. Chapter Nine shall return to this question in considering the frequency of all types of guardianship.

With regard to abandoned infants, the most striking innovation of Byzantine society was the establishment of Christian philanthropic institutions capable of accepting helpless infants and providing them with the nurture they needed in order to survive. Neither the ancient *polis,* nor the Greco-Roman temples, nor the agents of the pre-Con-

---

126. See Macrides, "Substitute Parents," pp. 1–9, esp. p. 3, where the author assumes that adoption was more important than welfare institutions in providing for orphans and children of destitute families.

stantinian imperial government supported any services such as those provided by Makrina's monastery in fourth-century Anatolia. One of the oldest of these orphanages and by far the most famous was Zotikos's Orphanotropheion in Constantinople. From its humble origins in the fourth century it grew into a powerful government agency, the directors of which sometimes controlled state policy. Since the Orphanotropheion became important not only as a philanthropic institution, but also as an educational center and as a major government bureau, it deserves detailed study in the following two chapters.

VII THE ORPHANOTROPHEION
ADMINISTRATION

 At the center of the Byzantine program to assist orphans stood the great Orphanotropheion of Constantinople, founded by Saint Zotikos probably during the reign of the emperor Constantius and still functioning nine hundred years later at the beginning of the fourteenth century. As the orphanage of the imperial city in a society that the capital dominated politically, economically, and culturally, it is not surprising that this philanthropic institution eclipsed all other orphan schools, whether those controlled by bishops or those attached to monasteries. It is surprising, however, that it also eclipsed all the other charitable institutions of the empire, including some of the large imperial hospitals of Constantinople. Its director, the *orphanotrophos,* came to supervise not only the Orphanage proper, but a wide range of philanthropic services, including an emergency grain supply of some sort for Constantinople.

The Orphanotropheion evolved into such a sprawling institution with such a complex administrative structure that I must devote two chapters to explain it adequately. This present chapter will examine the administrative structure of the institution and the duties of the orphanage director. The following chapter (Chapter Eight) will focus on the orphan school proper by presenting as much information as the sources reveal about its curriculum, its teachers, and its students.

Before beginning our survey, it will be useful to discuss briefly how Byzantine sources identified the Orphanage of Constantinople. The citizens of the Byzantine capital originally referred to the city's principal asylum for homeless children as the Orphanage of Zotikos, after its fourth-century founder. In many of their novels, however, the emperors of the fifth and sixth centuries identified the institution simply as the pious Orphanotropheion.[1] Sometime before 638, the emperor Herakleios issued the last decree that used the name Zotikos Orphanotropheion.[2]

Several decades earlier, the emperor Justin II had constructed a large church within the precincts of the Orphanotropheion, a church he dedicated to the apostles Peter and Paul.[3] Although thereafter most sources continued to call the orphan asylum the Orphanotropheion, a few texts began identifying the institution as that of Paul.[4] References to the apostle Peter seem to have fallen out of use, but occasionally the busts of both the apostles appeared on the lead seals used by *orphanotrophoi*.[5] Beginning with the twelfth century, however, Byzantine sources made more frequent use of the name Paul. For example, when Cyril Phileotes praised the emperor Alexios for his generous support of the orphanage, undoubtedly in the same location as the ancient Zotikos asylum for homeless children, he called the institution the Orphanotropheion of Paul. Moreover, Leo of Rhodes, a teacher at the Orphanage during the twelfth century, addressed a prayer to Saint Paul as the sole patron of the institution.[6]

PREEMINENCE

In studying the Orphanotropheion, one must first consider its preeminent position among all other philanthropic institutions of the empire and also the high rank that its directors enjoyed in both the church hierarchy and the state bureaucracy. The clearest evidence that Zotikos's Orphanage outranked all other charitable institutions comes from the imperial legislation of the fifth century.

1. *JCod*, 1.3.34 (35), identifies the Orphanage in Latin as *orphanotrophium; JNov*, 120.1, uses the Greek ὀρφανοτροφεῖον.

2. Novel 4 (Herakleios), RP, 5: 240.

3. Theophanes, 1: 244.

4. Genesios, 1.9 (pp. 8–9).

5. Zacos, nos. 1261 (anno 550–650) and no. 1268 (late seventh or early eighth century); Schlumberger, p. 380 (sixth century).

6. *Vie de Cyrille le Philéote*, 47.6 (p. 230); for Leo of Rhodes, see *Vaticanus Palatinus gr*, 92, fols. 145ᵛ and 207ᵛ.

As we learned in Chapter Three, Leo I issued a decree in 472 that granted the Orphanotropheion and all its properties and dependent agencies the same legal and fiscal privileges that then belonged to Hagia Sophia or would be given in the future to the patriarchal church of Constantinople.[7] At that time, no other philanthropic institution in the capital or the provinces enjoyed this status. Seventy years later Justinian conferred these same privileges on the Hospital of Saint Sampson, also one of the original charities of Christian Constantinople.[8] Thereafter, no emperor granted this status to any other philanthropic institution. When in the eleventh century Constantine IX established his vast Mangana palace and attached a hospital and *gerokomeion* (old-age home) to it, he never extended to these philanthropic foundations the privileges of Hagia Sophia, nor a century later did the emperor John II Komnenos grant such rights to his famous Pantokrator Xenon.[9]

At the beginning of the twelfth century, after her father Alexios I had refurbished the Orphanotropheion, Anna described the complex as a city within a city. Several decades later, Theodore Prodromos hailed the Orphanage as "Mount Sion," the citadel of the New Jerusalem. Byzantine rhetoricians frequently employed such biblical allusions, but in this speech Prodromos composed such a long and detailed metaphor that it is difficult to believe that he did not conceive of the Orphanotropheion as the premier symbol of the empire's spiritual superiority.[10]

The high status of the officials, both ecclesiastical and imperial, who directed Zotikos's Orphanage, also reflected the institution's importance. As early as 458, the *orphanotrophos* played an important part in the ecclesiastical politics of Constantinople. In that year Gennadios became bishop of the capital city with the support of Akakios, the *orphanotrophos*.[11] Thirteen years later Akakios himself ascended the patriarchal throne.[12]

7. *JCod*, 1.3.34 (35).

8. *JNov*, 131.15.

9. Miller, "Introduction to the 1997 Edition," *Birth*, pp. xix–xx.

10. Anna Komnena, *Alexiad*, 15.7.4 (3: 215); Prodromos, *Eisiterios* (PG, 133: 1271).

11. *Theodoros Anagnostes*, p. 106.

12. Evagrios, 2.11 (p. 63). Rodolphe Guilland has written the only study devoted to the *orphanotrophoi* of Constantinople; see Guilland, "Études," pp. 205–21.

Andrew of Crete, one of the most influential ecclesiastical figures of the Byzantine Dark Ages (seventh and eighth centuries), served for some time as the *orphanotrophos* of the Zotikos's foundation. Andrew was born in Damascus and entered religious life as a monk attached to the Church of the Resurrection in Jerusalem. Andrew first arrived in Constantinople as an envoy of the Jerusalem church to the new emperor Justinian II (685–695 and 705–711). On this visit, Andrew decided to stay in Constantinople. After he had passed some years living as a contemplative monk, the emperor Justinian had him ordained a deacon of Hagia Sophia. Shortly after that, Andrew took over the office of *orphanotrophos*. He managed the Orphanage with such skill that the emperor chose him as metropolitan of Gortyna on Crete. In this case, heading the Orphanotropheion served as a springboard to one of the most important bishoprics of the early eighth century.[13]

From the reign of Michael III (843–863) comes perhaps the most conclusive evidence that the Orphanage held the primary place of honor among philanthropic institutions. In describing the customs during the ninth century that commemorated Palm Sunday, *The Book of Ceremonies* assigned the *orphanotrophos* the leading role during a formal reception in the Triklinos, a palace throne room that had been built in the days of Justinian I. The ceremony began when the *orphanotrophos* entered the Triklinos, approached the emperor, and handed him a number of small crosses which the sovereign was to distribute to select officials. Thereupon, the *orphanotropos* left the throne room to return leading a procession that included the *sakellarios* (treasurer) of Hagia Sophia, the sacristan of the church of the Virgin at Blachernai, and six directors of the oldest hospitals of Constantinople together with the two demarchs of the capital.[14]

The *ordo* of this ceremony clearly illustrated the primacy of the *orphanotrophos* and the institution he supervised with respect to other philanthropic agencies, including the prestigious hospital of the emperor Theophilos and the ancient Sampson Xenon. Moreover, it linked the

---

13. *Vita Andreae*, pp. 171–75.

14. *De cerimoniis*, 1.41 (1: 160–62). Bury, "Ceremonial Book," pp. 419–27, argues that the section of the *Book of Ceremonies* describing the Palm Sunday procession dates from the reign of Michael III.

orphanotrophos not only with the other famous philanthropic institutions of the city, but with the ceremonial leaders of the capital's *demos* and with two churches, Hagia Sophia and the Blachernai church. Hagia Sophia functioned as the city's cathedral, and since the time of the Avar siege of 626 the Blachernai church had served as the repository of Constantinople's palladium, the robe of the Virgin. The Palm Sunday ceremony thereby emphasized the Orphanotropheion's prominent place among the urban institutions of Constantinople.[15] Since the ceremony occurred on Palm Sunday, it also reinforced the imagery of Constantinople as the New Jerusalem.

Evidence collected from lead seals used by successive *orphanotrophoi* confirms these literary sources. An eighth-century orphan director held the high court title of *patrikios,* a rank often associated with provincial *strategoi* (military governors).[16] Several *orphanotrophoi* of the ninth and tenth centuries received the rank of *protospatharios,* also an honor held by many *strategoi.*[17]

In the eleventh and twelfth centuries, key political figures often held the post of *orphanotrophos.* The eunuch John from Paphlagonia served as an advisor under the emperors Basil II and Romanos III and then became the chief decision maker in the government of his brother, Michael IV (1034–1041). As prime minister (mesazon), John also held the post of *orphanotrophos.*[18]

In the administration of Manuel I (1143–1180), Alexios Aristenos became one of the highest judicial officials of the empire *(dikaiodotes)* at the same time he supervised the Orphanage.[19] Before the fall of Constantinople to the soldiers of the Fourth Crusade, John Belissariotes

---

15. Miller, *Birth,* pp. 80–81, discusses the order of the hospital directors who participated in the ceremony. They approached the emperor in an order that reflected the prestige of the institutions that they supervised. Since the *orphanotrophos* preceded all other officials participating in the Palm Sunday commemoration, the institution he headed surely outranked all other philanthropic institutions of Constantinople. With regard to the Church of the Blachernai and the Virgin's Robe, see Janin, *Églises,* pp. 161–70, and Cameron, "Virgin's Robe," pp. 42–56.

16. Zacos, no. 2395.

17. Zacos, nos. 1795, 1841a, 1842b, and 3181.

18. For the biography of John the Orphanotrophos, see Janin, "Ministre," pp. 431–43. See also the vivid account in Psellos, *Chronographia,* 4.12–15 (1: 126–33).

19. Darrouzès, *Tornikès,* pp. 54–56. For the office of *dikaiodotes,* see *ODB,* 1: 624.

held the chief financial office of the state *(megas logariastes)*, also an important judicial office *(protasekretis)*, and served as *orphanotrophos*.[20] The directors of no other hospital, *gerokomeion*, or almshouse of Constantinople occupied high-level government positions such as these at the same time they were managing their philanthropic institutions.[21]

The evidence reviewed so far proves beyond a doubt the primacy of the Orphanotropheion among Byzantine charitable agencies during the centuries before 1204. It also enables us to identify another important *orphanotrophos*, Nikephoros, who occupied the patriarchal throne from 798 to 811. According to his biographer Ignatios, Nikephoros began his public career as an imperial official. He subsequently left his job and withdrew to a secluded hermitage to lead a life of prayer and study, but here he also gave freely to the poor and needy. His generosity won him such fame that the government of Constantine VI and Irene appointed him director of "the greatest *ptocheion* of Constantinople."[22]

In the light of the evidence presented above, it is now possible to identify this greatest *ptocheion* of the capital as the Orphanotropheion for the following reasons. First, *ptocheion* is a general expression for a wide range of philanthropic institutions. Several sources, in fact, referred to the leprosarium of Zotikos as a *ptocheion* and to the orphan director as a *ptochotrophos*, the name generally used for the head of a *ptocheion*.[23] Second, as our preceding discussion has shown, the Orphanotropheion outranked all charitable agencies in the capital. Byzantine sources reveal no other philanthropic institution that could possibly be described as "the greatest *ptocheion* of Constantinople." We can therefore safely place Nikephoros beside Andrew of Crete as another example of a man who directed the Orphanage before he moved on to high ecclesiastical office.

20. Choniates, *Orationes*, 1: 147 and 2: 159. For the offices, see *ODB, sub vocibus*.

21. Miller, *Birth*, p. 113, demonstrates that directors *(xenodochoi)* of some hospitals held honorary titles such as *spatharios* and *protospatharios*, but so far no evidence has been found that hospital directors held high government offices at the same time that they administered their philanthropic institutions.

22. *Vita Nicephori*, pp. 146–59, esp. p. 152: τοῦ μεγίστου πτωχείου τῶν κατὰ τὴν βασιλίδα ἐπιτροπεύειν προτροπῇ βιαίᾳ τῶν κρατούντων ἡ χάρις ἠξίωσε. . . .

23. The oldest extant version of the *Vita Zotici* (from the eleventh century) refers to the first Orphanage director as Ζωτικοῦ τοῦ πτωχοτρόφου (Aubineau, "Zoticos," p. 71). See also Philes, poem 43 (pp. 47–48).

ADMINISTRATION

The administrative history of the Orphanotropheion is difficult to reconstruct because no detailed document has survived that outlines its management structure and its staff organization. We have no sources regarding the Orphanotropheion that provide the wealth of information that the twelfth-century Pantokrator Typikon contains regarding the Pantokrator Xenon and its adjacent *gerokomeion*.[24] Nevertheless, it is possible to glean pieces of information from widely scattered sources to obtain some notion of how Constantinople's Orphanage was administered.

As we saw in Chapter Three, the Orphanotropheion no doubt began as one of the principal philanthropic agencies under the bishop of Constantinople. During Gennadios's tenure as patriarch (458–471), however, his *oikonomos*, Markianos, decentralized church administration by reorganizing most of the churches and all the prominent philanthropic establishments as independent institutions.[25] Thus, in the legislation of Leo I and Justinian, the Orphanotropheion appeared as an independent pious house responsible for its own property.[26]

In addition to the orphanage director, Justinian's Novel 120 (544) referred to *chartoularioi* attached to the Orphanotropheion, officials who approved major property decisions. For example, if the *orphanotrophos* decided to lease property, use property as security for a loan, or exchange property, the *chartoularioi* of the institution had to swear alongside him that these contracts would not harm the financial well-being of the Orphanage.[27] Such *chartoularioi* existed in many philanthropic institutions; they were in charge of keeping records and usually had some legal expertise as well.[28]

The ninth-century *Kletorologion of Philotheos* offers the most detailed outline of the Orphanage's administrative staff. Under the *orphanotrophos*, it listed, first, the *chartoularioi* of the house, that is, of the orphanage proper, and second, the *chartoularioi* of the Zotikos leprosarium. This list therefore indicated that the Orphanage was managed

24. Cf. *Typikon Pantokrator*, pp. 83–111.   25. *Theodoros Anagnostes*, p. 106.

26. *JCod*, 1.3.34 (35); *JNov*, 120.1; *JNov*, 131.15.   27. *JNov*, 120.5.

28. Miller, "Sampson Hospital," p. 126.

separately from the leprosarium.[29] Such a separation dated back at least to the sixth century, when Justin II allotted a substantial annual revenue to the Orphanage with the stipulation that a specific amount be transferred to a separate account for the leprosarium.[30]

After the two groups of *chartoularioi*, the *Kletorologion of Philotheos* listed the *arkarios*, a treasurer whose duties remain obscure, and finally the *kouratores*. In this context the term *kourator* does not refer to the guardians of older orphans (as does the cognate Latin *curator*), but rather to managers of specific properties belonging to the Orphanotropheion.[31]

A letter written by the monastic reformer Theodore of Stoudios in the early ninth century contains an interesting passage that possibly refers to a woman serving as a *chartoularios* in the Orphanotropheion. In the letter, addressed to the *orphanotrophos* Leo, Theodore referred to Leo's wife as the Lady Chartoularia.[32] Byzantine writers often addressed the wife of a Byzantine official with the feminine form of her husband's title; for example, a polite Byzantine might address the wife of a man who held the rank of *protonotarios* as *protonotarissa*. But writers less often used feminine forms of an office name such as *chartoularios*.[33] Moreover, as *orphanotrophos*, Leo no doubt held some honorary rank such as *spatharios* or *protospatharios*. Thus, Theodore should have addressed the *orphanotrophos*'s wife as *spatharia*, not as *chartoularia*. It is therefore possible that Theodore referred to Leo's wife as *chartoularia* because she had obtained some legal training and had at some time in the past worked as a *chartoularios*. Had she perhaps worked beside her husband in the Orphanage?[34]

All the extant sources agree that Zotikos founded his orphanage as

29. *Kletorologion of Philotheos*, p. 123.

30. Leo VI, *Novel*, pp. 377–78 ; cf. Aubineau, "Zoticos," chap. 12 (p. 82).

31. *Kletorologion of Philotheos*, p. 123.

32. Theodore of Stoudios, *Ep.* 29 (pp. 80–82), esp p. 82: Κυρία Χαρτουλαρέα.

33. See, e.g., Maria Kastorissa with the title of *patrikia* in the eleventh century (*Peira*, 17.19 [p. 67]) or Eudokia with the title of μεγάλη παπίαινα in the fourteenth century (MM, 1: 17). Although the *papias* had been an office in the tenth century, during the thirteenth century it had become an honorary title (*ODB*, 3: 1580).

34. Cf. Gavitt, *Charity*, p. 153. In this detailed study of the fifteenth-century Ospedale degli Innocenti in Florence, Gavitt found that one of the treasurers of the institution, a certain Bartolomeo, had a wife who was also employed in the orphanage as a supervisor of female volunteers who worked with the children.

an ecclesiastical organization. He himself served as a priest of Constantinople, as did Nikon, the orphanage director in 472.[35] Justinian's novels always classed the Orphanotropheion among the independent ecclesiastical foundations of the capital.[36] At the end of the seventh century, Andrew of Crete first became a deacon of Hagia Sophia before he received the office of orphanage director.[37] A hundred years later, during the patriarchate of Tarasios, the *orphanotrophos* was still closely linked to the church of Constantinople. According to his biographer, the future patriarch Nikephoros was supervising the Orphanage and its related welfare agencies at the same time he was managing a substantial part of the resources of Hagia Sophia. Nevertheless, the same *vita* stated that the emperors Constantine and Irene, not the patriarch, selected Nikephoros as *orphanotrophos*.[38] Although the Orphanotropheion was always considered an ecclesiastical institution, the emperors exercised considerable authority over it, as Nikephoros's appointment demonstrates.

According to the Legend of Saint Zotikos, Constantius had heavily endowed the Orphanotropheion early in its history.[39] The emperors Leo I, Justinian, and Herakleios had issued laws to regulate its operations.[40] Moreover, seals that date from the seventh, eighth, and ninth centuries prove that some *orphanotrophoi* held secular court titles of honor and thus enjoyed close ties to the imperial government. The orphan director Stephen from the late seventh century ranked as a *koubikoularios,* and the eighth-century Prokopios was a *hypatos* (honorary consul). The obverse of Stephen's seal, twin busts of Saints Peter and Paul, demonstrates that he headed the Orphanage of Constantinople.[41] There is little doubt that the other seals also belonged to directors of the ancient Zotikos Orphanotropheion.

Several years after the *orphanotrophos* Nikephoros had become pa-

---

35. For Zotikos, see Miller, "Zotikos," p. 372, and Aubineau, "Zoticos," pp. 92–95; for Nikon, see *JCod,* 1.3.34(35).

36. *JNov,* 120.1; *JNov,* 131.15.   37. *Vita Andreae,* p. 174.

38. *Vita Nicephori,* p. 152.

39. Aubineau, "Zoticos," no. 11 (pp. 80–82); Philostorgios, p. 225.

40. For Leo I, *JCod,* 1.3.31 (32) and 1.3.34 (35); for Justinian I, *JNov,* 120 and 131.15. For Herakleios, Novel 4 (RP, 5: 240).

41. Zacos, no. 1268 (Stephen) and no. 3171 (Prokopios).

triarch, the emperor Nikephoros (802–811) carried out some major re-organization that substantially increased the emperor's supervision of the Orphanage. According to the historian Theophanes, who disliked Emperor Nikephoros's financial policies, the newly crowned sovereign canceled tax exemptions that the Orphanage had enjoyed, probably by grant of his predecessors, Constantine and Irene. In addition, Nike-phoros placed the best properties belonging to the Orphanotropheion and other philanthropic houses under the control of officials managing the imperial estates.[42]

These measures as described by Theophanes would have substan-tially reduced the revenues of the Orphanage and endangered its sur-vival. The historian Genesios, however, mentioned the institution as still functioning a few years later at the close of Michael I's reign (811–813).[43] Instead of confiscating the Orphanage's estates, Nikephoros apparently changed the status of the Orphanotropheion by classifying it as a state institution. As a result, the *orphanotrophos* appeared on a list of state officials drawn up in 842–843.[44] Thereafter, subsequent lists of government officials always included the orphanage director. In the *Kletorologion of Philotheos,* the most detailed of these documents, the *or-phanotrophos* appeared as the fifty-sixth government official, after the two curators of imperial estates and the master of requests, a judicial official.[45] In another section, the *Kletorologion* classified the *orphan-otrophos* as one of eleven financial bureaus of the government.[46]

Despite this reclassification, however, some orphanage directors af-ter 811 still came from the clergy. The learned patriarch Photios ad-dressed a letter to his antagonist, the deacon and *orphanotrophos* George, a man who later played a prominent part in the anti-Photian synod of 869. George clearly functioned as an active member of the Constantinopolitan clergy.[47] During the same period, Photios apparent-ly forced the metropolitan of Nicaea to renounce his episcopal see to

42. Theophanes, 1: 486–87.   43. Genesios, 1.9 (pp. 8–9).

44. *Préséance,* p. 51.

45. For the *Kletorologion of Philotheos,* see *Préséance,* p. 103; for tenth-century lists, see *Préséance,* pp. 251 and 271.

46. *Préséance,* p. 107.

47. Photios, *Ep.,* 136 (pp. 186–87) and Mansi, 16: 135–36.

assume control of the Orphanotropheion in Constantinople.[48] In both these cases the sources clearly imply that these clergymen directed the Orphanotropheion of the capital, not an institution attached to a provincial bishopric.

John the Paphlagonian, perhaps the most famous *orphanotrophos*, controlled the Byzantine government for a number of years under his brother, the emperor Michael IV (1034–1041). Before entering imperial service, John had put on the habit of a monk, which he never laid aside during his time in office.[49] Two of his official seals described him as monk and *orphanotrophos*.[50] It has surprised some historians that John, the emperor's first minister, remained in the post of *orphanotrophos*, a high position but below the top echelons of the official bureaucracy. John no doubt continued to serve as *orphanotrophos* throughout the reign of Michael IV because both church canons and imperial legislation banned monks and clerics from holding official positions in the government. As we saw in Chapter Five, however, jurists interpreted the duty of all Christians to care for orphans and other needy persons as offering an exception to this rule.[51] Thus, both church and government would have considered the office of *orphanotrophos* the most appropriate post for a monk such as John to have filled.

In addition to John in the eleventh century, at least two other monks served as *orphanotrophoi* during the twelfth century. The emperor Alexios wrote a special legal opinion to answer a question posed by the *orphanotrophos* in his regime, a monk named Metrophanes. About sixty years later, the emperor Manuel I (1143–1180) addressed a similar legal opinion to another monk *orphanotrophos* named Basil Anzas.[52] Rarely did practicing monks fill any other high government posts.

Several sources have revealed a great deal about the official career of Alexios Aristenos, an orphan director of the twelfth century. The fa-

---

48. *Vita Ignatii*, PG, 105: 573.   49. Psellos, *Chronographia*, 4.14 (1: 130).
50. Schlumberger, pp. 379–80.

51. For a discussion of this issue, see Chapter Five, regarding clerics and monks as guardians.

52. For Metrophanes, see Tiftixoglu and Troianos, "Unbekannte Kaiserurkunden," p. 146. For Basil Anzas, see the comments of Magdalino, "Innovations," p. 159, and note 49.

mous literary figure Theodore Prodromos described Alexios as belonging both to the palace and to the Great Church and in another passage as a member of both the senate and the clergy.[53] Alexios apparently began his career in the clergy, but he soon took on government posts such as that of *nomophylax* (an official in charge of legal education) and *orphanotrophos*. Eventually, he assumed the prestigious judicial office of *dikaiodotes* while at the same time becoming manager *(oikonomos)* of Hagia Sophia, clearly an ecclesiastical post. When, in 1157, the patriarch Loukas Chrysoberges insisted on a stricter interpretation of the canons banning clerics from secular duties, Aristenos had to step down from his job as *dikaiodotes*. In commenting on this affair, the canonist Theodore Balsamon did not record that Aristenos also had to give up his post as orphan director, but shortly thereafter Michael Hagiotheodorites, a palace official with no known church affiliations, assumed the responsibility of managing the Orphanotropheion.[54]

This survey of the evidence clearly demonstrates that *orphanotrophoi* were appointed both from among imperial officials and from among deacons and priests of Constantinople; John the Orphanotrophos and at least two twelfth-century men even wore the monastic habit while serving as orphanage directors. It seems reasonable therefore to conclude that the Byzantines considered the Orphanotropheion as belonging both to the sphere of the government and to that of the church. In fact, in a legal decision of the early twelfth century, the emperor Alexios explicitly stated that the Orphanotropheion enjoyed the legal and fiscal privileges both of a religious institution and of a government financial office.[55]

This dual nature of the Orphanotropheion not only effected its legal status, it also shaped the administration of its school for orphans. Several twelfth-century sources describing the Orphanotropheion's teaching staff state that both the emperor and the patriarch of Constantinople enjoyed supervisory rights over the school. In a speech retracing the career of his former teacher, Stephen Skylitzes, Theodore Prodromos mentioned that the emperor had initially appointed Skyl-

53. Prodromos, *Gedichte,* Poem 56b (p. 463); Prodromos, *Eisiterios* (PG, 133: 1274).
54. Darrouzès, *Tornikès,* pp. 54–56; see also PG, 140: 253c.
55. Tiftixoglu and Troianos, "Unbekannte Kaiserurkunden," p. 143.

itzes as a teacher at the Orphanotropheion, but later when Skylitzes was about to be promoted to the highest supervisory post on the teaching staff, his enemies tried to block his appointment by appealing not to the emperor, but to the patriarch.[56] Circa 1150, a teacher at the orphan school, Leo of Rhodes, addressed several appeals to the *orphanotrophos* Alexios Aristenos. In one of the prose works, Leo asked Aristenos to represent him before the patriarch and obtain for Leo a release from burdensome teaching duties. In his poem, Leo prayed that Saint Paul, the patron of the Orphanotropheion, would help win him a respite in his work by softening the heart of the patriarch.[57]

According to Leo, the patriarch, not the emperor, normally made decisions regarding teaching posts at the Orphanotropheion, at least during the twelfth century.[58] Robert Browning showed that during this same century grammar instructors at the Orphanage sometimes advanced to hold one of the principal teaching posts attached to Hagia Sophia. For example, Constantine Stilbes taught for twelve years at the Orphanage school before becoming *didaskalos* of the Apostle, one of the highest ranking teaching positions of the cathedral school.[59]

The authority that the patriarch exercised over the Orphanage school may have begun when the emperor Alexios reorganized the schooling system at Constantinople in 1107.[60] It is also possible, however, that patriarchal supervision went back to the origins of the Orphanotropheion. We will examine further the Orphanage school and the extent of patriarchal authority in the next chapter.

FINANCES

In a study of the Orphanage's administration, one must also consider finances. How did the Orphanotropheion sustain the services it

56. Prodromos, "Monodie," pp. 8–9.

57. *Vaticanus Palatinus gr.*, 92, fols. 207–8 *(schedos)*; fols. 145ᵛ–146 (poem). These works have not been edited.

58. *Vaticanus Palatinus gr.* , 92, fol. 146: οὕτω περ ἴσως τληπαθοὺς ἀνδρὸς χάριν / τῷ πατριάρχῃ φράξε τῆς οἰκουμένης. / δίδαξον αὐτὸν τοὺς μακροὺς ἐμοὺς πόνους.

59. Browning, "Patriarchal School I," pp. 174–76; Stilbes, *Prolusione,* pp. 47–52.

60. Magdalino, *Empire,* pp. 273–75; but see also Magdalino, "Reform Edict," pp. 199–218, in which Magdalino stresses how little is known about the development of the Patriarchal School in Constantinople. At this point, it is unclear how important Alexios's reform edict was in restructuring the educational system in the capital.

provided homeless children and other needy people? According to the Arian historian Philostorgios, the emperor Constantius contributed to the sustenance of a group of orphans and those who cared for them.[61] As we saw in Chapter Three, one way he might have provided for these children was by endowing the philanthropic institutions of Zotikos, including the saint's orphan asylum, with revenues from the state treasury and with properties carved from the most productive imperial estates. According to one version of Zotikos's *vita,* the emperor also confirmed the transfer of the saint's own private property to the ownership of his institutions.[62] A hundred years later, the *orphanotrophos* Nikon, the successor of Zotikos as *orphanotrophos,* administered a collection of churches, monasteries, philanthropic agencies, and the lands that sustained these institutions.[63]

Justinian's Novel 120, issued in 544, described the resources of the Orphanotropheion as consisting primarily of property that the orphan director and his *chartoularioi* were not to sell, but were to lease out on emphyteutic leases.[64] Novel 131 recognized the right of the *orphanotrophos* to appear in court as the person exercising legal rights and duties over the property, that is, he was responsible for the management of the Orphanage's property just as a guardian bore all legal rights and duties on behalf of his ward.[65]

Archaeologists have discovered a boundary marker belonging to one of the Orphanage's estates, a marker found near the Byzantine city of Apameia in Thrace. The inscription on the stone reads: "The boundary delineating the property of the Orphanotropheion and of Aitherios, the illustrious curator of the properties leased by him in emphyteusis." Manuel Gedeon has dated this marker to the reign of Justinian.[66] The inscription confirms that the Orphanotropheion was leasing at least some of its property according to the rules Justinian had set down and that it owned property located in Thrace.

During the seventh century, the Byzantine Empire suffered tremendous losses of territory. The Arab armies seized the wealthy provinces

61. Philostorgios, p. 225.
62. Aubineau, "Zoticos," no. 11 (pp. 80–82).
63. *JCod,* 1.3.34(35).   64. *JNov,* 120.1 and 5.
65. *JNov,* 131.15.   66. Gedeon, p. 27.

of Syria, Palestine, and Egypt and made agriculture difficult in much of Asia Minor. Bulgars and Slavs overran most of the Balkans. By the end of the century, the Byzantines considered it a military triumph when the emperor Justinian II managed to lead troops from Constantinople to Thessalonike by land.[67] It is not surprising, therefore, that the Orphanotropheion had few resources available to support its operations when Andrew of Crete became its director during this same Justinian's reign. Through his honest and wise management, however, Andrew succeeded in restoring the Orphanotropheion to economic health.[68]

As we saw above, in the early ninth century, the emperor Nikephoros I reorganized the Orphanotropheion's income and established new methods of managing the institution's landed property. Theophanes' description of these changes indicated that some of the Orphanage's properties were being farmed by *coloni* (dependent peasants—*paroikoi* in Byzantine Greek).[69]

During the tenth and eleventh centuries, the surviving sources rarely mention the Orphanotropheion or its finances. The *Chronicle* of Kedrenos, however, does record that an earthquake in 1034 damaged both the leper asylum of Zotikos and the Orphanage proper. The emperor Romanos III repaired both of these institutions at the same time he built some new aqueducts and cisterns for the city.[70]

At some point before the accession of Alexios I (1081), the Orphanotropheion again fell on hard times. The twelfth-century historians Michael Glykas and John Zonaras both claim that prior to Alexios's reign the Orphanotropheion had ceased to function.[71] Just as in the seventh century the Arabs had seized or pillaged most of the eastern provinces, so too in the second half of the eleventh century the Turks occupied or ravaged large stretches of Asia Minor. After the Battle of Mantzikert (1071), the Turks impeded agriculture in all of Asia Minor. If Glykas and Zonaras correctly recorded that the Orphanotropheion was unable to operate its philanthropies prior to 1081, then the institution must have derived much of its income from lands in Asia Minor.

---

67. Ostrogorsky, *History*, p. 130.   68. *Vita Andreae*, no. 5 (p. 174).
69. Theophanes, 1: 486–87.   70. Kedrenos, 2: 503–4.
71. Glykas, p. 621; Zonaras, p. 744.

When Alexios seized the throne in 1081, the empire faced almost in-
surmountable difficulties. The Turks occupied Anatolia; Pechenegs
were raiding the Balkan provinces; and Robert Guiscard's Normans
were advancing from the west. During his remarkable reign, Alexios
managed to defeat these enemies and reestablish the empire as a major
power in the Middle East. As part of his program to revivify the Byzantine state, Alexios allotted new resources to the Orphanotropheion so
that it could resume its philanthropic activities and even expand its traditional services.

Anna Komnena's description of her father's restored Orphanage of
Saint Paul included some details on how he financed it. Alexios granted
new landed estates to the Orphanotropheion, confirming these gifts by
chrysobull (the most solemn imperial document, sealed with a golden
bull). He also provided revenues from the seas, as Anna phrased it. This
probably referred to Alexios's grant of some docks in Constantinople
to the Orphanage.[72] We know from other sources that during the
eleventh century philanthropic institutions owned many docks in the
capital.[73] The emperor also created several offices to keep the accounts
of the institution's finances, perhaps a reference to the two bureaus of
chartoularioi mentioned earlier. Anna stressed that her father also established careful methods of auditing how these *chartoularioi* managed the
Orphanotropheion's extensive properties.[74] Since there is no previous
reference to such audits, it is possible that Alexios introduced some new
procedure to protect the institution from financial abuses. Together
with the Turkish invasions, such abuses in administering the Orphanage's endowment might have contributed to its collapse prior to 1081.

As a result of Alexios's reforms, the Orphanotropheion was able to
reopen its orphan school and to support many poor and disabled persons as well. Anna described the indigent of the Orphanotropheion as
those who formerly had nothing, but now resembled owners of great
estates who leisurely passed their days while the emperor and his officials labored as their stewards.[75]

---

72. Anna Komnena, *Alexiad*, 15.7.5–7 (3: 215–16).
73. Attaleiates, pp. 277–78.
74. Anna Komnena, *Alexiad*, 15.7.7 (3: 217).
75. Ibid., 15.7.5 (3: 215).

The archives from the monastery of the Lavra on Mount Athos preserve two documents describing estates that Alexios granted to the Orphanotropheion as part of his restoration. The first document, drafted in 1104, stated that the Lavra monastery owned an estate not far from Thessalonike. The Lavra monks claimed that this property was so far away from their monastery that it presented spiritual dangers for the monks to manage it. Thus, they requested that the emperor take this estate known as Barzachanion and give them in exchange other properties closer to their monastery. Alexios agreed; he took possession of Barzachanion, assigned it to the Orphanotropheion, and gave the monks in exchange two imperial estates closer to Mount Athos.[76]

Alexios's chrysobull described in one passage how Barzachanion passed under public authority and in another how the emperor granted it to the Orphanotropheion. In the second chrysobull, dated 1111, the monks of Lavra surrendered two estates, Peristerai and Tzechlianes, to the emperor, who then gave these lands to the public treasury, defined explicitly by this same chrysobull as the office (sekreton) of the Orphanotropheion.[77]

By classifying the lands of the Orphanotropheion together with the imperial estates the Lavra documents prove that in the twelfth century the system established by the emperor Nikephoros I was still functioning, namely, that the government considered the lands of the Orphanotropheion part of its fixed resources managed by one of the state sekreta, that is, the office of the Orphanotropheion.

As Anna Komnena stated and as the Lavra documents confirm, the emperor was ultimately responsible for the material resources of the Orphanotropheion. He and the officials he appointed including the orphanotrophos managed the estates on behalf of the orphans and other needy persons. As we noted above, however, the patriarch was also involved in the Orphanotropheion, but not directly in managing its resources.

One of the Lavra documents included a survey of the Barzachan-

76. *Actes de Lavra*, no. 56 (1: 292–93).
77. Ibid., no. 58 (1: 303).

ion estate. It consisted of 6,962 *modioi* of land, or roughly 6.2 square kilometers. Slightly more than half the land, 3,549 *modioi,* consisted of good agricultural land or rich pasture; rough mountain terrain made up the remaining 3,413 *modioi.* Of the fifteen *paroikoi* (serfs or *coloni*) who worked the land of Barzachanion, eleven owned one team of oxen and four owned two teams. In addition, the estate possessed a water mill which ran only in the winter and a garden area. This survey provides evidence that just as in the days of Nikephoros's reforms, *paroikoi* worked some of the Orphanotropheion's lands.[78]

Twelfth-century sources offer some compelling evidence that not all *orphanotrophoi* managed the great wealth of the Orphanage honestly. Indeed, it would be surprising if a prestigious foundation such as the Orphanotropheion, richly endowed by Alexios I with estates and other resources, did not attract the cupidity of unscrupulous bureaucrats. Toward the end of the reign of John II (1118–1143), Theodore Prodromos described the return of Alexios Aristenos to the office of *orphanotrophos* as the very salvation of the institution. Although Prodromos's extravagant praise might have been due to the excesses of Byzantine rhetoric, his phrases leave the impression that other *orphanotrophoi* had not managed the resources of Saint Paul's Orphanage as successfully as Aristenos had during his initial tenure as orphanage director.[79]

A second encomium, written by Niketas Choniates in the 1190s, leaves no doubt that previous *orphanotrophoi* had mismanaged the property of the Orphanage and embezzled money. In praising the *orphanotrophos* Belissariotes, Choniates stressed that this virtuous official had never offered money to become director of the Orphanotropheion, nor had he used his office to make himself wealthy. According to Choniates, Belissariotes knew that God would blow away like chaff any wealth gained from defrauding orphans or the poor. Belissariotes never dared to appropriate anything from the resources of the Orphanotropheion for his own use, and he guarded the property of the institution from the greed of others. That Niketas Choniates praised Belissar-

78. Ibid., no. 56 (1: 293). Byzantine *modios* measurements are very difficult to convert into modern area measurements. Experts have had great difficulty in determining exact equivalencies since the Byzantines used so many different kinds of *modioi.* See *ODB,* 2: 1388.

79. Prodromos, *Eisiterios* (PG, 133: 1268).

iotes for his honest management of the Orphanotropheion implies that other *orphanotrophoi* had not been as conscientious in governing the institution as had Belissariotes.[80]

How often did *orphanotrophoi* steal from the institution they supervised? Justinian had required that, when a person was appointed *orphanotrophos, xenodochos* of a hospital or hospice, bishop, or *oikonomos* (steward) of a diocese, he take an inventory of his private property. Moreover, this same law stipulated that the new *orphanotrophos* could only will by testament the property listed in the inventory. Justinian's rule therefore discouraged stealing large tracts of land in the interests of the orphan director's family, but it was less effective in stopping embezzlement of liquid funds for personal use.[81] It is impossible to determine how frequently *orphanotrophoi* defrauded the Orphanage, but Choniates' speech demonstrates that intentional mismanagement definitely occurred.

When the crusaders seized Constantinople in 1204 and subsequently established the Latin Empire, many Byzantine philanthropic institutions were destroyed. We know that the Western soldiers sacked the famous Sampson Xenon next to Hagia Sophia and that, as a result, it ceased to function as a medical hospital. After the restoration of the Greek state in 1261, the Sampson did not reopen its hospital wards.[82] The ancient Panteleemon Xenon, founded in the sixth century, also lay in ruins when the emperor Michael VIII liberated Constantinople. It remained in this state until a monk named Niphon spent his private fortune to refurbish it in 1340.[83]

We have no similar evidence documenting the fate of the Orphanotropheion under the Latins. We know only that the emperor Michael VIII (1259–1282) decided to restore it as part of his effort to return Constantinople to its former glory. The historian Pachymeres described how Michael reestablished the clergy at the Church of the Holy Apostles and at the Church of the Blachernai and then reopened a school for grammar at the old Orphanotropheion. He allotted mon-

80. Choniates, *Orationes, logos XV* (1: 154–55).
81. Malalas, 18.11 (p. 359).
82. Miller, "Sampson Hospital," pp. 128–30.
83. *Actes de Lavra*, no. 123 (3: 20–26). See also Miller, *Birth*, p. 195.

ey to pay for teachers at the school and to provide stipends for the students.

According to Pachymeres' brief account, Michael VIII restored only the grammar school at the Orphanotropheion. We cannot tell whether the children who studied there were orphans or simply boys who needed stipends to support their schooling.[84] According to a poem, written a few decades later circa 1316, however, the Orphanotropheion was once again providing many philanthropic services including the care of orphans, services that it had previously offered in the prosperous days of the Comnenian emperors.

This poem was written by the prolific poet Manuel Philes sometime before his death circa 1320 and dedicated to an *orphanotrophos* named Tryphon Kedrenos. In these verses, Philes described Tryphon as helping orphans, assisting the crippled, providing help for the blind, and feeding the hungry, all charitable activities which, according to Anna Komnena, the great Orphanage, restored by her father, accorded the poor and needy of early-twelfth-century Constantinople. Moreover, Philes described Tryphon as sponsoring the baptism of many children. As we shall see in the next chapter, the *orphanotrophos* had been associated with the baptism of orphans since the late ninth century, if not before. Although it is possible that Philes' poem is simply repeating traditional phrases describing orphan directors in centuries past, the lively details of his poem and the description of Tryphon's administrative and legal activities in the western provinces give the impression that the poet was striving to present details from contemporary reality.[85]

How long after Tryphon served as its director did the Orphanotropheion continue to operate a school for children and other philanthropic services? We shall return to this question at the end of this chapter. At this point, however, let us examine more closely what philanthropic work the Orphanage and its various departments actually performed.

---

84. Pachymeres, 4.14 (1: 283–84). See also the comments of Failler, "Pachymeriana," pp. 190–93.

85. Philes, poem 43 (pp. 47–51). See also Dölger, *Aus den Schatzkammern*, no. 74/7 (pp. 206–8), dated January 1316, which refers to an *orphanotrophos* named Tryphon Kedrenos. This is no doubt the same *orphanotrophos* to whom Philes dedicated his poem.

GOOD WORKS

Among the many sources that mention the Orphanotropheion, Anna Komnena's description alone provides us with detailed information concerning this vast institution's many charitable operations. She mentioned residences for poor people and living quarters for disabled men and women, a category that included the elderly. According to Anna, each handicapped resident had a specific person assigned to help him or her. Thus, a young person, paid by the Orphanotropheion, aided an old woman; an assistant who could see guided a blind man; another assistant with sound limbs helped a resident who was missing a foot; and mothers of other children nursed abandoned infants. Anna emphasized that Alexios was trying to imitate Christ. Although the emperor was unable to heal miraculously those who had suffered crippling maladies or maiming accidents, he could hire servants fit physically and mentally to assist each one of the people who sought help at the Orphanotropheion.[86]

Anna's description indicates that the residences for the poor and disabled formed a circle, probably enclosing the entire precinct of the Orphanotropheion. This circle of buildings had two storeys of apartments both for the residents and those who served them. On the highest point within the precinct, on what Anna called the acropolis of Constantinople, stood the sixth-century church of Saint Paul. Anna described how Alexios secured a numerous staff of clerics for Saint Paul's as well as paid for a choir of both men and women to sing antiphonal hymns at the church.

Near Saint Paul's, Anna described convents Alexios maintained for deaconesses. Anna also mentioned that her father constructed a large monastery for Iberian nuns who had previously wandered about the city whenever they visited Constantinople. All these monastic buildings Anna located off to the left of the Church of Saint Paul as one approached from the gate. To the right of the church she described the school for orphans.

---

86. Anna Komnena, *Alexiad*, 15.7.4–7 (3: 215–16). For the entire section on the Orphanage, see *Alexiad*, 15.7.4–9 (3: 214–18).

Zonaras also praised Alexios's work in rebuilding the Orphanotropheion. Confirming Anna's account, Zonaras stated that the emperor admitted many old people as residents at the Orphanage and built inns where nuns and monks could reside. Neither Anna nor Zonaras described in any detail the facilities for the homeless children, although Anna did offer some fascinating information on the teaching and learning procedures at the orphan school.[87]

Sources from later in the twelfth century provide evidence that Alexios's reconstructed Orphanotropheion continued to function under his successors. At the end of John II's reign (circa 1140), Theodore Prodromos described the many crippled persons who lived at the Orphanage together with homeless children.[88] At the end of the century, Niketas Choniates also listed the disabled residents at the Orphanotropheion—the blind, the lame, those who were missing a hand or a foot.[89] As we saw above, Philes' poem dating from the early fourteenth century repeated many of the details found in the twelfth-century sources and thereby provides evidence that Michael VIII restored at least some of the services that the Comnenian Orphanotropheion had performed.[90]

Anna's lengthy description of the Orphanotropheion presents us with a philanthropic institution that not only nurtured and educated orphans, but provided a host of other charitable services as well. Anna's account also implies that most of what Alexios established on the acropolis of Constantinople began with him. As Anna expressed it, "[the emperor] built in this place another city."[91] Reliable sources, however, demonstrate that the emperor Justin II first constructed the Church of Saint Paul in the sixth century, and the many texts examined in Chapter Three have shown that Zotikos first opened the original Orphanage and the leprosarium in Pera during the second half of the fourth century.[92] How many of the other agencies that Anna listed as her father's work had actually existed earlier?

87. Zonaras, p. 745; cf. Anna Komnena, *Alexiad*, 15.7.4–9 (3: 214–18).
88. Prodromos, *Eisiterios* (PG, 133: 1270–73).
89. Choniates, *Orationes, logos XV* (1: 154–55).
90. Philes, poem 43 (pp. 50–51).
91. Anna Komnena, *Alexiad*, 15.7.4 (3: 215).
92. Regarding the Church of Saint Peter and Paul, see Theophanes, 1: 244.

Two stories from the sixth century prove that already in the reign of Justinian the Orphanotropheion was maintaining hostels for visiting monks. According to the monastic biographer Cyril of Skythopolis, a superior of the Great Lavra in Palestine named Gelasios planned to visit Constantinople to support the condemnation of Theodore of Mopsuestia. Gelasios's opponent, Askides, however, tried to block Gelasios's visit by ordering the officials of the patriarchate, of the palace, and of the Orphanotropheion not to receive him. Cyril's account makes clear that one of the three places most likely to offer a visiting monk lodging in Constantinople was the Orphanage.[93]

The second story, one from a collection of ascetic tales, recounts how an anonymous superior of a monastery in Asia Minor, probably on the coast of Asia Minor, came to Constantinople because of some problem in his community. He stayed at the Orphanotropheion together with many other monks including some heretical ones. The story described these ascetics gathered around an open hearth for warmth.[94]

Some rooms at the Orphanotropheion could also be used for imprisoning wrong doers. In his entertaining book of advice for success, the eleventh-century general Kekaumenos warned his son not to get involved in contracting to collect imperial revenues. Kekaumenos illustrated the danger by recounting the case of a relative who took on a tax contract and ended up imprisoned at the Orphanotropheion. Kekaumenos did not provide enough details to determine if the relative had contracted to collect revenues specifically for the Orphanotropheion, which, as we have demonstrated, was considered an imperial financial bureau, or had agreed to collect the regular state tax. From his account, however, we know that at least in some circumstances the government imprisoned at the Orphanotropheion revenue collectors who could not pay what they owed the state.[95]

I have so far found no examples of crippled, blind, or aged persons at the Orphanotropheion before Alexios's reorganization. It is therefore possible that the emperor added the outer circuit of hostels that

93. *Vita Sabae*, pp. 194–95.
94. "Vies et récits," tale 9 (pp. 54–55).
95. Kekaumenos, *Strategikon*, chap. 95.

Anna described in great detail. Moreover, archaeologists have identified walls on the site of the Orphanotropheion that date from the Comnenian era.[96]

On the basis of Anna's description, it is clear that Alexios restored the Orphanotropheion as the largest philanthropic institution of Constantinople. He endowed it with new lands to finance its many services, and constructed some additional buildings. As our survey has indicated, however, most of the services that Anna attributed to her father's initiative the Orphanotropheion had, in fact, been providing for many centuries. Alexios's primary contribution was repairing the damage the institution had suffered during the difficult years following the reign of Romanos IV (1068–1071).

To fulfill its charitable mission, the Orphanotropheion had to secure a steady supply of grain to feed the poor of Constantinople. According to one version of his *vita*, the first *orphanotrophos*, Zotikos, had commandeered so much grain and other supplies for the needy residents of his leper asylum that he caused a serious food shortage in Constantinople. This version of the *Vita Sancti Zotici* dates from the tenth or eleventh century and does not present a factual account of fourth-century events, but it does show that Constantinopolitans believed that the Orphanotropheion's many philanthropic agencies required huge supplies of food.[97] Anna Komnena stated that rivers of wine and wheat poured into the Orphanotropheion from its many vast estates to feed the countless number of people residing there.[98]

Procuring sufficient food, chiefly wheat, was thus a fundamental task of the *orphanotrophos*. As a result, three separate Byzantine sources compare successful orphanage directors with Joseph, the favorite son of the Hebrew patriarch Jacob. According to his eighth-century biography, Andrew of Crete restored the resources of the Orphanage, like a wise Joseph. The allusion here was clearly not to Joseph's fight with his brothers, but to his subsequent success in Egypt where his correct interpretation of the pharaoh's dreams not only won

96. Mango, *Développement*, p. 34, and note 66.

97. Miller "Zotikos," chap. 9 (pp. 355–56) and chap. 11 (p. 359); see also the commentary to the text, pp. 341 and 370–72.

98. Anna Komnena, *Alexiad*, 15.7.5 (3: 215).

Joseph his freedom, but saved the country from the ravages of famine (Gen 41).[99]

In a twelfth-century encomium, Nikephoros Basilakes also compared the *orphanotrophos* Alexios Aristenos to Joseph because, like the hero of Genesis, the orphanage director had saved a great multitude from starvation. Basilakes added, however, that there was one great difference between Joseph of Egypt and Aristenos. In nourishing the starving Egyptians, Joseph had deprived them of their lands; Aristenos, on the other hand, fed the hungry people of Constantinople and left them in possession of their property (Gen 47:13–26). Basilakes also identified Aristenos as a *sitodotes,* a term occasionally used in Hellenistic and Roman times to describe a *polis* official who managed the grain supplies. In the early fifth century (A.D.), Synesios, the bishop of Cyrene, selected the same term to refer to the *prefectus annonae,* the imperial bureaucrat responsible for supplying Constantinople with grain.[100] Prodromos's speech in honor of Aristenos also mentioned that the *orphanotrophos* had provided food for many poor people.[101]

The third source to compare an *orphanotrophos* to Joseph was the early-fourteenth-century poem of Manuel Philes written to honor the orphanage director Tryphon. According to Philes' verses, the people of Byzantium considered that Tryphon had become another Joseph because he had gained prominence by feeding the city's hungry.[102] Thus, Philes' poem as well as the twelfth-century encomium by Basilakes suggest that *orphanotrophoi* helped in feeding the poor of Constantinople.

It is possible that the *orphanotrophoi* began to play a part in supplying food to the poor of the capital at the end of the seventh century when the emperor Justinian II assigned the new orphanage director, Andrew of Crete, the task of supervising not only the Orphanotropheion, but also the nearby *diakonia* of Eugenios. According to Andrew's *vita,* the new director,

99. *Vita Antreae,* no. 5 (p. 174).

100. Basilakes, *Aristenos,* chap. 32 (p. 25). With regard to the office of *sitodotes* in ancient *poleis,* see Lidell-Scott, *sub voce.* For *sitodotes* as the Greek term for the *prefectus annonae,* see Synesios, Ep. 87 (PG, 66: 1456 A).

101. Prodromos, *Eisiterios,* PG, 133: 1269 and 1271.

102. Philes, poem 43 (p. 49).

. . . swept away the orphanhood of the one pious house [the Orphan-otropheion] through his fatherly assistance and drove away completely the hard times of the second pious house [the *diakonia* of Eugenios] and fed the poor with an undiminishing supply of bread, as another wise Joseph, appearing to the poor, not in Egypt, but in the houses of God for the poor.[103]

Thus, Andrew fed the poor through his administration of both phil-anthropic institutions.

From other sources, we know that pious houses known as *diakoniai* began to function in Constantinople during the sixth century. One of the principal services of these new philanthropic institutions was to provide free baths for poor people, but in his study of Byzantine bread tokens John Nesbitt has shown that as early as the seventh century *diakoniai* began issuing lead tokens to the poor that could then be re-deemed for food.[104] Nesbitt's research therefore suggests that Andrew of Crete became a new Joseph for the poor of Constantinople primari-ly because he administered the Diakonia of Eugenios. Given the prox-imity of this *diakonia* to the Orphanotropheion, the orphanage direc-tors who succeeded Andrew of Crete probably continued to manage the pious house of Eugenios.

Another expansion of the *orphanotrophos's* charitable responsibilities occurred at the end of the eighth century when Tarasios became patri-arch of Constantinople. Tarasios is best known for his role in helping to defeat iconoclasm at the Ecumenical Council of 787, but he also was famous for his work in reforming church-run charities in the Byzantine capital.

Sometime after becoming patriarch, Tarasios decided to reorganize distribution of grain for the Constantinopolitan poor by eliminating from the list of recipients those who were not in need and subsequent-ly augmenting the portions allotted to the truly indigent. In the words of Tarasios's biographer Ignatios the Deacon, the patriarch became an-other Joseph.[105] This same Ignatios credited the *orphanotrophos* at that

103. *Vita Andreae*, no. 5 (p. 174).

104. For *diakoniai*, see Miller, *Birth*, pp. 130–32; Marrou, "L'origine orientale," pp. 95–142; Nesbitt, "Byzantine Copper Tokens," pp. 67–75.

105. *Vita Tarasii*, p. 402.

time, the future patriarch Nikephoros, with helping to manage Tarasios's reform. According to Ignatios, the Orphanage director not only managed the largest *ptocheion* in Constantinople (that is, the Orphanotropheion), but he also took charge of administering a section of the Great Church, no doubt the offices involved in Tarasios's expanded grain distributions.[106]

From the surviving sources one cannot reconstruct exactly what role the Orphanotropheion played in feeding the population of Constantinople. Did the *orphanotrophos* continue to feed the poor beyond the walls of the Orphanage by administering *diakoniai* such as that of Eugenios, or did he come to supervise some centralized grain reserve as the twelfth-century Basilakes implied when he called Aristenos a *sitodotes*? Despite these unanswered questions, the evidence strongly suggests that the duties of the *orphanotrophos* included not only feeding the many residents of the Orphanage, but also distributing food to a wider circle of indigent citizens throughout Constantinople.

THE ORPHANOTROPHOS AS JUDGE

The ninth-century *Kletorologion of Philotheos* unmistakably listed the *orphanotrophos* among the financial officials of the government. Since the time of the emperor Nikephoros I and his fiscal reforms, the Orphanage's many estates were classed as imperial land. Thus, the *orphanotrophos* took his place beside the *sakellarios*, the *logothetes* of the *genikon* and of the *stratiotikon*, and the curators of imperial estates as one of the top financial bureaucrats of the state.[107] Other sources, however, described the Orphanage director as a legal official. A letter of the eleventh-century intellectual Michael Psellos referred to the *orphanotrophos* as a judge who possessed expertise in the fine points of Roman law.[108] Psellos's contemporary, Eustathios Rhomaios, described a complicated legal case that the *orphanotrophos* had considered as the magistrate of first instance.[109]

How long had the *orphanotrophos* exercised the responsibilities of a magistrate, and what were the cases he adjudicated? Just as in our

106. *Vita Nicephori*, p. 152.
108. Psellos, *Ep.* 240 (pp. 290–91).

107. *Kletorologion of Philotheos*, p. 107.
109. *Peira*, 15.12 (p. 53).

study of the Orphanotropheion's role in supplying Constantinople with grain, so too regarding the director's judicial responsibilities, the sources do not provide precise answers, but they leave no doubt that the *orphanotrophos* exercised judicial powers.

The emperor Leo I's law of 472 offers the first indication that the *orphanotrophos* had to possess some knowledge of the Roman law or be advised by someone who did. According to Leo's constitution, the *orphanotrophos* should function as a guardian or curator for all the minor children in the Orphanage. He had to represent the children under his tutelage in court and to protect their persons, their property, and any business affairs that might have involved them.[110]

We have no statistics regarding the number of children at the Orphanotropheion from any period and we have no idea what percentage of the orphans had substantial property to administer. In view of Leo's legislation, however, it would seem that a sizable number of the orphans owned property and that the *orphanotrophos* and his *chartoularioi* had to devote considerable time to protecting their wards from legal difficulties.

The legislation of the Isaurian emperors Leo III and Constantine V (717–775) transformed the *orphanotrophos* into a magistrate. As we saw in Chapter Four, the original *Ecloga* required that all orphans of Constantinople whose parents had died without establishing tutors pass directly into the care of the Orphanage or of a monastic community in the capital.[111] Apparently, this rule placed too many children in the Orphanotropheion and the monastic schools, because a revised version of the *Ecloga* gave the *orphanotrophos* the power to appoint guardians for orphans without *tutores testimentarii* rather than have all these children assigned to institutions. In effect, this rule made the *orphanotrophos* a new *praetor tutelarius,* the ancient Roman official of the capital, last mentioned in a law of Justinian.[112]

The *orphanotrophos* continued to serve as a magistrate who assigned *tutores* and *curatores* until the close of the ninth century when the

110. *JCod*, 1.3.31 (32).
111. *Ecloga*, 7 (p. 198).
112. *Ecloga privata aucta*, 8.2 (pp. 28–29). For the last reference to the *praetor tutelarius*, see *JCod*. 1.4.30 (anno 531).

Macedonian emperor Leo VI altered the guardianship laws as part of his attempt to overturn the legal system of the Isaurian emperors. As a result of Leo's legislation, the quaestor assumed responsibility for cases involving orphans and their tutors and curators.[113] In the *Peira*, the eleventh-century judge Eustathios Rhomaios stated explicitly that the quaestor appointed guardians in cases where the original tutor had died while his ward was still a minor.[114]

Despite the emergence of the quaestor as the magistrate who ordinarily exercised jurisdiction over testaments and issues involving guardians, the *orphanotrophos* continued to function as a judge. In an eleventh-century dispute involving a lease of property belonging to the Gerokomeion of Saint Helias, the *orphanotrophos* first heard the parties involved and then forwarded the case to Eustathios Rhomaios, at that time a judge on one of the high courts of the Hippodrome. After issuing a legal ruling regarding the categories of philanthropic institutions, Eustathios returned the case to the *orphanotrophos*'s court for a decision regarding the status of the Gerokomeion of Saint Helias, that is, to determine if it had been founded by an emperor or empress or by a private person.[115] It is unclear why the *orphanotrophos* had jurisdiction in this case. Perhaps, as head of the principal charitable organization of the capital, he heard the dispute because it involved a philanthropic agency in or near Constantinople.

In Psellos's letter concerning an unnamed *orphanotrophos*, the learned author stated specifically that the orphan director served as a judge, but Psellos added that the *orphanotrophos* had to know about vulgar pupillary substitutions and the rules for restoring property to an orphan, two subjects intimately linked to adjudicating last testaments and disputes regarding guardianship, the kinds of cases that, according to Eustathios Rhomaios, the quaestor had handled since the legislation of Leo VI.[116] To complicate the matter further, the twelfth-century legal manual the *Ecloga Basilicorum* stated that a number of high judicial officials including the *droungarios* (of the *vigla*) and the master of requests could assign tutors or empower lower magistrates

---

113. Leo VI, *Novel*, 44 (pp. 177–81).
115. *Peira*, 15.12 (p. 53).

114. *Peira*, 16.5 (p. 55).
116. Psellos, *Ep.* 240 (pp. 290–91).

to do so.[117] Given the present state of research, it is impossible for us to distinguish the competence of the quaestor from that of the *orphanotrophos* or to determine how these officials shared responsibility regarding issues of guardianship with the *droungarios* or the master of requests. The evidence, however, demonstrates that the Orphanage director continued to function as a judge after the reforms of the Macedonian emperors.

From the twelfth and fourteenth centuries comes additional evidence that men who held the office of Orphanage director had trained in the law and were thus prepared to function as judges. At the end of John II's reign (1143), Alexios Aristenos simultaneously held the office of *orphanotrophos* and that of *nomophylax,* the official who supervised legal education in Constantinople.[118] In his encomium of Aristenos, Basilakes described the *orphanotrophos*'s education as having culminated in the study of justice.[119] Sometime after 1143, Aristenos obtained one of the highest judicial offices of the twelfth-century bureaucracy, the post of *dikaiodotes.*[120]

Like Aristenos, John Belissariotes, *orphanotrophos* at the end of the twelfth century, also pursued the study of law. As a boy, he had frequented the law courts to hear the lawyers argue their cases.[121] Also like Aristenos, Belissariotes held a number of judicial posts, including one of the highest (the post of *protasekretis*), at the same time he served as *orphanotrophos.*[122] Two fourteenth-century orphanage directors, Tryphon Kedrenos and Leo Bardales, also concentrated on the study of law and filled judicial posts. Like Belissariotes, Leo Bardales came to hold the office of *protasekretis.*[123]

Although we know only a very few of the people who functioned as orphanage directors from the twelfth through the fourteenth century,

117. *Ecloga Basilicorum,* pp. 251–52.

118. Prodromos, *Eisiterios* (PG, 133: 1269). See also another oration by Prodromos in honor of Aristenos (PG, 133: 1258–68).

119. Basilakes, *Aristenos,* 22–23 (pp. 19–20).

120. Darrouzès, *Tornikès,* pp. 54–56. See also Balsamon, PG, 137: 45.

121. Choniates, *Orationes, logos XV* (1: 151).

122. Choniates, *Orationes,* 2: 159.

123. For Tryphon Kedrenos, see Philes, poem 43 (pp. 47–51). For Leo Bardales, see Sevcenko, "Léon Bardalès," pp. 248–58.

all those about whom we have adequate information had studied law as part of their training and held some high judicial office in addition to managing the Orphanotropheion. On the other hand, no source from these late years indicates whether or not the *orphanotrophos* adjudicated cases by virtue of his office as director. Theodore Prodromos portrayed Alexios Aristenos sitting in judgment, but at the time of Prodromos's speech Aristenos also held the office of *nomophylax* which by the twelfth century included in its scope judicial duties.[124]

In the final analysis, we cannot determine the legal disputes which the *orphanotrophos* adjudicated, and after Eustathios Rhomaios's reference to the case of the Elias Gerokomeion, we have no evidence that orphanage directors continued to act as judges, but the sources leave no doubt that some *orphanotrophoi* had gained fame as legal experts.

The judicial responsibilities of the *orphanotrophos* probably derived from his position as an official closely linked to the city of Constantinople. Just as *orphanotrophoi* had exercised a role in guaranteeing the capital's grain supply, so too they possessed magisterial competence within the jurisdiction of Constantinople. As evidence of this, one should recall that, during the period from the mid-eighth century to the legal reforms of the Macedonian emperors at the end of the ninth century, the *orphanotrophos* judged guardianship cases within the capital city, a judicial function that the urban prefect had previously performed.

THE END OF THE ORPHANOTROPHEION

When did the Orphanotropheion cease to function? The anonymous *Treatise on the Offices*, attributed by the manuscripts to Kodinos, states explicitly that the *orphanotrophos* had cared for orphans, but at the time when this treatise was composed had ceased to have any specific duties.[125] According to this same treatise, many of the other ancient offices of the empire no longer corresponded to specific administrative functions and had become merely honorary titles held by the emperor's advisors.

---

124. Prodromos, *Eisiterios* (PG, 133: 1269).
125. Pseudo-Kodinos, *Traité*, 185, ll. 17–20.

Careful analysis of the *Treatise on the Offices* has demonstrated that this text shares some passages with the memoirs of the emperor John VI Kantakouzenos, completed in the 1360s. On the basis of these passages and other details in the text, scholars have established that the *Treatise* was written sometime after John Kantakouzenos gained control of Constantinople (February 1347).[126]

As we saw earlier, the emperor Michael VIII had restored the Orphanotropheion after he had regained the capital in 1261. In fact, he refurbished it along with two key churches in Constantinople, the Holy Apostles and the Theotokos Church of the Blachernai. Philes' poem in honor of Tryphon Kedrenos provides good evidence that the emperor Michael had reestablished most of the philanthropic services that the Orphanage had performed in the twelfth century. Philes described the *orphanotrophos* Tryphon as bread for the hungry, clothing for the naked, a missing limb for the crippled, and a father to the orphan (see Sirae 4:10). He even described Tryphon as giving birth to new children through baptism, a clear allusion to the orphanage director's role in catechizing non-Christian orphans.[127]

A letter dating from the same period also indicated that the Orphanage was still functioning. The historian Nikephoros Xanthopoulos wrote this message to an unnamed *orphanotrophos*. In it, Xanthopoulos implored the *orphanotrophos* to fulfill his duties to nourish the poor by assisting a destitute man whom Xanthopoulos had befriended. This document does not refer to an orphan school, but it does portray the *orphanotrophos* as a man who was duty-bound to assist the needy. The editor dates this letter to the years just prior to 1320.

We thus have evidence that the *orphanotrophos* still supervised philanthropic services prior to 1320, but no longer performed such work after February 1347. Apparently, the Orphanotropheion had ceased to function sometime between 1320 and 1347, the period of Byzantium's civil wars. I would suggest that the Orphanotropheion finally closed during the most destructive of these wars, the clash between John Kan-

---

126. *ODB*, 2: 1135. For the history of Cantacuzenus's civil war, see Nicol, *Last Centuries*, pp. 191–216.

127. Pachymeres, 4.14 (1: 283–84). Philes, poem 43 (pp. 47–51).

takouzenos and the Palaeologan regency government of Anna of Savoy and the patriarch Kalekas. John Kantakouzenos himself wrote that this civil war had destroyed almost everything and had reduced the great Roman Empire to a feeble shadow of its former self.[128]

Rodolphe Guilland has demonstrated that documents both from the archives of Athos and from Constantinople prove that imperial officials continued to bear the title *orphanotrophos* until the fifteenth century, but after 1320 no sources mentioned the Orphanotropheion, its school, or its other philanthropic services.[129] Moreover, the *Treatise of the Offices* clearly states that, by the end of the civil wars (February 1347), the title *orphanotrophos* no longer referred to the supervisor of a philanthropic institution but had become a purely honorary title. It is therefore probable that the famous orphanage of Constantinople had ceased functioning by the mid-fourteenth century, approximately nine hundred years after its foundation.

128. Cantacuzenus, 3.1 (2: 12).
129. Guilland, "Études," pp. 205–21.

VIII   THE ORPHANOTROPHEION
THE ORPHAN SCHOOL

 According to Anna Komnena, her father, Alexios, placed a grammar school for the children of the Orphanotropheion to the right of the ancient church of Saint Paul.[1] The historian Zonaras also credited Alexios with having first established this orphan school.[2] In support of these two accounts, many other sources from Theodore Prodromos's oratory to the writings of Constantine Stilbes described this grammar school for orphans as having functioned continually throughout the twelfth century.[3] But did Alexios really found this school ex nihilo, as Anna and Zonaras claimed, or did the emperor simply reestablish an ancient institution, just as he refounded the Church of Saint Paul and the monastic *xenodocheia* we discussed in the previous chapter?

We have already examined how the Byzantine state and the Byzantine Church administered the Orphanotropheion and discussed some of the philanthropic services it provided. In this chapter we will first review the evidence that the Orphanage of Constantinople supported a school for many centuries prior to the reign of Alexios. Second, we will explore what sort of education the orphan school provided for its wards. Third, we will examine the organization of its teaching staff

1. Anna Komnena, *Alexiad*, 15.7.9 (3: 217).
2. Zonaras, p. 745.
3. See the wide range of sources presented in this chapter and also Miller, "Orphanotropheion," pp. 83–104. See also the interesting article on the school at the Orphanotropheion by Mergiali-Falangas.

and identify at least a few of the instructors who taught the courses. Finally, we will discuss what information survives about the students at the Orphanotropheion.

SCHOOLING BEFORE ALEXIOS

In describing Alexios's restoration of the Orphanotropheion, Zonaras emphasized that the emperor "established in addition" a grammar school both for orphans and for children of indigent parents. The emperor appointed teachers *(didaskaloi)* and tutors *(paidagogoi)* and provided *annona* allotments *(siteseis)* for both instructors and students.[4] Anna's account also indicated that Alexios's restoration had introduced sophisticated new methods to teach classical Greek to the orphans.[5] The many references to the Orphanotropheion from the centuries prior to the reign of Alexios, on the other hand, provide no direct evidence of a grammar school for homeless children; this is true even of the sources from the reign of Justinian, a period from which many documents have survived. From the decades after Alexios's foundation, however, writers frequently mentioned the grammar school of the Orphanotropheion.[6] The evidence therefore indicates that Alexios established a new grammar school at the Orphanage, an institution that developed into one of the Byzantine capital's prominent educational centers.

Although no evidence has survived to prove the existence of a grammar school at the Orphanotropheion prior to Alexios's reign, it is difficult to believe that this well-endowed orphanage, the most prominent philanthropic institution in the empire, failed to offer its wards some kind of education since many other group homes for children in the provinces, whether episcopal, monastic, or private, placed great emphasis on educating the homeless children in their care. We saw

---

4. Zonaras, p. 745: (Alexios) ἀλλὰ μὴν καὶ μοναζόντων καὶ μοναζουσῶν ἐν αὐτῷ ἐδείματο καταγώγια· πρὸς δὲ τοῖς καὶ διδασκαλεῖον γραμματικῶν ἵν᾿ ἐν αὐτῷ διδάσκοντο παῖδες ὀρφανοὶ ἢ γονέων ἀπόρων. . . .

5. Anna Komnena, *Alexiad*, 15.7.9 (3: 217–18).

6. E.g., Basil Pediadites, a teacher at the orphan school, was identified in a manuscript as μαΐστωρ τῆς σχολῆς τῶν γραμματικῶν τοῦ Παύλου. (Browning, "Patriarchal School [II]," pp. 20–22). Moreover, Prodromos referred to the children of the Orphanotropheion as having studied grammar (Prodromos, *Eisiterios* [PG, 133: 1270]).

how the fourth-century *Apostolic Constitutions* required that bishops in the region around Antioch provide training in a craft for male orphans.[7] At the same time, Basil of Caesarea placed the orphans he protected into a monastic school that taught grammar, biblical studies, and, according to Basil's famous letter on education, the Greek classical writers as well.[8]

Because Basil exercised such wide influence throughout the provinces of the Byzantine Empire and because his ideas continued to shape church institutions for many centuries after his death, the schooling he provided for orphans at Caesarea doubtless inspired many other bishops and monastic superiors to found similar programs for homeless children. For example, in the late fourth century, Euthymios, abandoned by his mother and uncle, received an education at the episcopal school in Syrian Melitene, an education that incorporated many of the procedures Basil had designed for his educational institution at Caesarea. Similarly, in the sixth century, Alypios, abandoned by his family, learned to read the Holy Scriptures at an episcopal school in Paphlagonia. In the early tenth century, Peter and his little brother, having lost their parents, studied both sacred and profane literature at a monastery school probably located in Constantinople.[9]

Although Anna's description of Alexios's twelfth-century building and reorganization provides the first detailed picture of a fully developed academic program at the Orphanotropheion, as early as the fifth century the emperor Leo I made a clear reference to teaching the children residing there. In 472, Leo promulgated a law that exempted the orphanage director from undergoing any audit regarding the property of orphans under his supervision. In addition, the law emphasized that, like a loving father, the *orphanotrophos* was to care for all the children deprived of parents and was to educate them with parental affection.[10] Although this law provided no specific evidence regarding a

---

7. *Constitutiones Apostolorum*, 4.2 (2: 172).
8. Basil, *Interrogatio XV*, PG, 31: 953. For classical Greek literature, see *Ad adulescentes de legendis libris gentilium*, Basil, *Ep.* (4: 390).
9. *Vita Euthymii*, p. 11; *Vita Alypii*, p. 149; *Vita Petri Argivorum*, pp. 1–5.
10. *JCod*, 1.3.31 (32).

school within the precinct of the orphan asylum, it assumed that the head of the institution would arrange some sort of training for his wards.

The examples of orphan schools in other provincial towns, the wide influence of Basil's rules at Caesarea, and this law of Leo I provide strong evidence that the Orphanotropheion maintained some sort of educational program as early as the fifth century. A closer inspection of the sources, however, will not only demonstrate beyond any doubt that a school had existed at the Orphanage of Constantinople since the 400s, but also will provide some information on what subjects the children were expected to study while residing at the institution.

THE CURRICULUM

Because we have no *typikon* or imperial *chrysobull* regulating the procedures at the Orphanotropheion in general nor the organization at the orphan school in particular, it is impossible to reconstruct exactly the course of studies that the children followed. A careful reading of scattered references, however, does reveal that the institution provided instruction in at least three areas of study: music, Christian doctrine, and Greek grammar. The first sources that allude to disciplined training at the Orphanotropheion refer to a choral music program of some sort.

From the mid-fifth century, ten years earlier than Leo's law regarding the education of children at the Orphanotropheion, comes indirect evidence that the orphans of this institution were singing in an organized choir. According to Zacharias of Mytilene, a Syrian Monophysite, the people of Constantinople used to go to the Orphanage to hear a choir chant songs composed by Timokletos, the brother of the *orphanotrophos* Akakios.[11] Why did these people go to the Orphanotropheion? There was no prominent church at the Orphanage until a century later when Justin II built the church of Saints Peter and Paul there. Perhaps Timokletos performed his songs at the Orphanotropheion because his brother, the orphanage director, allowed him the

---

11. Zachariah of Mitylene, 4.11 (p. 80).

use of the facilities. Since Timokletos was a Monophysite, he might have been banned from other locations within Constantinople. It is more likely, however, that the inhabitants of Constantinople came to the Orphanotropheion to hear the children sing Timokletos's songs. Moreover, later Greek sources and several Latin texts from papal Rome will demonstrate conclusively that singing formed an important part of the training program at the Orphanage in Constantinople.

Descriptions of Byzantine court ceremonies from the late ninth and tenth centuries occasionally refer to the presence of an orphan choir at celebrations within the palace and at prominent churches in Constantinople. The *Kletorologion of Philotheos* mentions an orphan choir that participated in an elaborate feast at the palace to celebrate the Epiphany. After one of the dinner courses had been served, two domestics of Hagia Sophia entered the imperial dining hall, one leading adult singers and the other directing a choir of orphans. After the patriarch had given a special blessing, the two groups of singers alternated in chanting antiphonal hymns.[12]

According to the *Book of Ceremonies,* on the Feast of the Purification (2 February), an orphan choir stood on benches and greeted the emperor with songs as he entered Hagia Sophia through the main doors. These benches were probably a series of risers to allow the shorter boys in the back to watch the choir conductor. The *Book of Ceremonies* stated that the orphans were to chant the customary acclamations on behalf of the emperor, probably invocations for the sovereign's health and for victory over the enemies of the empire.[13] On the Feast of the Annunciation (25 March), the orphans sang at an outdoor ceremony held in the forum.[14] On the day after Easter, the orphans participated in a liturgical celebration at the Church of the Holy Apostles.[15]

Neither the *Book of Ceremonies* nor the *Kletorologion of Philotheos* stated that this orphan choir came from the Orphanotropheion, but another ninth-century source indicated that the well-known orphan choir, the one that no doubt participated in imperial ceremonies, was trained at the Orphanage. The *Vita Sancti Antonii junioris* (early ninth

---

12. *Kletorologion of Philotheos*, pp. 185–87.   13. *De cerimoniis*, 1.36 (27) [Vogt, 1: 140].
14. Ibid., 1.39 (30) [Vogt, 1: 153].   15. Ibid., 1.10 [Vogt, 1: 69].

century) recounted the story of a girl from an aristocratic family who lay dying from a serious disease. Those in charge of her care summoned singers "according to the custom of the Orphanotropheion."[16] From the wording of this *vita*, it is not clear whether the singers, described simply as *psaltes*, were the orphans themselves or cantors who sang in the manner of the Orphanotropheion. In either case, however, the passage proves that the Orphanage was well known for a particular kind of singing, probably the antiphonal chanting that the orphan choir performed at the imperial feast on the Epiphany.

From a century earlier (late seventh century) comes more evidence that the Orphanotropheion maintained a singing program for its children. The renowned *orphanotrophos* Andrew of Crete gained a reputation in Constantinople not only as a man of great philanthropy, but also as a composer of songs. In fact, he introduced to the capital a new form of liturgical music, known as a *kanon,* which Kosmas the Melode and John of Damascus had developed in Andrew's home province of Palestine. Andrew himself composed what was to become the most famous of these hymns, called the Great Kanon, which the Orthodox Church subsequently established as a special song for Holy Week.[17] It is impossible to determine whether Andrew received the post of *orphanotrophos* because of his musical ability, but it is probable that he, like the fifth-century Timokletos, composed some of his songs for the orphan choir to sing. One possible example is his long *kanon* for Palm Sunday with its references to the children of the New Jerusalem welcoming Jesus with hymns.[18]

Additional evidence regarding a music program for orphan children comes not from Constantinople, but from Rome. In describing Roman ecclesiastical customs and institutions during the seventh and eighth centuries, the *Liber Diurnus* reproduced a document regarding a Roman orphanage under papal control. According to this document, a pope of the late seventh century, possibly Pope Sergius I (687–701), saw that the orphan home had ceased to function because it lacked suffi-

16. *Vita Antonii junioris,* pp. 211–12.
17. *ODB,* 1: 92–93; Auzépy, "Carrière," pp. 1–12.
18. Maisano, "Inno inedito," pp. 523–71, esp. p. 523.

cient income. The pope restored the orphanage by endowing it with new resources so that it could provide for "the assembly of infants" and could "minister to the little children." According to the *Liber Diurnus*, the orphanage had existed for some years prior to its decay and subsequent restoration by Pope Sergius I.[19]

This late-seventh-century document provides the earliest reference to a Roman orphanage under the pope. Earlier sources do not mention it, not even the voluminous correspondence of Pope Gregory I (590–604), which contains much detailed information on Roman ecclesiastical and urban institutions at the beginning of the seventh century. Scholars have therefore assumed that the papal orphanage originated in the mid-seventh century.[20] During these same years (640–680), Byzantine religious and cultural influence in Rome grew stronger as Greek monks and clergy migrated from the eastern Mediterranean lands—Syria, Palestine, Asia Minor, and the Balkans—to Italy in general and to the ancient city on the Tiber in particular. The emperor Constans II augmented the Greek presence in Rome when he and his court visited the city in 663. Sometime during these "Byzantine" decades, the Roman *orphanotrophium* was founded, probably with the help of Greek immigrants. That Roman documents referred to this orphan home as the *orphanotrophium*, a term clearly derived from Byzantine Greek, strengthens this conclusion.[21]

In stating the reasons why the pope had reestablished the Roman *orphanotrophium*, the document in the *Liber Diurnus* not only mentions the pope's desire to help the young children but also his wish to ensure "that the order of song not die out and disgrace of the house of God not ensue." In other words, the Roman *orphanotrophium* maintained a children's choir that had a significant role in papal ceremonies.[22] In fact, singing formed such a major part of the regimen at the orphanage that people in Rome began referring to the institution not as the orphanage, but as the *Schola Cantorum.*

19. *Liber Diurnus*, V.97 (pp. 176–78). See also Waesberghe, "Schola Cantorum," p. 114.

20. Waesberghe, "Schola Cantorum," pp. 114–17.

21. Cavallo, "Cultura italo-greca," pp. 503–8. See also Riché, *Education*, pp. 345–52 and esp. p. 345: "Rome was a Byzantine city in the seventh century."

22. *Liber Diurnus*, V.97 (p. 177).

Several ninth-century papal *vitae* from the *Liber Pontificalis* state explicitly that the contemporary Schola Cantorum had formerly been called the *Orphanotrophium*.[23] The biography of Pope Sergius II proves that this name change had occurred as early as 800. According to his *vita*, the future pope Sergius II lost both his parents by the time he reached the age of twelve. Pope Leo III, the man who crowned Charlemagne, accepted responsibility for the little boy and placed him in the Schola Cantorum to learn his letters and mellifluous singing. When he was old enough, the boy joined the clergy of Rome—also a common career choice for many children raised in Byzantine orphanages, as we saw in Chapter Five. In 844, this former orphan was selected as bishop of Rome. As pope, Sergius II assigned new revenues to restore his old home, the Schola Cantorum. The *vita* added that people had formerly referred to the *Schola* as the *Orphanotrophium*.[24]

Obviously, training in music formed the core of the educational program at the Roman orphanage, but what evidence do we have that this Roman asylum was modeled on the Orphanotropheion in Constantinople? We have already emphasized two reasons for holding that the Roman Church patterned its orphanage on the famous institution of Constantinople. First, the Roman Church opened its orphanage sometime during the seventh century when Greek clergy began to settle in the Western capital in substantial numbers. Second, papal documents always referred to the orphan home as the *Orphanotrophium*, a term clearly derived from Byzantine Greek and not found in any earlier Latin sources.

Besides this evidence, scholars have uncovered additional information that establishes that the Orphanotropheion of Constantinople inspired its Roman counterpart. First, liturgists and musicologists have discovered that a new form of chant developed in Rome during the seventh century. Although these scholars disagree as to the nature and significance of some of these innovations, they all identify strong Byzantine influence as the key element in inspiring Roman liturgical changes of the mid-seventh century. The Dutch scholar S. van Dijk be-

---

23. *Liber Pontificalis*, 2: 92 (Pope Sergius II, 844–847); ibid., 2: 195 (Pope Stephen V, 885–891).
24. *Liber Pontificalis*, 2: 86 and 2: 92.

lieves that the creation of a new papal choir, the Schola Cantorum, and a novel method of singing occurred under Pope Vitalian (657–672), the bishop of Rome who welcomed the Byzantine emperor Constans II to the Western capital. Van Dijk also claims that Vitalian founded the Schola Cantorum, that is, the Roman *Orphanotrophium*, as part of a wider program to imitate Byzantine imperial ceremonies.[25]

Philologists have uncovered a second piece of evidence, far more conclusive than that based on musicological studies. Just prior to 1143 (250 years after Byzantine influence disappeared in Rome), a canon of Saint Peters named Benedict completed a treatise known as the *Liber Politicus*. In it Benedict described many papal ceremonies, including popular celebrations held in public piazzas. In depicting two of these outdoor celebrations, one held on Laetare Sunday (the fourth Sunday in Lent) and the other on the Saturday of Easter Week, Benedict mentioned that a children's choir chanted Greek songs. In describing the Laetare Sunday festival, Benedict transcribed the full text of one Greek song the children chanted. By the twelfth century, knowledge of Greek had died out in Rome, but Benedict was able to write down the verses using Latin characters. From this transcription, modern philologists have succeeded in restoring the original Greek text.[26]

Although Benedict did not mention that the choir came from the Schola Cantorum, he did state that both of these celebrations took place in the square next to the Church of Saint John Lateran where the principal buildings of the Schola Cantorum were located. John the Deacon, an official in the administration of Pope John VIII (872–882), however, provided a much earlier description of these same festivities during Easter Week, and in his account the prior of the Schola Cantorum played the major role in the burlesque associated with these piazza celebrations.[27] Since the Greek words recorded by Benedict two

25. Waesberghe, "Schola Cantorum," pp. 115–17, holds that the Schola Cantorum was under Byzantine influence, but that it was linked to a more traditional urban chant and liturgical celebrations in the churches of Rome. Van Dijk, "Urban and Papal Rites," pp. 465–72, on the other hand, asserts that the new Schola Cantorum had nothing to do with the urban liturgical rites of Rome, but was part of the policy of Pope Vitalian to model the papal court on the rich ceremonies of the Byzantine imperial court.

26. Patala, "Chants grecs," pp. 512–30; for the Greek text of the song, see pp. 519–23.

27. John the Deacon (Hymnodites), *Cena*, p. 870. For a lengthy discussion of the life of John the Deacon, see Arnaldi, "Giovanni Immonide," pp. 33–83.

hundred years later included several lines addressed to the head of the children's school, it is clear that the singers who had originally chanted this song came from the Schola Cantorum.[28]

Where did these Greek chants come from? Analysis of the Greek text shows a Byzantine origin. First, the language is Greek, not Latin. Second, one line of the song referred to the emperor as the *Basileus*, by the seventh century the official title of the Byzantine ruler.[29] Finally, another line expressed a wish for imperial victory, in the words of the song "Romania conquers."[30]

That this song used *Romania* to refer to the Roman Empire proves a Byzantine origin for at least some of these verses. Before the Fourth Crusade (1203–1204), the West used the term "Romania" to refer to the Romagna, the former exarchate of Ravenna, not to denote the entire Roman state. In the Byzantine East, however, the term "Romania" came to mean the East Roman Empire, especially in contrast to the barbarian world. A sixth-century inscription from Sirmium asked God to save Romania from the Avars. Thus, the children's victory acclamation surely came from the East, not from Italy.[31]

In conclusion, the children of the Schola Cantorum continued to sing Greek hymns as late as the twelfth century, songs which originated in the early days of the institution's history when it had functioned primarily as an orphanage. Such Greek songs had been introduced into the children's repertoire by Byzantine clergy and officials who came to Rome during the seventh century. There can be little doubt, therefore, that those who organized the Roman orphanage patterned it on the older Orphanage on the citadel of Constantinople. It is likely too that sections of the Greek song recorded by Canon Benedict closely followed Byzantine hymns chanted by the orphan choir of Constantinople.

After reviewing all the evidence both from Rome and from the city of Byzantium, we can conclude that music formed a significant part of

28. Patala, "Chants grecs," p. 519, ll. 1–4: Οἰκοδέσποτα, χαῖρε. / Χαῖρε, μετὰ παντὸς δέους ὁρῶ, / ὁρῶ εἰς τὸ μέλλον. / Ὁ καιρὸς εἰσῆλθε.

29. Ibid., 520 line 22: βασιλέα εἴσειδα.

30. Ibid., 522 line 58: Ῥωμανία νικᾷ.

31. *ODB*, 3: 1805.

the orphans' training at the Orphanotropheion of Constantinople. Thus, we can safely accept Zacharias of Mitylene's reference to the songs of Timokletos as proof that as early as the fifth century the children of Zotikos's Orphanage were learning choral singing.[32] It is possible, however, that the singing program began even earlier, when the Orphanotropheion had first opened.

As we saw in Chapter Three, Zotikos had probably established his philanthropic agencies including the Orphanotropheion sometime during the reign of Constantius (337–361). These years had seen intense competition among the contending theological factions that were vying for control of local churches. Music played a part in this competition. Even before the Council of Nicaea (325), Arius had composed songs for his supporters to sing in the streets of Alexandria.[33] Later on, the moderate Arian party that crystalized around Bishop Makedonios of Constantinople also won fame for its all-night vigils and antiphonal choirs of both men and women.[34] After the victory of the Nicean faction at the Council of Constantinople (381), the Arian party of Constantinople continued to support singing and elaborate processions at their churches beyond the walls of the city.[35] In such an atmosphere that promoted music, but especially choral singing, both as part of Christian worship and as a weapon of propaganda, it would have been natural for Zotikos or one of his successors to have organized the children into a choir.[36]

We have evidence for elaborate choirs at the Church of the Anastasia, the headquarters of the Nicaean party in Constantinople when Theodosius became emperor in 379. Moreover, Gregory of Nazianzos described these choirs together with a group of orphans and widows, although he did not state explicitly that the children were also singing.[37] If the Nicaeans were using elaborate choirs before 379, we

32. Zachariah of Mitylene, 4.11 (p. 80).

33. Philostorgios, p. 13.

34. Gregory of Nazianzos, *Oratio XLI: In Pentecosten* (PG, 36: 440); Sozomenos, 7.21.6–8 (p. 334); *Vita Sancti Auxentii* (PG, 114: 1380). See also Miller, "Orphanotropheion," p. 89.

35. Sozomenos, 8.8.1–6 (pp. 360–61); Sokrates, 6.8 (p. 325).

36. See the evidence presented in Chapter Four that Zotikos was one of the followers of Makedonios. See also Miller, "Orphanotropheion," pp. 88–90.

37. Gregory of Nazianzos, *Poemata di seipso*, 17 (PG, 37: 1260).

can be sure that the moderate Arians, who controlled the official church of Constantinople as well as Zotikos's Orphanage, had even more impressive musical performances. In view of the later importance of an orphan choir in Constantinople, it is tempting to postulate that children from Zotikos's Orphanage were chanting in the newly constructed Hagia Sophia as early as the reign of Constantius II.

Whether the orphans began to sing in the fourth century or several decades later at the time of Timokletos, such instruction in music fit the ancient Greek model of education that church leaders like Basil of Caesarea were adopting for Christian schools. Black-figured vases demonstrate that Athenian children of the fifth century B.C. had received training in music as part of their basic schooling.[38] Hellenistic schools continued this musical tradition. Third-century (B.C.) inscriptions describe how the cities of Teos and Chios paid for music teachers and sponsored public examinations in both singing and playing musical instruments. Moreover, in Hellenistic cities specially trained children's choirs performed at important civic and religious festivities. Influenced by such Greek traditions, Augustus established a choir of *amphithaleis* children to sing on the Palatine Hill at the Saecular Festival of 17 B.C.[39] In view of the important place music held in classical (that is, pre-Christian) education and its role in the development of popular Christian liturgical ceremonies, one can easily understand why the children both at the Orphanotropheion and at the other church-run schools learned to sing.

Our study has shown that from the time of Timokletos, if not earlier, the children of the Orphanotropheion received instruction in choral singing. How long did the Orphanage of Constantinople continue to emphasize music teaching? All the extant references to the orphan choir come from the ninth and tenth centuries, the era that produced detailed manuals of the complicated imperial ceremonies. The orphan choir disappeared from Byzantine sources thereafter. One text that survives from the twelfth century, however, indicates that the Or-

---

38. Golden, *Childhood*, pp. 62–63; Webster, *Potter*, pp. 57–59.

39. Marrou, *History*, pp. 189–91. For the description of Augustus's ceremonies, see Horace, *Carmen saeculare*.

phanotropheion continued to emphasize choral singing even after the emperor Alexios restored and possibly reorganized the institution.

Theodore Prodromos, who spent most of his life teaching at the Orphanotropheion, wrote a commentary to the original seventh-century *kanones* composed by Kosmas the Melode and John Damascene for the feasts of the Lord.[40] In his dedication, Prodromos claimed that the *orphanotrophos* Constantine had requested that he prepare this commentary.[41] Recent research on the manuscripts containing Theodore Prodromos's works has shown that his commentary on these hymns was recopied many times and that it came to serve as the standard Orthodox interpretation of these festal *kanones*.[42] That a twelfth-century *orphanotrophos* showed enough interest in a collection of hymns to request a detailed study and that the resulting commentary assumed a central position in the scholarship on Byzantine church music suggest that choral singing retained a significant place in the curriculum of the Orphanotropheion in the years after Alexios Komnenos's reign.

An analysis of twelfth-century texts, combined with a careful reading of a few passages from earlier sources, reveals that, in addition to music, the curriculum at the Orphanotropheion included disciplined study of Christian doctrine. As we saw in the opening chapter, when the emperor Alexios returned from his campaign of 1116 against the Turks, he brought back with him many orphans from the war-torn districts of Asia Minor. When he reached Constantinople, he found relatives to serve as guardians for some of these homeless children. Of the orphans who had no relatives, he assigned those with some understanding of their Christian faith to monastic schools in the capital; but those remaining who had no religious training he sent to the Orphanotropheion.[43]

The *Vita Sancti Cyrili* provides a more detailed picture of Alexios's policy regarding orphans without proper Christian education. According to his biographer, Saint Cyril praised Alexios for the work he had

40. *Theodori Prodromi commentarios*, pp. 1–2.
41. Ibid., pp. 1–2.
42. Hörandner, *Prodromos*, p. 44.
43. Anna Komnena, *Alexiad*, 15.7.1–3 (3: 213–14).

performed through the Orphanage of Saint Paul, an institution where the emperor had provided food for the hungry, had given drink to the thirsty, and had sheltered the homeless (Matt 25: 35–40). Cyril especially lauded Alexios, however, for ransoming captives, both adults and children, from among the Turks, captives who had begun to adopt the practices and beliefs of the godless (that is, the Moslems). These people the emperor had saved from the prison of godlessness and brought into "the light of the sun of justice." Cyril was unable to mention all those from every tongue whom the emperor had saved through Christian instruction and baptism at the Orphanotropheion.[44]

According to Saint Cyril, Alexios expected the staff at the Orphanotropheion to teach children such as those the emperor had brought with him from Asia Minor the doctrines of Christianity in preparation for baptism. Some of these children had come from Christian families, but because of the Turkish invasions they had never been given any religious instruction and presumably had not received baptism. Other children Alexios had taken from barbarian peoples. Cyril mentioned that the emperor had captured or ransomed children, especially from among the Scythians, that is, the Pechenegs and the Turks.[45]

In describing the students studying at the orphan school, Anna Komnena vividly portrayed the ethnic diversity of the student body. She mentioned Latins from Italy and France studying diligently, Scythians learning the Hellenic language, boys from Rome learning to write Greek, and unlettered Byzantines mastering proper classical Greek.[46] In his eulogy of his teacher Stephen Skylitzes, Theodore Prodromos stated that his former instructor's duties at the Orphanotropheion had included initiating both barbarians and Greeks into the mysteries of the pure Greek language.[47] In his eulogy of Anna Komnena, George Tornikes also mentioned orphans and widows from many races at the Orphanotropheion.[48]

In fact, the number of foreigners at the Orphanage of Saint Paul

44. *Vie de Cyrille le Philéote,* chap. 47.4–7 (pp. 229–31).
45. Ibid., chap. 47.6–7 (pp. 230).
46. Anna Komnena, *Alexiad,* 15.7.9 (3: 218).
47. Prodromos, "Monodie," p. 7.
48. Tornikès, "Éloge d'Anne Comnène," p. 319.

probably outnumbered the Byzantine children. The thirteenth-century chronicler sometimes identified as Theodore Skoutariotes believed that Alexios designed the new orphan school solely for foreign children taken in war.[49] Moreover, twelfth-century sources increasingly referred to the Orphanotropheion as dedicated to Saint Paul and dropped any reference to the institution's association with Saint Peter. The teacher Leo of Rhodes prayed to Saint Paul as the sole patron of the Orphanage.[50] Since Christian tradition considered Paul the apostle to the Gentiles, he served as the ideal heavenly advocate for an institution that devoted much of its energy to Christianizing barbarians.

During the second half of the twelfth century, Constantine Stilbes taught on the staff of the Orphanotropheion. His principal responsibility, as he himself stated, was to teach the Gospels to those outside the feast, that is, to those who had not yet been baptized.[51] Stilbes taught catechism for twelve years to non-Christian children at the Orphanotropheion before he was appointed, first, *didaskalos* of the Psalter, and then *didaskalos* of the Apostle, two of the three principal posts for catechetical teachers in Constantinople.[52]

It is clear from the *Vita Sancti Cyrili* and from Stilbes' career that foreign children as well as semi-Islamicized orphans from Asia Minor received instruction in Christian doctrine. Anna's description of grammar lessons, however, emphasized a second mission the school fulfilled, that of Hellenization. The teachers of the orphan school not only catechized their pupils, but they also taught them the intricacies of ancient Greek.[53]

Did the emperor Alexios first conceive this mission to Christianize and Hellenize the children of the barbarians? Several earlier sources indicate that he did not initiate this policy of accepting non-Byzantine orphans. In an obscure letter addressed to an unknown *orphanotrophos*, Michael Psellos stated that Bulgarians and Scythians were aware of the

49. *Synopsis chronike* (Skoutariotes), pp. 177–78.
50. *Schedos, Vaticanus Palatinus gr. 92*, fol. 208, and poem, *Vaticanus Palatinus gr. 92*, fol. 145ᵛ.
51. Stilbes, *Prolusione*, chap. 4 (p. 48).
52. Browning, "Patriarchal School(II)," pp. 26–32.
53. Anna Komnena, *Alexiad*, 15.7.9 (3: 218).

orphan director's conduct in protecting the property of the children in his care.[54] It is difficult to determine what exactly Psellos is referring to in this passage, but his words imply the presence of barbarian children at the Orphanotropheion. Why else would Scythians or Bulgarians be concerned about how the orphan director performed his duties?

The ninth-century *Kletorologion* presents stronger evidence. According to this text, on the Wednesday of Easter Week, the *orphanotrophos* played the leading role in a ceremony to introduce to the emperor those recently baptized at the celebration of the Resurrection.[55] The tenth-century *Book of Ceremonies* described the same service, but in greater detail. The *orphanotrophos* entered the imperial banquet hall dressed in splendid robes. Six newly baptized adults and six orphans followed him. Since the *Kletorologion* only mentions the newly baptized, it is probable that these orphans had received baptism at Easter alongside of the six adults. The *orphanotrophos* anointed the foreheads of the newly baptized, and then the emperor gave them each a kiss of fellowship.[56]

These two guidebooks for imperial ceremonies show that the *orphanotrophos* played a major part in preparing non-Christians for baptism. Since we know from the *Vita Sancti Cyrili* that the Orphanotropheion was preparing barbarians and war refugees for the sacrament of Christian initiation in the twelfth century, these earlier sources offer good evidence that this program began several centuries earlier.[57]

When did the practice of instructing non-Christians begin at the Orphanotropheion? There are no references prior to the *Kletorologion*, which associate either the *orphanotrophos* or his institution with catechizing barbarians. The famous orator Themistios, however, indicated in a speech he made before the emperor Theodosius I sometime in the 380s that, as early as the fourth century, Roman (that is, Byzantine) philanthropy formed a part of the empire's strategy to assimilate the barbarians. In his speech, Themistios claimed that the Goths had conquered Roman armies of the East and West, but when they crossed

---

54. Psellos, *Ep.* 240 (p. 290).
55. *Kletorologion of Philotheos*, p. 207.
56. *De cerimoniis*, 1.21 (12) [ed. Vogt, 1: 82–83].
57. *Vie de Cyrille le Philéote*, chap. 47.6 (p. 230).

the Haimos Mountains of northern Thrace, they were subdued "by piety, justice, mildness, and *philanthropia.*" According to Themistios, *philantropia* was motivating the East Romans to care for the sons of the Goths and to nurture their daughters.[58]

Themistios's meaning in this speech is not clear. He possibly was referring to the actions of private individuals who had adopted Goth children, abandoned by their tribe in its wanderings, or to the imperial policy of taking hostages. The emperor Constantine had initiated the practice of seizing barbarian children from beyond the Danube and holding them hostage in Constantinople to ensure the good behavior of the Germanic tribes.[59] It is also possible that monasteries or philanthropic institutions had accepted some of these Goth children and raised them as Roman (that is, Nicaean) Christians. Were some also cared for at the Orphanotropheion of Zotikos?

There is no evidence of barbarian children at the Orphanotropheion before the composition of the *Kletorologion* in the ninth century. Themistios's speech, however, indicates that, even as early as the fourth century, the Byzantine government had begun to see the value of philanthropic programs in winning the goodwill of barbarian tribes.

The *Kletorologion* and the *Book of Ceremonies* show that the emperor Alexios did not begin the practice of catechizing barbarian orphans and adult prisoners of war, but he did widen the scope of the program to include the many semi-Islamicized refugees from Asia Minor. Throughout the twelfth century the Orphanotropheion continued to perform this service. Even after its restoration by the emperor Michael VIII in the late thirteenth century, preparing children for baptism still formed part of the Orphanage's program. In praising the *orphanotrophos* Tryphon Kedrenos, Manuel Philes congratulated this orphan director for having given birth to so many children, not through natural birth, but through the regeneration of baptism.[60]

From the ninth through the fourteenth centuries, the Orphanotropheion prepared barbarian orphans and some adults for baptism. The

---

58. Themistios, *Oratio 34*, chap. 463 (p. 78) and chap. 466–67 (p. 82).
59. Thompson, *Visigoths*, p. 10.
60. Philes, poem 43 (p. 49).

sources, however, provide little indication of how the Orphanage of Constantinople organized its catechism lessons. Constantine Stilbes and perhaps Leo of Rhodes taught Christian doctrine to the children during the twelfth century, but the sources have left no trace of the methods these teachers employed.[61] On the other hand, far more information has survived with regard to the third course of studies at the Orphanotropheion, Greek grammar.

As we have seen, the earliest evidence of a school at the Orphanotropheion—Timokletos's songs of the mid-fifth century—indicates that the children were receiving training in choral singing. We can safely infer that along with instruction in music, the orphans also were taught to read and write Greek. Instruction in *grammata* (reading and writing Greek) had formed a basic subject in the primary schools of the classical world since the days of Periclean Athens. Moreover, one of the central figures in the development of Greek academic life, the philosopher Aristotle, stressed the importance of learning to read and write as the key to knowledge in many other fields.[62] In this tradition, Basil of Caesarea required that the students of his monastic school also learn their letters, though he replaced at least some of the readings from ancient literature with stories from the Sacred Scriptures.[63]

Basil's rules for his monastic school set the pattern for subsequent Byzantine academic programs, whether directly under bishops or supervised by monasteries. When the young Saint Nicholas entered the monastery of Stoudios in the late ninth century, the superior assigned him to the school to learn his letters.[64] In the tenth century Peter the bishop of Argos established a school for orphans that included both training in crafts and instruction in reading and writing for some of the children.[65]

The most significant evidence for a basic reading and writing curriculum at the Orphanotropheion of Constantinople comes not from

---

61. Stilbes, *Prolusione*, chap. 4 (p. 48). For Leo of Rhodes, see below at note 112.

62. For classical Athens, see Golden, *Childhood*, p. 62; for Aristotle's views, see his *Politica*, 1338a.

63. Basil, *Interrogatio XV* (PG, 31: 953).

64. *Vita Sancti Nicholae Studitae* (PG, 105: 869–72).

65. *Vita Petri Argivorum*, pp. 7–8.

provincial episcopal schools or from monasteries, but from the Western capital at Rome. The *Liber Pontificalis* mentioned that Pope Leo III entrusted an orphan boy in his care to the Schola Cantorum to learn how to read and to sing "mellifluously."[66] Since the Roman Schola Cantorum had been modeled on the Orphanotropheion of Constantinople, the *Liber Pontificalis* provides strong evidence that the orphans at the Byzantine asylum also learned to read and write as they trained to sing for the emperor and people of the Eastern capital.

No literary sources before the twelfth century, however, provide any details on how the students at the Orphanotropheion learned to read and write ancient Greek. The first such details come from the pages of Anna Komnena's *Alexiad*. After mentioning that the emperor Alexios had established the grammar school for the orphans, Anna described one of the teachers surrounded by his students who were engaged either in copying what the princess called *schede* or were passionately discussing grammar questions. In her rhetorical fashion, Anna pictured two prominent elements of the Orphanotropheion's program to teach Greek: writing *schede* and preparing for oral contests.[67]

Until recently, Byzantinists did not understand exactly what Anna meant by *schede*. The ancient Greek word referred to a riddle or puzzle. Even now, scholars do not fully comprehend all the variations of this instructional exercise. Anna herself caused confusion by claiming that *schede* were an innovation of her own generation.[68]

The earliest use of the term *schedos* for a form of teaching exercise comes from the letters of Michael Psellos. In one of his epistles, Psellos describes two bright students who had managed to finish all the *schede* that Psellos had provided them and were now asking him to write new ones.[69] In the letter, Psellos implied that he had copied *schede* when he had been in school, that is, in the 1020s.[70] Moreover, two of Psellos's contemporaries, Christopher of Mytilene and John Mauropous, both referred to students who engaged in *schede* contests of some sort.[71] Thus, grammar teachers were using *schede* at least a hundred years be-

---

66. *Liber Pontificalis*, 2: 86.
67. Anna Komnena, *Alexiad*, 15.7.9 (3: 218).
68. Ibid., 15.7.9 (3: 218).
69. Psellos, *Ep.* 16 (p. 20).
70. Ibid. See also comments of Schirò, "Schedografia," p. 13.
71. See Schirò, "Schedografia," p. 13 and pp. 17–18.

fore Anna's generation.[72] When Anna asserted that teaching with *schede* was an innovation, perhaps she was referring not to the use of the first *schede*, but to the introduction of a new form of this exercise.

Recent research has shown that, in fact, a new type of *schedos* did appear in the early twelfth century, a form associated with teachers at the Orphanotropheion. Theodore Prodromos and Stephen Skylitzes, both instructors at the orphan school of Constantinople, won fame for developing innovative *schede* that were becoming popular with students and other grammar teachers at the same time Anna was composing her history of her father's reign.[73] In his eulogy in honor of Theodore Prodromos, Eugenianos stressed that Prodromos had raised the *schedos* to a new art form. In Eugenianos's words, Prodromos had made the *schedos* "an intellectual psalm."[74]

Several modern studies on twelfth-century *schede* have analysed a number of these new grammatical exercises and have shown that they were in fact extended word puzzles. By making use of changes in the pronunciation of Greek over the centuries, the writer of a good *schedos* used ioticisms, changes in consonant pronunciation, and variations in marking off the words in a phrase to produce a text with several possible meanings. Students had to take the *schedos* prepared by the teacher and rewrite it in such a way as to discover its true meaning according to the rules of classical Greek grammar and orthography.[75] Thus, Anna correctly portrayed the students at the Orphanotropheion busily writing *schede*.[76]

In his excellent study of twelfth-century *schede*, Ioannis Vassis has published two of these puzzles composed by Theodore Prodromos.[77] Since Prodromos spent most of his life teaching at the Orphanotropheion, students at the orphan school probably used these *schede* or ones similar to them. Moreover, the first of these two compositions, dedicated to Saint Nicholas, begins by addressing the students as a

---

72. This is the conclusion of Schirò, "Schedografia," pp. 12–14, and of Garzya, "Literarische," pp. 3–4.

73. Garzya, "Literarische," pp. 3–4; Vassis, "Graeca," pp. 1–14.

74. Eugenianos, "Monodie," pp. 461–62.

75. Garzya, "Literarische," pp. 3–6; Vassis, "Graeca," pp. 1–14.

76. Anna Komnena, *Alexiad*, 15.7.9 (3: 218).

77. Vassis, "Graeca," pp. 14–19.

chorus. Is this a reference to the orphans' choir or simply to a group of children? The *schedos* also includes a reference to Saint Nicholas's role in assisting orphans.[78]

To have transcribed Prodromos's two *schede* correctly would have required a high degree of proficiency in ancient Greek. The first of these *schede* begins with the sentence, "Φέρε, χορέ, τῷ μύρον εἰ αἰρῇ νικολάῳ τὸ ὄνομα προσοίσομεν τὸ σύνηθες" (Come, chorus, we shall present the customary praise to Nicholas, if he should bear the perfume). To transcribe this sentence correctly and eliminate the non sequitur "if he should bear the perfume," the students needed to write, "Φέρε, χορέ, τῷ Μύρων ἱερεῖ Νικολάῳ τὸ ὄνομα προσοίσομεν τὸ σύνηθες" (Come, chorus, we shall present the customary praise to Nicholas, the bishop of Myra). Even well-trained modern philologists would find it difficult to convert "εἰ αἰρῇ" into "ἱερεῖ." In fact, in working with manuscripts containing these *schede*, modern scholars have failed to realize that the many ioticisms, misspellings, and apparently meaningless phrases were done on purpose, and as a result they have credited these anomalies to scribal errors.[79]

The two *schede* published by Vassis indicate that the Orphanotropheion provided an education beyond the primary level. Students at the orphan school were receiving a thorough training in classical Greek, far more rigorous than they would have needed simply to sing the psalms. Since there is no evidence before the twelfth century of the students at the Orphanotropheion working with *schede* or receiving anything beyond rudimentary instruction in reading and writing, it is possible that this advanced training in classical Greek began with the emperor Alexios's restoration program. This would perhaps justify Zonaras's and Anna's claims that the first Comnenian emperor had founded the grammar school at the Orphanage.

As a teaching tool, the *schede* did not win universal praise. Immediately following her description of the Orphanage students recopying their *schede*, Anna bitterly condemned the use of these word puzzles. She claimed that such games were replacing the texts of the classical

---

78. Ibid., pp. 14–16.
79. Browning, "Codice," p. 25.

authors and were thereby destroying liberal education *(enkyklios paideusis)*.[80] Another important scholar of the twelfth century, John Tzetzes, attacked the use of *schede* as the barbarizing work of ignorant hucksters.[81] The renowned scholar Eustathios of Thessalonike was more moderate in his judgment, but he too described these puzzles as word labyrinths.[82]

At least one modern scholar has seen the twelfth century's fascination with these *schede* as an indication of the age's cultural flaw: an overzealous striving to preserve pure classical Greek. In this all-consuming effort, the Byzantine masters of the *schede* destroyed the natural wellsprings of creativity in literature, that is, an appreciation of the vernacular.[83] But other scholars, such as Alexander Kazhdan, Ann Epstein, and Karl Krumbacher, have praised the *schedos* as a valuable new tool for teaching ancient Greek more effectively to a wider range of students.[84]

A final verdict about whether the *schede* retarded or enhanced Byzantine civilization must await further study of these difficult texts. At present, not many of these scholastic exercises have been published, and only a few scattered articles have addressed the topic. Although it is impossible to judge the overall success of *schede* as teaching tools, we can state that they came to play a predominant role in education and even rose to become a new form of literature. As we have seen above, the Orphanotropheion was one of the institutions that fostered their use.

In addition to writing *schede,* Anna mentioned that the students at the orphan school were also passionately engaged in answering grammatical questions.[85] These students were not simply discussing grammatical issues; they were preparing for some sort of public debate or contest. A hundred years earlier, Psellos had referred to one of his students who had copied no *schede* and had participated in no *logoi,* the

80. Anna Komnena, *Alexiad,* 15.7.9 (3: 218).
81. Tzetzes, *Historiae,* 9.701–8 (p. 372).
82. Eustathios, *Odysseam,* 2: 211 *(ad* T line 436).
83. Basilikopoulos-Ioannidou, pp. 188–99.
84. Kazhdan and Epstein, *Change,* p. 123; Krumbacher, *Geschichte,* pp. 590–92.
85. Anna Komnena, *Alexiad,* 15.7.9 (3: 218).

same two activities Anna described at the Orphanotropheion.[86] But what exactly were these *logoi?* A laudatory speech by Constantine Manasses provides the key to answering this question.

In 1167, Manasses wrote an oration in honor of Michael Hagiotheodorites, a man who held the office of *orphanotrophos* and also that of *logothete* of the *dromos.*[87] Manasses especially praised Hagiotheodorites for the time he spent, despite his many official responsibilities, with the children of the Orphanage. At contests held in the presence of the emperor, Hagiotheodorites would pose tricky questions for the boys in an effort to catch them up in grammatical or rhetorical errors. Manasses claimed that not a single student escaped the *orphanotrophos's* clever grammatical traps. According to Manasses's speech, these formal quiz sessions greatly amused the emperor Manuel I and his court.[88]

The students at the Orphanotropheion thus engaged in some sort of oral contests to display their mastery of Greek grammar. Basil of Caesarea had recommended such contests as one of the best methods to keep young students interested in their school work. As we saw in Chapter Five, competitions in academic subjects had not begun with Basil's *Regulae,* but had formed part of the educational program in many Greek cities of the Hellenistic period. This twelfth-century competition before Manuel I, however, is the first reference we have to contests specifically for the Orphanage students, but it is possible that, under the influence of Basil, the students of the Orphanotropheion had been competing in grammar quizzes of some sort for centuries.[89]

We have several references from the eleventh century to contests in copying *schede.* John Euchaites wrote a short poem that described a *schede* contest at the School of the Forty Martyrs, and Giuseppe Schirò

86. Psellos, *Ep.* 24 (p. 31).

87. Magdalino, *Empire,* pp. 256–57.

88. Manasses, "Unedierte Rede," p. 181. Manasses does not use the word "orphans," but describes the children as παισὶ τροφίμοις. Τρόφιμος, a term used in Sparta to refer to children of poor parents who were raised by wealthier families. Moreover, in many inscriptions from classical times the word meant a foster child (Lidell and Scott, *sub voce*). Since we know that at the time of the contests Michael Hagiotheodorites held the office of *orphanotrophos,* we can safely conclude that these foster children, these children of poor families, were in fact the students of the Orphanotropheion.

89. Basil, *Interrogatio XV* (PG, 31: 953); cf. Hellenistic contests described in Marrou, *History,* pp. 230–31.

discovered five anonymous poems that mention a nearly contemporary *schede* competition at the same school.[90] Moreover, a nine-line poem at the end of a twelfth-century *schedos,* preserved in the Marciana Library of Venice, refers to a contest of *schede* presumably held at the Orphanotropheion since the victor was to receive the crown of the school's patron, Saint Paul.[91]

In Anna's description of the Orphanage students, she seems to have been describing the youths as they practiced rewriting the *schede* and debating grammar points.[92] In both cases, then, the students were sharpening their skills for future contests. Some were practicing for a *schede* competition such as the one mentioned in the Marciana manuscript, while others were training for verbal contests such as Michael Hagiotheodorites conducted before the emperor Manuel I in 1167. Contests so dominated the academic life of the children at the orphan school during the twelfth century that one of their teachers, Leo of Rhodes, referred to his pupils as youths involved in contests and to his own labors as constantly weaving contentious words.[93]

These contests, but especially the preparation for them, thus formed a major part of the grammar curriculum at the Orphanotropheion. It is revealing that, when the emperor Michael VIII restored the institution after his reconquest of Constantinople in 1261, he provided not only funds for pupils' stipends and for teacher salaries, but also for purses to reward in a suitable fashion those students who excelled in *logoi,* probably the verbal contests in grammar.[94]

THE TEACHERS

The best information we have about the organization of the teaching staff at the Orphanotropheion comes from the pen of Theodore Prodromos, who himself spent much of his life as an instructor at the orphan school.[95] When Stephen Skylitzes died, Prodromos composed

---

90. For the poem of John Euchaites, see Schirò, "Schedografia," p. 18, note 21, which reproduces the text. For the anonymous poems, see ibid., pp. 27–29.

91. Browning, "Codice," p. 32.   92. Anna Komnena, *Alexiad,* 15.7.9 (3: 218).

93. *Vaticanus Palatinus gr. 92,* fol. 145ᵛ–146.   94. Pachymeres, 4.14 (1: 284).

95. Italikos, no. 1 (p. 61) indicates that Prodromos lived at the Orphanotropheion, as does Prodromos, *Eisiterios* (PG, 133: 1269).

an elaborate monody in honor of his deceased friend and former teacher. In the opening section of this speech, Prodromos described Skylitzes' early career at the Orphanage of Saint Paul.

Skylitzes had scarcely finished his education when he attained a position as an instructor at the orphan school. At that time, Skylitzes' brother held the supervisory teaching position on the school's faculty. While still very young, Skylitzes replaced his brother as the principal *(proedros)* of the school. Prodromos added that many others wanted this job and that they complained to the patriarch who had made the appointment. These envious ones alleged that Skylitzes was not old enough for the job of school supervisor.[96]

Prodromos's account proves that a number of instructors taught at the orphan school and that a principal, distinct from the *orphanotrophos,* supervised the academic side of the institution. Moreover, Prodromos revealed that as part of a promotion ceremony Skylitzes received a special blessing from the patriarch which included an anointing with holy chrism.[97] We know from a speech delivered by Michael Italikos in 1142, that he too received a special blessing and a ceremonial anointing with chrism when the patriarch Leo Stypes appointed him *didaskalos* of the Gospels.[98] Apparently, the patriarch controlled the instructional staff at the Orphanotropheion just as he did the highest teaching posts of Constantinople, the three *didaskaloi* of the Holy Scriptures attached directly to Hagia Sophia. The writings of another teacher at the Orphanotropheion, Leo of Rhodes, also described the patriarch as the highest authority over the orphan school.[99]

What exactly was the nature of the patriarch's control over the orphan school? As we saw in the preceding chapter, the Orphanotropheion had become an independent ecclesiastical institution in the fifth century.[100] The patriarch, therefore, enjoyed no legal power of ownership over the institution or its movable or immovable resources. Robert Browning has suggested that the patriarch's authority over the Orphanotropheion rested on an organization of education in Constantinople

---

96. Prodromos, "Monodie," pp. 8–9.   97. Ibid., p. 9.
98. Italikos, no. 10 (p. 118).
99. *Vaticanus Palatinus gr. 92,* fol. 207ᵛ and fol. 146.
100. *Theodoros Anagnostes,* p. 106

that had turned the orphan school into a division of a larger, centralized system under the bishop of the capital city.[101] In a recent article on the organization of education in the Byzantine Empire, Ugo Criscuolo has maintained that the patriarch's control over schools arose not from an organizational structure, but from the ancient Christian concept that teaching represented an episcopal ministry and that in a sense all instructors in a Christian society functioned as representatives of the bishop. This would explain why the director of the orphan school received an anointing with chrism from the patriarch's hands.[102]

Prodromos's eulogy of Skylitzes, however, states that the emperor also played a role in confirming a new principal for the orphan school.[103] Moreover, a *schedos* written by another teacher at the Orphanage indicates that the *orphanotrophos* held considerable power over the school as well.[104]

From the evidence available one cannot establish the lines of command at the school exactly, but it does seem clear that the principal or *proedros* supervised a number of teachers. The school principal in turn was responsible to the *orphanotrophos* as the administrative head of the entire institution, but the *proedros* also stood under the patriarch who supervised the instructors at the Orphanage as ministers sharing in his episcopal teaching office. Finally, the emperor, both as sovereign and as the chief patron of the Orphanotropheion, had ultimate authority over the entire philanthropic operation.

Prodromos's speech in honor of Skilitzes also provides a few details on the personal qualities of Skylitzes as a teacher. He spent many hours working on *schede* with his students, often in private sessions. He always wore a smile and tried to emphasize the good qualities of his students' work. Prodromos stressed that at one point in his life Skylitzes decided to take up the philosophy of poverty. According to Byzantine usage, this meant that Skylitzes had become a monk.[105]

In describing Skylitzes' new life of poverty, Prodromos never re-

101. Browning, "Patriarchal School (I)," pp. 167–76.
102. Criscuolo, "Chiesa," pp. 378–79 and p. 385, note 37.
103. Prodromos, "Monodie," pp. 8–9.
104. *Vaticanus Palatinus gr. 92*, fols. 207–207ᵛ.
105. Prodromos, "Monodie," pp. 10–11.

ferred to a specific monastery. Since monasticism was a much looser institution in the Eastern Church than it became in the Latin Western Church, it was possible for Skylitzes to lead a monastic life in Byzantium without in fact joining an ascetic community. Skylitzes became a monk in that he began to wear the simple garb of a monk, to practice strict fasting and celebacy, and to adopt other aspects of an austere lifestyle.[106]

Sometime in the reign of the emperor John II (1118–1143), Skylitzes was selected as metropolitan of Trebizond. He was consecrated bishop when he was only thirty years old. Consequently, he could not have served as principal of the orphan school for very many years.[107] That a principal of the orphan school could advance directly to an important see such as Trebizond indicates that by the twelfth century the school of the Orphanotropheion enjoyed a prominent place in the eyes of both the government and the church of Constantinople.

In addition to Prodromos and Skylitzes, we know of three other teachers at the Orphanotropheion during the twelfth century: Leo of Rhodes, Constantine Stilbes, and Basil Pediadites. Leo wrote two colorful works, a short *schedos* and a poem, that contain some interesting information about his teaching career at the Orphanotropheion. In the *schedos,* he mentioned that he had held several lower ranks on the teaching staff before assuming a supervisory role. Leo did not state that he served as *proedros,* but it is possible that he held this top rank in the school. He also claimed to have filled several other important offices at the orphan school. Leo's *schedos* thus depicts a teaching staff with more ranks than Prodromos mentioned in his funeral oration for Skylitzes.[108]

Leo did not enjoy teaching at the Orphanotropheion. In his poem he compared his work there to the brick-making labors of the Hebrews enslaved in Egypt.[109] He claimed that he had toiled in the orphan

---

106. Ibid., p. 10. Regarding Byzantine monasticism, see Hunger, *Reich*, pp. 229–98. See also Elm, *Virgins*. Although Elm's book deals specifically with women and the ascetic tradition of the fourth century, she makes some valuable observations about Byzantine monasticism in general and has included an excellent bibliography.

107. Prodromos, "Monodie," pp. 9–10.

108. *Vaticanus Palatinus gr. 92*, fols. 207–207ᵛ.

109. Ibid., fol. 146.

school for twenty years, longer than most of the instructors.[110] More-over, he complained that at his advanced age, he found it too difficult to teach children. As he stated in his poem, "I am worn out in address-ing the tribes of infants."[111]

It is difficult to determine exactly what subjects Leo taught. He re-peatedly referred to his job as a *mystagogia*, a term used to describe preparation for baptism.[112] His statement that he taught tribes of in-fants might also indicate that he was preparing young barbarian refugees for Christian initiation. In another place, however, he com-plained about his having to weave together contentious words, proba-bly a reference to the grammar or *schede* contests.[113] Perhaps during his twenty-year service, he taught both catechism and Greek grammar to the children.

After more than twenty years of service in the orphan school, Leo's petitions to his direct superior, the *orphanotrophos* Alexios Aristenos, and to the patriarch met with success. He finally received the metro-politan see of Rhodes.[114]

Constantine Stilbes briefly mentioned his teaching post at the Or-phanotropheion in the speech he delivered circa 1200 upon his appoint-ment as *didaskalos* of the Apostle. In the 1180s he had begun his teach-ing career at the orphan school where he worked for twelve years before advancing to the high rank of *didaskalos* of the Psalter. In his speech, Stilbes stated specifically that he had taught the Gospels, that is, that he had prepared the barbarian and semi-Islamicized children for baptism.[115] Stilbes made no mention of having taught Greek gram-mar, and in fact, the list of *schedos* authors that Robert Browning as-sembled from his study of *schede* manuscripts does not include Stilbes's name.[116] It is therefore possible that Stilbes only taught reli-gion at the institution.

In the course of his speech, Stilbes did not complain about his work

110. Ibid., fols. 207–207ᵛ.
111. Ibid., fol. 145ᵛ: κέκμηκα καὶ γὰρ προσλαλῶν βρεφυλλίοις.
112. Ibid., fols. 207–207ᵛ.
113. Ibid., fol. 145ᵛ: πλέκων ἀπεῖπον τοὺς ἁμιλλοτηρίους (λόγους).
114. *Hierarchia*, 1: 203.   115. Stilbes, *Prolusione*, pp. 47–48.
116. Browning, "Codice," pp. 21–34.

at the Orphanotropheion as Leo had, but he did make a veiled reference to his low salary.[117] His economic situation no doubt improved when he left the orphan school to take up a more prominent teaching post at Hagia Sophia, that of *didaskalos* of the Psalter. Sometime before 1204, he became metropolitan of Kyzikos on the shores of the Marmora Sea.[118]

With regard to Basil Pediadites, we know only that he taught grammar at the Orphanotropheion in the second half of the twelfth century. During his early career at the Orphanage, he apparently wrote some blasphemous poems, and as a result, lost his teaching post. He later regained his job and redeemed his reputation in the eyes of the patriarchal supervisors because, prior to 1200, he was made metropolitan of the western city of Kerkyra.[119] We have no idea of the contents of these blasphemous poems. He might have written them in a misconceived effort to amuse his young students.

Of the five men whom we know taught at the Orphanotropheion and concerning whom we have found some biographical information—Skylitzes, Prodromos, Leo, Stilbes, and Pediadites—four advanced to the high ecclesiastical office of metropolitan bishop. Only Theodore Prodromos seems to have remained all his life at the Orphanotropheion. His lack of success in attaining high ecclesiastical office despite his renown as a writer and rhetorician has puzzled modern scholars and may also explain why contemporaries began referring to him as Ptochoprodromos.[120] We shall discuss Prodromos's career later in this chapter with respect to the students at the Orphanotropheion.

THE STUDENTS

With regard to the teachers at the Orphanotropheion, the sources provide a few details about the bureaucratic organization of the staff. With regard to the students—the orphans and poor children accepted at the school—on the other hand, the surviving documents offer al-

117. Stilbes, *Prolusione*, pp. 47–48.
118. Browning, "Patriarchal School (II)," pp. 26–32.
119. Ibid., pp. 20–22.
120. Kazhdan, *Studies*, p. 87. For an early reference to the writer as Ptochoprodromos, see Mercati, "Testament," p. 46.

most no information. We do not know how the administrators of the Orphanotropheion structured the students' daily routine or how they fed and housed the children. At what time did classes start, when and where did the students take their meals, and when did they retire in the evening? No direct evidence has survived from Constantinople concerning their living arrangements, but fortunately the ninth-century Roman writer John the Deacon provides a glimpse of the dormitory at the Schola Cantorum. In his *Vita Sancti Gregorii*, John described the boys sleeping together in a dormitory hall, not in private rooms.[121] Since officials at Rome had presumably modeled the Schola Cantorum on the Orphanotropheion of Constantinople, it is likely that they had also copied the method of housing the children from their Byzantine archetype.

Did the orphan students wear uniforms? The *vita* of Saint Theophano described members of a children's choir, possibly the chorus from the Orphanotropheion, as wearing wreaths on their heads at the wedding of Emperor Leo VI and the young Theophano at the end of the ninth century.[122] These wreaths were a traditional headdress for nuptial celebrations, but this passage demonstrates only that choir singers, including the children of the Orphanotropheion chorus, wore special garb for their performances. No sources survive, however, that indicate that the orphans wore uniforms during their daily routines.

The centuries prior to the emperor Alexios's rebuilding efforts have left only one meager piece of information regarding student organization at the Orphanotropheion. A lead seal that Gustave Schlumberger dated to the tenth or eleventh century bears the inscription, "Seal of the first students of the Orphanotropheion" or perhaps "Seal of the first of the students of the Orphanotropheion."[123] In either case, the seal indicates some sort of structure in the student body of the orphan school.

Fortunately, the twelfth century offers a few more details about student organization. Nikephoros Basilakes composed a strange oration against a political enemy whom he identified with the pseudonym Bo-

---

121. John the Deacon (the Hymnodites), *Vita Sancti Gregorii* (PL, 75: 241–42).
122. *Vita Theophano,* chap. 11 (p. 6).
123. Schlumberger, p. 379.

goas, the name of Alexander the Great's close companion. In the speech, composed in 1157, Basilakes provided a sketch of Bogoas's parents and of his childhood, a sketch that also recounted Bogoas's years as a student at the Orphanotropheion.[124]

According to Basilakes, Bogoas's father had eked out a meager existence as a fisherman. His father had tried to find a wife in Sinope, a town on the coast of the Black Sea from which he conducted some of his fishing expeditions, but the impoverished fisherman had had no success. He pushed north to a barbarian land near the Sea of Azov where a famine was raging. Here he found a starving Scythian woman who agreed to marry him. Bogoas was born of this nuptial union. As Basilakes contemptuously described his enemy's origins, Bogoas was "the by-product of food for the poor and the fruit of famine."[125]

Bogoas's father brought him to Constantinople without his barbarian mother. Since the poor fisherman did not have enough money to raise little Bogoas, he decided to give the child to an uncle. As we have seen, uncles frequently accepted the role of guardian in Byzantine society. The father then disappeared from Bogoas's life. Unfortunately, the uncle also had insufficient resources, and although he had promised to love Bogoas and to provide for his care, the poor man decided to hand the boy over to the teachers of grammar, an obvious reference to the Orphanotropheion which had become the grammar school par excellence in twelfth-century Constantinople.[126]

At the Orphanotropheion, Bogoas met one of the senior students who subsequently became his mentor. The older boy daily worked with Bogoas and came to play the leading role in his education. He both inspired Bogoas intellectually and gave him opportunities to practice his grammar lessons.[127] That an older male student assumed a teaching role with respect to Bogoas may represent a tradition at the

---

124. Basilakes, *Adversus Bogoam*, pp. 92–110. See also Magdalino, *Empire*, pp. 277–84, who suggests that this Bogoas was Soterichos Panteugenos, the orthodox patriarch of Antioch (resident in Constantinople).

125. Basilakes, *Adversus Bogoam*, chaps. 12–13 (pp. 99–100).

126. Ibid., chap. 13 (pp. 100): ὁ δὲ (the uncle) γραμματοδιδασκάλοις ἐκδίδωσιν. Cf. Browning, "Patriarchal School (II)," pp. 20–22, where Basil Pediadites is identified in a manuscript as μαΐστωρ τῆς σχολῆς τῶν γραμματικῶν τοῦ Παύλου.

127. Basilakes, *Adversus Bogoam*, chap. 13 (p. 100).

Orphanage that had its origins in the monastic rules of Basil of Caesarea. As we saw in Chapter Five, Basil made use of the best among
the older students as monitors of the younger children.[128] Subsequent
episcopal and monastic schools followed Basil's example and instituted
the same practices.[129] One would expect a similar system at the Orphanotropheion.

It is also possible that Bogoas was assigned to work with the older
student to train in the use of *schede* in preparation for forthcoming
contests. Psellos's comments in his letters and the eleventh-century poems describing *schede* competitions all indicate that students both
trained for and competed in *schede* events in pairs.[130] Bogoas and his
older friend possibly formed such a *schede* team.

Basilakes' declamation against Bogoas thus revealed that the orphan school used a kind of mentoring program by assigning younger
students to work with older boys who were doing well in their studies.
Basilakes' speech, however, added some additional information concerning student life at the Orphanotropheion. According to Basilakes,
Bogoas and his mentor were involved in an erotic relationship. When
the younger boy noticed that his student tutor admired his youthful
beauty, Bogoas willingly submitted to the older boy's desires. Basilakes' account did not directly criticize this aspect of their relationship;
rather he focused on Bogoas's immaturity in desiring to continue such
behavior after he grew older. Bogoas so wanted to remain in this homosexual relationship that he had himself castrated to preserve his
youthful looks. Basilakes, of course, presented this act as a sign of Bogoas's depraved nature.[131]

Was Basilakes telling the truth in his speech against Bogoas? Obviously, Basilakes exaggerated in composing this vicious attack on a political enemy, but should we accept as fact the story about the homosexual relationship? Since Basilakes described this erotic relationship in
its initial stage as admirable, he probably did not intend to use it as his
principal attack on Bogoas's moral character. On the other hand, Basi-

128. Basil, *Interrogatio XV* (PG, 31: 953).
129. See *Vita Euthymii*, p. 11.
130. Schirò, "Schedografia," pp. 11–29, but esp. p. 23.
131. Basilakes, *Adversus Bogoam*, chap. 13 (pp. 100–101).

lakes might have invented the story of the homosexual activity and portrayed it as a positive aspect of Bogoas's educational experience to drive home even more forcefully his main point, Bogoas's utter moral depravity.

In the final analysis, one cannot accept all the specific details that Basilakes presented in this speech regarding Bogoas and his mentor. There are simply too many exaggerations in Basilakes' highly vituperative oration to take all of it seriously. Nevertheless, that Basilakes chose to describe his enemy as having had a male lover while a student at the Orphanotropheion indicates that his hearers had reason to believe that such a relationship could have occurred, given what they knew about education in general and conditions at the Orphanotropheion in particular. I therefore believe that Basilakes' speech does provide evidence that homosexual relationships, particularly between older students and their younger wards, did occur. How often these relationships developed we cannot determine, but Basilakes implied that they were not rare, a point he did not need to make in attempting to portray Bogoas as abnormally evil.

According to Basilakes, Bogoas left the orphan school to join the clergy of Constantinople. He associated also with a group of politically active monks with connections at the imperial court.[132] In his excellent book on twelfth-century Byzantine society, Paul Magdalino has suggested that Basilakes used the name of Bogoas to disguise the identity of his actual target, Soterichos Panteugenos, patriarch of Antioch. If Magdalino is right, then, the case of "Bogoas" shows that students from the Orphanotropheion could rise to extremely high positions within the Byzantine Church.[133]

That a student from the Orphantotropheion came to hold a high position in the ecclesiastical hierarchy fits what we have seen at other orphan schools. In the ninth century, the orphan Peter left a monastic school to become bishop of Argos, and he in turn was succeeded as local shepherd by a man who had grown up in the orphanage Peter himself had sponsored.[134] At Rome, the ninth-century pope Sergius II had

132. Ibid., chap. 15 (p. 101).
133. Magdalino, *Empire*, pp. 277–84. See also Magdalino, "Bogoas," pp. 47–63.
134. *Vita Petri Argivorum*, pp. 1–6 and 17.

begun his training in music and grammar as one of the orphan students at the Schola Cantorum.[135] Thus, one should not find it surprising that Bogoas, abandoned successively by his fisherman father and his impoverished uncle, was able to rise to the highest ranks of the Byzantine clergy, thanks to the excellent education he received at the Orphanotropheion.

Not all orphans succeeded, however. Constantine Stilbes dedicated one of his poems to an orphan and former student who seems not to have benefitted materially from his education at the Orphanotropheion. Stilbes began his poem by praising this former student's intelligence: he was a boy who had shone like the morning star among his fellow pupils.[136] Nevertheless, he failed to find a place in Constantinople and finally died in the provincial city of Patras, abandoned by friends, an orphan without a home or even a city. He passed away in a philanthropic institution, probably a *gerokomeion* or a *xenon,* where the hospital workers washed him, fed him, quenched his thirst, and finally closed his eyes in death.[137]

Why did Stilbes' student fail in life, despite his success in his studies? Of course, a historian cannot answer such a question, even if sufficient documentation had survived. So many psychological factors would have contributed to his material failure and his death in a philanthropic institution in western Greece. Nevertheless, since Stilbes' poem did not mention that this orphan student had ever joined the clergy, one should consider the possibility that graduates from the Orphanotropheion, as well as those from other monastic or episcopal schools, had little opportunity open to them other than joining a monastery or the ranks of the local clergy. Since the children raised in orphanages would have had no living family members willing or able to serve as their guardians, they also would have lacked sponsors in their adult lives to assist them in building careers. Such may have been the fate of Stilbes' student who died a stranger in a strange land.[138]

In addition to Bogoas and Stilbes' student, the twelfth-century

---

135. *Liber Pontificalis,* 2: 86 and 92.   136. Stilbes, *Monodia,* p. 88, ll. 1–3.

137. Ibid., pp. 89–90, ll. 27–44.

138. Ibid., p. 89, l. 29: Τίς ὀρφανὸν συνῆξεν ἄπολιν, ξένον; p. 90 line 44: Θάπτουσι Πάτραι μακρόθεν με (the dead student speaking) πατρίδος.

sources perhaps reveal another former student of the Orphanotropheion, one of Byzantium's most prominent literary figures, Theodore Prodromos. This writer's life history has posed many problems for modern scholars who have tried to reconstruct his biography from casual remarks in his writings and those of his colleagues. In his detailed essay on Prodromos, Alexander Kazhdan stated that despite Prodromos's fame in his own time and his popularity among modern scholars, much remains obscure about his family and his career.[139] Other scholars have emphasized contradictory statements that Prodromos made about his own childhood and youth.[140] A careful rereading of these statements, however, provides four reasons for believing not only that Prodromos had lost his parents during his youth, but also that he studied at the Orphanotropheion.

First, in his eulogy of Stephen Skylitzes, Prodromos stated explicitly that he himself had studied under Skylitzes and had worked closely with him in learning the art of *schedos* writing. Before becoming metropolitan of Trebizond, Skylitzes had taught at the Orphanotropheion, but in no other school.[141] It is possible that Skylitzes had instructed Prodromos as a private student, but no evidence exists that at the orphan school teachers were allowed to take on paying pupils. Stilbes' complaint about his low salary at the Orphanotropheion suggests that the instructors did not have an opportunity to augment their income.[142] Moreover, Prodromos did not claim to have been Skylitzes' private pupil. The easiest explanation for Prodromos's account is to assume that the future orator, poet, and romance writer had studied at the Orphanotropheion while Skylitzes was teaching there.

Second, regarding his family, Prodromos never mentioned his mother. She apparently died early in his life.[143] He did mention his father, however. In explaining why he chose the academic life, Prodromos recounted how his father once placed him on his knee and advised him to take up scholarship as a sure road to success.[144] In a second poem,

---

139. Kazhdan, *Studies*, p. 87.
140. See Wolfram Hörandner's brief biography in Prodromos, *Gedichte*, pp. 21–32.
141. Prodromos, "Monodie," pp. 8–10.   142. Stilbes, *Prolusione*, pp. 47–48.
143. See Eugenianos, "Monodie," p. 456.
144. Prodromos, *Gedichte*, poem 38 (pp. 378–79).

however, Prodromos stated that he had been taken in by relatives and raised by them.[145] In this latter passage, Prodromos used the verb that in classical Greek meant to support an adopted child.[146] To reconcile these two statements, one must assume that Prodromos had lived with his father as a small boy, but at some point his father either died or left him in the care of relatives.

Third, in a poem, written in demotic Greek, Prodromos claimed that the empress Irene, wife of Alexios I, had provided him sustenance as a little boy while he had lived with his books and lessons.[147] In another poem, Prodromos made the strange statement that God had handed him over to wise lords with whom he had contended and won the prize.[148] One can resolve these seemingly contradictory statements by assuming that Irene sponsored Prodromos for admission to the Orphanotropheion, where the boy then gave himself over to studies as he himself stated in his demotic poem. Moreover, such an interpretation unravels the meaning of his second statement concerning the wise lords with whom Prodromos contended: they were the teachers and older student mentors whom Prodromos was able to defeat in *schede* contests or the grammatical *logoi*.[149]

The fourth argument hinges on Prodromos's subsequent career. As an adult, he taught for many years at the Orphanotropheion, where he gained a reputation for his clever *schede*.[150] In his speech in honor of Alexios Aristenos's reappointment as *orphanotrophos*, Prodromos referred to the Orphanage as his home.[151] Moreover, in his last years, Prodromos retired not to a monastery or to the estate of a relative or friend, but to a *gerokomeion* where he was confined, as his friend Eugenianos stated, not because of his age, but because of illness. Prodro-

145. Prodromos, *Gedichte*, poem 59 (pp. 479–80): ὑφ' οἷς (relatives) ἀναχθεὶς εὐσεβῶς ἀνετράφην.

146. Cf. *Anthologia graeca*, 9.254 (Phil.): ἡ δ' εὔπαις (the mother speaking) θετὸν υἱὸν ἀνήγαγον.

147. Prodromos, "Nuova poesia," p. 399.

148. Prodromos, *Gedichte*, poem 38 (p. 380).

149. Ibid., p. 380, l. 95: ὅττι σοφοῖς κυρίοις με θεὸς μέγας ὦπασε δμωόν, / οἷς παραεθλεύσω καὶ ἀέθλια ἐσθλ' ἀνελοίμην·

150. See above.

151. Prodromos, *Eisiterios* (PG, 133: 1269).

mos's last days in a *gerokomeion,* probably the one attached to the Orphanotropheion, resembled the fate of Stilbes' orphan student who also finished his life in a philanthropic institution in Patras, far away from Constantinople.[152]

The surviving sources reveal so little about the students of the Orphanotropheion that modern scholars do not know if the school accepted girls as well as boys. As we saw in Chapter Five, Basil's school in fourth-century Cappadocia allowed female children to enter, and the private orphanage in ninth-century Prousa cared for an equal number of boys and girls. As both episcopal and monastic schools came to focus increasingly on preparing their wards either for the clergy or the ascetic life, however, girls disappeared from many orphan schools except those attached to women's religious communities.[153] It is therefore likely that the Orphanotropheion excluded female children from its program, but we have no documents that prove that girls were not admitted there.

The Orphanotropheion thus provided its wards with a multifaceted education that included training in music, Christian doctrine, and reading and writing. After the emperor Alexios's reorganization, it also offered its students superior training in Greek grammar and probably rhetoric. Its program enabled some students to rise from poverty to exalted church offices. But did it meet the needs of most orphans in Constantinople? We have no indication of the numbers of students it trained or what criteria the institution used to admit children. Did the Orphanotropheion's Christianization program designed for barbarians and refugees gradually limit the number of native Greek orphans from Constantinople and the provinces who entered the institution? As the orphan school gained in prestige to become one of the leading academic centers of the Byzantine capital, did powerful families place their orphaned younger brothers, nephews, or cousins in this well-financed educational institution?

We saw in Chapter Three that as early as the fifth century some

---

152. Eugenianos, "Monodie," p. 460; cf. Stilbes, *Monodia,* pp. 88–90.
153. See Chapter Five.

children at the Orphanotropheion had inherited considerable proper-ty.[154] Did this wealthy element gradually grow until, by the twelfth century, it excluded the truly impoverished street urchins of Constan-tinople from the sophisticated grammar lessons of Stephen Skylitzes or Theodore Prodromos? These are questions that at present cannot be answered with certainty. In describing the students at the orphan school, however, Anna Komnena provided a valuable clue. She stated that some of the native Greek children at the Orphanotropheion could not read or write and were in the process of learning their letters.[155] It is difficult to imagine that the orphans of powerful families would have been completely illiterate upon entering the Orphanotropheion. Anna's observation indicates that at least some of the students at the orphan school came from poor families. The example of Bogoas may also offer an example of a truly needy child accepted at the institu-tion[156] Nevertheless, one cannot determine how closely the elaborate Orphanotropheion of twelfth-century Constantinople followed the ex-ample of its fourth-century founder, Zotikos, who designed the chari-ties he established for the outcasts of society.

154. *JCod*, I.3.31(32).
155. Anna Comnena, *Alexiad*, 15.7.9 (3: 218).
156. Basilakes, *Adversus Bogoam*, chaps. 12–13 (pp. 99–100).

IX   DID IT WORK?

 Despite the Judeo-Christian belief that the God of the universe especially loved orphans and protected them with a father's care, the Byzantines recognized that from a worldly point of view *orphania* was the greatest disaster that could befall a child. Archbishop Demetrios Chomatianos described how it caught children when they were too young and too inexperienced to manage their own affairs. As a result, it often scattered their possessions both to relatives and to outsiders. According to Chomatianos, Byzantine law was unable to protect such children from all the evils of orphanhood, but it did provide the help of guardians. The archbishop frankly admitted that relatives and friends frequently despoiled the property of orphans, but he saw the Byzantine laws of guardianship as providing at least some protection against the greed of sinful men and women.[1]

Was Chomatianos's faith in the Byzantine system of guardianship justified? The following chapter will examine to what degree the Byzantine laws of guardianship and adoption, backed up by the church-run orphanages, actually protected children who had lost their parents. The lack of records makes such an inquiry extremely difficult. Whereas historians who study Renaissance orphanages in Italy or foundling homes in eighteenth-century France have at their disposal records of how many children entered or left an institution in any given year, how many died while in the orphanage or left to lead normal

---

1. Chomatianos, no. 84 (p. 369).

adult lives, no such evidence exists for the Byzantine Empire.[2] In fact, only two sources have survived from the one thousand years of East Roman history that offer any indication of how many children Byzantine orphanages housed at any one time. Moreover, no official records exist from any region at any period that reveal how many children were assigned guardians either through the *tutela legitima* or the *tutela testamentaria*. The only indication of how many children were under the supervision of guardians comes from the tax records discussed in Chapter One.[3]

In addition to the lack of any statistical data, one should consider also the difficulty of evaluating child care. What constitutes success? As we saw in the previous chapter, of the two children identified as having studied at the Orphanotropheion, Bogoas and Stilbes' student, one succeeded and the other failed in terms of material goals. But was Bogoas truly successful because he achieved a secure position in the clergy? Since the Orphanotropheion provided an environment where Bogoas could engage in homosexual activity and even castrate himself, many observers both in Byzantine times and today would classify his training there as a failure. On the other hand, Stilbes' student died in poverty, but perhaps in sanctity; at least he left one of his former teachers deeply grieved by his death. From a spiritual point of view, then, one might evaluate the experiences of these two orphans far differently.[4]

Despite these difficulties, this chapter will examine the Byzantine system of orphan care simply to determine whether it protected orphans from physical want by providing food, shelter, and some education. Whether it succeeded in fostering moral and spiritual growth is a question beyond the ken of human scholarship.

Although no records survive that provide any statistical information

---

2. For an example of how complete the records are from some orphanages of Renaissance Italy, see Gavitt, *Charity*, who presents a thorough study of the Ospedale degli Innocenti of Florence from 1410 to 1536.

3. Theodore of Stoudios, *Ep.* 211 (p. 333) refers to the early-ninth-century orphanage outside Prousa (see Chapter Five, p. 133). *Typikon Kecharitomene*, chap. 5 (p. 41), describes a twelfth-century monastery for women that was always to care for two orphan girls.

4. For Bogoas, see Basilakes, *Adversus Bogoam*, chaps. 12–15 (pp. 99–101); for Stilbes's student, see Stilbes, *Monodia*, pp. 88–90.

concerning the results of guardianship or record vital statistics of children raised in orphanages, we do have the seventy-seven cases that have provided valuable information on the orphans of the Byzantine Empire. An analysis of these seventy-seven children, combined with a consideration of several general statements concerning the fate of orphans during the Byzantine centuries, will give us some indication of whether the East Roman system in fact succeeded in aiding orphans.[5]

GUARDIANSHIP

When the emperor Alexios I returned from Asia Minor bringing with him the many war orphans of Anatolia, he first turned to the Roman laws of guardianship to find relatives to care for these children; he only resorted to orphanages for those boys and girls with no family members in Constantinople who were willing to accept them.[6] An analysis of the seventy-seven orphans also indicates that guardianship formed the backbone of the Byzantine system to shelter orphans. Of these seventy-seven children, only eighteen were raised in orphanages, ten had no tutor or curator, and the remaining forty-nine received guardians or adopting parents.

East Roman emperors and intellectuals, however, sometimes expressed doubts concerning the effectiveness of guardianship. The pagan orator Themistios stated that at the beginning of Theodosius's reign (379), he had seen orphan boys and girls from the most prestigious families stripped of their property by greedy guardians and left to wander penniless in the streets of Constantinople. According to Themistios, the emperor Theodosius's intervention, not the ministrations of faithful guardians, rescued these children from poverty.[7] A Christian contemporary of Themistios and a future bishop of Constantinople, John Chrysostom, revealed that family guardians were often ineffective in protecting their wards from the machinations of friends and relatives.[8]

In the sixth century, the emperor Justinian frankly admitted that he

---

5. For these seventy-seven cases, see Chapter One and the Appendix.

6. Anna Komnena, *Alexiad*, 15.7.3 (3: 214).

7. Themistios, *Oratio 34*, no. 462 (p. 76).

8. Chrysostom, *In epistulam ad Romanos homilia XVIII* (PG, 60: 581–82).

had adjudicated many cases where guardians had turned against the children they were obliged to protect. What is even more shocking, Justinian claimed that, before their appointment as guardians, one would have supposed these men to have been well suited morally to serve as the protectors of their relatives. As a result of his experiences, Justinian designed rules to exclude from guardianship two groups of people, debtors and creditors of the orphan, people whom the emperor suspected might use guardianship to defraud their wards.[9]

In totally revising the ancient rules of *tutela* and *cura*, the eighth-century emperor Leo III issued the strongest condemnation of the Byzantine guardianship system in Title Seven of his *Ecloga*. Here Leo stated that, before his revision, lay tutors and curators had habitually consumed the property of the orphans whom they had promised to protect. As a result of the failure of the guardianship program, inherited from ancient Rome, Leo transferred many orphans to the care of the Christian group homes, run by bishops and monasteries, and in Constantinople to the Orphanotropheion.[10]

The legislation of the ninth-century emperor Leo VI also described how guardians abused the orphans in their care. Leo focused on a particular abuse: male guardians who sexually assaulted the female children whose *tutela* they had assumed. Leo VI considered such abuse common enough to warrant new legislation that would confiscate offenders' property and transfer it to the estates of their victims.[11]

Despite these many negative statements concerning guardians, one should not forget the sentiment of the learned bishop and legal expert of the thirteenth century Demetrius Chomatianos, who stated that the law in fact offered orphans strong protection through the institution of guardians and curators. Despite abuses, Chomatianos thought that *tutela* and *cura* shielded orphans from suffering even greater misfortunes.[12] An examination of our seventy-seven orphans offers some support for Chomatianos's confidence.

From among the seventy-seven cases of children who had lost both parents, ten did not receive guardians either through the testament of their parents or through the rules of *tutela legitima*. Of these ten chil-

9. *JNov,* 72 (anno 538).
11. Leo VI, Novel 34 (137–39).
10. *Ecloga,* 7 (p. 198).
12. Chomatianos, no. 84 (p. 369).

dren, only one had a happy life compared to the other nine who suffered in their youth. This means that 90 percent of the children without guardians had problems in their childhood. Of the remaining sixty-
seven orphans who either had guardians or foster parents, or who
entered orphanages, twenty-two had negative experiences, that is, 33
percent of the orphans under some form of guardianship. A check of
these results against the possibility that these figures were due simply
to chance shows that there is a high probability that the lack of
guardians and no other factor produced such a high percentage (90 percent) of unhappy childhoods among the ten compared with the 33 percent among those orphans with legal protectors.[13]

In addition to the argument based on a statistical analysis, we
should examine a few specific examples. The one and only case of an
orphan without a guardian whose life turned out more happily than
anyone would have dreamed possible in fact shows how difficult life
was for children without guardians. According to the seventh-century
Pratum Spirituale, a wealthy aristocrat of Constantinople decided to
give away all his property to the poor. Later, when he was about to die,
he appointed no human guardian for his now destitute son, but left the
boy in the care of Jesus Christ. After his father's death, the boy was
wandering through the streets of the capital when he decided to enter
a church to pray. The boy did not know that in the same church a rich
woman and her daughter had been pleading with God to direct them
in choosing a husband. As the aristocratic lady was begging God to
send a husband for her girl, the orphan youth entered the church.
When the wealthy woman questioned him and heard the story of his
father, she decided that Christ had served the boy as a most effective
guardian and had found his ward a wealthy and virtuous bride, her
own daughter.[14]

Although this story recounts the case of a youth who succeeded in
finding a comfortable place in society despite his lack of a regular

---

13. Dr. Chapman McGrew, a colleague at Salisbury University, has verified that a chi-
square table of these statistics indicates that there is a less than 1 percent chance that some
factor other than the presence or lack of guardians influenced the success or failure of
these orphans. Dr. McGrew cautioned, however, that one of the cells in the chi-square
table had a low frequency rate.

14. John Moschos, *Pratum spirituale*, chap. 201 (PG, 87.3: 3089).

guardian, its tone demonstrates that worldly experience had taught most Byzantines that children without living parents needed guardians to govern their affairs, and especially to find them suitable husbands or brides. In effect, only a miracle could save an orphan without a guardian.

The ninth-century Paul suffered a fate more typical of orphans without guardians. First, Paul's father perished in a naval battle against the Arabs; second, his older brother Basil joined a distant monastery; finally, his mother died without leaving him a guardian. When Basil sent a companion monk to invite his younger brother to visit him at the monastery, the messenger found that Paul had lost all his property and was being forced by the neighboring peasants to tend their pigs, one of the least prestigious jobs in an agricultural community. Only after repeated efforts was Basil able to liberate Paul from the villagers' control.[15]

Another example comes from the patriarchal court of thirteenth-century Constantinople. The patriarch Gregory of Cyprus adjudicated the case of three Turkish orphans whose father had converted to Christianity, joined the Byzantine army, and received a land grant in the form of a *pronoia* (a conditional grant of income from land in return for military service). When their father died, the boys lost the *pronoia* and had no one to serve as their guardian. Their pitiable laments made everyone cry including Patriarch Gregory who promised to find the boys some assistance from the emperor.[16]

George Kouritzes, who lived in thirteenth-century Ohrid, represents the most typical case of an orphan without a guardian. His father died when he had been very young. His mother naturally acted as George's legal guardian, but she was forced to sell most of their property to make ends meet. When George was ten, she sold a vineyard that had belonged not to her, but to George's father. Shortly thereafter she died. Left without a guardian, George simply took to the open road. As Chomatianos phrased it, "his *orphania* persuaded him to love traveling," a statement that implied that being without a guardian

---

15. *Vita Pauli Junioris*, chaps. 2 and 3 (pp. 20–23).
16. Gregory of Cyprus, *Ep.* 159 (p. 119).

forced some children to wander from place to place. Finally, when George reached age twenty-five, he returned to his home village and sued Sylvester, the man who had purchased the vineyard of his father, on the grounds that George's mother had not complied with the Roman law rule requiring a magisterial *decretum* to sell an orphan's property. George eventually got two-thirds of his vineyard back.[17]

George's case not only demonstrates how orphans without guardians often found no place in settled society, but it also illustrates that as an adult a clever orphan could use the guardianship laws to reclaim at least some of the family property.

The sources we have reviewed here present strong evidence that guardianship offered at least some protection to orphans, as Chomatianos claimed. Without this institution children who had lost both parents had little chance of a materially happy life.

Did the Byzantine rules of *tutela* and *cura* find the best possible guardians for orphans? One Byzantine innovation—preferring birth mothers over all other relatives unless the father stipulated differently in his will—assured the optimum protectors for the children. As we saw in Chapter Four, Byzantine law supported the rights of birth mothers in every situation, even where the child was illegitimate. Other Byzantine innovations apparently opened up guardianship to other women—older sisters, for example. By substantially widening the pool of potential guardians, these innovations helped to protect children from the worst fate: having no guardian at all.

By granting women and eunuchs the right to adopt homeless children, Byzantine law also expanded protection by offering orphans a wider field of potential foster parents. Indeed, adopting women provided happy environments for five out of the eight successful adoptions found in our sample of seventy-seven children.[18]

In one area, however, Byzantine law failed to improve the lot of orphans. Our seventy-seven cases clearly show that adult older brothers who accepted guardianships did not protect their younger siblings nearly as well as uncles protected their nephews and nieces. Of the seven

17. Chomatianos, no. 91 (pp. 401–4).
18. Leo VI, *Novel*, nos. 26 and 27 (pp. 101–11).

orphans for whom older brothers served as guardians, six, or 86 percent, had bad experiences. Of the seventeen orphans whom uncles protected, six, or 35.3 percent, had unhappy childhoods. Unfortunately, there are not enough cases in this sample to make any statistically valid statement as to whether the difference in outcome was due to the nature of the guardians or simply to chance. Nevertheless, the results suggest that older brothers did not fulfill the role of guardian as well as uncles did. A review of a few specific cases will underscore this point.

Circa 400, in the ancient town of Athens, a girl by the name of Athenais lost her parents. Her father had written a will in which he divided all his property between his two sons and left his daughter Athenais only a legacy of one hundred *nomismata*. At this time, it was still legal to exclude some children, especially females, from the inheritance. As we learned in Chapter Four, the emperor Justinian later changed this law.

The chronicler Malalas who recounted Athenais's experiences, did not say that the brothers served as the guardians of their sister's person and of her one hundred *nomismata*, but since they would have served as her *tutores* by rules of the *tutela legitima* and since Malalas did not mention Athenais's father's having appointed a *tutor testamentarius*, they surely acted as her guardians. Moreover, the rest of the story supports such a conclusion.

Athenais asked her older brothers for an equal share in the inheritance. A fight ensued which resulted in the two brothers driving Athenais from her family home. As an orphan, she sought refuge with her mother's sister. This maternal aunt did an excellent job in guarding Athenais's virginity, perhaps the prime responsibility of guardians in the case of female orphans. After a while, the maternal aunt took the girl to live with her paternal aunt in Constantinople. There the two older women resolved to introduce Athenais to the empress Pulcheria, the sister of the reigning emperor Theodosius II, so that the girl could explain what she had suffered at the hands of her brothers.

Athenais presented her case so effectively and so impressed Pulcheria both with her beauty and her intelligence that the empress decided that the girl would make an excellent wife for the emperor. Athenais agreed to become a Christian, married Theodosius, and reigned with the Christian name of Eudokia. Following the example of the Old Testament Joseph, Athenais did not punish her brothers, but rewarded them with high government offices.[19]

The thirteenth-century records of Demetrios Chomatianos include two additional examples of brothers as guardians, cases we have already studied with respect to the legal institutions of guardianship. The first recounted the ordeal of John Achyraites. After he had lost both his parents, his adult brother Constantine became guardian for John, then only nine years old, and his thirteen year-old brother Leo. Despite his mother's faith in him as a protector of his younger brothers, Constantine deserted the boys by joining the army and squandered all of their property.[20] The second case involved four brothers who were orphaned and received as their guardian an adult half brother named Ganadaios. In the course of protecting these boys, Ganadaios expropriated all their movable property. The orphans had to appeal their case many times until finally Chomatianos granted them a fair hearing.[21]

When one considers Byzantine inheritance laws, it is easy to understand why older brothers made poor guardians. Ancient laws both at Athens and at Rome allowed the father to dispose of his property in any way he wished. Thus, a father might decide to grant his entire estate to his eldest son and leave only a small legacy to the younger children. Following this ancient custom, Athenais's father had arranged his estate to exclude his daughter from the inheritance.[22] Christianity, on the other hand, encouraged parents to divide up their property into equal shares for all their children including female offspring. In fact, Saint Basil condemned as immoral the practice of preferring one child over another in composing a testament.[23] In the sixth century, the emperor Justinian incorporated the Christian concept of equal shares into the Roman law of inheritance. As a result of his legislation, all children were to receive equal parts of the family property unless they had tried to kill their father, to burn down the family home, or to commit some other grave offense.[24]

Under the ancient Greco-Roman system, an adult brother as the

19. Malalas, 14.4 (pp. 273–75).   20. Chomatianos, no. 84 (pp. 369–78).
21. Ibid., no. 83 (pp. 365–68).   22. Malalas, 14.4 (pp. 273–75).
23. Basil, *Homiliae in hexaéméron, Homilia VIII* (pp. 459–61).
24. Käser, *Roman Private Law*, p. 358; *JNov,* 18 and 115.

first-born male often became the heir to all his family's property. In such a case, the job of guarding over his younger siblings fit well with his role as heir and executor of his father's last testament. The elder brother simply preserved the legacies his father had granted to the younger children while he supervised his wards' upbringing and education. Under the Justinianic system, on the other hand, the adult brother's role as coheir with his siblings clashed with his duty to guard their shares. The adult brother now bore sole responsibility for managing all aspects of the family property, including paying his father's debts, but he enjoyed an inheritance right only in his portion of the family inheritance. In such a situation, it was easy for the adult brother to take some of his siblings' property, even unintentionally. We have an example of exactly such a situation in a papyrus document dated 567.

In Chapter Four we discussed this case which described the legal problems of Psates, the eldest brother in a family of five children from the region of Aphrodito in Egypt. After the death of both the parents in the mid-sixth century, Psates assumed the guardianship of his four siblings. After her marriage, Psates' sister sued him for failing to turn over her share of the inheritance. During his guardianship Psates had not kept adequate records and had delayed in handing over the pots, pans, and other household items he had promised to his sister, but the magistrate did not find him liable for squandering or embezzling the woman's fair share of the inheritance. Psates had simply managed his parents' estate without keeping careful records. When one considers all the payments Psates had made while guardian—making good his father's debts, repairing family buildings, and paying the wet nurse for the youngest child—it is easy to see how some guardian brothers were tempted to transfer part of the property due their younger sisters and brothers to their own accounts.[25]

Even before Byzantine legislation required that parents leave all their children equal shares of their property, fights among brothers and sisters over their inheritance shares occurred so frequently that these family disputes came to symbolize strife and confusion. Thus, in

25. *PLond*, 1708.

a late fourth-century sermon on the wisdom of God's creation, John Chrysostom compared the divine harmony of the heavens with the constant battles among selfish siblings, icons of fallen human nature, over their shares of the family's wealth.[26]

A careful review of the six cases in which brothers performed poorly as *tutores* confirms these impressions because, in five of these six examples, guardian brothers were involved in property disputes with their sibling wards. In only one case did a brother guardian fulfill his duties poorly for any other reason, and that was Saint Antony of Egypt who left his little sister with a community of virgins so that he could seek the Lord in the desert wilderness.[27]

Uncles, on the other hand, did not suffer such conflicts of interest. They usually had their own households and their own estates. They did not enjoy the status of coheir with their wards. Only in the case of the death of the orphan—or of the several orphans where there was more than one child—would uncles have entered upon their wards' estates. Although a few uncles no doubt reached such a level of greed that they murdered their nephews and nieces, I have found no such cases from Byzantine times. In other words, it would have required far more treachery for an uncle to seize a major portion of his ward's property than it would have for a brother to embezzle more than his legal share of the family substance. Moreover, some elder brothers might even have felt justified in seizing more because of the labors and responsibilities they bore in managing the guardianship of their siblings' persons and property.

A careful examination of five cases in which uncles did not adequately fulfill their guardianship duties confirms this interpretation. (The sixth case does not provide enough information for discussion.) In contrast to the bad brother guardians, bad uncle *tutores* did not perform poorly because of property disputes. Two of the four negative cases involved quarrels over marriage arrangements. The fourth-century Egyptian Amoun had to marry a woman whom his uncle guardian had selected for him. Amoun, however, had never wanted a wife be-

---

26. John Chrysostom, *In librum Isaiae "Ego Dominus Deus feci lumen"* (PG, 56: 144–45).
27. *Vita Antonii*, chaps. 1–5 (PG, 26: 840–48).

cause of his desire to lead the life of a monk.[28] In the sixth century, George Chozebites also fought with his uncle over marriage. George's guardian wanted the youth to marry his own daughter. George managed to escape his uncle and fled to the protection of his adult brother who had joined a Palestinian monastery.[29]

The other three uncles who did not fulfill their duties as guardians neglected their wards. In the first case, a fourth-century bishop found himself too busy to take care of his two wards and tried to find another person to take over his guardianship role.[30] In the second case, originally described in a fifth-century Syrian text, Saint Abramios failed to notice that one of the young monks in his community had conceived a sexual desire for Abramios's niece and, as a result of the saintly uncle's negligence, was able to seduce her.[31] In the third case, from sixth-century Egypt, the uncle found his female ward a good husband, but after the man's premature death the uncle did not continue to take an active interest in his niece.[32]

In five cases, dutiful uncle guardians provided such a good education for their wards that these children eventually became famous. The renowned monastic leader Plato of Sakkoudion lost both his parents during a plague that struck Constantinople while Constantine V ruled the empire (741–775). One of his uncles accepted responsibility for him and trained him in keeping accounts for the imperial treasury. Plato gained such skill in this profession that he amassed a fortune from his job and added this to his paternal estate, which his virtuous uncle had preserved intact. Despite his success, Plato decided to renounce the world and take up the monastic lifestyle. Eventually, he became superior of the monastery of Sakkoudion and a prominent leader in the movement to restore icons.[33]

The patriarch Michael Keroularios (1043–1058) served as guardian for his two nephews, both of whom received excellent educations. The youngest, named Constantine, rose to fill a high government post.[34] Nikephoros Gregoras became one of the leading intellectual

---

28. Palladius, *Lausiaca*, chap. 8 (pp. 40–42).   29. *Vita Georgii Chozebitae*, pp. 95–98.
30. *POxy*, no. 2344.   31. *Vita Abramii*, pp. 935–36.
32. Maspero, no. 67005.
33. Theodore of Stoudios, *Homilia XI* (PG, 99: 804–8).
34. Psellos, *Encomium ad Cerullarium*, pp. 351–52.

figures of the fourteenth century after having lived under the protection of his uncle guardian John, the metropolitan of Herakleia. Bishop John not only provided for Gregoras's physical needs, but he personally taught him philosophy and introduced him to the works of Plato.[35]

John Argyropoulos, the prominent fifteenth-century intellectual, also was orphaned at a young age and received his education through the auspices of his uncle. Argyropoulos excelled in Aristotelian philosophy and in the practice of medicine. He eventually migrated to Italy, where he became a leading cultural figure, first in Florence and later in Rome.[36]

Athanasios, the founder of the great Meteora monastic center, lost both his parents shortly after his birth in 1305. His paternal uncle accepted responsibility for the boy and raised him as though he were his own child. Although the uncle died before Athanasios had reached adulthood, he had instilled in the boy a love of learning that led Athanasios first to the lecture halls of secular literature in Thessalonike and eventually to the true knowledge of monasticism.[37]

Despite the evidence that normally uncles made better guardians than adult brothers, Byzantine law continued to uphold the ancient Roman rule that an adult brother had a greater legal right to exercise guardianship than an uncle did. On the other hand, one should consider that Byzantine emperors and their legal advisors could not have altered this ancient rule of law without threatening the stability of nuclear family units which often survived the death of both parents. Even after both father and mother died and several siblings had reached adulthood, the family often remained together. As we saw above, Athenais naturally continued to live with her brothers as a family unit until she asked for a larger share of her father's estate and was expelled by her male siblings.[38]

In the early thirteenth century, when John Petraliphes and his wife died, their children continued to live together. All of John's sons accepted responsibility for the care of the family property and for the

---

35. Gregoras, "Vie de Jean," chaps. 12–14 (pp. 53–63).
36. Argyropoulos, *Comédie*, p. 37; *ODB*, 1: 164–65.
37. *Vita Athanasii (Meteora)*, pp. 239–41.
38. Malalas, 14.4 (pp. 273–75).

guardianship of their young sister Theodora. They jointly protected her and negotiated her marriage to Michael, the ruler of Epiros.[39]

Although in assigning the office of guardian, Byzantine law gave brothers precedence over uncles, a survey of the seventy-seven cases indicates that uncles actually assumed the position of tutor or curator more often (in eighteen cases) than any other relatives. After uncles, brothers accepted the responsibility of guardianship in seven cases, more often than other family members except uncles. Moreover, a survey of the 167 households recorded in the tax register prepared for the Athos monastery of Iberon in 1301 clearly supports the evidence of the seventy-seven cases. This register shows that in eighteen houses nephews and nieces were living with uncles while in sixteen houses siblings were living with their older brothers.[40] Not all of these younger brothers, however, were minors. In some of these households, perhaps the majority, adult brothers had simply chosen to remain together as a family unit, a practice widespread in other Mediterranean countries such as Italy.[41]

The ninth-century *vita* of Saint Makarios also suggests that Byzantines considered uncles the most likely guardians for orphans. According to the *vita*, Makarios was born in Constantinople circa 780. After losing both his parents at a tender age, one of his relatives accepted responsibility for his care. The author of the *vita* knew only that Makarios received as guardian a male relative, but he added that when people later recounted the saint's early years, they naturally assumed that the relative was Makarios's uncle.[42]

FEMALE ORPHANS

A reading of the seventy-seven cases shows clearly that female orphans had more problems in childhood than did their male counterparts. Of the seventy-seven cases, forty-six cases involved only male orphans and twenty-six only female orphans; the other five cases either

---

39. *Vita Theodorae* (PG, 127: 904–5).
40. Dölger, *Aus den Schatzkammern*, pp. 35–51.
41. Cooper, "Patterns," pp. 277–78.
42. *Vita Macarii*, pp. 141–44.

dealt with both brothers and sisters or did not identify the sex of the ward. Of the forty-six males, eighteen children experienced serious problems under their guardians while twenty-three lived happily under their tutors. In five cases, the sources did not reveal the outcome of the guardianship.

Of the twenty-six female orphans, however, only eight had good experiences while sixteen suffered injustices. Again, the number of cases is too small and the difference not great enough to exclude the possibility that these variations have resulted from chance. Still, it is important to note the difference and to examine a few specific cases of orphan girls that support these findings.

Circa 300, the mother of Gregory of Nyssa was born in central Anatolia. Gregory, one of the most prolific authors among the Fathers of the Greek Church, wrote an account of his mother's difficult childhood. At an early age, she conceived a desire to follow the monastic lifestyle, but both her parents died before she could fulfill her ambition. Because of her physical beauty, many men sought her hand in marriage. So many desired her with such passion that there was grave danger that someone would attempt to take her by force. Gregory implied that some might even have desired to rape her. In order to protect herself, Gregory's mother finally decided to abandon her dream of the monastic life and accept a pious husband to act as her guardian *(phylax)*. Gregory's account suggested that his mother had not received a family guardian capable of protecting her from the threat of abduction or sexual assault at the hands of some of her suitors.[43]

A papyrus from sixth-century Egypt provides even a more vivid picture of the dangers facing an orphan girl, dangers that continued long after she had found a husband. During the reign of Justinian, a woman named Sophia appealed to the duke of the Thebaid, one of the military governors of Egypt, for assistance in recovering her child. To enlist the duke's support, Sophia recounted her trying experiences.

Early in her life, Sophia lost both her parents. As one would expect, she moved in with her uncle and aunt, who served as her guardians, although Sophia did not use the official terminology for this function.

43. *Vita Macrinae*, pp. 142–44.

Her uncle and aunt managed to find her a husband with whom Sophia soon conceived a child. Before she had weaned the baby boy, however, her husband suddenly died. According to Sophia, the tax collectors of her village then connived with her deceased husband's brothers to deprive her of the property that her spouse had left to her and to her child (the husband's legal heir). Sophia yielded the property and fled with her baby. She did not indicate why she refrained from opposing her in-laws or why her former guardian relatives (her uncle and aunt) did not assist her in protecting her interests. She did state, however, that her child had no protector, perhaps a reference to the baby's lack of a male guardian. Since this case took place in the reign of Justinian, Sophia herself could have served as her child's legal guardian, if she had reached the age of twenty-five. In her deposition to the court, however, Sophia made no reference to her own age.

Sophia soon found a second husband to support her. He had children by a previous marriage, but he expelled these from his house to make room for Sophia and her baby. Sophia mentioned the expulsion of the children of the first wife without any qualifying statement as though it were the natural result of a second marriage. Her testimony here inadvertently confirmed the arguments of Byzantine bishops against second marriages.

Sophia's troubles were only just beginning. Shortly after her second marriage, Semouthes, a local magnate, seized her new husband because of some pledge the man had made to a village official named Jeremiah. Apparently, the husband had stood surety for a loan on behalf of Jeremiah or had borrowed money directly from Jeremiah. Senouthes so mistreated Sophia's new spouse that he died while still in captivity. Senouthes now seized Sophia for his own pleasure, but when she refused his sexual advances he threw her into a private jail. After the local magistrate ordered Sophia's release, Senouthes continued to hold her for a while before finally letting her go.

Jeremiah, the local official to whom Sophia's husband had owed money, now confiscated all the property that had belonged to her second husband. Again destitute, Sophia sought the assistance of a company of Macedonian soldiers who offered her protection from the local Egyptian officials. Nevertheless, she lost custody of her child,

whom the treacherous Jeremiah now claimed. In fact, Sophia decided
to appeal to Duke Flavius Marinos in order to recover her little boy.[44]

Sophia's many misfortunes demonstrate how vulnerable she was as
an orphan and a woman. Perhaps some of her problems were the result of bad luck. Her first husband had died suddenly; her second husband had confronted the wrong man, the magnate Senouthes. It seems
unlikely, though, that she would have suffered so many injustices if she
had not lost her parents or had possessed more effective guardians. As
in the case of Makrina, being a woman also made her vulnerable to inappropriate sexual advances by Senouthes. Fortunately for Sophia, the
Macedonian soldiers refrained from exploiting her helpless situation.

Sexual exploitation clearly threatened female orphans. Among the
twenty-six girls without parents, four ended up as prostitutes or, at the
very least, as women of loose morals. From fifth-century Egypt comes
the story of Paesia who lost her mother and father while still a young
girl. Since she was a good Christian and an admirer of the desert her-
mits, she turned her house into a *xenodocheion* for traveling monks. For
some time, she honorably received these holy men and provided them
lodging. After a while, however, her resources ran low; some evil men
convinced her that she could survive only by turning to prostitution.
She eventually accepted their advice and became a successful prostitute. She even made enough money to have servants and assistants.
Saddened by the moral collapse of their former benefactress, the her-
mits dispatched the monk John to convince Paesia to repent. After
masquerading as a customer, John managed to enter Paesia's chamber
and easily convinced her to abandon her sinful ways.[45]

We have already discussed briefly the second girl orphan who also
became a prostitute, the little niece of Saint Abramios. She lived with
her pious uncle for many years after the death of her parents, but when
she fell victim to the sexual advances of one of the monks, she fled her
uncle's protection and became a prostitute. As in the case of Paesia,
Abramios managed to find his niece and rescued her from her sinful
profession.[46] The third case involved the wealthy pagan girl of Alexan-

44. Maspero, no. 67005.
45. *Apophthegmata Patrum, Appendix ad Palladium* (PG, 65: 217–20).
46. *Vita Abramii*, pp. 935–37.

dria whose parents left her no guardian. After charitably giving away all her property, she also took up prostitution, only to be rescued by angels and the saving waters of baptism.[47]

The fourth orphan girl came from eleventh-century Anatolia. The girl's father, a officer in the Anatolikon *theme* (military province), was captured by Moslems. In prison for many years, he finally made a vow to God that he would become a monk and visit the Holy Land if God would liberate him from his Saracen captors. Shortly thereafter, the Moslems released him. Right away he donned the monastic habit as he had promised, but instead of going on the pilgrimage he decided to visit his home. Not far from his old residence, he met a poor woman who offered him food and lodging. In the evening, the devil tempted him, and he slept with the woman. Afterwards, he began to talk with her to learn something about the fate of his family and friends.

During this conversation, the woman recounted her own life. Her father had left her home when she had been very young. He had either died in battle or in captivity. Shortly after he had marched out to war, her mother died. The villagers seized all the family property and drove her and her two younger brothers out of their home. She traveled to a nearby village where she had been laboring to support herself and the boys. The story did not state that she had become a prostitute, but the ease with which the monk met her and gained access to her house shows that she had become a woman of low morals and most likely practiced some form of prostitution to help in supporting her siblings. The monk suddenly realized that this woman was his own daughter. He fled in shame, but eventually realized that God had punished him for failing to keep his vow to visit the Holy Land.[48]

Perhaps of greater significance than these random examples is Novel 34 of the emperor Leo VI. As we saw above, Leo drafted this law to correct abuses in the behavior of guardians. The novel identified as one of the most common examples of nefarious guardians those male protectors of orphan girls who sexually assaulted their helpless wards.[49] That Leo had to frame a specific law to control this type of

47. John Moschos, *Pratum Spirituale,* chap. 207 (PG, 87.3: 3097–3100).
48. *Vita Lazari,* chap. 63 (p. 529).
49. Leo VI, *Novel,* no. 34 (pp. 137–39).

abuse among guardians provides additional evidence that such behavior occurred frequently.

In describing the life of his mother, Theoktiste, Theodore of Stoudios revealed another problem besides sexual exploitation that faced girl orphans. Theoktiste had lost her parents in an epidemic that struck Constantinople in the reign of Constantine V (741–775). In fact, she was the sister of Plato of Sakkoudion, the successful monastic leader we discussed above. Whereas Plato received excellent training under the tutelage of his guardian uncle, Theoktiste had been given no education at all. Theodore of Stoudios stated explicitly that she had never learned to read because of her *orphania*. Although Theodore described in detail Plato's guardian, he never mentioned who had cared for his mother and had failed to provide her with basic reading skills. After referring to his mother's illiteracy, he praised her successful efforts as an adult to teach herself to read.[50]

From what we know about ancient Greece and Rome as well as about other premodern societies, it is not surprising that a male orphan received a good education while his sister did not even learn to read or write. What is surprising in this example, however, is that Theodore identified the cause of Theoktiste's illiteracy as her *orphania*, not her sex. In other words, he thought that upper-class families normally taught their daughters to read.

OFFICIALS

In recounting her misadventures in sixth-century Egypt, the young widow Sophia revealed the many difficulties that could beset a female orphan, even after she married, but her story suggests that not only relatives and in-laws caused such problems, but also Byzantine officials and magistrates who sometimes victimized orphans without families to protect them. Government officials seized property that Sophia had claimed as her own on two separate occasions. After the death of her first spouse, tax collectors cooperated with the brothers of Sophia's deceased husband to divest her and her child of any inheritance. After the

50. For the *orphania* of Theodore of Stoudios's mother, see *S. Theodori Studitis laudatio in matrem* (PG, 99: 884–85); for the *orphania* of her brother Plato, see Theodore of Stoudios, *Oratio XI* (PG, 99: 805–9).

death of her second husband, a village official called the *boethos* confiscated what Sophia had gained from the second marriage. This *boethos,* the evil Jeremiah, not only seized the property, but he took custody of her boy as well, an act that led Sophia to bring her case before the duke of the Thebaid.[51] How common was such unjust behavior among Byzantine officials?

The ninth-century *vita* of Saint Gregory Dekapolites also portrayed a government official who defrauded orphans, this time in the Byzantine province of southern Italy near Reggio. This bureaucrat named Merkouras managed public lands, probably the lands belonging to the emperor's estates *(kouratorikia).* Merkouras confiscated properties for the government when private owners died without leaving any heirs. If circumstances permitted, Merkouras made sure that some large estates lacked heirs by murdering the orphan children who would have claimed the property as the rightful successors. This is the only case alleging the murder of orphans that I have discovered from Byzantine times.[52]

One of the cases Chomatianos heard in the early thirteenth century also dealt with the problem of officials who violated the rights of orphans. Two *archontes* living near Skopje confiscated property from orphan brothers named George and Melas Litoboes after the death of their guardian. It is interesting that in filing a complaint against these *archontes,* George characterized them as barbarians because they displayed such ignorance of Roman (that is, Byzantine) law. George also claimed that the Bulgarian regime that temporarily controlled the region around Skopje had allowed the forceful seizure of orphans' property, something that a true Roman administration would never have tolerated.[53]

One legal source of the early twelfth century complained not that Byzantine magistrates mistreated orphans, but rather that they often listened too sympathetically to the complaints of such children. The eldest Keroularios brother, Michael, received the guardianship over his

---

51. Maspero, no. 67005.

52. *Vie de Saint Grégoire le Decapolite,* chap. 11 (p. 55).

53. Chomatianos, no. 59 (pp. 261–64).

younger siblings when their father, Constantine, died suddenly. Since Constantine failed to draft a will, Michael feared that his younger brothers might charge him with some abuse of the guardianship laws. Michael apparently believed that Byzantine judges often sided with young orphan plaintiffs against guardians without examining the facts of each individual case.[54]

In the final analysis, it is impossible to determine how often magistrates and administrative officials violated the rights of orphans by seizing their property, by permitting their sexual abuse, or by killing them, or how often they supported orphans without listening to the legitimate claims of guardians or other adult relatives. Enough evidence survives, however, to assert that abuses definitely occurred.

A more significant question is whether or not orphans had easy access to law courts whenever their rights had in fact been violated, or whether or not the orphans of the lower classes were able to use the courts to protect themselves and their meager property. These questions address the most important issue regarding any legal system: How accessible were its tribunals to all ranks in society? Again, not enough sources describing specific guardianship cases survive to provide any statistically valid statement, but one should consider the surviving records of Chomatianos's court, records that include one hundred and ten cases dealing with Roman private law issues. Of this total, thirteen involved guardianship cases, some of which dealt with people of relatively humble origins.[55] Certainly, the dispossessed Jewish boy Manuel represented an orphan who owned very little. He only managed to survive after his stepfather took his land by becoming a professional cook. Despite his Jewish background and his menial profession, he was able to get a hearing before Chomatianos and eventually to regain his property.[56] How common were such cases? Did Chomatianos win renown in the thirteenth century as a legal expert precisely because he was willing to hear the little person's complaints?

54. Novel 19 (Alexios I), JGR, 1: 292–96.
55. Chomatianos, nos. 24, 32, 42, 59, 63, 81, 82, 83, 84, 85, 90, 91, and 95.
56. Chomatianos, no. 85 (pp. 377–82).

ORPHANAGES

If orphans had no relatives willing to accept the responsibility of guardianship, Byzantine society normally expected that the Christian Church would protect them by placing them in some type of group home. How successful were these Byzantine orphanages in raising their wards to be happy and productive subjects of the empire? As we saw in Chapter Eight, we were unable to arrive at any conclusions about the Orphanotropheion, both because we know facts about so few people who lived and studied there and because it is impossible to determine what constitutes a successful adult life. As with the Orphanotropheion, so too with episcopal, monastic, and private orphanages: research cannot determine how well they performed their essential task of feeding, protecting, and educating their wards. The sources, however, do preserve the record of some success stories, most of them saints.

In the late fourth century, the orphaned Euthymios entered the episcopal school of Melitene and rose to the rank of presbyter, after which he assumed the responsibility of supervising all the monasteries of the diocese. Moreover, his older companion at the school, Akakios, eventually became bishop of Melitene. Although the sources do not state that Akakios was an orphan, his achievements and those of Euthymios demonstrate how successful pupils of the episcopal school could be, at least within the clergy.[57]

In the sixth century, the orphan Alypios grew up in the episcopal school of Paphlagonian Adrianople. He too rose rapidly in the ranks of the local clergy and was eventually ordained a deacon. The bishop then entrusted him with the important post of *oikonomos*, the officer who managed the financial aspects of the local church.[58]

In the early tenth century Saint Peter, the future bishop of Argos, lost both his parents while he was still very young. He and his little brother entered a monastic school in Constantinople. Peter excelled in his studies and eventually was selected as bishop of Argos in central

---

57. *Vita Euthymii*, pp. 9–12 and pp. 32–33.
58. *Vita Alypii*, chaps. 2–4 (pp. 148–50).

Greece. Peter, in turn, sponsored an elaborate orphanage in his diocese which he designed especially for victims of the constant Arab raids. When Peter died, one of the orphans from his school succeeded him as bishop and also wrote the fascinating *vita* that has preserved the record of Peter's achievements.[59]

In the late eleventh century Blasios came as an infant to the monastery of Saint Philip in Sicily. We do not know whether his parents or relatives abandoned him or offered him as an oblate to the monastery. In any case, he was raised and educated in the ascetic community and at the proper time donned the monks' habit. When the monastery's founder drafted a *typikon* for the community of Saint Philip, he designated Blasios to succeed him as superior.[60] In twelfth-century Constantinople, Athanasios, the superior of the Mamas monastery, had many of the same experiences as Blasios. The monks of the monastery of Philanthropos had accepted Athanasios when he had been a baby; they fed him, educated him, and at a suitable time tonsured him. Before Athanasios was chosen to be superior of the Mamas community, the monks of the Philanthropos had selected him to serve as *oikonomos* of their community.[61]

All of these orphans succeeded by remaining either in the clergy of the episcopal church that supported their school or by joining the monastery that had originally accepted them. I have found no examples of orphans from these institutions who entered secular life. This might result from the nature of the sources—saints' biographies and monastic *typika*—but it is also possible that youths in these group homes had the best chances for success if they remained within the ecclesiastical structure. The life stories of the two twelfth-century graduates of the Orphanotropheion, Bogoas and Stilbes' student, point to the same conclusion.

Despite the successes of these saints and monastic leaders, Byzantine sources also have left evidence that some children did not flourish in these orphan schools. As we saw in Chapter Five, the thirteenth-century bishop of Naupaktos, John Apokaukos, admitted that he had en-

<hr>

59. *Vita Petri Argivorum*, pp. 1–17. 60. *Typikon of Saint Philip*, pp. 197–201.
61. *Typikon Mamas*, p. 259.

countered many problems at his orphanage. He stated that God had blessed him with a large number of orphans, but also that many of these children hated him without cause. Some had tried to flee the institution, while others had maligned him in the company of other bishops.[62]

Some of the students at Apokaukos's orphanage displayed antisocial behavior. We have already discussed Apokaukos's favorite student, John the Thief, who liked to steal eggs at Easter time. John had more serious problems, however. Apokaukos described how he often wandered off and how he failed to listen attentively and usually rushed to do a chore before he properly understood his instructions.[63]

Another orphan at Apokaukos's school, however, displayed far more erratic behavior. Apokaukos accepted him at the age of ten. His mother was still living, but she was so poor that she could not provide him with shoes or clothing. After having fed, clothed, and educated the youth, Apokaukos ordained him as a cleric in the church of Naupaktos and even promoted him to a high post *(lausynaktes)*. The former orphan, however, eventually deserted his church office and ran off with the wife of another cleric. He traveled around with her to towns and villages until he seduced a young virgin. Still burning with lust, he left this girl to go in search of other women. All the time, he ignored his desperately poor mother, leaving her without the care and affection of her own child.[64]

From the fourteenth century comes another example of orphan children under stress in these group homes. One of the nuns at the Theodora convent in Thessalonike took in a baby girl abandoned by her mother. The nuns fed her and cared for her until she reached the age when she could carry out chores around the convent. At the time when the nuns thought the girl had reached sufficient age to help around the convent, she developed an illness—the source describing her plight claimed she was possessed by a demon—and could not control her bowels. She constantly soiled her clothes and her bedding. The

62. Apokaukos, *Epistolai*, no. 27 (pp. 85–86); Apokaukos, "Dyrrachena," pp. 572–73.
63. Apokaukos, *Epistolai*, no. 100 (pp. 150–52).
64. Apokaukos, "Dyrrachena," pp. 572–73, and Apokaukos, "Symbole," pp. 233–34.

nuns were on the point of getting rid of her when the saintly archbish-op of Thessalonike and champion of the Hesychast monks Gregory Palamas miraculously cured her of her incontinence.[65]

The story of the little girl possibly reflects another problem at Byzantine orphanages, especially those attached to monasteries. These fourteenth-century nuns appear to have been more interested in using the orphan girl as a servant than in providing her with a good educa-tion. In this regard, one should consider several earlier examples. In the fifth century, at the Egyptian monastery of Abba Gelasios, the monks assigned one of the boys they had taken in as an infant or young child to work in the kitchen.[66] At the eleventh-century monastery of Chris-todoulos on the island of Patmos, the monks accepted orphans and even abandoned infants, but they probably employed these children as servants, once they were of sufficient age.[67] Anna Komnena's passage provides the strongest evidence that in fact many monasteries accepted such children to use as servants.

When the emperor Alexios returned to Constantinople from his campaign of 1116, Anna described how he entrusted the native-born Byzantine orphans without living relatives in the capital to the care of local monasteries. Anna emphasized that Alexios instructed the superi-ors of these ascetic communities not to use these children as slaves. Rather, he ordered that the orphans be raised as free persons and be deemed worthy of a complete education culminating in the study of the Holy Scriptures. That Alexios had to set such conditions for en-trusting the children to these monasteries demonstrates that some as-cetic communities did indeed accept orphans and abandoned children to use as servants, and according to Anna's own words, even as slaves.[68]

In some cases the monks treated these young servants very harshly. Regarding the kitchen boy at the fifth-century monastery of Abba Gelasios, the *Apophthegmata Patrum* recorded how the cellarer placed this orphan in charge of cooking a fish, while the monk left on an er-rand. Alone in the kitchen, the boy was unable to control his desire to

65. *Encomium Gregorii Palamae auctore Philotheo* (PG, 151: 629).
66. *Apophthegmata Patrum, Appendix ad Palladium* (PG, 65: 148–49).
67. *Typikon Christodoulos*, p. 83 and p. 86.
68. Anna Komnena, *Alexiad*, 15.7.3 (3: 214).

taste this wonderful fish. When the cellarer returned and found the orphan devouring the fish, he flew into a rage and began kicking the boy
so hard that he killed him on the spot. Overcome with fear, the cellarer picked up the orphan and carried him to the saintly Abba Gelasios
who miraculously restored the child to life. Abba Gelasios instructed
the cellarer not to tell anyone about the miracle, but the *Apophthegmata Patrum* did not mention whether Gelasios also warned him not to
kick the kitchen boy again.[69]

It is impossible to know how frequently monks physically abused
children in their care. The fourth-century *Apostolic Constitutions* advised bishops and natural fathers not to spare the rod in disciplining
young children.[70] Many centuries later, John Apokaukos recommended whipping and even blows with a stick to discipline the orphans
at the episcopal school of Naupaktos.[71] As we saw in Chapter Five,
Apokaukos's penchant for physical punishment probably explains why
the orphans disliked their bishop and why some of them fled his
school.

In employing harsh physical punishments, however, episcopal and
monastic school masters were simply following the accepted mode of
disciplining children. The fourth-century church father Gregory of
Nazianzos recommended whipping as an effective way to impress on
children how to behave. John Chrysostom observed that parents expected teachers to beat their children regularly. For some Byzantines,
the teacher's whip even came to symbolize education. In a society that
considered corporal punishment an integral part of the educational
process, one would assume that orphans were whipped just as the children of living parents were. The sources, however, do not reveal how
frequently such beatings were excessive and resulted in physical
injury.[72]

Despite these problems, monastic and episcopal schools were well
respected for their teaching methods. As we saw in Chapter Four, the

69. *Apophthegmata Patrum, Appendix ad Palladium* (PG, 65: 148–49).

70. *Constitutiones Apostolorum*, 4.11 (2: 188).

71. Apokaukos, *Epistolai*, no. 100 (pp. 151–52) and no. 101 (p. 152).

72. Regarding physical punishments in Byzantine schools, see Tsantelas, "Kakopoiese,"
pp. 532–36.

eighth-century emperor Leo III had such faith in these orphanages that he preferred to entrust boys and girls who had lost both parents to the care of monastic or episcopal schools rather than to leave them with family guardians.[73] Leo's system of institutional care never completely replaced the Roman guardianship system, however, and by the end of the ninth century the emperor Basil I had dismantled Leo's legal reforms and restored traditional guardianship.

The tenth-century *vita* of Saint Theodore of Kytheron presents the only evidence that some of those who supervised care for homeless children saw advantages in finding foster parents for the children over placing them in monastic or episcopal schools. According to the *vita*, Theodore was born to wealthy parents from the town of Korone in the Peloponnesus. When he reached age seven, Theodore's mother and father dedicated him to the service of God by enrolling him in the clergy of the local church. They handed him over to the bishop of Korone to be educated in an episcopal school, probably similar to the one opened at about the same time by Peter, bishop of Argos.

Shortly after Theodore began to study at the school both his parents died, leaving the boy an orphan. Since these episcopal schools were equipped to care for orphans, it would have been easy to have left Theodore in the episcopal school, especially since no relatives came forward to assume the boy's guardianship. This was not to be Theodore's fate, however. A friend of Theodore's parents, a priest from Nauplion, offered to adopt the boy and raise him as his own. The *vita* does not indicate whether the bishop actively sought someone to adopt Theodore, but it is certainly possible that he did. One should recall that the *Apostolic Constitutions* not only required that bishops assume responsibility for orphaned children, but also that they make an effort to locate good Christian families to adopt some of the male children. In any case, Theodore left the episcopal school and moved to Nauplion to live with his adopted family.[74]

In 1116, the emperor Alexios also showed a preference for family care over group homes. The emperor entrusted the Byzantine orphans

---

73. *Ecloga*, 7 (p. 198).

74. *Vita Theodori (Kytheron)*, pp. 282–83; cf. *Constitutiones Apostolorum*, 4.1–2 (2: 170–72).

to monastic schools only when he was unable to locate *tutores* according to the Roman law rules. Alexios did not mention adoption as an option, but he might have expected that the monastic superiors to whom he entrusted the orphans without guardians would help at least some of these children to locate adults willing to adopt them.[75]

ADOPTION

As we saw in Chapter Six, adoption formed a part of the Byzantine child welfare system, even though Anna Komnena did not specifically mention it in describing Alexios's distribution of orphans. The sources, however, provide no accurate information concerning how frequently nonrelatives adopted orphans or how successful such parents were in caring for homeless children. Of the seventy-seven orphan cases, ten involved children who were adopted compared with forty cases in which relatives came forward as guardians. Regarding this comparison, however, there are not enough samples to eliminate chance as the reason why guardians appear more common than adopting parents.

Of perhaps greater significance are the figures derived from tax surveys. The tax records from three thirteenth-century villages, located in Asia Minor and the coastal islands, demonstrate that from a total of fifty-one households two provided care for underage relatives, a nephew and a young sister, probably cases of guardianship, but that no households sheltered adopted children.[76]

From villages in the territory around Thessalonike, the tax records of 1401 reveal 167 households. Of these, seventeen households included nephews or nieces, in most cases examples of uncle guardianships, and fifteen households contained siblings. Compared to these relatively large numbers of probable guardianship cases, only two households listed adopted children among their members.[77] These tax records thus

75. Anna Komnena, *Alexiad*, 15.7.3 (3: 214).

76. For these tax records of the thirteenth century, see MM, 4: 13–14 (anno1235) and MM, 6: 215–16 (anno 1263).

77. For the tax records of the fourteenth century, see Dölger, *Aus den Schatzkammern*, pp. 35–51.

support the indication of the seventy-seven cases, that is, that guardians cared for more orphans than adopting parents did.

Four of the ten adoption cases came from the lives of saints. One of these *vitae*, probably from the fourth century, described how Clement of Ankyra was adopted by a holy woman who later joined her foster son in his charitable activities on behalf of abandoned children in Asia Minor. Another *vita* from the eleventh century recounted how Athanasios the Athonite was taken in by a wealthy woman of Trebizond who raised him with a number of other foster children.[78]

In only two of these nine adoption cases did the foster children end up alienated from their adopting parents, and in both these the disputes involved marriage plans. The most serious of these two cases concerned a wealthy widow named Eudokia who decided to adopt a seven-year-old girl at the beginning of the fourteenth century. Eudokia loved the girl almost as her own child and gave her some of her personal property in addition to a substantial dowry. When the adopted daughter grew older, however, she deliberately disobeyed Eudokia and married a man without her foster mother's approval. Eudokia immediately sought the return of all her property by citing her foster daughter before the patriarch's court.[79]

Such disputes between adults and children over marriage arrangements, however, were not limited to adopting parents and their foster sons or daughters. We saw above that conflicts over marriages often caused bad feelings between orphans and uncle guardians. Indeed, the eleventh-century *Peira* devoted two of its longest chapters to discussing marriage problems, including disputes between birth parents and their children, a good indication that such fights occurred just as frequently in natural families as they did in those established by guardianship or adoption laws.[80]

In the final analysis, we can say little about how effective adoption was in protecting Byzantine orphans. With regard to frequency, the ev-

---

78. See the *Vita Clementis* (PG, 114: 821–24) and the *Vitae duae antiquae* (*Vita A*, pp. 5–6) of Saint Athanasios the Athonite.

79. MM, 1: 17–18. See also the example of the adopted daughter's marriage in *Récits de Paul*, chap. 12 (pp. 96–97).

80. *Peira*, 25. 1–17 and 49. 1–37 (*JGR*, 4: 93–113 and 196–210).

idence suggests that adoption played less of a role than guardianship did in securing homes for children, but we have no solid evidence of this. The ninth-century *vita* of Saint Theodore provides the only indication that Byzantine society made an effort to find foster homes for children rather than commit them to institutional care.[81]

SLAVERY

Anna's account of her father's orphan settlement implied that, had Alexios not insisted that the orphans from Asia Minor remain free, some monasteries would have enslaved these children. Since the reign of Justinian, however, the law had required that adults who took in abandoned babies raise these children as free persons. In view of Justinian's rules, which were never revoked by subsequent emperors, how could twelfth-century Constantinopolitan monasteries have contemplated using Alexios's orphans as slaves?[82] A collection of miraculous tales and a letter of the classical scholar John Tzetzes provide valuable clues to answering this question.

First, the tenth-century *Tales of Monemvasia* recounts the miraculous story of a local *archon* from the Peloponnesus who maintained a private orphanage. Here the *archon* instructed the orphans in reading and in the tenets of the Christian faith. According to the *Tales*, the *archon* had purchased at least one of these children as a slave; this boy had come from Scythia where he had never been baptized.[83] Second, in his Letter 80, written in the mid-twelfth century, John Tzetzes complained about a Bulgarian slave boy whom the metropolitan of Dristra had sent him as a gift. Tzetzes stated that the boy was too young to do any work, and that Tzetzes himself was spending all of his time and money feeding the child and a second slave boy whom Tzetzes owned. In exasperation, Tzetzes groaned that he himself was constantly serving as a nourisher of orphans (Tzetzes used the verb *orphanotropheo*) rather than receiving any material benefits from his young slaves.[84]

Both of these sources describe slave orphans of barbarian origin,

---

81. *Vita Theodori (Kytheron)*, pp. 282–83.
82. Anna Komnena, *Alexiad*, 15.7.3 (3: 214); cf. *JCod*, 8.15.3 and *JNov*, 153.
83. *Récits de Paul*, chap. 9 (pp. 76–78).
84. Tzetzes, *Ep*. 80 (pp. 119–20).

one from Scythia and the other from Bulgaria. Probably these children had been captured either by Byzantine military forces in combat or by barbarian armies who then had sold these captives to international slave dealers. Since the children had been captured beyond the borders of the empire in some form of military action, they escaped the protection of Justinian's novels which only applied to babies abandoned by parents within Byzantine territory. In 1116, the emperor Alexios had also been carrying out a military campaign in Asia Minor when he came into possession of the orphans he subsequently brought to Constantinople. Thus, he realized that some monastic superiors might have considered these children as prisoners of war and therefore as slaves and not have educated them as free persons.

A final example from the early fifteenth century demonstrates even more clearly the link between slave orphans and combat beyond the empire's borders. This example comes not from the pen of a Byzantine witness, but from a Florentine writer and performer named Andrea Mangabotti (di Barberino). Sometime before 1431, Andrea wrote a popular chivalric romance in Italian about a knight named Guerrino Meschino. Guerrino's father, Milone, a Frankish prince, had seized Durazzo and conquered all of Albania in order to marry the beautiful princess Fenisia. Several months after Fenisia gave birth to Guerrino, the previous rulers of Durazzo returned with a vast army and took the city by storm. The conquerors imprisoned Milone and Fenisia, but Guerrino's nurse managed to flee the palace with the infant and find a ship setting sail from the harbor.

The high seas offered no refuge, however. Moslem pirates attacked the boat, killed the governess, and then sold Guerrino, still in swaddling clothes, as a slave in the Byzantine port of Thessalonike. Epidonios, the man who purchased Guerrino, lived in Constantinople and soon took the baby to the Byzantine capital where the kindly man raised him as his own son.[85]

Although the Florentine author wrote this romance solely for entertainment and borrowed many themes from French chivalric tales, the

---

85. No modern edition of *Guerrino Meschino* exists. See, however, the summary in Osella, *Guerrin Meschino*, pp. 39–63, as well as the discussion of the manuscripts and printed editions, pp. 19–39.

medieval *Romance of Alexander,* and ancient literature, some of the details about the Byzantine Empire reflected the early fifteenth century.
For example, when Guerrino reached manhood, he proved himself to
the emperor by helping to defeat the Turks who were besieging Constantinople. One of the details that no doubt reflected reality was the
link between combat in the southern Balkans, Mediterranean piracy,
and a slave market in Thessalonike.[86]

It is also interesting that Andrea portrayed Guerrino's experience in
Constantinople as positive. Although Epidonios had purchased Guerrino as a slave, he had the boy baptized and adopted him. When Epidonios finally had his own son, he raised the two boys together. This Florentine romance thus provides additional evidence that the Byzantines
sometimes relied on adoption to provide care for abandoned children.

THE SYSTEM

This evaluation of Byzantine orphan care has revealed many defects in the system. Byzantine observers including the emperor Justinian readily admitted that some guardians either neglected their wards
or used their legal powers to despoil the orphans in their care.[87] The
traditional method of designating guardians by degrees of relationship
(grandfather, brother, uncle, cousin) in some cases passed over poten-
tially the best guardian, a well-established uncle, in favor of an imma-
ture and jealous older brother. If no relatives were willing to accept
the labors of guardianship, the orphanages—whether monastic, episcopal, or private—offered food, shelter, and in many cases an excellent
education, but with these group homes came the risks of physical
abuse at the hands of overly harsh teachers and the possibility of sexual abuse from other students. A third option for orphan children was
adoption, but we have no idea how often it occurred. Certainly, Anna
Komnena did not mention it as one of the avenues the emperor Alexios pursued to secure stable environments for the orphan refugees and
captives from Asia Minor.

---

86. Osella, *Guerrin Meschino,* pp. 41–42. See the monograph on late Byzantine slavery by
Köpstein, esp. pp. 56–84. Several Byzantine writers state explicitly that it was licit to enslave
barbarians, but not *homophyla.*

87. *JNov,* 72 (anno 538).

Although the Byzantine system of orphan care obviously could not guarantee happy childhoods and stable environments for all the orphans of the empire, it did offer a remarkably varied approach to the problem of children who had lost their parents. Clearly, this system did not emerge at once as a result of a carefully thought-out plan orchestrated either by the imperial government or by the Orthodox Church. Rather, it had evolved over many centuries to meet needs as they arose.

Our study has shown that the creative forces that shaped Byzantine orphan care came from the interactions of Greek and Roman laws and customs with the moral imperatives of Christianity. As soon as Constantine accepted the new religion, he turned his attention to the protection of orphans. First, he changed the laws of guardianship to offer greater protection to the orphan wards, and then he experimented with ways to discourage abandonment of infants.

By implementing far stricter controls on the behavior of guardians, Constantine inadvertently stimulated a number of later developments in the system of orphan care. As Constantine and the subsequent Christian emperors imposed ever more stringent regulations on the behavior of guardians, fewer men were willing to accept the burdens. This, in turn, led to legislation that opened up guardianship to women, first to mothers, then to grandmothers, and eventually, in practice, to all female relatives of orphaned children. At the same time, these laws forced some wealthy orphans into the group homes that Christian leaders had been organizing to care for a continually growing number of children without parents.[88]

In order to discourage natural parents or slave owners from abandoning their infants, Constantine extinguished any right such heartless people might claim later on to take back their children. Constantine hoped that his changes in the law would encourage people who found such abandoned babies to raise them as their own slaves or their adopted children. Two centuries later, Justinian legislated that people who took in exposed infants could no longer enslave them, but had to raise them as free children, either by adopting them or by accepting responsibility for them in some informal manner.[89]

88. See Chapter Three.
89. See Chapter Six.

The group homes also evolved over the centuries. In the pre-Constantinian Church, bishops assumed responsibility for raising orphans and trying to locate adults willing to adopt them. During the course of the fourth century, however, monasteries of both men and women began to accept orphans to raise within the ascetic community. Moreover, as early as the fifth century, we have evidence of a private group home founded by an aristocratic woman of Constantinople.[90]

This system of orphanages grew large enough during subsequent centuries that the emperor Leo III (717–741) thought that episcopal, monastic, and private group homes would be able to care for all children whose parents had died without leaving a proper testament ordaining a *tutor testimentarius*.[91]

The Byzantine state obviously played a key role in the development of orphan care by altering the laws governing guardianship and adoption and by encouraging bishops and monasteries to develop schools that could provide a stable environment and a good education for homeless children without guardians. The government encouraged these orphanages by granting fiscal privileges to churches and monasteries and by outright donations of land or money. It is unclear, however, if the state had any role in promoting private orphanages.

A ninth-century aristocrat named Moschos founded a private orphanage outside the Bithynian city of Prousa, an institution large enough to care for eighty boys and girls. To construct his orphanage, Moschos seems to have received no help from the emperor. In fact, Moschos strongly supported Theodore of Stoudios and other monks who were resisting the reigning emperor Leo V's attempt to suppress the use of Christian icons. Moschos's orphanage, apparently free from any government supervision, offered a safe haven for Theodore and other active opponents of the imperial government and its religious policies.[92]

The Byzantine state perhaps exercised its greatest influence on the system of orphan care through its support of the Orphanotropheion of Constantinople. From the earliest days of Zotikos's Orphanage, the

---

90. Proklos, *Homélie* 26 (pp. 182–83).   91. *Ecloga*, tit. 7 (p. 198).
92. Theodore of Stoudios, *Ep.* 211 (p. 333).

emperors had sustained this institution through substantial land grants and special privileges. In the ninth century, the emperor Nikephoros I simply took over the Orphanotropheion and incorporated the entire institution into the state administration. As we saw in Chapter Seven, the *orphanotrophos* subsequently took his place alongside other government bureaucrats as part of the imperial state hierarchy.

In the early eleventh century, the emperor Romanos III financed repairs to the Orphanotropheion, and at the end of the century Alexios I Komnenos refurbished the entire institution and endowed it with new rural estates and urban properties. As a result of Alexios's major refinancing of the institution, the Orphanotropheion became one of the leading schools in the empire, counting among its faculty some of the most renowned scholars and writers of the twelfth century.[93]

As early as the fifth century, the Orphanotropheion of Constantinople became the premier philanthropic institution in all the empire. It is not clear, however, that it held a correspondingly significant place in serving the needs of orphan children within the East Roman state. After Nikephoros I reorganized the Orphanotropheion as a government agency, the emperors increasingly used it to promote Christianization and Hellenization among neighboring barbarians. By the twelfth century, when the institution's prestige as a school reached its zenith, most of the orphan children who lived and studied there probably came from outside the empire.[94]

Despite its significance as an institution for foreign students, the Orphanotropheion did have an impact on the system of care for native Byzantine orphans. First, it always took in some native Greek orphans, as Anna Komnena indicated in her description of the student body.[95] Second, it served as a paragon of academic excellence that could inspire bishops and monastic superiors in charge of schools and group homes in Constantinople and the provinces. Third, its prominent location on the acropolis of the capital, its extensive lands and urban properties, and the high rank of its director among government officials served as constant reminders that a truly Christian state had to place

93. For the repairs of Emperor Romanos III, see Kedrenos, 2: 503–4.
94. See the arguments in Chapter Eight.
95. Anna Komnena, *Alexiad*, 15.7.9 (3: 218).

the welfare of orphans at the very center of its governmental program.

Although orphanages clearly did not care for the majority of homeless children in the Byzantine Empire, they certainly represented the most innovative side of the child care system in the East Roman state. From the great Orphantropheion of Constantinople to the orphan asylum at Prousa which was large enough to shelter eighty boys and girls, from the monastic school of Basil with its elaborate student organization to the thirteenth-century group home of Bishop Apokaukos at Naupaktos, these institutions had no parallel in the cities of Classical Greece, in the provinces of the High Roman Empire, or even in the Jewish society of Palestine despite the emphasis the Hebrew Scriptures placed on God's special love of orphans.[96] Orphanages were innovations of Christian communities, institutions that the Byzantine state readily supported to supplement the traditional guardianship laws of the ancient world.

Christian orphanages, however, were not unique to the Byzantine Empire. Many sources also refer to them in the world of Latin Christianity. It will therefore be useful to examine briefly orphan care in Western Europe both to supplement the information we have discovered regarding Byzantine group homes and schools and to link more closely our discussion of Byzantine orphans with the modern history of helping homeless children.

96. There is some evidence that the Essenes took in orphans to raise them at Qumram; see Fitzmyer, p. 19.

X EPILOGUE
THE WEST

 During the fifteenth century, the silk merchants of Florence hired the renowned Renaissance architect Filippo Brunelleschi to build a beautiful orphanage for their city. The silk merchants decided to name this new institution the Ospedale degli Innocenti.[1] A millennium earlier in Constantinople the wealthy woman whom Patriarch Proklos had praised for her charity and civic devotion had dedicated her church and orphan home to the same Innocents, the infants whom Herod had murdered according to Matthew's Gospel (2:1–12).[2] Did these two institutions share more than a name? Although separated by one thousand years of history and sustained by two very different cities, Renaissance Florence and Constantinople in the early Byzantine period, did these orphanages give expression to the same religious and cultural values?

To answer this question satisfactorily would require several more monographic studies concerning orphan care in Western European lands because the medieval civilization of Italy and the rest of Latin (Catholic) Europe lacked the cultural unity of the Byzantine world. The society of Anglo-Saxon Wessex differed radically from that of the Lombard towns in Italy. Even within the Italian peninsula, Venice had a far different social, political, and economic structure than did its rival

---

1. For the most thorough study of the foundation of the Ospedale degli Innocenti, see Gavitt, *Charity,* pp. 33–105.

2. Proklos, *Homélie 26,* pp. 174–83.

Genoa. Therefore, I will limit the discussion in this chapter to posing and answering five questions concerning the care of orphans in Latin Europe. Addressing these questions should open paths for future research on orphan care in Western Europe and also offer some new insights on Byzantine programs for assisting boys and girls without living parents.

First, did Western Europeans inherit the Byzantine laws of guardianship? Second, did they have similar episcopal schools that could offer asylum to orphans as well as train young clerics? Third, did Latin monasteries take in orphans as Greek monasteries did in the East Roman Empire? Fourth, did orphans in Western group homes learn to sing in special choirs as the children of Byzantine orphanages did? Fifth, what sort of care did the Knights of Saint John, a Western crusading order, offer to homeless children in twelfth-century Jerusalem? Examining this last question provides additional evidence of a close link between Byzantine philanthropy and Western medieval institutions. Moreover, it also has important consequences for the future study of the great orphanages of Renaissance Italy such as the Innocenti of Florence, the Ospedale Maggiore of Milan, and the Ospedale di Santo Spirito at Rome.

The first question regarding the Byzantine laws of guardianship is perhaps the most difficult of these five to answer since the legal history of Western Europe after the fall of the Roman Empire is so complex.[3] Nevertheless, one can generalize that the Byzantine reforms in guardianship did not reach the Latin half of the empire during the late ancient period. First, because Constantinople ceased to rule the Latin provinces for any extended period after Constantine's death in 337, these regions did not incorporate into their legal practice the fundamental reforms in guardianship law that Theodosius I introduced, even though these novels were also issued in the name of the Western emperor, Valentinian II. Second, Western legal practice failed to implement Justinian's novels regarding orphans, even though that emperor tried to reestablish the legitimate Roman state in Italy. Finally, after 410

---

3. Chomatianos, no. 84 (p. 369), clearly identified legal guardianship as the principal protection for orphans in the Byzantine world.

barbarian rulers in the Western provinces began to introduce their own customs, a practice that had a profound impact on the laws of some regions.

With the rise of the Carolingian Franks (687–842) and the subsequent spread of feudal relationships and land tenure, even the *tutela* of pre-Byzantine Roman law disappeared in many areas of the former Western Empire. In place of Roman guardianship, the Franks introduced feudal wardship, a Germanic institution that took no interest in the welfare of orphans.

According to Frankish custom, the possession of feudal property depended upon a warrior's ability to fulfill his obligation to fight for his military superior, whether that was the king himself or a local baron, count, or duke. If a warrior were unable to fulfill his military duties, he lost his property, his fief. These warriors, the medieval knights, became the dominant class of landowners in Western Europe throughout the Middle Ages.

If one of these knights died and left a son too young to assume his father's military obligations, his superior or lord assumed control of the orphan's property until the boy was old enough to fight. Since feudal law represented a return to a more primitive stage in legal development, women could play no part in guardianship, just as they could not perform such duties in pre-Christian Greek and Roman law.

In some areas, the lord appointed another adult warrior to serve as the *baillistre,* that is, to fulfill the boy's military obligation in his place. In other regions, the lord possessed the fief directly until the orphan became an adult. If the orphan were a girl, the lord had the obligation to find his female ward a husband who could fight. This feudal wardship had very little in common with Roman *tutela* since the Frankish guardian, whether the lord himself or the *baillistre,* had no obligation to preserve the orphan's property intact. The feudal guardian could use all the revenues of the fief for himself and was subject only to a vague requirement to train a male orphan to fight or to find an orphan girl a capable husband.[4] Feudal law did not subject the guardian to an audit,

---

4. For the institution of wardship, see Bloch, *Feudal Society,* pp. 201–3, and Pollock and Maitland, *History,* 1: 317–26.

did not require an inventory of the minor's property, and did not place a general *hypotheca* over the guardian's other property as security for proper management of the orphan's estate.[5]

In Italy, Roman *tutela* managed to survive, but in France and England the Frankish wardship became a fundamental part of the law.[6] Even though feudal law applied only to the lands of the warrior aristocrats, it had an effect on all aspects of customary law. For example, the English common law never developed the idea of a universal guardian to protect an orphan who inherited nonmilitary property (that is, not subject to feudal obligation). When, in the thirteenth century, English judges began to protect orphans, they could only postpone all legal actions for or against minors until the children reached age twenty-one, since the common law had no concept of *tutela*.[7]

Under feudal law, lords could easily exploit their wardship rights for gain, especially if these lords wielded great power. The Norman kings of England often abused their wardship powers by excessively exploiting lands that fell under their protection and even selling their wardships to the highest bidders. Complaints over such abuses played a major role in the high nobles uprising against King John in 1215.[8]

Although Roman law was eclipsed throughout Western Europe in the barbarian and subsequent feudal age, it never died out in Italy. During the twelfth century, legal scholars from the school of Bologna expanded the study of Roman law and even began to lobby for its use as the dominant legal system throughout Italy and the rest of Europe.[9] These Bolognese scholars studied and taught the Roman law in its early Byzantine form, Justinian's *Corpus juris civilis*, which included the East Roman reforms of *tutela*.[10] As a result of this revival of Justinianic law, Byzantine guardianship regulations were gradually reintroduced to the West and replaced many negative aspects of feudal wardship.

Even in England, the strongest defender of feudal law, the Roman law *tutela* slowly reappeared, first in the courts of the church and by

---

5. One of the issues of the Barons' War in England (1263–1264) was the demand of vassals that the lords should be subject to an audit (Pollock and Maitland, *History*, 1: 322).

6. Bloch, *Feudal Society*, pp. 201–2.   7. Pollock and Maitland, *History*, 2: 443.

8. Sayles, *Medieval England*, pp. 395–401.   9. Knowles, *Evolution*, pp. 155–63.

10. Helmholz, "Canon Law," p. 216.

the fifteenth and sixteenth centuries in the court of the chancellor, who used his powers to supplement the common law in order to appoint effective guardians with some of the powers of the Roman tutor.[11] Thus, by the early modern period, Western Europe had restored the Roman law of guardianship and, through the *Corpus juris civilis,* had accepted many of the Byzantine innovations.

Careful study of late medieval ecclesiastical records from England and France also shows that these Western judges developed the office of *tutela* in the same way as Byzantine magistrates of the tenth and eleventh centuries had done. Just as in the East, judges in the ecclesiastical courts of the Latin world recognized only guardians appointed by testament and those appointed by magistrates (Justinian's *tutela Atiliana*). The *tutela legitima* disappeared as a distinct category and was simply classified as a magisterial appointment.[12]

With regard to the second question, whether Western bishops placed orphans in their schools for future priests and deacons, the Latin sources clearly reveal that they did. According to a grave inscription, a fourth-century pope, probably Liberius (352–366), had begun his career in the Roman Church as a homeless infant, taken in by pious believers and "nurtured at the breasts of faith." When Liberius was old enough, he entered the ranks of the lectors. After he reached adulthood, he was ordained a deacon, and finally in 352 the Christian community of Rome selected him as bishop to lead the most important church in the Latin half of the empire.[13]

Liberius's *cursus honorum* mirrored almost exactly some of the ecclesiastical careers of Byzantine orphan clerics. About fifty years later in the eastern province of Syria, we have seen that Euthymios's mother abandoned her three-year-old boy by offering him to the Church of Melitene. Bishop Otreios accepted Euthymios and joined him to a group of lectors living with him at the episcopal palace. After giving Euthymios a sound education, the bishop ordained him a deacon and then a priest. Unlike Liberius, however, Euthymios turned away from

---

11. Ibid., pp. 211–45.
12. Ibid., pp. 225–27.
13. *Liber pontificalis,* 1: 209–10. Cf. Chapter Four, notes 21 and 22.

the active life of the urban clergy to become a monk of the desert, but two of Euthymios's close friends in the lector school did eventually advance to hold the episcopal office of Melitene.[14]

Not only at Rome, but also in the Western provinces, bishops were establishing schools for children who served as lectors while they trained to become deacons and priests of the local church. These schools not only trained future clerics, but just as in the Byzantine provinces they offered a means of providing care and training for orphans and destitute children. In late-fourth-century North Africa, Julianus, bishop of Vazaritanum, accepted the care of a very young boy from an indigent family. Rather than raise the boy himself, however, Julianus intrusted him to a brother bishop, Epigonius of Mapsaliensis, who baptized the child and educated him to serve as a lector.[15]

According to an inscription from sixth-century Gaul, the bishops of Viviers had established a tradition that they should make every effort to nurture orphans.[16] In seventh-century Spain, the fourth synod of Toledo (held in 633) required that bishops maintain a boarding school for young children who wanted to become deacons or priests. The synod also stated that the local church should assume the guardianship of any orphans who had been placed in this school.[17] Finally, we have already considered the example of the Roman Church which in the seventh century built an *orphanotrophium* where the orphans learned to sing and prepared themselves to enter the higher clergy as deacons or priests. In at least one case, a former student of the orphanage ascended the throne of Saint Peter as Pope Sergius II.[18]

With respect to the third question, concerning monasteries, here too Western sources indicate that monks of the Latin world took in orphans just as they did in the Greek Christian tradition. Saint Augustine referred to consecrated virgins in fourth-century North Africa who collected exposed infants and brought them to the church for baptism.[19] Apparently these nuns near Hippo were practicing a disci-

14. *Vita Euthymii*, pp. 8–13 and p. 32.
15. *Concilia Africae*, pp. 190–91 (anno 397).
16. *Inscriptions chrétiennes*, no. 483 (2: 207–10).
17. *Concilium Toletanum IV*, cap. 24 (Mansi, 10: 626).
18. See Chapter Eight, p. 216.
19. Augustinus, *Ep.* 98 (p. 527).

pline of charity similar to the program that Makrina had established for her community of virgins in fourth-century Cappadocia. Makrina's nuns collected infants abandoned along the roads and byways of central Anatolia and raised them in their community of female ascetics.[20] In seventh-century Gaul, the Frankish queen Bathilda convinced her husband, King Clovis II of Neustria, to organize a program to purchase child slaves. After freeing the children, Balthildis entrusted them to the care of monasteries to receive food, shelter, and training to enter the cloister.[21]

Orphans often came under the tutelage of monasteries through oblation. According to the ninth-century oblation records of Saint Germain des Prés, relatives other than parents frequently dedicated children to the monastery. Some, if not most, of these relatives were serving as informal guardians who for whatever reason were unable to raise these children and hence decided to dedicate them to God by placing them in the monastery.[22] In exactly this fashion, on the Byzantine island of Lesbos, the relatives of the orphan girl Theoktiste believed that they were not able to care for her and thus dedicated her to a community of nuns. Theoktiste entered the monastery on Lesbos at the same time relatives were bringing orphan oblates to the Frankish monastery of Saint Germain.[23] In his study on simony and oblation, Joseph Lynch has shown that relatives continued committing orphans to monasteries in the West well into the twelfth century.[24]

With regard to the fourth question, about music, Latin sources also describe a strong tradition of training in music, especially in choral singing, as an integral part of education for children in episcopal group homes. We have already examined how the music program at the Roman *orphanotrophium* came to dominate the curriculum to such an extent that by the ninth century Romans began to call the institution the Schola Cantorum.[25] The Roman church, however, clearly had modeled this school on the Orphanotropheion of Constantinople, and thus one could argue that it did not represent a native Latin institution. Other

---

20. Cf. *Vita Macrinae*, no. 26 (p. 232).   21. *Vita Balthildis*, pp. 493–94.
22. See Boswell, *Kindness*, p. 245, note 54.   23. *Vita Theoctistis*, pp. 228–29.
24. Lynch, *Simoniacal Entry*, pp. 45–47 and p. 59, note 83.
25. See Chapter Eight.

sources, however, indicate that purely Western episcopal schools outside Rome had also been employing music to train future clerics since the fifth century. From the time of Saint Augustine, African sources prove that young lectors were learning to sing as part of their seminary training.[26] In sixth-century Gaul, Gregory of Tours described a bishop, Nicetius of Lyons (552–573), who began training the little children at his episcopal school to sing as soon as they were able to speak. Although Gregory did not specifically mention that any of the children at the school were orphans, he did stress how young some of them were, an indication that these children had either been orphaned, abandoned, or offered as oblates to the church of Lyons.[27]

A German legend of the Late Middle Ages demonstrates how the popular consciousness had come to link orphans and choral singing. According to this legend, an anonymous archbishop of Cologne rescued eight babies who were about to be thrown into the Rhine River. Under questioning by the archbishop, the servants who were carrying out this heinous deed confessed that their mistress had given birth to nine children and that she had decided to keep only one baby and throw the others into the river. Rather than track down the mother, the archbishop decided to raise the infants himself. As they grew older, he began to train them to sing as a small choir. Ten years later, he finally visited the true parents and took his choir of orphans with him. During the course of his stay, the children's singing so enthralled the couple that they began to wish that these orphans could be their own offspring. When they revealed to the archbishop their secret desire, he explained to them what had actually occurred.[28]

The tradition of orphan choirs continued to develop in Western Europe through the Renaissance and early modern period. In the sixteenth century, the city of Naples founded several new orphanages for boys which focused their schooling program on training the children in choral singing. By performing in ceremonies at the royal court, singing for funerals, and chanting for liturgical services in the city's many churches, the orphan choirs were able to supplement their insti-

26. Caglio, *Jubilus*, pp. 184–89.
27. Gregory of Tours, *Liber vitae patrum*, 8.2 (p. 692).
28. Walter, "Sage," pp. 851–53.

tutions' income from landed endowments. Moreover, some of the graduates of these orphan schools became famous as musicians throughout Italy.[29] At Venice during the eighteenth century, one of the best-known composers of baroque music, Antonio Vivaldi, spent his entire professional life teaching music to the orphan girls of the Pietà orphanage. From 1703 to 1740, he gave singing lessons and taught the violin to the children. During his career at this orphan home, Vivaldi sometimes held the post of choir director. Moreover, he composed his most famous works for the girls to perform. Since Vivaldi was also an ordained priest, he may have considered his lifelong career at the Pietà as part of his clerical vocation to assist those in need.[30]

Lovers of music throughout eighteenth-century Europe praised the high quality of the orphan choir at the Pietà. Popular opera singers even went there to hear the girls' performances because they hoped to improve their own singing by studying the soloists in the choir. The high quality of the orphanage chorus no doubt owed a great deal to Vivaldi's tireless labors in training the girls.[31]

The French Enlightenment philosopher Jean Jacques Rousseau described a visit he himself made to the Pietà in 1743, just after Vivaldi's death, to hear a performance of the choir. According to Rousseau, the girls sang Sunday vespers for the public, but they never showed their faces. Rather, they performed modestly from behind a screen. Rousseau claimed that they sang so beautifully that he instantly fell in love with them. He used his personal connections with one of the Pietà directors to meet the soloists. When he finally saw them, however, he was surprised that many had suffered disfigurements of various sorts—pockmarks or permanent injuries to their eyes—the traces of their harsh lives before entering the orphanage. Nevertheless, Rousseau was charmed by their perfect manners.[32]

Rousseau's colorful description, confirmed by many other accounts, reveals striking similarities between the performances of the girls at the Pietà in eighteenth-century Venice and the orphans who sang at

29. Concerning the orphan choirs of Naples, see Di Giacomo, *Conservatorio*, passim.
30. Pincherle, *Vivaldi*, pp. 15–38.
31. Ibid., p. 20.
32. Rousseau, *Confessions*, Part 1, Book 7 (1: 481–82).

the Orphanotropheion of fifth-century Constantinople. Just as at the Pietà, the orphans of Byzantium sang for the public on Sundays. Moreover, they chanted songs written especially for them by the famous composer Timokletes, in the same manner as the Pietà choir sang the works of Vivaldi.[33]

By the eighteenth century, the Pietà accepted only female abandoned infants and girls who had lost their parents. Not all of these girls sang well enough to perform in the choir. Only an elite group, the *figlie del coro*, participated at the Sunday vespers. An elite group of singers had emerged also at the Orphanotropheion. In the late ninth century, Philotheos referred to the children's choir that sang for the emperor on Epiphany as the orphans *tou souphragiou* (the approved orphans), probably a special group of gifted singers similar to the *figlie del coro*.[34]

One cannot demonstrate that the Venetians modeled the music program at the Pietà on the ancient tradition of the Orphanotropheion at Constantinople, nor that they imitated some Western institution closer to home, such as the Schola Cantorum of medieval Rome. Rather, the Pietà emerged from a strong Christian tradition of group homes that had emphasized music as part of the educational program in the Byzantine East as well as the Latin West from at least the fifth century.

Music reoccurs frequently in the history of orphan care and in many different circumstances. For example, in the German city of Hamburg during the years 1778–1781, the city government conducted a vigorous debate concerning the proper method of caring for orphans. Should the city construct a new orphanage or close its old ones and move to a system of foster care in private homes? Progressive citizens voiced their opposition to orphan asylums because they created unnatural environments where children did not learn how to interact properly with adults. In such group homes, the children also failed to comprehend the nature of private property and personal responsibility so important to eighteenth-century liberalism. Opponents of foster care

---

33. Pincherle, *Vivaldi*, pp. 19–24; cf. Zachariah of Mitylene, 4.11 (p. 80).
34. Pincherle, *Vivaldi*, p. 24; cf. *Kletorologion of Philotheos*, pp. 185–87.

pointed out, however, that if the city closed its orphanages, the citizens would no longer be able to see and hear the orphan bands that participated in summer parades within the city. Eventually, Hamburg voted to build the new orphanage, which opened in 1785.[35]

In 1891, a Methodist minister from the southern United States, Reverend Daniel Jenkins, founded the first orphanage to shelter and educate African-American orphans. Jenkins had decided to open this institution after he began rescuing homeless boys he had met wandering the streets of Charleston, South Carolina. Both to support the orphanage and to provide training for the children, Jenkins organized a marching band that rapidly gained popularity in Charleston and eventually toured cities in the United States and in Europe.[36]

Obviously, these examples do not prove a continuous tradition extending from the fifth-century choir of the Orphanotropheion through Renaissance and Baroque Italy to the Jenkins Band of Charleston, but they do demonstrate that over the centuries in diverse cities of the Western world those who managed group homes for children recognized the virtue of music programs in educating homeless children. Singing in a choir or playing musical instruments in an orchestra or band taught the orphans valuable skills; it also inculcated in them pride in their personal abilities as well as the importance of working within a larger group. Did it play such an important role in the total educational program because it also met deeper emotional needs and helped to calm and comfort children who had no families?

The fifth question concerns the child care program supported by the twelfth-century hospital in Jerusalem, a large philanthropic institution belonging to the Western military order of the Knights of Saint John. Both from the rules of the order and from papal correspondence, historians have long known that this Jerusalem hospital offered medical services, including care by physicians and surgeons, to the resident poor of the Holy City and to Christian pilgrims. Moreover, research has shown that the medical services of this hospital were widely copied in the hospices and hospitals of Western Europe.[37] Only recently, how-

35. Jacobs, *Waisenhausstreit*, pp. 49–60.
36. Green, *Edmund Thornton Jenkins*, pp. 3–21.
37. Miller, "Knights," pp. 709–33.

ever, did scholars discover that the Knights also ran a large orphanage and foundling home in Crusader Jerusalem.

In 1988, an Austrian historian, Berthold Waldstein-Wartenberg, described an unpublished treatise on the Knights' hospital that he had seen in a manuscript of the Bayerische Staatsbibliothek (*Codex Clem.* 4620, folios 132v–39v). According to Waldstein-Wartenberg, this text included new information on the hospital's medical services, as well as an extended description of a program to care for orphans and abandoned infants. In 1998, Benjamin Kedar published the text and in his commentary stressed that the document contained much new information on how the Knights' hospital functioned just prior to Jerusalem's capture by Saladin in 1187. Neither Waldstein-Wartenberg nor Kedar, however, was able to discover who wrote the treatise.[38]

Immediately after having described the Knights' medical services both in their hospital and on the battlefield, this anonymous treatise added a detailed account of a program to aid women with infant children.[39] This program began by offering assistance to women who gave birth while they themselves were staying in the Jerusalem hospital. If these mothers were too poor or sick to care for their babies, they could leave them with nuns on the hospital staff who would locate wet nurses to nourish the children. For those mothers who had some form of housing near Jerusalem but were desperately poor, the hospital offered free clothing and blankets.

Besides helping indigent mothers willing to keep their babies, the Knights' program also assisted infants abandoned in and around Jerusalem. According to the anonymous treatise, some women simply left their babies in the streets, either because of hunger, or, in the writer's words, "because of a strange course of nature." People passing by often picked up the babies and brought the foundlings to the Hospital of Saint John, where the staff arranged for wet nurses.

The Knights' program also offered to mothers of twins the opportunity to leave one of the children at the hospital if these women

38. Kedar, "Twelfth-Century Description," pp. 3–5.

39. Ibid., pp. 21–22, reveals that the Hospitallers maintained mobile medical services to assist those wounded in battle against the Moslems. This is the only source to describe these services.

could not afford to raise both babies. In effect, these mothers of twelfth-century Jerusalem were able to use the Knights' hospital to aid in family planning.[40] Studying the archives of eighteenth-century Europe, historians have discovered that in a similar manner destitute families in Milan abandoned their second, third, or fourth child to the Ospedale Maggiore and to other city orphanages so that they could limit the number of mouths they had to feed.[41]

The anonymous treatise described another group of mothers who came to the hospital to discuss their family problems. If staff members determined that any one of these women suffered from a chronic illness and would be unable to raise her child, they accepted responsibility for the infant and assigned it a wet nurse. If the staff members determined that a woman could not care for the baby because of poverty, the hospital provided her with sufficient money to raise the child at her home.

Finally, the Knights' program assisted those desperate women who came to the gate of the hospital with their faces veiled because of shame. These unwed mothers simply left the infants at the threshold of the hospital and fled.

After describing how the babies arrived in the hospital's care, the anonymous treatise next explained what salaries the Knights paid to the wet nurses and how the orphanage staff supervised the conduct of these women. The hospital rules required that at frequent intervals the wet nurses bring the babies back to the orphanage so that one of the nuns *(sorores domus)* could inspect the children to be sure that they were receiving proper nutrition and suitable attention from the nurses.[42] At this point, the author of the treatise added an interesting observation. The nuns were to perform these inspections so that the wet nurses would not neglect their wards "as frequently happens in other places."[43] He thus implied that other orphanages existed that offered help to abandoned infants. The writer, however, did not mention who managed these institutions.

40. Kedar, "Twelfth-Century Description," pp. 24–25.
41. Cf. Hunecke, "Abandonment," pp. 125–32.
42. Kedar, "Twelfth-Century Description," p. 25.
43. Ibid., p. 25: *"ut mos est in alienis."*

This new information about the Knights' program for infants at their Jerusalem hospital poses a number of problems in tracing the history of orphan care both in the medieval West and in the Byzantine Empire. The scale of the child care program that the Knights of Saint John supported went far beyond what we have seen in other group homes in the West. Latin bishops had maintained episcopal schools primarily to train deacons and priests and only secondarily to nurture orphans. The same could be said of most Byzantine bishops. So also both Greek and Latin monasteries accepted oblate orphans to foster new members of their spiritual families, and only indirectly provided shelter for children without caring parents. The Knights of Saint John, however, designed their services solely to assist infants and young children either by providing direct subsidies to poor mothers or by taking in babies and raising them. Moreover, the anonymous treatise mentioned that other such institutions were functioning in Jerusalem and its surrounding territory, although they were not administered as efficiently. Since such philanthropic institutions did not exist in Latin Europe, did they come from the Byzantine world?

The Knights of Saint John were exclusively a Western order. Their members came principally from France, Italy, and Spain; their organization clearly evolved from the Latin monastic tradition. Nevertheless, the order had strong links to Byzantine society. First, their headquarters lay in Jerusalem, a city that had been subject to Moslem political authority since the seventh century, but that had preserved a strong Christian Greek and Syrian tradition. Second, the community of lay brothers that eventually became the Knights of Saint John adopted a sixth-century Byzantine church, dedicated to Saint John the Baptist, as the order's conventual chapel. Third, the Knights owed their foundation in the eleventh century to a group of Amalfitan merchants with strong ties to the Byzantine Empire.

The southern Italian city of Amalfi had risen to prosperity by trading with Constantinople. Moreover, during the eleventh and twelfth centuries, Amalfitans were the only Latin Christians to maintain a monastery on Mount Athos. Of even greater significance, the merchant Mauro, the chief supporter of the lay brothers whose community would eventually become the Knights of Saint John, had a permanent residence in Constantinople, and his son, Pantaleone, had received the imperial title of consul from the emperor Constantine X (1059–1067) for the support he gave to Byzantine interests in southern Italy.[44]

In view of the Knights' close ties to the Byzantine Empire and its church, one should carefully consider the possibility that they adopted their Jerusalem foundling home from Byzantine philanthropic institutions. In examining this possibility, however, one must also bear in mind that no evidence has so far surfaced in Greek sources that Byzantine group homes ever provided all the services for mothers and infants described by the anonymous author. Examples we have studied—especially John Apokaukos's episcopal school in thirteenth-century Naupaktos—indicate that Byzantine orphanage directors did not accept babies anonymously as the Jerusalem hospital did.

Although no Byzantine sources describe an institution exactly like the Knights' orphanage, one must avoid any conclusions based on an argument *ex silentio*. It is indeed possible that the *brephotropheia* of sixth-century Constantinople functioned in a manner similar to the Knights' orphan asylum.[45] Moreover, Anthousa's orphanage in the eighth century surely used some system similar to that of the Jerusalem hospital to rescue infants abandoned along the byways of the Byzantine capital. Finally, Anna Komnena described wet nurses breast-feeding babies at the Orphanotropheion in Constantinople.[46] Did these infants come under the care of the imperial orphanage through one of the means that the anonymous treatise described at the Jerusalem hospital?

In this regard, one should also consider that the anonymous author referred to other foundling homes that accepted babies and found them wet nurses. Were these services run by Greek or Syrian communities in or around Jerusalem that had continued to maintain Byzantine philanthropic institutions throughout the period of Arab domination?

---

44. The most complete history of the Knights of Saint John is Riley-Smith, *Knights*. See also Waldstein-Wartenberg, *Vassalen,* and the articles in *Military Orders* (see Kedar). For their connection with Byzantium, see Miller, "Knights," pp. 728–31.

45. *JCod*, 1.3; *JNov*, 7; *JNov*, 43; *ACO*, 3: 128–29.

46. For Anthousa, see *Menologium Basilii Porphyrogeniti* (PG, 117: 409); for the Orphanotropheion, see Anna Komnena, *Alexiad*, 15.7.6 (3: 216).

Since some researchers have suggested that the Knights' medical services were patterned on Moslem hospitals, the well-organized *bi-maristani,* one should also include Arab influence among the possible factors in shaping the Knights' orphan program in Jerusalem. Just like Christianity, Islam emphasized the importance of caring for homeless children, especially since Mohammed himself had lost both his parents at an early age. On the other hand, a careful study of charitable foundations in Egypt has uncovered no evidence of any orphanages there during the thirteenth or fourteenth century. One must nevertheless consider the possibility that Islamic institutions inspired some aspects of the Knights' foundling home services at the Jerusalem hospital.[47]

At present, we cannot determine what motivated the Knights of Saint John to organize such an elaborate orphan program in Jerusalem. Perhaps Byzantinists will discover more detailed sources that will reveal how the *brephotropheia* of Constantinople rescued infants or how the Orphanotropheion took in babies and found them wet nurses. Working with the Latin sources, western medievalists may uncover more precise information concerning the Knights just as in 1988 Waldstein-Wartenburg found new evidence in the anonymous treatise.

Although much remains unclear about the origins of the Knights' orphanage and foundling home, there can be no doubt that it played a major part in inspiring new philanthropic institutions in Western Europe. The regulations of the twelfth-century hospital of Montpellier in southern France reproduced many of the key chapters from the *Rule of Raymond du Puy* for the Jerusalem hospital. Through his careful collating of hospital regulations in France, Leon LeGrand has demonstrated that many thirteenth-century hospices in northern France including the Hôtel-Dieu of Paris were influenced by the procedures required in the Jerusalem hospital.[48] In the heart of Latin Christianity, at Rome, the Hospital of the Holy Spirit also modeled many of its regulations on those of the Knights' charitable institution in Jerusalem. The thirteenth-century rules of the Roman hospital even mentioned explicitly

47. With regard to Moslem influence on the Knights's hospital, see Riley-Smith, *Knights,* p. 335. With regard to Egypt, see Sabra, *Poverty,* pp. 88–85.

48. For the Rule of Montpellier, see Le Grand, "Le Maisons-Dieu," pp. 105–6; LeGrand, *Statuts,* pp. ix–xxv; Miller, "Knights," pp. 720–21.

that the institution was to accept abandoned babies and to provide special assistance to women who gave birth while staying in the hospital.[49]
Finally, the Knights of Saint John themselves maintained an orphanage
and foundling home as part of their Genoese hospital, the Commenda
di Prè. Records from 1373 show that this orphanage procured wet nurses for abandoned babies and provided dowries for the older orphan
girls at the institution.[50]

Until the discovery of the anonymous treatise, historians examining
Western child care programs had supposed that large orphanages specializing in the care of abandoned infants only appeared at the end of
the Middle Ages. John Boswell claimed that such institutions first began to operate in the fourteenth century. Challenging Boswell's conclusions, Volker Hunecke asserted that such orphanages did not open until the fifteenth century at the time the silk gild of Florence began
construction of the Ospedale degli Innocenti. During the 1400s large
orphanages and foundling homes were built in all the major Italian
cities: the Innocenti in Florence (1445), the Ospedale Maggiore in Milan
(1450s), the Pietà in Venice (1465), and the renovated Hospital of the
Holy Spirit in Rome (1470s). Although they disagree on many points,
both Boswell and Hunecke maintain that these large Italian orphanages had no medieval precedents.[51] The anonymous treatise clearly requires that social historians reexamine the origins of these Renaissance
institutions.

In view of the Knights' close ties with the East, the anonymous
treatise also demands a reevaluation of Western child care programs in
the context of both Islamic and Byzantine institutions. Since the fundamental cultural forces that shaped Western European society were
identical to those that underlay the East Roman world, scholars need
especially to compare Latin institutions with those of the Byzantine
East.

49. For the Rule of the Hospital of the Holy Spirit, see PL, 217: 1137–56 and esp. cap. 41
(col. 1146). See also Walter, "Sage," p. 835, note 15.

50. Luttrell, "Hospitallars," p. 77 and note 78. Regarding the Commenda di Prè, see
Commenda, esp. pp. 21–22.

51. Boswell, *Kindness*, p. 225 and pp. 430–34; Hunecke, "Abandonment," p. 119; Hunecke,
"Findelkinder," pp. 140–41.

In the final analysis it was clearly not an accident that the silk guild of Florence selected the same name for its fifteenth-century orphanage that a senatorial lady of Constantinople had used for her group home in the fifth century. Christianity and its Sacred Scriptures inspired Romans, Milanese, and Venetians of the Renaissance just as they had the people of Constantinople, Caesarea in Cappadocia, and Naupaktos. Moreover, the traditions of the Greco-Roman *poleis* fired the imaginations of Florentine merchants and artists just as they had fascinated Anna Komnena and the prominent instructors and *schede* masters of the Orphanotropheion. As a result, we should not be surprised that both the Latin West and Greek-speaking Byzantium evolved such similar institutions to care for homeless children.

This study has presented the Byzantine system of orphan care. It remains for Western medievalists to determine how and to what extent the East Roman program influenced child care institutions, first, at the Knights' hospital in Crusader Jerusalem, then in Italy at institutions such as the Commenda di Prè at Genoa or the Innocenti at Florence, and finally in orphanages throughout Western Europe. Future studies might also investigate whether striking similarities found in child welfare programs at orphanages of twelfth-century Constantinople, sixteenth-century Naples, or even twentieth-century Charleston arise from conscious imitation or from addressing common problems inherent in caring for children of any time or place. For example, why did orphanages in medieval Byzantium, eighteenth-century Italy, and modern Charleston, South Carolina, consider music a useful tool in educating and nurturing children? A comparative study of child care programs through the centuries might dispel the notion that human institutions and values mutate so rapidly that the experiences of the past are irrelevant to the problems of the present.

APPENDIX

SEVENTY-SEVEN ORPHAN CASES

The following is a list of the seventy-seven orphans whose childhood circumstances are recorded in a wide variety of primary sources from the Byzantine Empire. This list is arranged chronologically; each orphan case includes two lines. The first line consists of three entries. The first entry indicates when the orphan lived (either the date of the document or an approximation of when the events took place). The second entry states whether the orphan was a boy or girl, if the primary source includes this information. The third entry describes what sort of guardian or foster parent the child had, or, if the orphan was raised in a group home, what sort of orphanage cared for the boy or girl.

The second line of each orphan case identifies the primary source that refers to the orphan's upbringing. The first entry in this line provides the citation to the primary source. The second entry states the category to which this primary source belongs (saint's life, papyrus document, monastic *typikon*, oration, legal case, or narrative history).

1. 260s / girl / guardian brother
Vita Antonii (PG, 26:840–48) / saint's life (not the saint)

2. Circa 300 / girl / aunt (monastic superior)
Vita Febroniae, pp. 17–18 / saint's life (central figure)

3. Circa 300 / boy / adopted by woman
Vita Clementis (PG, 114:821–24) / saint's life (central figure)

4. Circa 336 / sex not mentioned / guardian uncle
POxy, no. 2344 / papyrus document

5. Anno 346 / two orphans (no sex) / guardian grandfather
PLond, no. 2235 / papyrus legal document

6. Fourth century / girl / no guardian
Select Papyri, doc. 165 (pp. 388–89) / letter

7. Fourth century / girl / guardian not mentioned
Vita Macrinae, pp. 142–44 / saint's life (central figure)

8. Fourth century / boy / guardian uncle
Storia Lausiaca, pp. 40–42 / pious tale (central figure)

9. Circa 372 / boy / guardian grandfather
Basil, *Ep.* 84 (2: 102–8) / letter

10. Fourth century / girl / adopting aunt
Storia Lausiaca, pp. 30–36 / pious tale (not central figure)

11. Anno 381 / boy / adopting uncle
PLips, no. 28 / papyrus contract

12. Late fourth century / girl / guardian (relationship unmentioned)
PLips, no. 41 / papyrus document

13. Late fourth ccentury / girl / guardian unknown
Vita Olympiadis, pp. 409–13 / saint's life (central figure)

14. Late fourth century / boy / episcopal school
Vita Euthymii, pp. 8–13 / saint's life (central figure)

15. Anno 407 / girl / guardian grandmother
Vie de Porphyre, pp. 74–79 / saint's life (not central figure)

16. Early fifth century / girl / brother guardians
Malalas, 14.4 (pp. 273–75) / narrative history

17. Fifth century / boy / monastery
Apophthegmata Patrum (PG, 65:148–49) / pious tale

18. Mid fifth century / girl / aunt and monastic superior
Vita Elisabethae, pp. 251–58 / saint's live (central figure)

19. Fifth–sixth centuries / girl / apparently no guardian
Apophthegmata Patrum (PG, 65:217–20) / pious tale

20. Sixth century / boy / episcopal school
Vita Alypii, pp. 148–52 / saint's life (central figure)

21. 536–539 / girl / no guardian
Moschos, *Pratum Spirituale* (PG, 87.3:3097–3100) / pious tale

22. Mid sixth century / girl / uncle and aunt guardians
Maspero, no. 67005 / papyrus court document

23. Circa 551 / boy and girl / uncle guardian
Maspero, no. 67026 / papyrus court document

24. Anno 567 / girl / guardian brother
PLond, no. 1708 / papyrus court document

25. Anno 570 / boy / adopted by male
Maspero, no. 67151 / papyrus testament disposing of property

26. Anno 570 / children (no gender) / guardian, superior of monastery
Maspero, no. 67151 / papyrus testament

27. Late sixth century / girl / guardian uncle
Vita Abramii, pp. 935–37 / saint's life (not central figure)

28. Late sixth century / boy / guardian uncles
Vita Georgii Chozebitae, pp. 97–100 / saint's life (central figure)

29. Late sixth–early seventh century / boy / no guardian
Pratum Spirituale (PG, 87.3:3089) / pious tale

30. Mid eighth century / boy / guardian uncle
Theodori Studitae oratio XI (PG, 99:804–8) / religious oration

31. Mid eighth century / girl / guardian not known
Oratio Theodori Studitae in matrem (PG, 99:884–85) / religious oration

32. Late eighth century / girl / guardian grandmother
Vita Annae, ActaSS, Nov. Propylaeum, cols. 173–78 / saint's life (central figure)

33. 780–842 / boy / guardian uncle
Vita Macarii, pp. 141–44 / saint's life (central figure)

34. Late ninth century / girl / monastery
Vita Theoctistis, pp. 228–29 / saint's life (central figure)

35. Late ninth century / boy / private orphan school
Récits de Paul, tale 9 (pp. 76–78) / pious tale

36. Late ninth century / girl / adoption by man
Récits de Paul, tale 12 (pp. 96–97) / pious tale

37. Early tenth century / boy / monastic school
Vita Petri Argivorum, pp. 7–8 / saint's life (central figure)

38. Tenth century / boy / no guardian
Vita Pauli junioris, pp. 20–23 / saint's life (central figure)

39. Tenth century / boy / adoption by relative and friend of father
Vita Theodori (Kytheron), pp. 282–83 / saint's life (central figure)

40. Tenth century / boy / guardian sister
Vita Nili, p. 263 / saint's life (central figure)

41. Tenth century / boy / adopted by woman (possible group home)
Vitae duae antiquae (Vita A), pp. 5–7 / saint's life (central figure)

42. Tenth century / girl / adopted by woman (possible group home)
Vitae duae antiquae (Vita A), pp. 5–8 / saint's life (not central figure)

43. Tenth century / boys / guardian uncle
anonymous, in Symean Magistros, no. 28 (p. 364) / letters

44. Tenth century / boy / episcopal school
Vita Petri Argivorum, pp. 1 and 17 / saint's life (not central figure)

45. Anno 1041 / boys / guardian uncle
"Cartulary of Saint Elias," pp. 139–41 / monastic *typikon*

46. Eleventh century / girl / no guardian
Vita Lazari, p. 529 / saint's life (not central figure)

47. Mid eleventh century / boy / guardian grandmother
Peira, 17.19 (*JGR,* 4:67) / law suit

48. Mid eleventh century / two boys / guardian uncle
(Patriarch Michael Keroularios)
Psellos, *Encomium ad Cerullarium,* pp. 351–52 / oration

49. Circa 1100 / boys / guardian elder brother
Novel 19 (*JGR,* 1:292–96) / imperial novel

50. Anno 1105 / boy / monastic school
Typikon of St. Philip, pp. 200–01 / monastic *typikon*

51. Mid twelfth century / boy / slave owner
Tzetzes, *Ep.* 80 (pp. 119–20) / letter

52. Mid twelfth century / boy / adoption
Typikon Kosmosoteira, chap. 107 (p. 70) / monastic *typikon*

53. 1150s / boy / Orphanotropheion
Basilakes, *Adversus Bogoam,* pp. 99–101 / oration

54. Anno 1159 / boy / monastic school
Typikon Mamas, p. 259 / monastic *typikon*

55. Circa 1200 / boy / Orphanotropheion
Stilbes, *Monodia,* pp. 88–90 / poem

56. Circa 1220 / boy / no guardian
Chomatianos, no. 32 (pp. 141–44) / court record

57. Circa 1220 / boys / guardian half sister
Chomatianos, no. 59 (pp. 261–68) / court record

58. Circa 1220 / boy and girl / guardian uncle and great uncle
Chomatianos, no. 63 (pp. 379–82) / court record

59. Circa 1220 / boy / guardian brother-in-law
Chomatianos, no. 82 (pp. 363–66) / court record

60. Circa 1220 / boys / guardian half brother
Chomatianos, no. 83 (pp. 365–68) / court record

61. Circa 1220 / boy / guardian elder brother
Chomatianos, no. 84 (pp. 369–78) / court record

62. Circa 1220 / boy / guardian stepfather
Chomatianos, no. 85 (pp. 377–82) / court record

63. Circa 1220 / boy / no guardian
Chomatianos, no. 91 (pp. 401–4) / court record

64. Circa 1220 / boy / episcopal school
Apokaukos, *Epistolai,* no. 27 (pp. 85–86) / letter

65. Circa 1220 / boy / episcopal school
Apokaukos, "Dyrrachena," pp. 572–73 / letter

66. Anno 1222 / boy / episcopal school
Apokaukos, *Epistolai,* no. 100 (pp. 150–52) / letter

67. Thirteenth century / girl / guardian brothers
Vita Theodorae (PG, 127:904–5) / saint's life (central figure)

68. 1283–1289 / boy / no guardian
Gregory of Cyprus, *Ep.* 159 (p. 119) / letter

69. Late thirteenth century / boy / monastery
Theoctisti Vita Sancti Athanasii, p. 13 / saint's life (not central figure)

70. Circa 1310 / boy / uncle guardian
Gregoras, "Le vie de Jean," pp. 33–34 and 55–63 / saint's life (not central figure)

71. Circa 1310 / boy / guardian uncle
Vita Athanasii (Meteora), pp. 239–41 / saint's life (central figure)

72. 1315–1319 / girl / adopted by woman
MM 1: 17–18 / court record

73. Mid fourteenth century / girl / monastery
Encomium Gregorii Palamae (PG, 151:629) / saint's life (not central figure)

74. Anno 1349 / girl / guardian grandmother
Actes de Xéropotamou, no. 26 (pp. 193–96) / legal document

75. Late fourteenth century / girl / adopted by woman
Chronicon Sphrantzes (pp. 46–48) / narrative history

76. Circa 1400 / boy / guardian uncle
MM, 2:406 / court record

77. Early fifteenth century / boy / guardian uncle
Argyropoulos, *Comédie,* p. 37 / invective satire

BIBLIOGRAPHY

AB. Analecta Bollandiana. Brussels, 1882– .

ACO. Acta conciliorum oecumenicorum. 4 vols. in 27 parts. Edited by Eduard Schwartz. Berlin and Leipzig: Walter de Gruyter, 1922–1974.

ActaSS. Acta Sanctorum. Antwerp, 1643–. 3rd ed. 71 vols. Paris, 1863–1940.

Actes de Lavra. 4 vols. Archives de l'Athos, 5, 8, 10, and 11. Edited by Paul Lemerle, A. Guillou, N. Svornos, and D. Papachryssandrou. Paris: P. Lethielleux, 1970, 1977, 1979, and 1982.

Actes de Xèropotamou. Archives de l'Athos, 3. Edited by Jacques Bompaire. Paris: Lethielleux, 1964.

Alexander, Paul J. "The Strength of Empire and Capital as Seen through Byzantine Eyes." *Speculum* 37 (1962): 339–57.

Alexios I. Alexios I Komnenos. Byzantine Texts and Translations, 4.1. Edited by Margaret Mullet and Dion Smythe. Belfast: Queen's University of Belfast, 1996.

Anna Komnena, *Alexiad.* Anna Comnène, *Alexiade.* 3 vols. Edited by Bernard Leib. Paris: Les Belles Lettres, 1937–1945. Translated into English by E. R. Sewter, *The Alexiad of Anna Comnena.* Baltimore: Penguin Books, 1969. Translated into German by Diether Reinsch. Cologne: DuMont Buchverlag, 1996.

Apokaukos, "Dyrrachena." "Δυρραχηνά." Edited by A. Papadopoulos-Kerameus. *BZ* 14 (1905): 568–74.

Apokaukos, *Epistolai.* "Unedierte Schriftstücke aus der Kanzlei des Joannes Apokaukos." Edited by N. A. Bees. *Byzantinische neugriechische Jahrbücher* 21 (1971–1974): 55–247 (pages are numbered separately in an appendix, "Aus dem Nachlasse von N. A. Bees").

Apokaukos, "Symbole." "Συμβολὴ εἰς τὴν ἱστορίαν τῆς ἀρχιεπισκοπῆς τῆς Ἀχρίδος." Edited by A. Papadopoulos-Kerameus. In *Sbornik satei posviashchennykh pochitateliami akademika i zasluzhennopu V. I. Lamanskomu,* vol. 1, pp. 227–50. Saint Petersburg, 1907.

Archaia Scholia. Τὰ Ἀρχαῖα Σχόλια εἰς Αἴαντα τοῦ Σοφόκλεους : κριτικὴ ἔκδοσις. Bibliotheke Sophias N. Saripolou, 34. Edited by George Christodoulou. Athens: Ethnikon kai Kapodistriakon Panepistemion Athenōn, 1977.

Argyropoulos, *Comédie.* "La comédie de katablattas: Invective byzantine du XVes." Edited by P. Canivet and Nicholas Oikonomides. *Δίπτυχα,* 3 (1982–1983): 5–97.

Arnaldi, Girolamo. "Giovanni Immonide e la cultura a Roma al tempo di Giovanni VIII." *Bullettino dell' istituto storico Italiano per il Medio evo e archivio Muratoriano* 68 (1956): 33–89.

Athanagoras, "Thesmos." Athanagoras, Metropolitan of Paramythia and Parga, "Ὁ θεσμὸς τῶν συγκέλλων ἐν τῷ οἰκουμενικῷ πατριαρχείῳ." Ἐπετερὶς τῆς Ἑταιρείας τῶν Βυζαντινῶν Σπουδῶν, 4 (1927): 3–38.

Athenagoras, *Legatio pro Christianis.* Patristische Texte und Studien, 31. Edited by Miroslav Marcovich. Berlin and New York: Walter de Gruyter, 1990.

Attaleiates, *Michaelis Attaliotae historia.* CSHB, 50. Edited by Immanuel Bekker. Bonn, 1853.

Attaleiates, *Ponema. JGR* 7: 409–97.

Aubineau, Michel, ed. "Zoticos de Constantinople: Nourricier des pauvres et serviteur des lépreux." *AB* 93 (1975): 67–108.

Augustine, *Ep. S. Aureli Augustini Hipponiensis episcopi epistulae.* Corpus scriptorum ecclesiasticorum Latinorum, 34.2. Edited by A. Goldbacher. Vienna: F. Tempsky, 1898.

Auzépy, Marie-France. "La carrière d'André de Crète." *BZ* 88 (1995): 1–12.

Bas. Basilicorum Libri LX. 17 vols. (including scholia). Edited by H. J. Scheltema and N. van der Wal. Groningen: Wolters, 1953–.

Basil, *Ep. Saint Basil: Letters.* 4 vols. Edited and translated by Roy D. Deferrari and Martin R. McGuire. Cambridge, Mass.: Harvard University Press, 1961.

Basil, *Interrogatio XV.* Basil of Cappadocia, *Regulae fusius tractatae* (PG, 31: 951–58).

Basil, *Homiliae in hexaemeron.* Basile de Césarée, *Homélies sur l'hexaéméron.* 2nd ed. Edited by S. Giet. SC, 26 bis. Paris: Les Éditions du Cerf, 1968.

Basilakes, *Aristenos.* Nikephoros Basilakes, *In Alexium Aristenum,* in *Nicephori Basilacae orationes et epistolae,* pp. 10–25. Edited by Antonius Garzya. Leipzig: Teubner, 1984.

Basilakes, *Adversus Bogoam.* Nikephoros Basilakes, *Adversus Bogoam,* in *Nicephori Basilacae orationes et epistolae,* pp. 92–110. Edited by Antonius Garzya. Leipzig: Teubner, 1984.

Basilikopoulou-Ioannidou, Agne. Ἡ ἀναγέννησις τῶν γραμμάτων κατὰ τὸν ιβ΄ αἰῶνα εἰς τὸ Βυζάντιον καὶ ὁ Ὅμηρος. Βιβλιοθήκη Σοφίας Ν. Σαριπόλου, 14. Athens: Ethnikon kai Kapodistriakon Panepistemion Athenōn Philosophike Schole, 1971.

BGU. Berliner griechische Urkunden. Ägyptische Urkunden aus den königlichen Museen zu Berlin. 4 vols. Berlin, 1895–1912.

Bloch, Marc. *Feudal Society.* Translated by L. A. Manyon. Chicago: University of Chicago Press, 1961.

Boswell, John. *The Kindness of Strangers: The Abandonment of Children in Western Europe from Late Antiquity to the Renaissance.* New York: Pantheon Books, 1988.

Brock, Sebastian P., and Harvey, Susan A., eds. and trans. *Holy Women: Holy Women of the Syrian Orient.* Berkeley and Los Angeles: University of California Press, 1987.

Browning, "Patriarchal School (I)." Browning, Robert. "The Patriarchal School at Constantinople in the Twelfth Century." *Byzantion* 32 (1962): 167–202.

Browning, "Patriarchal School (II)." Browning, Robert. "The Patriarchal School at Constantinople in the Twelfth Century." *Byzantion* 33 (1963): 11–40.

Browning, Robert. *The Byzantine Empire.* Rev. ed. Washington, D.C.: The Catholic University of America Press, 1992.

Browning, Robert. "Greek Influence on the Salerno School of Medicine." In *Byzantium and Europe: First International Byzantine Conference, Delphi, 20–24 July 1985*, pp. 189–94. Athens: European Cultural Center of Delphi, 1987.

Browning, Robert. "Il codice Marciano gr. XI.31 e la schedografia bisantina." In *Miscellanea Marciana di Studi Bessarionei*, pp. 21–34. Medioevo e Umanesimo, 24. Padua: Antinore, 1976.

Bury, "Ceremonial Book." Bury, John Bagnell. "The Ceremonial Book of Constantine Porphyrogennetos." *English Historical Review* 22 (1907): 209–27; 22 (1907): 417–39.

BZ. *Byzantinische Zeitschrift.* Munich, 1892– .

Caglio, A. T. Moneta. *Lo Jubilus e le origini della salmodia responsoriale.* Venice: San Georgio Maggiore, 1976–1977.

Cameron, A. "The Exposure of Children and Greek Ethics." *Classical Review* 46 (1932): 105–14.

Cameron, Averil. "The Virgin's Robe: An Episode in the History of Early Seventh-Century Constantinople." *Byzantion* 49 (1979): 42–56.

Cantacuzenus, John. *Historiarum Libri IV.* 3 vols. CSHB, 2, 3, and 4. Edited by L. Schopen and B. G. Niebuhr. Bonn, 1828–1832.

"Cartulary of Saint Elias." "History and Cartulary of the Greek Monastery of Saint Elias and Saint Anastasius of Carbone." Edited and translated by Gertrude Robinson. *Orientalia Christiana* 15 (1929): 121–275.

Cavallo, Guglielmo. "La cultura italo-greca nella produzione libraria." In *I Bizintini in Italia*, pp. 495–612. Milan: Libri Scheiwiller, 1982.

Chomatianos. *Demetrii Chomatiani archiepiscopi totius Bulgariae tractatus.* In *Analecta sacra et classica spicilegio Solesmensi parata*, Vol. 6: *Juris ecclesiastici graecorum selecta paralipomena.* Edited by Joannis Baptista Pitra. Paris and Rome, 1891.

Choniates, *Orationes. Nicetae Choniatae orationes et epistulae.* 2 vols. Corpus Fontium Byzantinae, 11.1 and 11.2. Series Berolinensis. Edited by Jan-Louis van Dieten. Berlin and New York: Walter de Gruyter, 1972.

Christophilopoulos, Anastasios. "*Σχέσεις γονέων καὶ τέκνων κατὰ τὸ βυζαντινὸν δίκαιον.*" Athens: Nomikon, 1946.

Chronicon Paschale. CSHB, 16 and 17. Edited by Ludwig Dindorf. Bonn, 1838.

Chronicon Sphrantzae. Georgio Sfranze. *Cronica.* Edited by Riccardo Maisano. Rome: Accademia nazionale dei Lincei, 1990.

Clement. *Paedagogus.* GCS, 12. Edited by Otto Stählin. Berlin: Akademie-Verlag, 1972.

CodTheo. Codex Theodosianus. 2 vols. in 3 parts. Edited by Theodor Mommsen and Paul M. Meyer. Berlin: Weidmann, 1905.

Cohn, Marcus. "Jüdisches Waisenrecht." *Zeitschrift für vergleichende Rechtswissenschaft, einschliesslich der ethnologischen Rechtsforschung* 37 (1919–1920): 419–45.

Commenda di Prè: Un Ospedale genovese del medioevo. Edited by Giorgio Rossini. Genoa: Istituto poligrafico e zecca dello stato, 1992.

Concilia Africae. Concilia Africae, a. 345–a. 525. Corpus Christianorum, series latina, 149. Edited by C. Munier. Turnholt: Brepols, 1974.

Connolly. See *Didascalia Apostolorum.*

Constantelos, Demetrios. *Byzantine Philanthropy and Social Welfare.* 2nd ed. New Rochelle, N.Y.: Caratzas, 1991.

Constitutiones Apostolorum. Les constitutions apostoliques. 3 vols. SC, nos. 320, 329, and 336. Edited by Marcel Metzger. Paris: Les Éditions du Cerf, 1985–1986.

Cooper, J. P. "Patterns of Inheritance and Settlement by Great Landowners from the Fifteenth to the Eighteenth Centuries." In Jack Goody, Thomas Thirsk, and E. P. Thompson, eds., *Family and Inheritance: Rural Society in Western Europe, 1200–1800,* pp. 192–312. Cambridge: Cambridge University Press, 1976.

Corpus juris civilis. Vol. 1: *"Institutiones" and "Digesta."* Edited by Theodor Mommsen and Paul Krüger. Berlin: Weidemann, 1928: reprint, 1952. Vol. 2: *Codex Justinianus.* Edited by Paul Krüger. Berlin: Weidemann, 1929; reprint, 1952. Vol. 3: *Novellae.* Edited by R. Schöll and W. Kroll. Berlin: Weidemann, 1929; reprint, 1952.

Crifò, Giulliano. *Rapporti tutelari nelle Novelle Giustinianee.* Pompei: Morano Editore, 1965.

Criscuolo, Ugo. "Chiesa ed insegnamento a bisanzio nel XII secolo: Sul problema della cosidetta Accademia patriarchale." *Siculorum Gymnasium* 28 (1975): 373–90.

Crook, John. *Law and Life of Rome.* Ithaca, N.Y.: Cornell University Press, 1967.

CSHB. Corpus Scriptorum Historiae Byzantinae. 50 vols. Bonn: W. Weber, 1828–1897.

Dagron, Gilbert. *Constantinople imaginaire: Études sur le recueil des Patria.* Paris: Presses universitaires de France, 1984.

Dagron, Gilbert. "Les moines et la ville: Le monachisme à Constantinople jusqu' au Concile de Chalcedoine (451)." *Travaux et Mémoires* 4 (1970): 229–76.

Dagron, Gilbert. *Naissance d'une capitale.* Paris: Presses universitaires de France, 1974.

Daphnis and Chloe. Longus: Daphnis et Chloe. Edited by Michael D. Reeve. Leipzig: Teubner, 1986.

Darrouzès, *Tornikès. George et Dèmètios Tornikès, Lettres et discours.* Edited by Jean Darrouzès. Paris: Éditions du Centre National de la Recherche Scientifique, 1970.

De cerimoniis. De cerimoniis aulae byzantinae. Le livre des cérémonies. 2 vols. Edited by A. Vogt. Paris: Les Belles Lettres, 1935–1939.

De scientia politica dialogus. Menae patricii cum Thoma referendario de scientia politica dialogus. Edited by Carolus Maria Mazzucchi. Milan: Università Cattolica del sacro Cuore, 1982.

Demosthenes 4: Private Orations XXVII–XL. Edited with an introduction by A. T. Murray. Cambridge, Mass.: Harvard University Press, 1965.

Didascalia Apostolorum. Didascalia et Constitutiones Apostolorum. Edited by Francis Xavier Funk. Paderborn: Ferdinandi Schoeningh, 1905. English translation based on Syriac version of the text by R. H. Connolly. *Didascalia Apostolorum: The Syriac Version Translated and Accompanied by the Verona Latin Fragments.* Oxford: Clarendon Press, 1929.

Dig. See *Corpus juris civilis,* vol. 1.

Di Giacomo, Salvatore. *Il Conservatorio dei poveri di Gesù Cristo e quello di S. M. di Lareto.* Collezione settecentesca, 27. Naples: Sandron, 1928.

Dölger, Franz, ed. *Aus den Schatzkammern des Heiligen Berges, 155 Urkunden und 50 Urkundensiegeln aus 10 Jahrhunderten.* Munich: Münchener Verlag, 1948.

DOP. Dumbarton Oaks Papers. Washington, D.C., 1941–.

Duncan-Jones, Richard. "The Purpose and Organization of the Alimenta." *Papers of the British School at Rome,* n.s. 19 (1964): 123–46.

Durliat, Jean. *De la ville antique à la ville byzantine: Le problème des subsistances.* Collection de l'École Française de Rome, 136. Rome: École Française de Rome, 1990.

Ecloga. Ecloga: Das Gesetzbuch Leons III. und Konstantinos' V. Forschungen zur byzantinischen Rechtsgeschichte, 10. Edited by Ludwig Burgmann. Frankfurt: Löwenklau, 1983.

Ecloga ad Prochiron mutata. See *JGR,* 6: 217–318.

Ecloga Basilicorum. Forschungen zur byzantinischen Rechtsgeschichte, 15. Edited by Ludwig Burgmann. Frankfurt: Löwenklau, 1988.

Ecloga privata aucta. See *JGR,* 6: 12–47.

Elm, Susanna. *Virgins of God: The Making of Asceticism in Late Antiquity.* Oxford and New York: Oxford University Press, 1994.

Enfance abandonnée et société en Europe, XIVe–XXe siècle. Collection de l'École Française de Rome, 140. Rome: École Française de Rome, 1991.

Epanagoge. See *JGR,* 2: 236–368.

Epanagoge aucta. See *JGR,* 6: 57–216.

Eugenianos. "Monodie." "Monodie di Nicétas Eugénianos sur Théodore Prodrome." Edited by L. Petit. *Vizantijskij Vremennik* 9 (1902): 446–63.

Eusebios, *De martyribus Palaestinae.* In Eusebius, *Werke,* Vol. 2: *Die Kirchengeschichte,* Part 2: *"Die Bücher VI bis X" und "Über die Märtyren in Palastina,"* pp. 907–50. GCS, 3. Edited by Eduard Schwartz. Leipzig: Heinrichs, 1908.

Eusebios, *Vita Constantini. Eusebius Werke,* Vol. 1.1: *Über das Leben des Kaisers Konstantin.* GCS, 57. Edited by Friedhelm Winkelmann. Berlin: Akademie-Verlag, 1975.

Eustathios, *Commentarii. Eustathii Archiepiscopi Thessalonicensis commentarii ad Homeri Iliadem pertinentes,* Vol. 4. Edited by Marchinus Van Der Valk. Leiden: Brill, 1987.

Eustathios, *Espugnazione*. Eustazio di Tessalonica, *La espugnazione di Tessalonica*. Edited by Stilpon Kyriakides. Palermo: Istituto siciliano di studi bizantini e neoellenici, 1961.

Eustathios, *Odysseam*. *Eustathii archiepiscopi Thessalonicensis commentarii ad Homeri Odysseam*. 2 vols. Edited by J. G. Stallbaum. Leipzig: Weigel, 1825–1826.

Evagrios. *The Ecclesiastical History of Evagrius with the Scholia*. Edited by Joseph Bidez and Leon Parmentier. London: Methuen, 1898.

Failler, A. "Pachymeriana nova." *REB* 49 (1991): 171–95.

Fenster, Erwin. *Laudes Constantinopolitanae*. Miscellanea Byzantina Monacensia, 9. Munich: Institut für Byzantinistik und Neugriechische Philologie, 1968.

Fitzmyer, Joseph. *The Dead Sea Scrolls and Christian Origins*. Grand Rapids, Mich.: Eerdmans, 2000.

Forrest, Alan. *The French Revolution and the Poor*. New York: St. Martin's Press, 1981.

Gardner, Jane. *Women in Roman Law and Society*. Bloomington: University of Indiana Press, 1986.

Garzya, Antonio. "Literarische und rhetorische Polemiken der Komnenenzeit." *Byzantinoslavica* 34 (1973): 1–14.

Gavitt, Philip. *Charity and Children in Renaissance Florence: The Ospedale degli Innocenti, 1410–1536*. Ann Arbor: University of Michigan Press, 1990.

GCS. Die griechischen christlichen Schriftsteller der ersten Jahrhunderte. Leipzig and Berlin: Akademie-Verlag, 1897–.

Gedeon, Manuel I. "Παλαιᾶς εὐωρίας θράκωα κέντρα." *Thrakika* 7 (1936): 5–34.

Genesios. *Iosephi Genesii regum libri quattuor*. Corpus fontium historiae byzantinae, 14. Series Berolinensis. Edited by Anni Lesmüller-Werner and Hans Thurn. Berlin and New York: Walter de Gruyter, 1978.

Glykas. *Michaelis Glycae annales*. CSHB, 27. Edited by Immanuel Bekker. Bonn, 1836.

Golden, Mark. *Childhood in Classical Athens*. Baltimore and London: Johns Hopkins University Press, 1990.

Goldhill, Simon. "The Great Dionysia and Civic Ideology." *Journal of Hellenic Studies* 107 (1987): 58–76.

Green, Jeffrey P. *Edmund Thornton Jenkins: The Life and Times of an American Black Composer, 1894–1926*. Westport, Conn.: Greenwood Press, 1982.

Gregoras "Le vie de Jean, Métropolite d'Héraclée du Pont." Edited by Vincent Laurent. *Archeion Pontou* 6 (1934): 1–67.

Gregory I, *Dialogi. Grégoire le Grand: Dialogues, Vol. 2: Livres I–III*. SC, 260. Edited by Adalbert de Vogüe and translated by Paul Antin. Paris: Les Éditions du Cerf, 1979.

Gregory of Cyprus, *Ep.* "Epistulae Patriarchae Gregorii Cyprii." Edited by Sophronios Leontopolis. *Ekklesiastikos Pharos* 4 (1909): 97–128.

Gregory of Nazianzos, *Ep. Gregor von Nazianz: Briefe*. GCS, 53. Edited by Paul Gallay. Berlin: Akademie-Verlag, 1969.

Gregory of Nazianzos, *In laudem Basilii*. In *Grégoire de Nazianze: Discours funèbres*, pp. 58–230. Edited by Fernand Boulenger. Paris: Picard et fils, 1908 (= PG, 36: 493–605).

Gregory of Tours, *Liber vitae patrum*. In *Monumenta Germaniae Historica, Scriptorum rerum Merovingicarum*, vol. 1, part 2, pp. 661–744. Hannover: Inpensis Bibliopolii Hahniani, 1885.

Guilland, Rodolphe, "Études sur l'histoire administrative de l'empire byzantin: L'orphanotrophe." *REB* 23 (1965): 205–21.

Hagemann, Hans-Rudolf. *Die Stellung der Piae Causae nach justinianischem Rechte*. Basler Studien zur Rechtswissenschaft, 37. Basel: Helbing and Lichtenhahn, 1953.

Hands, Arthur R. *Charities and Social Aid in Greece and Rome*. London: Thames and Hudson, 1968.

Helmholz, R. "The Roman Law of Guardianship in England, 1300–1400." In *Canon Law and the Law of England*, pp. 211–45. London and Ronceverte: Hambledon Press, 1987.

Hexabiblos. Constantini Harmenopuli manuele legum sive hexabiblos. Edited by G. E. Heimbach. Leipzig: Weigel, 1851; reprint, Aalen, 1969.

Hierarchia ecclesiastica orientalis: Series episcoporum ecclesiarum Christianarum orientalium. 2 vols. Edited by Giorgio Fedalto. Padua: Messaggero, 1988.

Homer: Iliad, Books XIII–XXIV. 4th ed, rev. Edited by D. B. Monro. Oxford: Clarendon Press, 1897.

Hörandner, *Prodromos*. See Prodromos, *Gedichte*.

Hunecke, Volker. "The Abandonment of Legitimate Children in Nineteenth-Century Milan and the European Context." In John Henderson and Richard Wall, eds., *Poor Women and Children in the European Past*, pp. 117–35. London and New York: Routledge, 1994.

Hunecke, Volker. "Findelkinder und Findelhäuser in der Renaissance." *Quellen und Forschungen aus italienischen Archiven und Bibliotheken* 72 (1992): 123–53.

Hunger, Herbert. *Reich der neuen Mitte: Der christliche Geist der byzantinischen Kultur*. Graz, Vienna, Cologne: Verlag Styria, 1965.

Inscriptions chrétiennes de la Gaule antérieures au VIII e siècle. 2 vols. Edited by Edmond Le Blant. Paris: Imprimerie impériale, 1855, 1865.

Inst. See *Corpus juris civilis*, vol. 1.

Italikos. *Michel Italikos: Lettres et discours*. Archives de l'orient Chrétien, 14. Edited by Paul Gautier. Paris: Institut Français d'Études Byzantines, 1972.

Jacobs, Josef. *Der Waisenhausstreit: Ein Beitrag zur Geschichte der Pädagogik des 18. und 19. Jahrhunderts*. Quakenbrück: Handelsdrückerei C. Trute, 1931.

Janin, *Église*. Janin, Raymond. *Le géographie ecclésiastique de l'empire byzantin. Première partie: Le siège de Constantinople et le patriarcat oecuménique. Vol. 3: Les églises et les monastères*. 2nd ed. Paris: Institut Français d'Études Byzantines, 1969.

Janin, Raymond. "Un ministre byzantin: Jean l'Orphanotrophe (XIe siècle)." *Échos d' Orient* 30 (1931): 431–43.

JCod. See *Corpus juris civilis,* vol. 2.

JGR. Jus Graecoromanum. 8 vols. Edited by Karl E. Zachariä von Lingenthal, with the help of Ioannes and Panagiotes Zepos. Athens: Phexi and Son, 1931; reprint, Aalen, 1962.

JNov. See *Corpus juris civilis,* vol. 3.

John Moschos, *Pratum spirituale,* PG, 87.3: 2851–3112. Translated into English by John Wortley, *The Spiritual Meadow.* Cistercian Studies Series, 139. Kalamazoo, Mich.: Cistercian Publications, 1993.

John the Deacon (Hymnodites), *Cena. Ioannis Diaconi versiculi de Cena Cypriani.* In *Monumenta Germaniae historica, Poetarum latinorum medii aevi,* vol. 4, pp. 857–900.

Jolowicz, Herbert F. "The Wicked Guardian." *Journal of Roman Studies* 37 (1947): 82–90.

Jolowicz, Herbert F., and Nicholas, Barry. *Historical Introduction to the Study of Roman Law.* 3rd ed. Cambridge: Cambridge University Press, 1972.

Jones, Arnold Hugh Martin. *The Later Roman Empire, 284–602.* Norman: University of Oklahoma Press, 1964.

Justin, *Apologia (Prima). L'apologie de Saint Justin philosophe et martyr.* Edited by Charles Munier. Fribourg: Éditions universitaires, 1995.

Käser, Max. *Das römische Privatrecht. Vol. 1: Das altrömische, das vorklassische, und klassische Recht.* Handbuch der Altertumswissenschaft, 10.3.3.1. Munich: Bech'sche Verlag, 1971. *Vol. 2: Die nachklassischen Entwicklungen.* Handbuch der Altertumswissenschaft, 10.3.3.2. Munich: Beck'sche Verlag, 1975.

Käser, Max. *Roman Private Law.* Translated by Rolf Dannenbring. Pretoria: University of South Africa, 1980. This translation is based on the tenth edition of *Römisches Privatrecht,* vols. 1 and 2, and Max Käser, *Das römische Zivilprozessrecht* (1966).

Kazhdan, Alexander. "'Constantin Imaginaire': Byzantine Legends of the Ninth Century about Constantine the Great." *Byzantion* 57 (1987): 196–250.

Kazhdan, Alexander. *Studies on Byzantine Literature of the Eleventh and Twelfth Centuries.* Cambridge: Cambridge University Press, 1984.

Kazhdan, Alexander, and Epstein, Ann. *Change in Byzantine Culture in the Eleventh and Twelfth Centuries.* Berkeley and Los Angeles: University of California Press, 1985.

Kedar, Benjamin. "A Twelfth-Century Description of the Jerusalem Hospital." In Helen Nicholson, ed., *Military Orders. Vol. 2: Welfare and Warfare,* pp. 3–26. Aldershot, U.K.: Ashgate, 1999.

Kedrenos. Cedrenus, Georgius. *Historiarum Compendium.* 2 vols. CSHB, 34 and 35. Edited by Immanuel Bekker. Bonn, 1838–1839.

Kekaumenos, *Strategikon. Cecaumeni Consilia et narrationes.* Edited by Genadij G. Litavrin. Moscow: Nauka, 1974.

Kippenberg, Hans G. "The Role of Christianity in the Depolitization of the Roman Empire." In S. N. Eisenstadt, ed., *The Origins and Diversity of Axial*

Age Civilizations, pp. 261–79. Albany: State University of New York Press, 1986.

Kislinger, Ewald. "Taverne, alberghi e filantropia ecclesiastica a Bizanzio." *Atti della Accademia delle scienze di Torino. Classe di scienze morali, storiche e filologiche* 120 (1986): 84–96.

Kletorologion of Philotheos. See *Préséance*, 67–235.

Knowles, David. *The Evolution of Medieval Thought.* New York: Knopf/Random House, 1962.

Köpstein, Helga. *Zur Sklaverei im ausgehenden Byzanz. Philologisch-historische Untersuchung.* Berlin: Akademie-Verlag, 1966.

Krause, Jens-Uwe. *Rechtliche und soziale Stellung von Waisen.* Witwen und Waisen im Römischen Reich, 3. Stuttgart: Franz Steiner Verlag, 1995.

Krause, Jens-Uwe. *Witwen und Waisen im frühen Christentum.* Witwen und Waisen im Römischen Reich, 4. Stuttgart: Franz Steiner Verlag, 1995.

Krumbacher, Karl. *Geschichte der byzantinischen Litteratur: Von Justinian bis zum Ende des oströmischen Reiches <527–1453>.* 2nd ed. Munich: Beck, 1897.

Kurylowicz, Marek. "Adoption on the Evidence of the Papyri." *Journal of Juristic Papyrology* 19 (1983): 61–75.

Laiou, Angeliki. "Contribution à l'étude de l'institution familiale en Épire au XIIIe siècle." *Fontes Minores* 6 (1984): 275–319.

Laskaris. See Theodore Laskaris, *Ep.*

Law and Society in Byzantium, Ninth–Twelfth Centuries. Edited by Angeliki E. Laiou and Dieter Simon. Washington, D.C.: Dumbarton Oaks, 1994.

LeGrand, Léon. "Les maisons-dieu, leur statuts au XIIIe siècle." *Révue des questions historiques* 60 (1896): 95–134.

LeGrand, Léon. *Statuts d'hôtels-dieu et de léproseries.* Paris: Picard et fils, 1901.

Leo VI, *Novel. Léon VI. Le Sage: Les Novelles. Texte et traduction.* Edited by P. Noailles and A. Dain. Paris: Les Belles Lettres, 1944.

Liber Diurnus romanorum pontificum. Edited by Hans Foerster. Bern: Francke Verlag, 1958.

Liber Pontificalis. Le Liber Pontificalis: Texte, introduction, et commentaire. 3 vols. Edited by L. Duchesne. Paris: Thorin, 1886–1957.

Liddell and Scott. Liddell, Henry G., Scott, Robert, et al. *A Greek English Lexicon.* 9th ed. Oxford: Clarendon Press, 1940; reprinted with supplement, 1968.

Lilie, Ralph-Johannes. *Die byzantinische Reaktion auf die Ausbreitung der Araber.* Miscellanea Byzantina Monacensia, 22. Munich: Institut für Byzantinistik und neugriechische Philologie der Universität München, 1976.

London, Ross D. "The 1994 Orphanage Debate." See *Rethinking Orphanages*, pp. 79–102.

Luttrell, Anthony. "The Hospitallers' Medical Tradition, 1291–1530." In Malcolm Barber, ed., *The Military Orders: Fighting for the Faith and Caring for the Sick*, pp. 64–81. Aldershot, U.K.: Variorum, 1994.

Lynch, Joseph H. *Simoniacal Entry into Religious Life from 1000 to 1260: A Social, Economic, and Legal Study.* Columbus: Ohio State University Press, 1976.

Macrides, Ruth J. "Substitute Parents and Their Children in Byzantium." In *Kinship and Justice in Byzantium, 11th–15th Centuries*, pp. 1–9. Aldershot, U.K.: Ashgate/Variorum, 1999.

Magdalino, Paul. "The *Bagoas* of Nikcphoros Basilakes: A Normal Reaction?" In Laurent Mayali and Maria M. Mart, eds., *Of Strangers and Foreigners (Late Antiquity–Middle Ages)*, pp. 47–63. Berkeley and Los Angeles: University of California Press, 1993.

Magdalino, Paul. *The Empire of Manuel I Komnenos, 1143–1180*. Cambridge: Cambridge University Press, 1993.

Magdalino, Paul. "Innovations in Government" In *Alexios I*, pp. 146–66.

Magdalino, Paul. "The Literary Perception of Everyday Life in Byzantium." *Byzantinoslavica* 48 (1987): 28–38.

Magdalino, Paul. "The Reform Edict of 1107." In *Alexios I*, pp. 199–218.

Maisano, Riccardo, ed. "Un inno inedito di S. Andrea di Creta per la dominica delle palme." *Rivista di storia e letteratura religiosa* 6 (1970): 519–72.

Malalas. *Ioannis Malalae Chronographia*. Corpus fontium historiae byzantinae, 35. Edited by Ioannes Thurn. Berlin and New York: Walter de Gruyter, 2000.

Manasses, "Unedierte Rede" "Eine unedierte Rede des Konstantin Manasses." Edited by Konstantin Horna. *Wiener Studien* 28 (1906): 171–204.

Mango, Cyril. *Le développement urbain de Constantinople (IVe–VIIe siècles)*. Traveaux et Memoires Monographies, 2. Paris: Diffusion de Boccard, 1990.

Mansi, Giovanni Dominico, ed. *Sacrorum conciliorum nova et amplissima collectio*. 54 vols. in 58 parts. Paris-Leipzig: Welter, 1901–1929; reprint, Graz, 1960–1961.

Maroi, Fulvio. "Intorno all' adozione degli esposti nell' Egitto romano." In *Raccolta di Scritti in onore di Giacomo Lumbroso (1844–1925)*, pp. 377–406. Milan: Aegyptus, 1925.

Marrou, Henri I. "L'origine orientale des diaconies romaines." *Mélanges d'Archéologie et d'histoire (École Française de Rome)* 57 (1940): 95–142.

Marrou, Henri I. *A History of Education in Antiquity*. Translated by George Lamb (translation of *Histoire del l'education dans l'antiquité*, 3rd ed.). New York: Mentor Books, 1964.

Maspero. *Papyrus grecs d'époque byzantine: Catalogue général des antiquités égyptiennes de Musée de Caire*. 6 vols. Edited by M. Jean Maspero. Cairo: Imprimerie de l'institut français d'archéologie orientale, 1910–1916.

Mateos, Juan, ed. *Le typicon de la grande église. Vol. 1: Le cycle des douze mois*. Orientalia Christiana Analecta, 165. Rome: Pont. Institutum orientalium studiorum, 1962.

Mazza, Mario. "Monachesimo Basiliano: Modelli spirituali e tendenze economico-sociali nell' impero del IV secolo." In *Basilio di Cesarea: La sua età, la sua opera e il Basilianesimo in Sicilia, Atti del Congresso Internazionale, Messina, 3–6 Decembre 1979*, 2: 55–96. Messina: Centro di studi umanistici, 1983.

Mercati, S. G., ed. "Un testament en faveur de Saint-Georges des Manganes." *REB* 6 (1948): 36–47.

Mergiali-Falangas, Sophia. "L'école Saint-Paul de l'orphelinat à Constantinople: Bref aperçu sur son statut et son histoire." *REB* 49 (1991): 237–46.

Metzer. See *Constitutiones Apostolorum.*

Miller, Timothy S. *The Birth of the Hospital in the Byzantine Empire.* Paperback edition. Baltimore and London: Johns Hopkins University Press, 1997.

Miller, Timothy S. "The Knights of Saint John and the Hospitals of the Latin West." *Speculum* 53 (1978): 709–33.

Miller, Timothy S. "The Orphanotropheion of Constantinople." In Emily Albu Hanawalt and Carter Lindberg, eds., *Through the Eye of a Needle: Judeo-Christian Roots of Social Welfare,* pp. 83–104. Kirksville, Mo.: Thomas Jefferson University Press, 1994.

Miller, Timothy S. "The Sampson Hospital of Constantinople." *Byzantinische Forschungen* 15 (1990): 101–35.

Miller, Timothy S., ed. "The Legend of Saint Zotikos According to Constantine Akropolites." *AB* 112 (1994): 339–76.

MM. Miklosich, Franz, and Müller, Joseph, eds. *Acta et diplomata graeca medii aevi.* 6 vols. Vienna: Gerold, 1860–1890; reprint, Aalen, 1868.

Monro. See *Homer.*

Montesquieu, *Esprit des lois.* Montesquieu, Baron de. *The Spirit of the Laws.* Translated by Thomas Nugent with introduction by Franz Neumann. New York: Macmillan, 1949.

Müller-Wiener, Wolfgang. *Bildlexikon zur Topographie Istanbuls.* Tübingen: Wasmuth, 1977.

Murray. See *Demonsthenes 4.*

Nani, "Threptoi." Nani, Teresa Giulia. "ΘΡΕΠΤΟΙ." *Epigraphica: Rivista italiana di epigrafia* 5–6 (1943–1944): 45–84.

Nardi, Enzo. "Giustiniano e l'adozione." *Atti della accademia delle scienze dell' Istituto di Bologna. Classe di scienze morali. Rendiconti* 74 (1985–1986): 47–63.

Nesbitt, John. "Byzantine Copper Tokens." In Nicolas Oikonomides, ed., *Studies in Byzantine Sigillography,* pp. 67–75. Washington, D.C.: Dumbarton Oaks, 1987.

Nicol, Donald M. *The Last Centuries of Byzantium, 1261–1453.* New York: St. Martin's Press, 1972.

Nicolai de Cusa cribratio Alkorani. Edited by Ludovicus Hagemann. Hamburg: Felix Meiner, 1986.

Novelles des empereurs Macédoniens concernant la terre et les stratiotes: Introduction, édition, commentaires. Edited by Nicolas Svoronos and prepared by P. Gounarides. Athens: Centre de Recherches Byzantines, 1994.

OCP. Orientalia Christiana Periodica. Rome, 1935–.

ODB. Oxford Dictionary of Byzantium. 3 vols. Edited by Alexander Kazhdan, Alice-Mary Talbot, Anthony Cutler, et al. New York and Oxford: Oxford University Press, 1991.

Orlandos, *Charagmata.* Orlandos, Anastasios, Τὰ Χαράγματα τοῦ Παρθενώνος. Athens, 1973.

Osella, Giacomo. *Il Guerrin Meschino*. Pallante: Studi di filologia e folklore, 9–10. Turin: Giovanni Chiantore, 1932.

Ostrogorsky, George. *The History of the Byzantine State*. Translated by Joan Hussey. New Brunswick, N.J.: Rutgers University Press, 1969.

Pachymeres. *Georgii Pachymeris De Michaele et Andronico Palaeologis libri XIII*. 2 vols. CSHB, 25 and 26. Edited by Immanuel Bekker. Bonn, 1835.

Palladios, *Dialogos*. *Palladios: Dialogue sur la vie de Jean Chrysostome*. 2 vols. SC, 341 and 342. Edited by Anne-Marie Malingrey. Paris: Les Éditions du Cerf, 1988.

Palladius, *Lausiaca*. Palladio, *La Storia Lausiaca*. Introduction by Christina Mohrmann, text by G. J. M. Bartelink, and Italian translation by Marino Barchiesi. Milan: Fondazione Lorenzo Valla, Mondadori, 1974.

Papadia-Lala, Anastasia. *Εὐαγὴ καὶ νοσοκομειακὰ ἰδρύματα στη Βενετοκρατουμένη Κρήτη*. Venice: Istituto ellenico di studi bizantini e post-bizantini di Venezia, 1996.

Patala, Zoï. "Le chants grecs du *Liber Politicus* du chanoine Benoît." *Byzantion* 66 (1996): 512–30.

Patlagean, Evelyne. *Pauvreté économique et pauvreté sociale à Byzance, 4e–7e siècles*. Paris: Mouton, 1977.

Patria Constantinopolis III. See Preger, Theodor, ed.

Patterson, Cynthia. "Not Worth the Rearing: The Causes of Infant Exposure in Ancient Greece." *Transactions of the American Philological Association* 115 (1985): 103–23.

Peira. See *JGR* 4: 11–260.

Peters, F. E. *The Harvest of Hellenism: A History of the Near East from Alexander the Great to the Triumph of Christianity*. New York: Simon and Schuster, 1970.

PG. Patrologiae cursus completus. Series graeca. 161 vols. Edited by Jacques-Paul Migne. Paris: Migne, 1857–1866.

Philes. *Manuelis Philae carmina inedita ex cod. c VII 7 Bibliothecae nationalis taurinensis et cod. 160 Bibliothecae publicae cremonensis*. Edited by Emidio Martini. Naples: Typis academicis, 1900.

Philostorgios. *Philostorgios: Kirchengeschichte*. 2nd ed. GCS, 21. Edited by Joseph Bidez with additions by Friedhelm Winkelmann. Berlin: Akademie-Verlag, 1972.

Photios, *Ep. Photii patriarchae Constantinopolitani epistulae et amphilochia*. Edited by Basil Laourdes and Leendert G. Westerink. Leipzig: Teubner, 1983.

Pieler, Peter E. "Rechtsliteratur." In Herbert Hunger, ed., *Die hochsprachliche profane Literatur der Byzantiner*, 2 vols., 2: 341–480. Handbuch der Altertumswissenschaft, 12.5.1–2. Munich: Beck, 1978.

Pincherle, Marc. *Vivaldi: Genius of the Baroque*. Translated by Christopher Hatch. New York: Norton Library, 1957.

PL. Patrologiae cursus completus. Series latina. 221 vols. Edited by Jacques-Paul Migne. Paris: Migne, 1844–1891.

PLips. Griechische Urkunden der Papyrussammlung zu Leipzig. Vol. 1. Edited by Ludwig Mitteis, with contributions by Ulrich Wilcken. Leipzig: Teubner, 1906.

PLond. Greek Papyri in the British Museum. Vol. 5. Edited by H. I. Bell. London: British Museum, 1917.

POxy. The Oxyrhynchus Papyri. London: Egypt Exploration Fund, 1898–1919, and Egypt Exploration Society, 1920–.

Pollock, Frederick, and Maitland, Frederic W. *The History of English Law before the Time of Edward I.* 2nd ed. 2 vols. Cambridge: Cambridge University Press, 1952.

Preger, Theodor, ed. *Scriptores originum Constantinopolitanarum.* 2 vols. Leipzig: Teubner, 1901–1907; reprint, New York: Arno, 1975.

Préséance. Les listes de préséance byzantines des IXe et Xe siècles: Introduction, texte, traduction et commentaire. Edited by Nicholas Oikonomides. Paris: Éditions du Centre National de la Recherche Scientifique, 1972.

Prochiron. See *JGR* 2: 114–228.

Prochiron auctum. See *JGR*, 7: 1-361.

Prodromos, *Eisiterios.* Theodoros Prodromos, Εἰσιτήριος τῷ αὐτῷ ὀρφανοτρόφῳ *(Alexios Aristenos).* PG, 133: 1268–74.

Prodromos, *Gedichte.* Theodoros Prodromos. *Historische Gedichte.* Wiener byzantinische Studien, 11. Edited by Wolfram Hörandner. Vienna: Akademie der Wissenschaften, 1974.

Prodromos, "Monodie." "Monodie de Théodore Prodrome sur Étienne Skylitzès métropolitain de Trébizonde." Edited by R. P. Louis Petit. *Bulletin de l'institut archéologique russe à Constantinople* 8 (1903): 1–14.

Prodromos, "Nuova poesia." "Una nuova poesia di Teodoro Prodromo in greco volgare." Edited by A. Maiuri. *BZ* 23 (1914–1919): 397–407.

Proklos, *Homélie 26.* In *L' homilétique de Proclus de Constantinople. Tradition manuscrite, inédits, études connexes,* pp. 174–83. Studi e Testi, 247. Edited by François J. Leroy. Vatican City: Biblioteca Apostolica Vaticana, 1967.

Psellos, *Ep. Michaelis Pselli scripta minora: Vol. 2. Epistulae.* Edited by Eduardus Kurtz and Franciscus Drexl. Milan: "Vita e pensiero," 1941.

Psellos, *Encomium ad Cerullarium.* Ἐγκωμιαστικὸς εἰς τὸν μακαριώτατον πατριάρχην κῦρ Μιχαὴλ τὸν Κηρουλλάριον. See Sathas, 4: 303–87.

Psellos, *Chronographia.* Michele Psello, *Imperatori di Bisanzio (Cronografia).* Edited by Salvatore Impellizzeri and translated by Silvia Ronchey. Milan: Mondatori, 1984.

Pseudo-Kodinos, *Traité des offices: Introduction, texte, et traduction.* Edited by Jean Verpeaux. Paris: Centre National de la Recherche Scientifique, 1966.

RE. Paulys Realencyclopädie der classischen Altertumswissenschaft. 24 vols. Revised and edited by Georg Wissowa and Wilhelm Kroll. Stuttgart: Metzler, 1893–.

REB. Revue des Études Byzantines. Bucharest, 1947–1948; Paris, 1949–.

Récits de Paul. Les récits edificants de Paul, évêque de Monembasie et d'autres auteurs. Edited by John Wortley. Paris: Centre national de la recherche scientifique, 1987.

Reeve, "Praefatio." In *Daphnis and Chloe,* pp. v–xix.

Rethinking Orphanages for the Twenty-first Century. Edited by Richard B. McKenzie. Thousand Oaks, Calif.: Sage, 1999.

Riché, Pierre. *Education and Culture in the Barbarian West.* Translated by John J. Contreni. Columbia: University of South Carolina Press, 1978.

Riley-Smith, Jonathan S. C. *The Knights of Saint John in Jerusalem and Cyprus (1050–1310).* London: Macmillan, 1967.

Rousseau, Jean-Jacques. *Les confessions.* 2 vols. Oeuvres de Jean-Jacques Rousseau. Paris: Le Livre de Poche, 1963–1965.

RP. Rhalles, Georgios, and Potles, Michael, eds. Σύνταγμα τῶν θείων ἱερῶν κανόνων. 6 vols. Athens: G. Chartophylax, 1852–1859.

Sabra, Adam. *Poverty and Charity in Medieval Islam: Mamluk Egypt, 1250–1517.* Cambridge: Cambridge University Press, 2000.

Saller, R. P. "Men's Age at Marriage and Its Consequences in the Roman Family." *Classical Philology* 82 (1987): 21–34.

Saller, R. P. "*Patria Potestas* and the Stereotype of the Roman Family." *Continuity and Change* 1 (1986): 7–22.

Sargenti, Manlio. *Il diritto privato nella legislazione di Costantino: Persone e famiglia.* Milan: Giuffrè, 1938.

Sathas, Konstantinos, ed. Μεσαιωνικὴ Βιβλιοθήκη. 8 vols. Venice and Paris: Cronou, 1872–1894; reprint, Athens, 1972.

Sayles, G. O. *The Medieval Foundations of England.* New York: A.S. Barnes and Co., 1950.

SC. Sources Chrétiennes. Paris: Les Éditions du Cerf, 1941–.

Schiavoni, Claudio. "Gli infanti esposti del Santo Spirito in Saxia di Roma tra '500 e '800: Numero, ricevimento, allevamento, e destino." In *Enfance abandonnée,* pp. 1017–64.

Schirò, Giuseppe. "La schedografia a Bisanzio nei secoli XI–XII e la scuola dei ss. XL martiri." *Bollettino della badia greca di Grottaferrata* n.s. 3 (1949): 11–29.

Schlumberger, Gustave. *Sigillographie de l'empire byzantin.* Paris: Leroux, 1884.

Schulthess, Otto. *Vormundschaft nach attischem Recht.* Freiburg: Mohr, 1886; reprint, New York: Arno Press, 1979.

Select Papyri. Vol. 1: Non-Literary Papyri, Private Affairs. With English translation by Arthur S. Hunt and C. C. edgar. Cambridge, Mass.: Harvard University Press, 1959.

Ševčenco, Ihor. "Léon Bardales et les juges généraux ou la corruption des incorruptibles." *Byzantion* 19 (1949): 247–59.

Sewter, E.R.A. See Anna Komnena, *Alexiad.*

Shepherd of Hermes. Hermas: Pastor. Die apostolischen Väter I: Der Hirt des Hermas. 2nd ed. GCS, 48. Edited by M. Whittaker. Berlin: Akademie-Verlag, 1967.

Sokrates. *Sokrates: Kirchengeschichte.* GCS, n.s. 1. Edited by Günther Christian Hansen. Berlin: Akademie-Verlag, 1995.

Sozomenos. *Sozomenos: Kirchengeschichte.* GCS, 50. Edited by Joseph Bidez and J. C. Hansen. Berlin: Akademie-Verlag, 1960.

Stengel. "Ἀμφιθαλεῖς," *RE* 1: 1958–59.

Stilbes, *Prolusione. Costantino Stilbes: La prolusione del Maestro dell' Apostolo.* Letteratura e civiltà bizantina, 2. Edited by Lia Raffaella Cresci. Messina: Edizione Dr. Antonino Sfameni, 1987.

Stilbes, *Monodia.* Stilbes, *Monodia.* In J. Diethart, ed., *Der Rhetor und Didaskalos Konstantinos Stilbes*, pp. 88–90. Vienna: Vienna Dissertation, 1971. See also the edition by Ugo Criscuolo: "Didascalia e versi di Costantino Stilbes," *Diptycha* 2 (1980–1981): 78– 97, text, 90–92.

Stroud, Ronald. "Greek Inscriptions: Theozotides and the Athenian Orphans." *Hesperia* 40 (1971): 280–301.

Suda. Suidae Lexicon. 5 vols. Edited by A. Adler. Leipzig: Teubner, 1928–1938.

Symeon Magistros. *Épistoliers byzantins du Xe siècle*, pp. 99–163. Archives de l'Orient Chrétien, 6. Edited by Jean Darrouzès. Paris: Institut Français d'Études Byzantines, 1960.

SynBas. Synopsis Basilicorum. See *JGR*, vol. 5.

Synopsis chronike (Skoutariotes). *Anonymou synopsis chronike.* See Sathas, 7: 1–556.

Taubenschlag, Raphael. *The Law of Greco-Roman Egypt in the Light of the Papyri 332 B.C.–640A.D.* 2nd ed. Warsaw: Panstwowe Wydawnictwo Naukowe, 1955.

"Testament d'Eustathios Boilas." "Le testament d'Eustathios Boilas (Avril, 1059)." In Paul Lemerle, ed., *Cinq études sur le XIe siècle byzantin*, pp. 15–63. Paris: Éditions du Centre National de la Recherche Scientifique, 1977.

Themistios, *Oratio 34. Die 34. Rede des Themistios: Einleitung, Übersetzung, und Kommentar.* Edited by Hugo Schneider. Winterthur: Keller, 1966.

Theoctisti Vita Sancti Athanasii. Edited by A. Papadopoulos-Kerameus. *Zapiski istoriko-filologiceskago fakul'teta Imperatorskago S.-Petersburgskago Universiteta* 76 (1905): 1–51.

Theodore of Stoudios, *Ep. Theodori Studitae Epistulae.* Corpus fontium historiae byzantinae, 31. Edited by George Fatouros. Berlin and New York: Walter de Gruyter, 1992.

Theodore Laskaris, *Ep. Theodori Ducae Lascaris epistulae CCXVII.* Edited by Nicholas Festa. Florence: Tipografia G. Carnesecchi e figli, 1898.

Theodori Prodromi commentarios in carmina sacra melodorum Cosmae Hierosolymitani et Ioannis Damasceni. Edited by Henricus M. Stevenson. Rome, 1888.

Theodoros Anagnostes: Kirchengeschichte. GCS, 54. Edited by Günther C. Hansen. Berlin: Akademie-Verlag, 1971.

Theophanes. *Theophanis Chronographia.* 2 vols. Vol. 1: Greek text; Vol. 2: Latin translation. Edited by Carolus de Boor. Leipzig: Teubner, 1883–1885; reprint, Hildesheim: Olms, 1963.

Theophanes Continuatus. In Immanuel Bekker, ed., *Theophanes Continuatus, Ioannes Cameniata, Symeon Magister, Georgius Monachus*, CSHB, 33, pp. 1–481. Bonn: Weber, 1838.

Theophylaktos of Ohrid, *Apologie de l'eunuchisme.* In Paul Gautier, ed., *Théophylacte d'Achrida: Discours, Traités, Poésies*, Corpus fontium historiae byzantinae, 16.1, pp. 288–331. Thessalonike: Association de Recherches Byzantines, 1980.

Thomas, John. *Private Religious Foundations in the Byzantine Empire.* Washington, D.C.: Dumbarton Oaks, 1987.

Thompson, E. A. *The Visigoths in the Time of Ulfila.* Oxford, U.K.: Clarendon Press, 1966.

Thurston, Bonnie Bowman. *The Widows: A Women's Ministry in the Early Church.* Minnasota: Fortress Press, 1989.

Tiftixoglu, Viktor, and Troianos, Spyros. "Unbekannte Kaiserurkunden und Basilikentestimonia aus dem Sinaiticus 1117." *Fontes Minores* 9 (1993): 137–79.

Tornikès, "Éloge d'Anne Comnène." In Jean Darrouzès, ed., *George et Dèmetrios Tornikès: Lettres et discours,* pp. 220–323. Paris: Editions du Centre National de la Recherche Scientifique, 1970.

Treadgold, Warren. *A History of the Byzantine State and Society.* Stanford, Calif.: Stanford University Press, 1997.

Tsantelas, "Kakopoiese." Tsantelas, Ioannis. "Κακοποίηση καὶ παραμέληση παιδιῶν ἀπὸ τοὺς γονεῖς μέ βάση τίς Βυζαντινές πηγές." *Βυζαντιναί Μέλεται,* 5: 532–42.

Typikon Blemmydes. In August Heisenberg, ed., *Nicephori Blemmydae curriculum vitae et carmina,* pp. 93–99. Leipzig, 1896.

Typikon Christodoulos. Rule, Testament, and Codicil of Christodoulos for the Monastery of Saint John the Theologian on Patmos. MM, 6: 59–90.

Typikon Kecharitomene. "Le typikon de la Théotokos Kécharitôménè." Edited by Paul Gautier. *REB* 43 (1985): 5–165.

Typikon Kosmosoteira. "Typikon du monastère de la Kosmosoteira près d'Aenos." Edited by Louis Petit. *Bulletin de l'institut archéologique russe à Constantinople* 13 (1908): 19–75.

Typikon Mamas. "Τυπικὸν τῆς ἐν Κωνσταντινουπόλει μονῆς τοῦ ἁγίου μεγαλομάρτυρος." Edited by Sophronios Eustratiades. *Hellenika* 1 (1928): 245–314.

Typikon of St. Philip. Typikon of the Monastery of Saint Philip in Demenna. In Giusseppe Spata, ed. and trans., *Le Pergamene greche esistenti nel grande archivio di Palermo,* pp. 197–210. Palermo, 1861.

Typikon Pantokrator. "Le typikon du Christ Sauveur Pantocrator." Edited by Paul Gautier. *REB* 32 (1974): 1–145.

Tzetzes, *Ep. Ioannis Tzetzae epistulae.* Edited by Petrus A. M. Leone. Leipzig: Teubner, 1972

Tzetzes, *Historiae. Ioannis Tzetzae historiae (Chiliades).* Edited by Petrus A. M. Leone. Naples: Libreria Scientifica Editrice, 1968.

van Dijk, S. J. P. "The Urban and Papal Rites in Seventh and Eighth-Century Rome." *Sacris Erudiri* 12 (1961): 411–87.

Vasiliev, Aleksandr A. *History of the Byzantine Empire.* 2 vols. Madison: University of Wisconsin Press, 1958.

Vassis, Ioannis. "*Graeca sunt, non leguntur.* Zu den schedographischen Spielereien des Theodoros Prodromos." *BZ* 86–87 (1993–1994): 1–19.

Vie de Cyrille le Philéote. *Vie de Saint Cyrille le Philéote, Moine Byzantin: Introduction, texte critique, traduction et notes.* Subsidia hagiographica 39. Edited by Étienne Sargologos. Brussels: Société des Bollandistes, 1964.

Vie de Jean Chrysostome. *Palladios: Dialogue sur la vie de Jean Chrysostome.* SC, 341. Edited by Anne-Marie Malingrey. Paris: Les Éditions du Cerf, 1988.

Vie de Porphyre. *Marc le Diacre, Vie de Porphyre, évêque de Gaza.* Edited by Henri Grégoire and M.-A. Kugener. Paris: Les Belles Lettres, 1930.

Vie de Saint Grégoire le Décapolite et les slaves macédoniens aux IXe siècle. Edited by Francis Dvornik. Paris: Libraire ancienne Honoré Champion, 1926.

Vie de Syméon. *La vie ancienne de S. Syméon Stylite le jeune (521–592).* Subsidia hagiographica, 32. Edited by Paul van den Ven. Brussels: Société des Bollandistes, 1962–1970.

"Vie et recits." "Vie et recits d'Anachorètes (IVe–VIIe siècles): Textes grecs inédits, extraits du méme ms." Edited by Léon Clugnet. *Revue de l'orient Chrétien* 10 (1905): 39–56.

Vita Abramii, *ActaSS*, Martii 2: 932–37.

Vita Alypii. "Vita Sancti Alypii Stylitae: Vita prior." In Hippolyte Delehaye, ed., *Les Saints Stylites*, Subsidia Hagiographica 14, pp. 148–69. Paris and Brussels: Société des Bollandistes, 1923.

Vita Andreae. *Vita Sancti Andreae.* In Athanasios Papadopoulos-Kerameus, ed., *Analekta hierosolymitikes stachyologiās*, vol. 5, pp. 169–79. Saint Petersburg, 1898.

Vita Antonii junioris. *Vita Sancti Antonii junioris.* Edited by Anastasios Papadopoulos-Kerameus. *Pravoslavnij Palestinskij Sbornik* 57 (1907): 186–216.

Vita Athanasii (Meteora). "Συμβολὴ εἰς τὴν ἱστορίαν τῶν μονῶν τῶν Μετεωρῶν." Edited by Nikos Bees. *Byzantis* 1 (1909): 237–60.

Vita Balthildis. *Vita Sanctae Balthildis.* In *Monumenta Germaniae Historica, Scriptororum rerum Merovingicarum*, vol. 2, pp. 475–508. Hannover: Impensis Bibliopolii Hahniani, 1889.

Vita Clementis. *Vita et certamen Sancti Clementis Ancyrani et sociorum.* PG, 114: 815–94.

Vita Danielis Stylitae (Epitome). In Hippolyte Delehaye, ed., *Les Saints Stylites*, Subsidia Hagiographica 14, pp. 95–103. Paris and Brussels: Société des Bollandistes, 1923.

Vita Elisabethae. "Sainte Élisabeth d'Héraclée abbesse à Constantinople." Edited by François Halkin. *AB* 91 (1973): 249–64.

Vita Euthymii. *Kyrillos von Skythopolis: Leben des Euthymios.* Edited by Eduard Schwartz. *Texte und Untersuchungen* 49, no. 2 (1939): 2–85.

Vita Febroniae. *Vita et martyrium Sanctae Febroniae.* *ActaSS*, June 7: 12–31.

Vita Georgii Chozebitae. *AB* 7 (1888): 95–144, 336–59.

Vita Lazari. *Vita Sancti Lazari in Monte Galesio.* *ActaSS*, Nov. 3: 508–606.

Vita Macarii. *Sancti Macarii monasterii Pelecetes hegumeni acta graeca.* *AB* 16 (1897): 140–63.

Vita Macrinae. Grégoire de Nysse, *Vie de Sainte Macrine.* SC, 178. Edited by Pierre Maraval. Paris: Les Éditions du Cerf, 1971.

Vita Matronae. Sanctae Matronae vita prima. ActaSS, Nov. 3: 790–813.

Vita Nicephori. Vita Sancti Nicephori. In Carolus de Boor, ed., *Nicephori archiepiscopi Constantinopolitani opuscula historica,* pp. 139–217. Leipzig: Teubner, 1880.

Vita Nili. Vita Sancti Nili abbatis, ActaSS, Sept. 7: 259–320.

Vita Olympiadis. Vita et translatio S. Olympiadis. Edited by Hyppolyte Delehaye. *AB* 15 (1896): 400–23.

Vita Pauli junioris. "Vita Sancti Pauli junioris in Monte Latro." Edited by Hippolyte Delehaye. *AB* 11 (1892): 5–74, 136–82.

Vita Petri Argivorum. Vita et conversatio Sancti Petri episcopi Argivorum. In Angelo Mai, ed,. *Patrum nova bibliotheca,* vol. 9.3, pp. 1–17. Rome, 1888.

Vita Sabae. Vita Sancti Sabae, by Cyril of Skythopolis. Edited by Eduard Schwartz. *Texte und Untersuchungen* 49, no. 2 (1939): 85–200.

Vita Tarasii. Ignatii diaconi vita Tarasii. Edited by I. A. Heikel. *Acta societatis scientiarum Fennicae* 17 (1891): 390–439.

Vita Theoctistis. De Sancta Theoctiste Lesbia, ActaSS, Nov. 4: 224–33.

Vita Theodori (Kytheron). In Nicholas A. Oikonomides, ed., "Ὁ Βίος τοῦα γίου τρίτ ου Θεοδώρου Κυθήρων," vol. 1, pp. 264–91. Πράκτικα τριτου πανιονίου συνεδρίου 23–29 Σεπτεμβρίου 1965. 2 vols. Edited by Ph. K. Boumpoulidos and M. Nestazopoulos. Athens, 1967–1969.

Vita Theophano. Vita I, in Eduard Kurtz, ed., *Zwei griechische Texte über die heilige Theophano, die Gemahlin Kaisers Leo VI,* Mémoires de l'académie impériale des sciences de St.-Pétersbourg 8.3.2, pp. 1–24. St.-Pétersbourg, 1898.

Vitae duae antiquae. Vitae duae antiquae sancti Athanasii Athonitae. Vita A, pp. 3–124; *Vita B,* pp. 125–213. Corpus Christianorum series graeca, 9. Edited by Jacques Noret. Turnhout: Brepols, 1982.

Vogt, Joseph. "Christlicher Einfluss auf Konstantin den grossen." In *Festschrift für Leopold Wenger zu seinem 70. Geburtstag,* vol. 1, pp. 118–48. Munich: Beck, 1944–1945.

Volk, Robert. *Der medizinische Inhalt der Schriften des Michael Psellos.* Miscellanea Byzantina Monacensia 32. Munich: Institut für Byzantinistik, neugriechische Philologie, und byzantinische Kunstgeschichte der Universität Münchens, 1990.

Volk, Robert. *Gesundheitswesen und Wohltätigkeit im Spiegel der byzantinischen Klostertypika.* Miscellanea Byzantina Monacensia, 28. Munich: Institut für Byzantinistik, neugriechische Philologie, und byzantinische Kunstgeschichte der Universität München, 1983.

Waesberghe, Joseph Smits van. "Neues über die Schola Cantorum zu Rom." In *Zweiter internationaler Kongress für katholische Kirchenmusik (Wien, 4–10 Oktober 1954),* pp. 111–19. Vienna: Böhlau, 1955.

Waldstein-Wartenberg, B. *Die Vasallen Christi: Kulturgeschichte des Johanniterordens im Mittelalter.* Vienna: Böhlau, 1988.

Walter, Ingeborg. "Die Sage der Gründung von Santo Spirito in Rom und das Problem des Kindesmordes." *Mélanges de l'École Française de Rome* 91 (1985): 819–79.

Webster, Thomas B. L. *Potter and Patron in Classical Athens.* London: Methuan, 1972.

Weidemann, Thomas E. J. *Adults and Children in the Roman Empire.* New Haven, Conn.: Yale University Press, 1989.

Wilberg, F. "'Ορφανοί," *RE* 18.1: 1197–1200.

"Will of Eustathios Boilas." "The Will of a Provincial Magnate, Eustathios Boilas (1059)." Translation with commentary by Spyros Vryonis. *DOP* 11 (1957): 263–77.

Wilson, N. G. *Scholars of Byzantium.* Baltimore: Johns Hopkins University Press, 1983.

Zachariä von Lingenthal, Karl E. *Geschichte des griechisch-römischen Rechts.* 3rd ed. Berlin: Weidemann, 1892.

Zachariah of Mitylene. *The Syriac Chronicle Known as That of Zachariah of Mitylene.* Translated by F. J. Hamilton and E. W. Brooks. London: Methuen, 1899.

Zacos, George. *Byzantine Lead Seals.* 2 vols. in six parts (vol. 1 coauthored with Alexander Veglery; vol. 2 coauthored with John Nesbitt). Basil and Berne: Augustin, 1972–1984.

Zonaras. Ioannis Zonaras, *Epitome historiarum.* Vol. 3. CSHB, 46. Edited by Theodor Büttner-Wobst. Bonn, 1897.

INDEX

Abandonment (infants), 8, 9, 141–44, 146, 148–52, 160–61, 165, 167, 173–74, 279
Ablavius, pretorian prefect, 149
Abraham, patriarch, 41
Abramios (guardian), 94–95, 137, 258, 263
Achilles *(Iliad)*, 23
Achyraites, John (orphan), 80, 255
acolytes, 45, 66, 112, 129
acropolis, 49, 51, 54, 76, 196–97, 281
adopted children, 20, 165–66, 168, 274, 279
adoption, 4, 8, 65, 140–42, 145, 161–74, 247, 253, 274–76, 278, 280
Adrianople, Paphlagonia, 153, 160, 268
Aegean Sea, 20–21
Africa, 47, 133, 149, 288, 290, 293
African-American orphans, 293
agnatic relatives, 32, 34, 75, 81–82, 135
Ainos, Thrace, 91
Ajax (Sophocles), 25–26, 28, 37–38
Akakios, bishop of Melitene, 120, 121, 268
Akakios, patriarch (472–89), 58, 77, 178, 212
Albania, 277
Alexander the Great, 239
Alexandria, Egypt, 11, 40–41, 46, 60–61, 87, 108, 110, 130, 219
Alexiad (Anna Komnena), 1, 2 n3, 4, 16, 20, 51, 227
Alexios I Komnenos, 1–3, 20, 30, 51, 83–84, 89, 104, 109, 128–29, 132, 177–78, 186–93, 196–200, 209–11, 221–23, 227, 229, 239, 244–43, 249, 271, 273–78, 281; Novel 19, 84–85, 104, 266–67
Alimenta, 31
almshouses, 3–4, 64, 127. *See also xendocheia* and *diakoniai*

Alypios, St., 153–57, 160, 211, 268
Amalfi, 296; Amalfitans, 296
Amoun (orphan), 257
amphithales, 24, 25, 42, 220
Anastasia Church, Cple., 61, 63, 219
Anastasios, emperor (491–518), 81
anathreptos, 172. *See also threptos*
Anatolia, 2, 124, 130, 173, 175, 191, 249, 261, 264, 289
Anatolian asceticism, 124. *See also* Eustathios, bishop of Sebasteia.
Anatolikon Theme, 269. *See also* Asia Minor
Andrew of Crete, St., 179, 181, 190, 199–201, 214
Andromache, 17, 24, 27
Ankyra, 64–65, 114, 121, 175
Anna Komnena, 1, 10, 16, 51, 67, 89, 109, 156, 191–99, 209, 222, 227, 246, 271, 274, 278, 281, 297, 300
Anna of Savoy, 208
annona, 70, 71 n82, 72–73, 110, 200, 210
Annunciation (25 March), 213
Anomoians, 62
Anthousa (daughter of Constantine V), 152, 155–56, 297
Antinoopolis, Egypt, 84, 171
Antioch, 11, 40, 113, 121, 158, 211, 241
Antony of Egypt, 130–31, 257
Anzas, Basil, *orphanotrophos,* 186
Apameia, Thrace, 189
Aphrodito, Egypt, 92–93, 256
Apokaukos, John, bishop of Naupaktos, 16, 123–27, 155–57, 269–72, 282, 297
Apophthegmata Patrum, 271–72

327

The Orphans of Byzantium: Child Welfare in the Christian Empire was designed and composed in Dante with Centaur display type by Kachergis Book Design, Pittsboro, North Carolina; and printed on sixty-pound Glatfelter Writers Offset Smooth and bound by Edwards Brothers, Inc., Lillington, North Carolina.